WOMEN
AND THEIR
FATHERS

Also by Victoria Secunda:

WHEN YOU AND YOUR MOTHER
CAN'T BE FRIENDS:
Resolving the Most Complicated Relationship
of Your Life

WOMEN
AND THEIR
FATHERS

THE SEXUAL
AND ROMANTIC
IMPACT OF THE
FIRST MAN
IN YOUR LIFE

VICTORIA SECUNDA

**Delacorte
Press**

Published by
Delacorte Press
Bantam Doubleday Dell Publishing Group, Inc.
666 Fifth Avenue
New York, New York 10103

Library of Congress Cataloging-in-Publication Data

Secunda, Victoria.
    Women and their fathers : the sexual and romantic impact of
the first man in your life / Victoria Secunda.
        p.   cm.
    Includes bibliographical references and index.
    ISBN 0-385-30268-1
    1. Fathers and daughters—United States. 2. Women—
United   States—Psychology. 3.   Intimacy   (Psychology)
I. Title.
HQ755.85.S432   1992
306.874′2—dc20   91-43138   CIP

Manufactured in the United States of America
Published simultaneously in Canada

June 1992

10 9 8 7 6 5 4 3 2 1
RRH

For Shel Secunda

Contents

Part Four. The Demystification of Men

Acknowledgments

This book could not have been written without the extraordinarily generous help of many people.

To the 150 daughters and 75 fathers who gave me hours of their time, courageously and movingly recounting their thoughts, feelings, and experiences, my gratitude is boundless. I found these people—who represent the socioeconomic and cultural spectrum —from two sources: first, from an ad I placed in the *Pennysaver,* a publication of classified advertisements that is delivered to virtually every home in Westchester and Putnam Counties, New York; second, through friends who gave me many names of people across the country. The trust these men and women placed in me will stay with me always. To protect their privacy, I have changed their names and all identifying characteristics.

In addition, I am greatly indebted to those researchers and social scientists who shared with me their professional expertise in interviews and, often, by sending me their writings. These authorities include:

Robert U. Akeret, Ed.D., psychoanalyst; Ellen M. Berman, M.D., clinical associate professor of psychiatry, University of Pennsylvania School of Medicine and director of the Women's Center, Philadelphia Psychiatric Center; Nina S. Evans, M.D., medical director and chief of psychiatry, Westchester Jewish Community Services, New York, and instructor and supervisor, Family Therapy, Divisions of Child Psychiatry and Public Psychiatry, Columbia University Psychiatric Institute; Judith M. Fox, psychoanalyst; Ronald Gaudia, M.S.W., deputy executive director, Westchester Jewish Community Services; Willard Gaylin, M.D., president of the Hastings Center and professor of psychiatry, Columbia University; Laurie D. Gilkes, M.S.W.; Marianne Goodman, M.D., associate clinical instructor in adult psychiatry at Mount Sinai Medical Center, New York; E. Mavis Hetherington, Ph.D., James Page, professor of psychology, University of Virginia; Louise J. Kaplan, Ph.D., psychologist and psychoanalyst; Clarice J. Kestenbaum, M.D., clinical professor of psychiatry and director of training, Division of Child and Adolescent Psychiatry, Columbia University College of Physicians and Surgeons; Margo King, Ph.D.; Daniel E. Korin, M.D.; Kenneth Lau, C.S.W., associate director, Child Abuse Training Project, Fordham University School of Social Work; David C. Leven, executive director, Prisoners' Legal Services of New York; James D. Meltzer, Ph.D., director of psychology and chief psychologist, St. Luke's/Roosevelt Hospital Center, New York; Avodah K. Offit, M.D., psychiatrist; Ross D. Parke, Ph.D., professor of psychology and Presidential Chair in Psychology, University of California, Riverside; Barrie Alan Peterson, M.Div., coordinator, office of student life, Rockland Community College, New York; Frank S. Pittman III, M.D., clinical assistant professor of psychiatry, Emory University School of Medicine, and adjunct professor of psychology, Georgia State University; Letty Cottin Pogrebin; Marlin S. Potash, Ed.D., psychologist; Barbara Schecter, Ph.D., professor of psychology, Sarah Lawrence College.

For research assistance and invaluable leads, I am indebted, as always, to Wendy Bloom, reference librarian, Mount Kisco (New York) Public Library; Lee Stark, reference librarian, and Teresa Strelek of the North Castle Public Library, Armonk, New York. Thanks also to James Hanniken, the National Organization for Men Against Sexism; Julius Marmur, Ph.D., of the Albert Einstein College of Medicine, Yeshiva University; Ruth F. Lax, Ph.D.; and Leonore Rosenbaum, M.S., assistant director, Westchester Self-Help Clearing House.

For reading portions of the manuscript and for their extremely helpful comments, I am grateful to Drs. Schecter and Potash.

I wish to thank also Carole Baron, publisher; Brian DeFiore, editorial director; and Larry Hughes and John Mooney, publicity department; of Delacorte, for their supportiveness and professionalism, and especially for their particular care and feeding of this author.

During the two years it took to research and write this book, I was in near-hibernation. These treasured friends cheered me on, often offering extremely useful suggestions: Barbara Coats, Sherry Suib Cohen, Judy Tobias Davis, Janet Elder, Linda Rodgers Emory, Judith Gerberg, Charlotte Gross, Mary Rodgers Guettel, Carole Hyatt, Ava Swartz Isaacs, Donna Jackson, Mary Alice Kellogg, Laurie Nadel, Nancy Offit, Jane Bryant Quinn, Ann McGovern Scheiner, Gene Secunda, Lilly Singer, Jane Morin Snowday, and Stephanie von Hirschberg.

My brother, Pat Simons, M.A. in counseling, once again provided love, editorial and psychological insights, and particular hand-holding above and beyond the call of sibling duty.

As I galloped toward my deadline, Catharine Henningsen and Barbara Mulrine helped to nail down footnotes, expunge computer demons, and assist me through the final days of manuscript preparation.

My agent, Elaine Markson, is an author's dream. She is unfailingly gracious and supportive, with words of wisdom and affection that constantly inspire me. I am also grateful for the particular kindnesses of her associates, Geri Thoma and Karin Beisch, who always supply help, professionalism, and cheerfulness in the arduous process of writing a book.

Six people deserve particular thanks and special praise:

Emily Reichert, executive editor of Delacorte Press and of Delta Books, edited this book with unflagging enthusiasm, high spirits, and a keen eye. Emily not only understands the writer's angst; she is also an editor of the old literary school, carefully reading and gently correcting the manuscript. She has been my booster from beginning to end.

Bob Miller, former editorial director of Delacorte and my editor for *When You and Your Mother Can't Be Friends,* acquired this book. His advocacy and graciousness have never been less than wholehearted.

Janet H. Gardner, a treasured friend and immensely talented writer and editor, read every word of this book. As she has done in the past, she saved me from syntactical carnage, mixings of metaphors, excesses of passion and italics, and sentences that go on and on and on. I will never be able to repay all her kindnesses and editorial generosity.

Nancy Rubin, another supremely gifted writer and cherished friend, went beyond the scope of routine comradeship in her encouragement and wise counsel. But for her many phone calls and assorted checkings-up, I could not have finished this manuscript with anything remotely resembling equanimity.

My daughter, Jennifer Heller, was a source of profound insights and much-needed humor. Her old soul, young heart, and particular understanding of the artistic process have made her a true soulmate.

Finally I wish to thank my husband, Shel Secunda. I cannot imagine writing this or any book—or article—without him. Nothing I write leaves my house without his superb editorial eye and brave criticism. In addition, he saw to it that our family did not go hungry (by shopping for and cooking groceries) or unclothed (he also did the laundry). He more than anyone is my champion. His love and encouragement of me and of my dreams have made him the yardstick by which I measure marriage and male-female friendship. For these and other blessings, I will forever be grateful to him.

VICTORIA SECUNDA

Introduction: Mystery Man

On an icy December day in the middle of researching this book, I defected from my computer to have a pre-Christmas lunch with four of my female friends. It's a tradition with us—we've known each other for years; we've shared each other's career triumphs and disasters and marital crack-ups; we've all put in time in therapy. This annual revelry is one that only a stint in the hospital could prevent.

Season's spirits animated the crowded restaurant where we met —the room glistened with ornaments, the air was filled with the comforting scent of pine and the cheerful sounds of Christmas carols softly oozing from unseen speakers.

Inevitably the conversation of our gang of five turned to family: Each of us was going to spend Christmas at her respective parental homestead.

"My mother is *already* a wreck—she's not speaking to my sister this week," said Paula, setting off smiles of recognition around the table. We were girding our filial loins for maternal button-pushing —the pointed questions, the guilt-inducing asides that, along with cranberries, would accompany the predictable turkey.

Suddenly Paula burst into laughter. "Listen to us!" she said. "Here we are, five smart, middle-aged women bitching about our mothers. *Again.* How come that's all we ever talk about?"

We guffawed in agreement. It was a tired but curiously satisfying topic of conversation in which we never seemed to lose interest.

"So," I offered, "let's talk about fathers instead."

An abrupt hush stalled our lively conversation. On the topic of fathers there were no wisecracks, no easy targets for jokes.

In all the years I had known these women, they had seldom mentioned their fathers, except in the most cursory, almost clinical terms: age, place of birth, and job pretty much covered Pop. No details, no nuances. No lingering delights or festering wounds. Just the facts. It was as though they had never considered Dad before. He was simply an amorphous, almost mythical presence in their childhoods.

But something about the Christmas season, the holiday of promise and nostalgia and mixed emotions, allowed these women to respond to my suggestion by looking back, pulling images of their fathers out of the past in mosaics of painful memory. And as they talked, it was with an air of wonder—surprise in their discovery that their fathers, to one degree or another, hadn't been there for them as much as they would have liked, or had failed them in some way, or just didn't know them.

Remarkably absent in these recollections was real rancor. Rather my friends conveyed a sense of dismay about the piecemeal role their fathers had played in their lives—a longing that, through the years, had been covered, like the snow gently falling outside, with the tacit, immutable assumption of "that's how fathers are."

Dismay hardly describes how most women feel about their mothers, as I discovered while researching and writing *When You and Your Mother Can't Be Friends,* an examination of the mother-daughter relationship.

When talking about their mothers, women could endlessly relate either tales of maternal tenderness or an almost "top *this*" litany of complaints. What characterized most mother-daughter relationships was *too much closeness:* Often they were bound together through obligation or rage or suffocating devotion. Mothers were too familiar to be mythical. The trick for daughters was learning how to separate from them, to detach without defecting.

But fathers were another story altogether. They were in some sense ephemeral, subject to their daughters' curious amnesia.

I decided that my next book had to be about fathers and daughters. I hadn't known my father all that well. He and my mother divorced when I was seven, a rupture that would divide us physically and emotionally and then, when he died, permanently. His absence left a hole in my life. For me men were alien creatures.

So I wanted to examine the father-daughter relationship, to see what I had missed: to find out what fathers teach their daughters about men, to discover how fathers prepare their daughters for their future romantic choices. I wanted to understand what women meant when they talked about their fathers—men who were both there and not there, men who were, it seemed, little more than a vague counterpoint to their daughters' childhoods.

Finding out about fathers is not easy. It's only in the last twenty years that they have been considered by the psychological community as much more than the "other" parent, taking a very distant second place to Mom.

But finding out about the father-daughter relationship is downright daunting.

Of all the pairings in the family, father/daughter is the least understood, least studied by social scientists, and lowest on the agendas even of "sensitive" American fathers who are struggling to avoid repeating the mistakes of the past—especially with their *sons.*

Which begins to explain why women don't know their fathers very well—most of them anyhow.

To be sure, there were among the women I interviewed those I envied. These women had fathers they could count on, fathers who were *available,* if only at the end of the day. These joyous and enriching attachments grew and deepened with the daughters' evolving needs and expectations and were a source of rock-sure dependability.

Those attachments were astonishingly rare. What characterized the rest was *too much distance:* separation, however involuntary, simply was the given. As one woman put it, "I loved my dad, but he wasn't real talkative. He was always working, or behind a newspaper, or in front of the TV. I'd take my problems to Mom instead."

The gaps in these father-daughter relationships, whether in intact, relatively happy families or those that were chilly or chaotic or shattered, were only a matter of degree. Nearly *all* the fathers had a kind of celebrity—like folk heroes, they were adored or feared from afar by their daughters. And most daughters simply assumed that it could never be otherwise. Hope characterized their intense feelings about Mom; resignation was the hallmark of Dad.

Fathers were, on some level, simply inexplicable, an eternal question mark. Only a handful of the women I interviewed were able to say, "My father was involved in my life in the healthiest, most loving way, even when we fought. Because of him I feel secure about myself as a woman and as a human being. Because of him I am comfortable in my own sexual skin."

Puzzling Connections

If Dad as "also-ran" parent is the conspicuous given in a woman's childhood, his impact on her femininity and identity is anything but obvious. That's because the clues don't show up until much, much later.

For it is not until a girl grows up and begins to fall in love that the father-daughter relationship, its gains and losses, becomes manifest. Only then does her ability to connect with a man other than her father—and in particular, her sexuality—get tested.

Not every woman wants or requires a man in her life; many women lead rich, fulfilling lives without partners. Some simply aren't ready for love—they first want to explore life as independent women, building careers and learning more about themselves and the world. Others are bona fide loners, quite content to lead lives of solitary intellectual richness, their emotional needs satisfied by close and affectionate friends and extended family. Still others have loving lesbian attachments that—save for procreation, and sometimes even then—satisfy their psychic needs and emotional and sexual yearnings.

But if and when a woman *does* want a loving partnership with a man, she will, however unconsciously, bring to it her childhood experience of her father.

The father-daughter relationship is the proving ground for a daughter's romantic attachments, her dress rehearsal for heterosexual love. Numerous studies point to the fact that a woman's capacity for a mutually loving and sexually fulfilling attachment is *directly* related to her relationship to her father.

And women who have difficulties in this area almost always had fathers who could not be counted on, or who were emotionally or physically unavailable, when they were growing up.

A loving mother is not enough to offset those difficulties.

According to research on female sexuality, women who have sexual conflicts and dysfunctions tend to think of males as the man who got away, or who at any time *might leave:* Men are not real, knowable, dependable. And if a woman expects on a gut level to be emotionally or physically stranded, she will have enough trouble achieving *trust,* let alone *sexual abandon.*

Without the belief that she can attract a loving, lovable man—which the well-fathered daughter takes for granted—a woman's romantic and sexual life can feel like very risky business indeed.

It is a psychological commonplace—because of the work of Freud—that fathers influence how their daughters relate to men, that little girls want to marry their daddies, and that the father-daughter-mother Oedipal triangle catapults a daughter into the outside world to find a man of her own.

It is a political commonplace—because of the women's movement—that the imbalance of power within the culture and the family reflects a male-dominated, patriarchal hierarchy, with women, *especially* daughters, at the bottom of the heap.

But such observations—profoundly, even maddeningly, true as they may be—do not in and of themselves answer these following questions:

• Why do so many little girls grow up to be women who are attracted *only* to men who do not meet their emotional needs?

• How did these men get that way? What causes so many tender and loving and spontaneous little boys to become men for whom those qualities are handicaps to be overcome, as though they were birth defects?

• With so many daughters experiencing "father hunger," how do they fill in the gaps in their histories, and in their present and future romantic attachments, without overloading them with unrealistic expectations?

• And how, finally, do women learn really to *talk* to their fathers and get to know them without idealization or defense or fear?

The goal of this book is to answer those questions and to close the gaps—to help women bring their fathers out of the shadows, so that the loving attachments they do form are not a series of guessing games or protective maneuvers or echoes of the past.

I interviewed 150 women, ranging in age from eighteen to seventy, of every socioeconomic stripe. I also interviewed 75 fathers —age thirty-eight to seventy-two—of daughters. I talked to dozens of authorities; I observed a men's consciousness-raising group and an incest-offenders therapy group; I read countless books and studies on gender and psychology.

All this research led me to one inescapable conclusion: Men and women, for all that they may feel like aliens to one another, do not start out that way. Something happens on the road from childhood to adult romantic love.

And what happens is this: The vast majority of people—whether male or female—begin life with fathers who were either emotionally or physically remote.

Daughters and sons tend to be loved by their fathers more in the breach, for a variety of psychological and cultural reasons. And the repercussions of that father-child chasm, that yearning by *both* sexes for a loving, available father, echo in all their adult intimate attachments, albeit in vastly different ways.

The Father-Daughter Puzzle. Many women understand, if only intellectually, that there *is* a connection between their relationships with their fathers and those with the men in their lives, but are able to apply that awareness only in the workplace. Reaping the rewards of feminism, they draw on memories of Dad—as problem solver, as decision maker—in learning how to compete with and work alongside men in the office.

But when it comes to their intimate, sexual attachments, their hard-won gains seem to evaporate in the dim light of a romantic setting, or the harsher glare of marital reality. Frequently they find themselves "acting differently" with a man at a party, on a date, or within a marriage. They jackknife back into childlike roles, behaving *just as they behaved toward their fathers,* looking to men to redress their childhood losses of Dad.

For many women it's as if they're two entirely different, mutually exclusive people: the worker and the lover, the competitor and the conciliator, the woman and the little girl.

Often they are trapped between two imperatives in their love lives: what they *want* and what they *need.* What they long for and what they get. Many women *say* they want a compassionate, sensitive man in their lives, yet when they find him, they often perceive him as "weak." Somehow love gets skewed: Love becomes equated with distance and loss.

And part of their confusion, their emotional double vision, is that *for most women fathers are mystery men.*

In 1990 a Virginia Slims/Roper opinion poll of women's attitudes over a twenty-year period was published. On the last page of the report analyzing its findings, there is this heading: "Shaping Women's Lives: Who's Been Most Important?"

Only 27 percent of the women cited "Father," whereas 53 percent cited "Mother." (As for men, 42 percent cited "Mother" and 41 percent cited "Father.")

Fathers are more mysterious to their daughters than to their sons. For one thing they are, obviously, of different genders. For another, fathers, whether married or divorced, tend to spend more time with sons than daughters. And of course fathers have traditionally left the bulk of parenting, especially of daughters, to mothers. (Even if Mommy has a job, somehow she seems to make more time for her children, taking them to the doctor or just sitting down for a chat.)

And if Dad isn't around all that much, if he's "always working," what's a daughter to do? *She'll invent him.*

Daughters fill in the blanks with illusions of what Daddy could be if only he didn't have to work so hard. They begin to think they are causing Daddy to keep his distance. They create fantasies to explain his emotional or physical absence.

Daughters solve the father-distance problem by trying to become that which *will* get Daddy's attention—in a sense, by reinventing themselves. They think, Maybe if I were prettier, or smarter, or more athletic, or Daddy's smiling, enchanting, entertaining, good little girl, maybe then he'd love me more. And if after trying to be all that, Daddy still doesn't love me, it must mean that there's something terribly wrong with me. Maybe if I were a boy . . .

It is an equation that makes perfect sense to a little girl: She needs her father. He provides a port in emotional storms with Mommy. He's protective, and he knows how to do things Mommy doesn't. If she loses Daddy, she loses her big strong man, and then "it's just Mommy and me."

When the daughter grows up and falls in love, she carries her fantasies with her. Now the man who courts her stokes hazy memories and impressions of Daddy's real or imagined love. If Daddy wasn't there to conjugate a man's love and dependability and encouragement, her expectations of her adult lovers become unrealistic and even overwhelming. The fantasies or fragmented reminiscences of Daddy become the standard by which she measures her partner. And when the man can't live up to the fantasies, or make up for her father's silences, she may feel twice betrayed.

The Father-Son Puzzle. A man cannot fulfill a woman's longings for her father for a variety of reasons, not the least of which is that in childhood he, too, may have felt confounded or betrayed by his *own* father.

I have discovered that most men don't know their fathers any better than women do. Distance is built into the father-son relationship just as it is in the father-daughter relationship. But the consequences are different: Most sons weren't taught what it means to *be* a loving man who is available.

In this sense paternal distance is even more damaging to men. For most of them it has never been considered "manly" to be in touch with their feelings because it would make them a "mama's boy." Without a role model of masculine sensitivity, they are often bereft of *any* intimate parental attachment.

Which is why they have trouble talking about their feelings.

This fact became abundantly clear during my interviews with men. What struck me was their initial uneasiness in sharing their inner lives and private thoughts. It was as though by stripping themselves of the sanctuary of male bluster and cloistered emotions, they were in some way endangered. And, as they would eventually explain, warming to the subject, that sanctuary—that emotional armor—was learned at Daddy's knee.

One man told me that when he was seven, his father's brother died, and his father burst into terrifying sobs. When he reached to comfort him, his father suddenly recoiled, raised his hands as though warding off a blow, and blurted, *"Don't.* I'll stop crying. *I'll be good."*

Another man said that when he was twelve, his father, whom he was accustomed to kissing every night before going to bed, held him away and said, "We can't do this anymore. You're too old for it now."

Most of these men were trained in childhood to conceal their vulnerabilities—to *become their fathers,* at least in terms of sequestering, even denying, their feelings.

And now, in their advancing years, they assessed the damage done by that training. Many of them felt that culturally prescribed, male-biased prestige was no substitute for a loving father who would give them the figurative and literal embrace of approval, the experience of masculine tenderness, the example of weeping without shame.

The price of their fathers' example was extraordinarily high. Having adopted the masculine stereotype, they tallied for me their losses: remote fathers; wives and lovers who perplex them; a paucity of intimate friendships with other men; children who grew up overnight while they were at the office.

For the majority of these men the language of love and emotionality is, if not altogether foreign, at least rusty. Without exception intimacy is a "female" skill every man I interviewed envies, but most are simply too embarrassed to call a male friend and say, "I'm having a lousy day—can we have lunch?"

Feminists might argue that sympathy for such male anguish is not unlike comforting the person whose truck just ran you over. Indeed, given the power imbalance in the real world, they have a point.

Many of the men I interviewed said that they *can* talk about their feelings, at least to their lovers, wives, sisters, mothers, female friends—or a female author; but, they admitted, they are far less good at returning the favor by *listening to women's feelings and identifying with them.* Instead they see women's emotions as problems to be fixed, like a broken clock.

No wonder women are a man's best friend—and no wonder women often have to go to *another woman* to find a best friend of their own.

Unraveling the Mysteries

If women are to know and become intimate with their partners in any meaningful way, either they must have experienced a loving, involved father *or they must understand the consequences of having been denied that experience.*

And when they realize that most people suffer from a similar affliction—father hunger—they have a solid basis for changing and improving their relationships with men.

In talking to women about their fathers, certain key issues emerged, which will be covered in this book, among them:

* *The Idealization of Fathers.* Daughters tend to fill in the blanks of their fathers' emotional and physical absences by seeing them as heroes. It is a way of keeping Daddy "close." In glorifying their fathers, they are able to separate more easily from their mothers. Moreover, idealizing fathers is a kind of psychic insurance—if Mommy is rejecting, at least there's always Daddy.
* *"Daddy's Little Girl."* Fathers are often easier on and more protective of daughters than sons, sometimes even preferring their little girls to their wives. Such favoritism can lead to a daughter's estrangement from her mother, overloading the connection to and dependence on Daddy. As a result the daughter, when she is grown, may remain childlike, believing she cannot live without a man.
* *Seasons of a Father's Life.* Research reveals that most men have a timetable for love, paternal or otherwise. Some fathers are good with little children, but most are busily building careers during their children's growing-up years. Fathers tend to pay attention to their emotional sides only in middle age. Consequently the seasons of a father's emotional life may collide with his daughter's: His midlife crisis, for instance, may coincide with her puberty.
* *Emotional Distance.* Because most men were raised not to be close to *either* of their parents—and because by cultural definition Dads are the also-ran parent, at least in the nursery—they often don't know how to be intimate with their children, *especially* their daughters. Example: When daughters reach adolescence and adulthood, the father end of a typical father-daughter telephone exchange is this: "You need money, right?" or "Hi. I'll put your mother on."
* *Opposites.* A father can't be a gender example to his daughter. That's both his strength and his weakness. He can be his daughter's haven when she has a fight with her mother, but he also fears his attraction to this miniature "woman."
* *Sexuality: Too Little "Closeness" or Too Much.* Love can be a land mine in the father-daughter relationship: The lines separating affection, flirtation, and sexuality often become blurred. How well Daddy navigates the sexual tides of the connection has enormous implications for father-daughter intimacy and, later, a daughter's romantic attachments. He may treat her like a "son,"

or "wife," or "mother," or "whore." Or, worst of all, as though she were invisible.

• *The Mother Factor.* Since Mom is usually around more than Dad, or is the primary caregiver, she colors her daughter's view of him and of men in general. Some mothers are jealous of father-daughter affection and try to sabotage it; others encourage the relationship *too much* through passiveness or excuse making. For good or ill, Dad is *interpreted* by Mom.

• *Siblings.* A father's preference for, or bias against, sons (many fathers consider daughters to be more malleable), or favoring one daughter over another, contributes to the erosion of the father-daughter relationship.

• *Stepfathers.* Since divorce is endemic in the culture, and since daughters are generally in the custody of mothers, a stepfather is often quasi-parent or divider of a daughter's loyalty to her father. Stepfathers are also potential usurpers of mothers' attention and allegiance to daughters. And since the stepfather is not a *real* father, sometimes—especially if he's flirtatious—he has the potential of seeming uncomfortably like a boyfriend to his stepdaughter.

• *Patterns in Paternal Love.* How all these issues are negotiated by a father depends on a number of variables, including temperament, birth rank, family and genetic history, cultural roots and financial context, and *especially the quality of his marriage.* The mix of these variables results in *general* behavioral categories among fathers, which are templates for their daughters' future romantic attachments:

> The Doting Father
> The Distant Father
> The Demanding Father
> The Seductive Father
> The Absent Father

• *Patterns in Daughters' Devotion.* Behavioral patterns in reaction to fathers, also colored by these variables, occur among daughters, including:

> The Favored Daughter
> The Good Daughter
> The Competitive Daughter

The Fearful Daughter
The Maverick Daughter

When women are able to examine their relationships with their fathers—and understand that their fathers are products of their own histories, gender training, and lessons in intimacy—they can begin to demystify men.

In that effort there is for daughters the potential for much understanding, much hope, and much joy.

The lucky women I interviewed who experienced in childhood their fathers' strength and affirmation and tenderness were able, as adults, to feel good about themselves as whole human beings. For these daughters men are not mysterious—rather they are real, human, knowable composites of both good and bad. Like their fathers the daughters approach all areas of their lives—work, love, friendship—with the ability to draw as much on their "masculine" strength for autonomy and productivity as on their "feminine" capacities to love and be loved.

These well-fathered daughters do not feel they have to judge themselves based on whether or not they have a man in their lives. But when and if they do form intimate attachments with men, their partnerships tend to be mutually nurturing and respectful and sexually satisfying.

Many other daughters discovered their fathers much later in life as their fathers, unschooled in the ways of intimacy and jolted by their proximity to the end their lives, awkwardly but poignantly came to terms with the losses of the masculine "ideal." Their daughters were able to form deeper and more meaningful attachments not only with their fathers but with the other men in their lives as well.

And some daughters, having discovered that their fathers were emotionally and/or morally bankrupt, learned to live without their fathers; at the same time they relinquished the need to believe that *all* men are brutes. These women held their fathers accountable either for their inability to love or for their cruelty. But they reached a twin awareness: that the forces that molded those men are egregious and must be changed and that they do not have to protect their fathers, and themselves, by eternally failing in love.

As adults women have the ability to dismantle their need to idealize or vilify the fathers of their childhoods. And in the process they can begin to sort out their ambivalent emotions about—and mixed messages to—the men in their lives.

By leaving childhood and childish expectations of "father" in the past, women can begin perceiving men in a way that will enable them—if they choose—to form loving, balanced, mature partnerships. They will be able to find the best that romantic love can provide: sexualized friendship between two whole, tender, strong people.

And the way for a woman to begin to do all that is to examine and resolve her relationship with the first man in her life:

Daddy.

PART ONE

First Love

1

▼▼▼▼▼▼▼

What Are Fathers For?

One night when I was eight, my dad took us to the movies. He's a strong, silent type—rugged, and very tall. Some kids behind us were making a lot of noise. My mom asked them to be quiet, and they said, "Shut your mouth, lady!" My father slowly rose to his feet, turned around, and said, "Excuse me?" The kids ran like hell out of the theater. I remember feeling so happy my dad was there—so protected and so safe.

—DORIS, THIRTY-FIVE

"Wait till your father gets home!"

The words periodically pierced the air on the Manhattan block where I grew up, a warning barked by frantic mothers—their heads jutting out of windows—pushed to the brink by children refusing to answer repeated summonses to dinner. Mothers had only to invoke the specter of Daddy, the Enforcer, and kids would instantly scramble indoors. The arrival of the man of the house meant *big trouble.*

Not for me. I couldn't *wait* for my father to come home.

When I think back on my childhood, two memories loom large. The first is the Thanksgiving I was five. My family and I had just consumed a lavish dinner, which rendered us stupefied.

My father, slumped on the living room couch, was near catatonic from a surfeit of food and brandy; I figured he needed cheering up. So I ran to my room, pulled on my ballet costume, returned to put on a recording of *Swan Lake,* and danced around the living room. His dour expression dissolved into a beguiled smile, as I knew it would.

I was always able to do that—delight my father with entertainments.

The other memory of him is that of smell, specifically of sawdust and cigarettes. In that same living room he had built bookcases to contain my parents' intellectual bounty: their enormous collection of books. Feverishly sawing and hammering, swallowed up by a fragrant cloud of wood chips and dust, he transformed the room overnight. One day the walls had been bare, the next they were striated with shelves stretching to the ceiling, my father poised on a ladder with a Camel dangling from his lips, delicately applying the last dollop of marine-blue enamel.

My father could do anything. To me he was the most wonderful, magical father there ever was. And he could delight me—enchant, really—as well, especially at bedtime, when the words in his lovingly shelved books burst into life. My father's sonorous voice brought Kipling's "great gray-green, greasy Limpopo River all set about with fever-trees" snaking right to the foot of my bed.

With my father life became an adventure. The minute he walked in the door at night, even the house seemed to take on a new energy, like a surge of electricity. Everything became charged, brighter, more colorful, more exciting.

And of course I couldn't wait to grow up and marry him.

With a father like that, my mother, no fragile flower, could only pale by comparison. And although he and I would later be estranged—he was in many ways the antithesis of a paternal paragon—it is my father who, of the two parents, provided the happiest memories of my childhood. Back then there were no ambivalences: My daddy loved me *no matter what.* My daddy would protect me. My daddy was perfect.

All fathers are, at first, heroes to their daughters, even when they're anything but heroic, even when they're away, even when they're tired or busy or angrily meting out punishments at the end of the day, or gone for good.

If mothers are to their children the domestic world, the humdrum, the predictable, the familiar and routine, fathers are the *other*—periodic, bigger, stronger, strange, *different.* Mothers represent the day, fathers the night—and the weekend, the holiday, the special dinner out.

I am, in part, describing a time preceding feminism and the divorce epidemic, a generation that shaped the fathers and most of the adult daughters who will be described in this book. Today the roles of women in the work force closely resemble those of their fathers; and many modern fathers are, arguably, becoming more like their mothers to children.

Theoretically both parents are able to provide for their children role models of achievement *and* tenderness, courage *and* compassion—able, as Toni Morrison, writing about black women, put it, to be "both safe harbor and ship . . . inn and trail."

But even with that generational caveat, not all that much has changed. Most children associate mothers with laundry and leftovers and Band-Aids and home. They associate fathers with the sights of cars, beaches, and ball games; the smells of grass clippings, sawdust, oil, sweat. The feel of whiskers against one's cheek. The sound of a rumbling, reassuring voice. The wider world, humming with possibilities.

Mommy is still the front-line parent, and Daddy is still the "other." Daddy is still "different." Daddy is still a daughter's defender, her hero, the first man in her life—no matter how old she is.

And daughters, more than sons, are often their fathers' particular delight; if a man is to yield to sentiment, it will likely be when describing his adored little girl.

Take Steve, a fifty-five-year-old criminal lawyer who prides himself on his intimidating courtroom style. Get him talking about his eighteen-year-old son, the high school quarterback, and he'll crow about the boy's football potential from day one. But get him reminiscing about his sixteen-year-old daughter, and his sharp features soften, his booming voice modulates to a bewitched awe.

> I was in the delivery room when she was born. The moment she wailed, in a voice I've come to know and dread—I remember it as clear as anything—I looked at this remarkable tiny thing, and my precise words were, "Oh, my goodness." It was just the wonder that this was my little girl.

What is it about the father-daughter attachment that gives it an air of unreality, of magic, of mystery? What makes the relationship so very different from that between mothers and daughters, or fathers and sons?

First Love, First Romance

For all children mothers are their first love, their first acquaintance with intimacy, touch, warmth, tenderness, sustenance. Infancy is a conspiracy between mothers and their babies, a bond that fathers can only helplessly witness, denied the profound pleasure and pain of giving birth. Fathers cannot experience the unique blending of bodies in pregnancy and breast-feeding that are the province of women alone.

Fathers, biologically at least, get second billing in the birthing process. Distant months ago they deposited the seed that would eventually result in bawling new life; but the main event, the center ring, belongs to mother and child.

Once they are home, father is demoted to *third* billing, displaced by the baby in his wife's previously undivided attention. To say that fathers often feel redundant and neglected, disenfranchised from the revolution in their lives now called "family," is to understate. Where once mother and father were merely a couple living together, playing house, the cadence of their lives virtually unbroken, now they snap into traditional roles, charted by memories of their own parents in the long-ago past. Marriage is forever changed when a child is born.

Most new fathers experience their own brand of emotional upheaval. Often they're downright envious of their wives' ability to have a baby, and even develop the paternal version of pregnancy symptoms, including exhaustion, weight gain, nausea, and backaches. But, let's face it, one cannot imagine that they envy the birth *process,* which one comedienne described as akin to having your lower lip pulled up over your head.

Fathers, galvanized into a new identity—Daddy—and new responsibilities, get into the act in other ways. If Mommy gets credit for childbirth, Daddy gets credit for penis power: A child is proof to the world that father truly is a *man,* a sexual, procreative creature, whose genitals, thank you very much, are in top working condition.

As one father, his face wreathed in a smile, put it, "I was delighted when my wife got pregnant. I'm macho enough for that to matter—that my sperm was, shall we say, viable."

Still, being a father is more than simply penis power. Mother may be a child's first love, but Dad quickly catches up in the baby's ardor. Men become fathers not simply by virtue of sexuality but because of their involvement. Perhaps in compensation for their biological redundancy, many fathers love to rock and hold their newborns, revealing an awkward kind of "infant hunger," a poignant need to bond that is physiologically denied them.

Babies know the differences between their mothers and fathers by as early as two or three months—particularly girls, who become attached to their fathers earlier than boys, for reasons that will be examined later in this chapter. Although all babies are emotionally connected to Mom earlier than to Dad, by the time they are around eight months old, they notice and need their fathers just as much as their mothers.

For good reason. According to Ross D. Parke, Ph.D., professor of psychology at the University of California, fathers, when left in charge of the baby, are *just as able as mothers* to respond to its cries of distress or loneliness or hunger, to feed and soothe the baby, to interpret what it is the baby needs. So important is this fatherly involvement that without it infants react more fearfully to strangers.

One of the greatest values of fathers, especially for daughters, is the very fact that they *are* costars in the parenting process. For without fathers the mother-daughter bond becomes *too* close, too mutually dependent. The father is crucial to what Margaret Mahler calls the "separation-individuation" of a daughter from her mother, because of the gender partnership of both "women": Mother is the daughter's genetic archetype, her role model in femininity. And daughter is the repository of all the mother's realized and unrealized hopes.

But whether a child is male or female, fathers are needed for their "otherness," to put a healthy wedge between mother and child, to be a haven from real or imagined maternal injustice or excessive hovering.

Most parents approach their firstborn child with dreams and self-doubts, joys and fears. But the dreams of mothers and fathers, shaped by tendrils of recollection, are spun into quite different forms.

A father brings to parenting a chorus of voices from his history, voices that evoke images of his own childhood. And so he watches his wife nurse his heir, or himself tenderly gives a bottle to the child, and begins to assert his role in the family. His dreams for that child, the ones that simmered for nine months, now become real in the baby's lusty cries or tranquil, innocent repose. And the dreams are instantly shaped by one fact alone: whether the infant is a *boy* or a *girl.*

While fathers cannot on a fundamental level know what it means to be either a mother or a daughter, they certainly know what it means to be a son. Having once been a "little man," they gaze at their own sons and see the boys they once were; they understand the biological engineering of their sons' bodies; they remember wet dreams, erections, pitched schoolyard battles for supremacy, brave efforts to hold back tears.

These voices from the past also conjure up images of *their fathers,* the man of the house, the head of the table, the arbiter of finances and family feuds, the parent sent downstairs to investigate a bump in the night or outside to peer under the hood of a recalcitrant car. Having a child ends forever a man's boyhood, if not his boyishness. Having a child means that the son has, in a real sense, *become* his father. Sons are for fathers a twice-told tale.

What, then, to make of a newborn daughter? It is here that the dreams of fathers for their children fork onto separate, gender-induced paths.

John Condry and Sandra Condry of Cornell University looked into the assumptions people make about children based on gender alone and how those assumptions get played out in parental behavior. The researchers asked 204 male and female college students to watch a videotape of a nine-month-old baby and to rate the emotional reactions of the child when presented with, among other things, a teddy bear, a jack-in-the-box, and a buzzer. Half the observers were told the infant was a "boy," the other half that it was a "girl."

The teddy bear produced in the baby reactions of pleasure, which the observers ranked as gender-neutral—that is, they could not tell from the baby's response whether or not it was a boy or a girl. The same uniformity of assessment—fear—occurred when the baby howled at the sound of the buzzer.

However, with the jack-in-the-box, which at first startled the baby and then caused it to scream, the observers tended to interpret the "girl's" reaction as one of fear and the "boy's" reaction as one of anger. But it was the *men* who perceived the greatest differences between the infant "boy's" and "girl's" reactions.

The researchers concluded that fathers tend to have more stereotypic perceptions of their children than mothers. Fathers *expect* their boys and girls to be different and as a result are more likely to *treat* those children differently. The child who is perceived to be afraid—a "female" trait—will need to be comforted; the child who is perceived to be angry—a "male" trait—will not.

Says Steve, fifty-four, the father of three girls,

> Sometimes I wish I'd had a son. I would like to do with a boy what I never did with my daughters. Physical things. Go to games, fly model airplanes, teach him about tools, and all that male crap. I never felt comfortable doing that with my girls. I wasn't going to wind up and really throw a ball at them *hard*. If I'd had a son, I'd probably want to take his hand off—just burn one in a couple of times.

For fathers, boys are familiar territory. Boys they *know*. Girls are simply a puzzle. It is no surprise, then, that most fathers, by a margin of nearly four to one, prefer boys to girls. In fact families with sons are somewhat less likely to divorce than those with daughters. And when there is a divorce, noncustodial fathers try harder to stay in touch with sons than with daughters.

This paternal bias for boys can be a mixed blessing for sons, who might respond, "Well, my dad sure has a funny way of showing it." Because fathers *are* a whole lot harder on, and expect more of, their sons than their daughters.

And it is against this background of bias and awkwardness that we begin to get an idea of why and how fathers behave as they do toward their daughters.

Daddy's Little Girl

"When I was born," writes John Cheever's daughter, ". . . it was my father [who] said, 'She'll have long blond hair and drive a sports car and we'll call her Susie.' "

Perhaps the most startling finding in the psychosocial studies I read regarding gender is this: Fathers—*much more than mothers*—are the dispensers of sex-role typing, beginning at birth.

Once babies are past the newborn stage, fathers gradually begin to push aside their natural ability to "mother" in a gender-neutral way—to nurture and accurately to read the emotions of their children—and instead assert not so much their parenthood as their parallel paternities: one for boys, the other for girls.

Says Dr. Parke, who has spent twenty years studying the behaviors of fathers with children,

> Women tend to be much more androgynous, and men tend to be somewhat traditional. Although there are pockets of men who are discovering their own capacities for being sensitive, there's a large percentage of men who still value the macho stereotypes, and that gets translated into activities that match boys and girls much more than women do.

Fathers often treat their little girls as though they might break. They hold their infant daughters more closely than they do their sons. According to one group of researchers, when simply looking at their newborns, they describe their sons as "firmer, larger featured, better coordinated, more alert, stronger, and hardier, while daughters [are] rated as softer, finer featured, inattentive, weaker, and more delicate."

Mothers tend to hold their babies primarily for caretaking—a required response for the child who needs to be fed, bathed, or changed—but fathers' involvement is more volitional: They tend to pick up their infants either to romp or because the babies want to be held.

Studies show that it is fathers, more than mothers, who love to roughhouse and be active with their kids. For this reason, fathers are often perceived by their children as simply being more fun than mothers. Part of their appeal may be that they are a novelty that never seems to wear off—they're just not around as much as mothers.

And when they *are* home, *it's playtime!* Many mothers have watched, aghast, as their husbands hurl their babies, especially their sons, into the air, scream *"Boo!"* or wildly swing them by their arms. Studies show that infants wriggle and squeal with delight when held by fathers more than when held by mothers. For daughters the "sex appeal" of men begins in this way—fathers as the source of all things exciting.

When it comes to toys, however, fathers tighten the gender-based screws: There will be no unisexuality, *especially* with their sons. While mothers generally allow both boys and girls to choose from an array of playthings, it is fathers who most often decree what is considered "appropriate" for sons and daughters.

Observe a father in a toy store with his toddler. Without knowing the child's gender, one can fairly easily guess its sex by seeing which toy the father eventually puts on his charge card. One father recalled for me just such an outing. "My son wanted a doll. Call me a sexist pig—I talked him into buying a truck instead." Less predictable are the purchases of mothers, who are not as insistant on toeing the toy/gender line.

By the time little girls are around two, when they discover that their sexual engineering is different from boys', and when they express pride in or frequently touch their genitals, many fathers feel uncomfortable with their daughters' "sexuality" and emotionally withdraw a bit from them. Then comes a long period when the daughter is something of a gender-neutral figure to Dad—not emphatically womanly, not particularly sexual—and he can once more unambivalently have fun with her. But when the daughter hits adolescence, her gender now blatantly obvious, Daddy may again beat a hasty emotional retreat.

Fathers treat their daughters differently in other ways as well. They're more protective of their daughters than their sons, and punish rambunctiousness in the former while rewarding it in the latter. Boys are allowed to cross the street at a younger age and to be out of the house for longer periods of time. Fathers also encourage their daughters' dependence by "helping" them, unbidden, with tasks far more often than they do sons. And while they want their sons to master a task, they want their daughters to have fun doing it.

Fathers are more likely to flirt with their daughters than mothers are to flirt with their sons. Moreover, it's not entirely true that dads don't talk. It's *how* they talk, and here, too, there are gender differences. In family gatherings fathers tend to interrupt and talk simultaneously with their children more than mothers and are more likely to direct their comments to sons than to daughters. When they do chat with their daughters, conversation tends to be sociable, whereas with sons conversation is likely to include threatening language and/or instruction.

For example, one man described his inability to resist with his sons—rather than his daughters—the impulse to lecture:

> My biggest problem is they'll ask me a question about, say, math, and I'll say, "Gee, that's really interesting, let me tell you all about quantum physics." I start with the assumption that my sons want to hear everything I know, and it's *not true*

—I can see the glaze set in their eyes. They'll say, "I just want to know how to finish this *one* problem, Dad."

What's *behind* all this paternal division of gender-linked labor? Why are fathers so hell-bent on creating dependent, demurring, fragile daughters, and tough, stoic, masterful sons? In my view there are four primary reasons:

- Homophobia
- A need for tenderness
- The incest taboo
- The family triangle

Homophobia

It could be said that a daughter learns to be "feminine" almost by default. For as much as a father wants to encourage his daughter to be womanly—the fine arts of which he usually leaves to his wife—it is far more urgent that his sons *not be.* Thus are the seeds of homophobia planted. Sons must not be girlish, not be sissies, not be homosexual—a concern far more prominent in fathers than in mothers.

For some fathers, especially those raised to adhere to rigid standards of masculinity, it is an instantaneous, if unconscious, cognitive leap from the son's picking up a doll to his becoming gay; from his becoming gay to being a social outcast; from there to his father's disgrace and humiliation in failing to provide the "proper" masculine role model—or, worst of all, being of dubious sexuality himself.

But it's no big deal if his darling daughter clomps around in Daddy's shoes, or plays in Little League, or becomes a tomboy— in fact Dad may secretly be pleased, even relieved. Not only is she flattering in her imitation of Dad—and does not, by virtue of being "just" a girl, challenge his potency and supremacy—she is also not yet enticing, not yet sexual, not yet at the point of leaving or replacing him.

But if his son plays "dress-up" with Mommy's frocks and jewelry and makeup, or gently cradles a doll, Dad gets rattled. Many fathers perceive a boyish girl as "spunky"; they perceive a girlish boy as "a mama's boy" or "a wimp" or an incipient "fag."

Even the most egalitarian, allegedly nonsexist of fathers.

Erica, thirty-two, recalls for me the moment when her husband —an avowed feminist—revealed his ambivalence about his nonsexist parental stance:

> We both were determined to raise our children androgynously. So when our daughter asked for a baseball mitt, and our son asked for a baby doll, we bought them. One day my son asked if he could take the doll to the supermarket, and I said, "Sure." But my husband wasn't crazy about the idea. He said, "You can play with it in the house. But if you go outside, why not leave it home." I couldn't believe it.

A Need for Tenderness

The second reason that fathers often treat their daughters with more delicacy, or at least benign neglect, is that fathers frequently crave their daughters' *nonsexual* tenderness. Says family therapist Dr. Frank Pittman, clinical assistant professor of psychiatry at the Emory University School of Medicine,

> We want our sons to compete with us, but we want our daughters to adore us. Our last hope is that our daughters may be able to see us as the fulfillment of our mothers' dreams for us—to be knights in shining armor. Our wives can never see us that way. A daughter's blind adoration may be the only time a man will ever get it from a woman.

And so we find fathers grunting and writhing with their sons on the floor in wrestling matches, or trying to demolish them on the tennis court, or giving them a slap on the butt. But we find them snuggling with their little girls on their laps, or caressing their hair, or holding hands with them on walks through the woods, or forfeiting tennis points to them on the court.

That often changes with anguishing abruptness in a daughter's adolescence.

Shifting Gears. When daughters begin to show evidence of sexuality—by menstruating, developing breasts, shucking their tomboyishness and primping for boys, most fathers recoil, as though their daughters' womanliness were a *deliberate* betrayal.

It is during daughters' teens that fathers make what is arguably their biggest mistake: They begin to withdraw their unalloyed adoration and instead hector them at the very time daughters need them most.

For just as Dad is beginning to pull back, teenagers tend to pull *way* back—all the way to childhood, or so it sometimes seems. They regress emotionally to what researcher Peter Blos calls "the second individuation-separation phase."

During the turbulent teens children embark on the bumpy transition from the world of the nursery to the world of adults. Where once they squared off into separate social camps—girls playing "house" with girls, boys playing ball with boys—now they begin to discover the opposite sex with immense fascination, even obsession. Childlike bodies are transformed from a kind of physical sameness to *obvious* differences. Sexual squaring off turns into sexual interest.

Paralleling these bodily changes is the regressive tug of the vastly simpler childhood years, as the teenager negotiates the raging hormones within and the terrifying outside world of adult challenges and heterosexual love. During these years teenagers ricochet between childlike dependence and a raucous trashing of all values parental. This replay of separation-individuation has the added dimensions of the teenager's intellectual seasoning, growing awareness of life's ambiguities, and libidinous hankerings. With one foot in adulthood, the other in childhood, they teeter between the two.

The adjustment of fathers to these changes is the stuff of sitcoms.

When the son starts pairing off with girls, a father is likely to send him into the connubial night with this two-word warning: "Be careful."

But when daughters start to date, to wear bikinis and jeans that would seem to cause gangrene, to put "gunk" on their faces, fathers become crazed. Fathers avert their bodies more with adolescent daughters, and even make less direct eye contact, than they did when the daughters lacked womanly contours.

And when they *do* look at daughters, they see not the girl but the *siren.* They grill her swains and imagine the worst—the plundering of their daughter's chastity and undivided filial devotion.

"Of course I gave my daughter permission to date," says Dan, chuckling, of his fifteen-year-old, "just as soon as she's forty-five, and with a guy who's ninety. And castrated."

Fathers can share their sons, but with daughters they have too much to lose: their sole source of unqualified, noncompetitive, worshipful love.

Fathers—not being female—compute a daughter's womanly body, not her immature emotions. They react to her readiness for sexual coupling, completely missing her emotional regression.

For the first time fathers hear the daughter's harsh judgments, which almost always begin with the words, *"Daddy, how could you!"*

One man, shaking his head with dismay, told me,

> The other day I drove my thirteen-year-old and her girl-friends to the movies. My wife had instructed me to put a lid on my "corny" jokes. To make sure I did as bidden, I started whistling. When my daughter got home, she screamed, *"How could you whistle? I was mortified!"* Jesus. I can't win.

Most fathers don't see the war within the daughter, her struggles with conflicting images of the idealized and flawed father, her temptation both to retreat to Daddy's lap and protection *and* to push out of his embrace to that of beau and of the world beyond home.

And they don't hear the implied questions in the daughter's confusing behavior: "Is it okay for me to grow up now? Is it okay for me to be a woman?"

And if they *do* hear those questions, the answer is likely to be *"Hell, no!"*

Says Dr. Marianne Goodman, associate clinical instructor in psychiatry at the Mount Sinai Medical Center in New York,

> Many fathers start picking on their daughters when the daughters are around eleven or twelve. They say, "How can you wear that? Take that stuff off your face!" The problem with fathers and adolescent daughters is that the father feels a natural attraction to a young woman who is adoring in a way that his wife no longer is. There are taboos imposed upon the attraction that make him feel that he is unnatural. His overcompensation is to put distance between himself and the

object of his attraction and confusion—his daughter. The easiest way is to devalue her by focusing only on her flaws.

The Incest Taboo

Part of Daddy's retreat is because of that very attraction, which for most fathers is totally unconscious. The unwritten rule against behaving seductively with one's opposite-sex child is, among other things, one way a father maintains a healthy distance from his little girl.

It is also one way to *keep* her a little girl, safely corralled by childhood and androgyny. But Daddy's retreat may be so abrupt that the daughter feels totally rejected.

Estelle, thirty-nine, put it this way:

> I was my father's favorite—until I was twelve. As a kid I would walk around in my underwear and leave the bathroom door open. But then I got a training bra. One day I was in the bathroom, and my father ran upstairs yelling, "Close that door!" From that moment on it was never the same. The affection left. He was really afraid of it—he kept the newspaper in front of him. From that day on, my brother was his favorite.

Certain feelings of attraction between parents and children are normal. Some parents experience a sense of their own sexuality when changing a child's diapers or feeling the baby's naked body against their own bare skin. And very young children often feel sexually stimulated when, say, they are bathed, and experience a delicious sense of pleasure when being stroked or held close.

Flirtatiousness between parents and their opposite-sex children—especially fathers with daughters—is also common. "How's my best girl?" and "Miss America better look for another job" and "I can't go to the office until I get my kiss" is part of the special father-daughter connection.

A few fathers told me that they simply *are* aroused by their adolescent daughters; the healthy ones accept their own arousability and do not cross the line between flirtation and seductive exploitation.

For it is *not* normal for parents to *act* on these feelings in an erotic way. And, as the horrifying incidence of sexual abuse of children, particularly girls, indicates, the barriers against incest are weaker than most people dare to imagine.

Still, for the majority of fathers, the incest taboo is so ingrained, so automatic, that they can't *imagine* the possibility of father-daughter attraction, let alone discuss it.

Consequently most fathers—especially since they've been trained to conceal their feelings—unconsciously or consciously believe that simply to *think* that their daughters are sexually attractive is actually to violate them, as though thought and deed were one; baiting or ignoring them is the surest libidinous defense.

The result is that daughters may perceive their fathers' behavior as disapproval and conclude that their fathers are either unpleasable or unloving—or that they themselves are unpleasing and unlovable.

The Family Triangle

When fathers withdraw from their developing daughters, they eagerly push mothers into the center of their daughters' lives—Mom becomes the buffer between sexually discomfited Dad and blooming child. Still, although father may be peering from the wings, he's very much a presence: Daughters discover a great deal about him *just by observing Mom.*

"Daddy's a very valuable commodity," says Dr. James Meltzer, director of psychology at Saint Luke's/Roosevelt Hospital Center in New York. "After all, Mommy wants him."

Which is why one cannot explore the father-daughter connection in splendid isolation from the family triangle. To do so is to forget one of the most important facts about being human: We are products of two parents, not one.

Any two-person relationship within the family is always influenced by a third—as in saying to a child, "My cousin Shirley was never nice to me when we were kids, and if you really love me, you'll have nothing to do with her." This is an example of what Dr. Murray Bowen and other family therapists call "triangling"—a component of "family systems" theory and therapy developed by Dr. Bowen that will be elaborated upon in Part Four.

What is being discussed here is the "family triangle"—the mother-father-child triad—in which we first learn what it means to be male or female and how to behave with members of the opposite sex.

For example, mothers are not simply models of femininity to their daughters but also examples of how a woman *reacts* to a man. Daughters learn about fathers, and men, not only by being with Dad but also by observing their parents' marital relationship—or its unraveling.

When mothers and fathers are supportive of each other, it makes each of their parental jobs infinitely easier. And parents who cannot bear being in one another's presence reveal as much, if not more, to a child about romantic love as anything the mother or father might say.

But parents are not, as we have seen, identical. They have a unique relationship, not only with each other but also with each child. Each makes a contribution to—or exacts a price from—individual sons and daughters. And each has a profound impact on the child's identity, which has an incalculably profound impact on that child's future relationships.

Numerous theorists have attempted to untangle with empirical tidiness the extraordinarily complex psychological connection between parents and their children. The original guru of the psyche —the ultimate arbiter of triangles—is of course Sigmund Freud.

According to Freud—whose work evolved in late-nineteenth-century, patriarchal Vienna—the organizing principle of the family is the Oedipal triangle between mother, father, and child, with father as the parent *in charge*. Drawing in part on what he acknowledged was an unfair cultural double standard—he blamed the social order for many of women's psychological problems—he formulated his theories about male and female identity.

Put simply, Freud believed that women—because they lack a penis—are morally, intellectually, and physically inferior to men. Consequently girls suffer from "penis envy"—without the wondrous organ, they are "wounded." Since mother, too, is minus a penis, she is also unfinished genital business, hence, horribly incomplete, a distinction that does not augur well for the mother-daughter relationship.

Enter the father, proprietor of the enviable appendage. What's a daughter to do about her terrible handicap? She will exchange her "wound" for fantasies of having her father's baby. But there's a hitch: Mom has Daddy—and his penis—all to herself. Hence she is archrival, to be got rid of, and Dad is elevated to beloved, idealized parent.

By the age of five or so, Freud believed, little girls give up the notion that they will seduce Daddy away from Mommy, because the price of doing so is the loss of mother's love, which the girl desperately needs. So she begins to put Oedipal things away and, instead, identifies with and becomes like her mother. Traces of her good/bad feelings for her father go underground until adolescence, when the girl has to make a choice: Dad or another man.

In her teens the daughter finishes the triangular Oedipal job by seeing her father (and her mother) through the prism of her chronological seasoning and hormonal changes—not as perfect and all-powerful but as good enough. So, too, does she see herself, as she leaves home for college or work or marriage, as good enough.

Unless, or course, something goes wrong—such as the father's absence or lack of involvement, or brutality, or excessive flirtatiousness or seductiveness—catastrophically altering the course of resolving her heterosexual yearnings and identity.

If the child is a boy, however, the Oedipal triangle works in quite another way. Boys *already* have a penis, but since Daddy's is grander and more elaborately garnished, they, too, suffer from "penis envy." But in this case envy includes rivalry for Mom, a no-win situation, given Daddy's power and the obvious preferability (to Mom) of Daddy's genital equipment. If the son were actually to succeed in "wooing" and winning Mom over, since father is bigger and stronger, the son might be punished—emotionally "castrated."

The son both longs for that early symbiosis with his mother, when she held him next to her body and nourished him with her breast, and fears it. For if he "chooses" Mom, his father will retaliate. To be loved by Dad, the little boy needs to renounce his first love: Mom. To play it safe, he must also banish all traces of her influence—her gentleness, her sensitivity—within his emotional wiring. Hence, Freud believed, sons bury their Oedipal desires by identifying with Dad.

Freud was a product of his stiffly formal, prudish times, when men laid down the law and were alleged to be the moral force of the world, and fragile women, feverishly repressing their sexuality, took to their beds with attacks of the vapors. Thus one cannot entirely separate his theories from the culture in which he lived.

Still, judging from the division of family labor that lingers to this day—Mom, working or not, in charge of the kids, Dad the primary breadwinner—the influence on one's identity of the family triangle hasn't changed a whole lot.

Feminist scholars, psychologists, and researchers, reworking Freud, still see men and women being raised in very different ways, which has an impact on how they ultimately treat their current or future partners and/or children.

Sociologist Nancy Chodorow, for instance, theorizes that mothers raise their daughters to *become* mothers or to have nurturing capacities. But mothers unconsciously—and, for the most part, unwittingly—discourage those qualities in their sons. Thus boys learn to be less invested in emotional commitments and almost totally invested in life and work outside relationships and the family. Because of the mother's huge responsibility for children in the nuclear family, and her devalued social importance in the culture, she plays a role in perpetuating male dominance.

Dr. Chodorow writes, "fathers often become external attachment figures for children of both genders during their preoedipal years. But the intensity and exclusivity of the relationship is much less than with a mother, and fathers are from the onset separate people and 'special.' "

The result is that for a daughter the loss of father's involvement can be compensated for, at least in part, by her ongoing connection to mother—and, later, by loving female friends.

But for a son, Chodorow argues, there is no such compensation: He must try to pattern himself on a man who probably is available to him only in the evening or on weekends, a man who may have little training in how to be close to anyone. To become a man, he must be *unlike his mother*—that is, he must not cry or express his pain or his need to love and be loved. He must deny his feelings.

To summarize Chodorow, daughters experience their fathers not so much by identifying with them as through their *relationship;* their closer bond—sometimes too close—is with Mom. Thus it is their autonomy that suffers. The reverse is true for sons, for whom *identification* with Dad, rather than emotional connection, is the primary tie. With boys it is relationships that suffer.

As these and other theorists make abundantly clear, the mother-father-child triangle is an immutable, ancient, and timeless fact of family: Little boys and girls *do* want to "marry" their mommies and daddies, because these are the first romantic figures in their lives. And when the resolution of the triangle is incomplete—when parents can't give *both* sons and daughters permission to grow into autonomous, secure, sensitive, sexual adults with partners of their own—it has ongoing consequences.

Resolving the Oedipal triangle is a tricky business, negotiated in the countless fits and starts of a child's emotional and physical growth. And unresolved triangles spill over into our adult lives and relationships.

Most men and women carry within them two voices from childhood, two models for "appropriate" human behavior—the "masculine" and the "feminine." And, depending on which parent was more influential in youth—as well as other variables, which will be discussed in a moment—sometimes they totally disavow one "voice," and the other takes over.

Here's how it works. Some men are drawn to strong women; these men are emotionally guarded with women as a defense against the "reengulfing" mother—that is, the woman who seems to be too maternal, too confining, too possessive. A doting woman may "feel" to him as though she were his own mother, an attraction vigorously to be deflected. For such men *all* things "female" —including therapy or their own tender inclinations—are threatening.

Other men are drawn to passive women, whom they treat as servants. Such women do not threaten a man's "power" or "masculine" identity. Yet a tender woman may nevertheless serve an important psychological purpose—she acts out his denied "feminine" side for him. On the surface he may hate in her the "weakness" he tries so hard to cover up in himself, but at the same time he needs her to do the "feeling" work for him.

In women we see similar patterns of romantic attraction. Some "strong" women are drawn to men who can be easily manipulated. These men act out the woman's disavowed "feminine" side.

Other women, who are ultrafeminine, coy, and dependent, whose "masculine" strengths were suffocated in childhood, may be attracted only to domineering men. These women see men as either big and strong or as spineless wimps. In furiously denying her own strength, such a woman may need an authoritative man to act out her ambition and anger—her "masculine" side—for her. She may be drawn to much older, or married, or unavailable, or— in extreme cases—brutal men.

In all these ways the family triangles of the distant, forgotten past—when we learned both what it means to be masculine or feminine and how men and women are "supposed" to behave with one another—are echoed in how we react as adults to members of the opposite sex.

"All right," a father, bombarded with all this data, might wearily admit, throwing up his hands in exasperation, "so I *do* treat my sons and daughters differently. But they simply *are* different. Are you going to tell me that they're the *same?"*

My answer would be a hearty "Yes. And No."

Men and Women: How Different Are They?

No one would reasonably argue that males and females are genetically, hormonally, physically, and emotionally identical. But with equal certainty it can be argued that men and women are, within a range of behaviors, talents, and personalities, more alike than they are different.

Which makes one wonder how Freud's theories would look if, as a young graduate student, he were formulating them today. For what he would witness is light-years away from turn-of-the-century Vienna. He would see about him women who are taking on many of the attributes of their own fathers as they move between the office, the day-care center, and home, or as they refuse to marry. He would see them going off to fight wars in, say, the Iraqi desert while their husbands mind the kids Stateside.

He would see a mere 27.5 percent of American families abiding by the traditional family roles of his time—Dad at work, Mom at home with the kids. He would see nearly a quarter of all American children living in households headed by women. He would see seven million children of gay and lesbian parents, and real estate laws defining a gay couple as a "family."

He would see male construction workers with hair grazing their shoulders or smartly bound in a ponytail, their earlobes sparkling with jewelry. He would see fathers present in delivery rooms and altogether anonymous in sperm-bank vials, resulting in some thirty thousand artificially inseminated births per year.

All of which raises the question: How different are men and women *really*? Let's begin with anatomy.

Biology. All embryos begin life as female. By six weeks or so sex genes begin to alter sexual development; male hormones are stimulated in the genetic male, while the genetic female continues along her gender path. When the newborn is around seven months old, male and female hormones go into hibernation, laying low until puberty.

Other biological factors are breathtakingly obvious: Boys have penises, which will later be employed in the service of procreation; girls have breasts for eventual feeding and uteruses for eventual reproduction. Infant girls tend to be less physically active than boys and have greater skin sensitivity and a keener sense of smell. Boys have greater muscle mass than girls, who have twice as much body fat. As they age, women thicken around the hips, men around the middle.

In the erogenous zone, male orgasm and the capacity for impregnation are simultaneous; women can become pregnant without having an orgasm. Nature provides real and unique incentives for women to make babies—the erotic pleasure of nursing makes breast-feeding something other than, say, washing the car. To sweeten the procreative deal, orgasm in women is intensified by the congestion of blood in the pelvic area, and each pregnancy boosts such congestion.

So far, so good. But since boys and girls tend to be treated differently from birth onward, it is nearly impossible to tell the difference between innate and learned behavior.

Not that researchers don't try.

Sociologist Alice S. Rossi splits the gender difference by arguing that human behavior cannot be assessed apart from biology—that is, hormonal development plays an important role in *the ease with which males and females learn (and unlearn) socially defined appropriate gender behavior.*

But questions *still* abound with frustrating inconclusiveness about what is inherent and what is learned.

To take just one example: Little boys exhibit greater visual acuity and spatial-relationship ability, while little girls are better with language. But is that nature or nurture? As we know, fathers are more specific and task-oriented in their behavior with sons, encouraging in them visual-spatial play, and more sociable and casually chatty with girls; research also shows that mothers imitate the sounds of their infant girls more than those of boys.

Given these findings, how, in this example, does one divine the intrinsic, "inherent" differences between the two sexes?

As for personality, there is evidence—also debated in some

quarters, as we shall see—that certain personality traits are inherited. One woman I interviewed who was adopted at birth found her biological father thirty years later and was stunned to see the similarities between them:

> First, we look alike—we have the same nose, the same mouth, the same ears, eyes and facial structure. Spookier is that we have the same speech patterns. We use the same words, timing and inflection. We have the same way of making jokes when we're uncomfortable. We also share some awful traits—bravado, wanting to be the center of attention, the life of the party.

But the nurture-nature debate *really* heats up on the question of aggression. Recent studies of the effect of genes on personality indicate that aggression may or may *not* be inherited. Leadership is said to be the characteristic most determined by genes; achievement and the need for intimacy are said to be least affected; and aggression falls somewhere in between.

Some theorists consider aggression to be an inherently male trait, depending on the degree of testosterone coursing through a man's body; hence most women, having less of the male hormone, are not innately assertive. Others disagree. Writes psychiatrist David W. Krueger, of the Baylor College of Medicine in Houston, "There is no substantial experimental evidence which proves that sex hormones are directly responsible for the sexual dimorphism of aggression or assertion."

How aggression is *interpreted* is a far more telling cultural index of who *ought* to be feisty and who ought not. For a man to assert himself is to fulfill his cultural and biological destiny—and to *fail* to do so is to be a disgrace to his sex. For a woman to assert herself is to be a "barracuda," a "ball-breaker," a "dyke."

As Rossi notes, often banished to the theoretical netherworld is the sight of a mother ferociously protecting her children, hardly a "pretty" or "passive" sight. So, too, is the singular cruelty of little girls to one another, as in "Let's not let her play with us today."

Then there is the notion of greater "male" intelligence, particularly in math and the sciences. This, too, has been called on the methodological carpet. Some researchers question the use of certain population samples in specific studies as the basis for generalizations about intelligence—as, for instance, the SAT test for college entrance. Results since 1972 have shown that males have done much better than females on the math portion and have a slight edge on the verbal portion. However, the majority of the test takers are women who are less affluent and less well educated than male test takers. As Janet Shibley Hyde, a professor of psychology, told *Newsweek,* "The men are a more highly selected sample: they're better off in terms of parental income, father's education and attendance at private school."

If the assumption based on such tests is that girls are less intelligent than boys, expectations of parents and teachers will reflect that assumption. So will the children themselves—a frightened or discouraged child simply will not test well.

"The only useful answer to the question, 'Who is smarter, a man or a woman?'," Estelle Ramey, M.D., professor emeritus of physiology at Georgetown University, told a reporter, "is, *Which* man and *which* woman?"

Then there is the matter of sensitivity, supposedly a "female" trait. "Most men are as capable of connecting emotionally as women," says Dr. Ellen Berman, clinical associate professor of psychiatry at the University of Pennsylvania School of Medicine. "Otherwise, there wouldn't be any male therapists."

The last word on the nurture/nature fracas belongs to psychologist and researcher Louise J. Kaplan, Ph.D.: "No biological trait," she told me, *"not one*—except, perhaps, blood type—is independent of environmental shaping."

Gender Identity. "One is not born, but rather becomes, a woman," Simone de Beauvoir observed. The same can be said of a man.

We know what "femaleness" is and is not—get undressed, look in the mirror, and you'll see. But being *female* and being *feminine* are not necessarily the same thing. Being feminine, to reframe Henry Higgins's definition of a "lady" in Shaw's *Pygmalion,* depends almost entirely on how you are treated. Femininity is a reciprocal process, a social evolution.

By the age of around eighteen months a child's gender identity —the sense that one is either a boy or a girl—is pretty much fixed. That sense is a result not only of toddlers' becoming aware of their differing genitals at this age; it is also because children begin to talk at approximately the same time. Researchers believe that the combination of biological sex awareness, cognitive ability, and how parents treat boys and girls coalesces into a general idea of what it means to be either one sex or the other.

"The basic imprint of gender," writes Dr. Krueger ". . . cannot be altered by therapeutic intervention." But, he adds, in a critically important distinction,

> The sex that is attributed to an infant during the initial two years of life . . . plays the *most important role of all possible variables, including genetic, hormonal, and anatomical factors, in the establishment of gender identity."* [Emphasis added.]

Thus there is a big difference between gender identity and gender role.

Gender Role. When Letty Cottin Pogrebin was conducting interviews for her book *Growing Up Free,* which made a strong case for nonsexist childrearing, she asked a number of fathers about their ideas of masculinity and raising sons. "One man said that he thought it was very important for a father to be a masculine role model and set the tone," she told me. She continued,

> I asked him to give me an example, and he said, "Well, I want him to know that men shake hands and don't kiss when they say hello and goodbye. So I started shaking hands with him to give him that feeling."
> I said, "How old was he at that time?"
> He said, "Three."

One problem in teasing out from this tangle what is considered one's "normal" gender role is that it is not necessarily what was considered "normal" when the women described in this book were growing up. Definitions of femininity and masculinity depend on the prevailing cultural and generational norms against which they are measured.

"Femininity" per se—as defined by the wearing of frilly clothes and makeup, "ladylike" body language, coquettishness, ability to cook or decorate a house, staying home to raise the kids—has, rightly so, come under attack for being a stereotype, particularly by feminists.

That which is considered "manly" is also debatable. With movies such as *Kramer versus Kramer, Tootsie, Mr. Mom,* and *Three Men and a Baby,* and books such as Robert Bly's *Iron John*—to say nothing of television personalities such as Fred Rogers, a decidedly gentle and nurturing man—one cannot categorically define what constitutes the quintessential man.

But opinions abound. And if one adheres to outdated, "traditional" generalities about each gender, one argues for the continued squaring off of men and women against each other.

The social structure that spawned most of our gender-linked assumptions and early twentieth-century psychosocial theories has all but vanished: Children are not raised solely by parents, isolated from the world; and growing numbers of them are brought up by one parent only. Beyond mother and father there is the steady, relentless beat of social messages from film, TV, and periodicals, which either shore up or sabotage lessons about gender roles first learned in the family.

Perhaps, suggests sociologist Joseph Pleck, it's a matter "not that we have to make men and women the same [but] that we do not have to strive so hard to make them different."

So what's "normal" femininity?

Writes Dr. Robert Stoller, who has closely examined this question, "Femininity . . . is not what *is* but what people *say it is,* an opinion."

Beginning at home.

Sorting It Out

A girl's sense of her womanly self depends only in part on how closely she has followed her mother's example in attire and actions, or how much she loves or hates or respects her. It is from *both* parents that a girl gains her basic identity. As Dr. Miriam M. Johnson put it, she learns about "maternal femininity" from her mother, but she learns about "heterosexual femininity" from her father.

There is no question that mothers color their daughters' views of their fathers. And, as we shall see in later chapters, other variables—including siblings, socioeconomic class, temperamental "fit," health, chance, and the passage of time—also modulate the father-daughter bond.

But the greatest impact on a woman's romantic choices and her ability to feel comfortable in her own sexual skin is how her *father* treated her in childhood.

The thousands of gestures and responses between father and daughter are woven into her identity as a woman *to whom a man responds in a special way.* And how she will react to future men — the theme of her romantic choices—will be an amalgam of all those grace notes of Dad through the years. She will be either secure or uncertain; flirtatious or "frigid"; demanding or compliant; defiant or meek; a mature, confident woman or a living doll.

The determination by a father of what is considered appropriate female behavior is negotiated in the countless interactions between him and his daughter throughout her growing up years. In the hidden reaches of the daughter's illusory memory she will, however unconsciously, measure the man of the moment against the first man in her life.

It is from her father that she begins to infer messages that will linger a lifetime—"I am, or am not, considered by men to be pretty, desirable, valuable, dependent, weak, strong, dim-witted, brilliant"; "men are, or are not, trustworthy, loving, predatory, dependable, available, dangerous."

If a daughter is unable to win her father's approval for her *self,* and not simply her achievements or "womanly" virtues, she may believe that she is unacceptable to other men, or she may choose men who can never measure up to her image of Daddy. She may believe that she can't live without a man—or that all men are no damn good.

So, what are fathers for? What is their unique value to girls? I believe a father can provide any or all of the following to his daughter:

One man's opinion—a viewpoint and way of being, a source of emotional and intellectual and tutelary richness that is different from Mom's.

One man's history—continuity from his past to her future, knowledge from his experience, his victories and failures.

One man's chemistry—his genes mingling with hers; his face and features, inflections and temperament, moods and instincts, all contributing to the alchemy of her personality.

One man's empathy—a haven from mother, a court of appeal, a source of perspective.

One man's body—his beard and scent, his frame and strength, his touch and sheltering arms, giving her the first, wondrous *feel* of a loving man's physical intimacy.

One man's charmed attention—a chance to rehearse, in a way that she cannot with her mother, what love with a man can be like.

One man's validation—a chance to voice and test her opinions, which he will not perceive as betrayals.

One man's adaptability—the capacity to weather with equanimity the seasons of his own life as well as hers.

One man's willingness to learn—from the triumphs and tragedies of her life, as well as his own.

Without any of that a daughter aches with questions. She has no dress rehearsals for heterosexual friendship and love—a handicap from which many women, their emotional histories littered with shattered hopes, never recover. Without a father's dependable involvement a woman is in some way forever incomplete, and "men" are so much theory.

A daughter needs a loving, available, predictable father or father figure who can be counted on, whether divorced or at home. She needs his best paternal intentions, even if his efforts occasionally fall short. She needs his maturity and limit setting and sexual oppositeness, so that she can function with confidence in the wider world of adult love and work.

For when a father gives his daughter an emotional visa to strike out on her own, he is always with her. Such a daughter has her encouraging, understanding daddy in her head, cheering her on—not simply as a woman but as a whole, unique human being with unlimited possibilities.

Alas, many daughters do not have that kind of father.

2

Silent Partner

My father and I had so distant a relationship that after he died, I can honestly say that I hardly ever gave him another thought. But I think of my mother often. I'll see the back of someone's head in a store and it will remind me of her, and I'll feel a pang. My father was just so inaccessible. How can you miss somebody who was there but just wasn't a part of your life?

—EMILY, FORTY-THREE

Emily is a treasured friend who, until our friendship reached the soul-baring stage, I envied for what appeared to be a seamless, charmed life.

Even her childhood seemed to have been idyllic. She was the adored only daughter of a loving mother and a father who was a highly respected scholar and teacher. Emily graduated at the top of her Ivy League class, married a successful lawyer, and had three children, for whom she has replicated her perfect past.

Except that it wasn't perfect. Her mother was too possessive, too needy, to allow Emily completely to separate from her—an issue with which Emily still wrestles. And her father was anything but affectionate or available. He was always holed up in his study, not to be disturbed. He took almost no interest in her friendships, her doubts, her joys—indeed, anything except her report cards.

And so Emily married a man who, she *thought*, would be the antithesis of her father. "I didn't choose him because he'd make an ideal husband," she says. "I married him because he'd make a wonderful father: The day I saw how tender he was with his nieces was the day I accepted his proposal."

Emily's husband is indeed responsive to his children. But when it comes to *her* emotional needs, it's as though they don't exist. "Why is it," she once asked me rhetorically, "that the only time he takes me seriously is when I'm screaming at the top of my lungs?"

Why indeed. For if you scratch below the glossy surface of many "enviable" marriages, often you'll find a disenchanted wife whose husband finds the landscape of her emotions as uninteresting as the moon's. And if she *really* examines the relationship, she may discover that there once was a man in her life *who was just like that:* her father.

But such women usually have trouble making that connection, because this is not the stuff of police blotters or television bulletins. This is the stuff of intangible, emotional loss—of unexplainable wounds that linger, like a bruise, from an injury that is long forgotten.

This, in fact, is the stuff of fathers who are silent partners within the family.

If in my research I hoped to discover that my experience with my father was unique, I was sadly disappointed: When it comes to fatherhood and its repercussions in a woman's life, it's not so much a question *that* fathers are uninvolved with their children; rather, it's how extraordinarily widespread the phenomenon is. Especially for daughters.

Study after study bears out this melancholy observation.

Dr. Stella Chess, for example, in her almost four decades of researching children and individuality, has found that one of the few recurring themes among children is their difficulties in getting closer to Dad.

And, according to the data gathered for her book *Daughters: From Infancy to Independence,* only two of the more than thirty women she studied had unalloyed memories of loving, attentive fathers. "We were unprepared for the predominantly negative outpouring from the rest," she writes. Most daughters had figuratively to dance for father's approval—and even then weren't altogether sure they'd get it.

To take another example, Dr. Seymour Fisher, in his ground-breaking, five-year study of the sex lives of three hundred women, found that among women who have trouble reaching orgasm, most had fathers who were emotionally or physically absent during their childhoods. Their fathers simply couldn't be depended upon.

The seminal study of the father-daughter relationship, and the one to which virtually all subsequent researchers refer, was conducted in 1972 by E. Mavis Hetherington, professor of psychology at the University of Virginia. In it she explored the effect of father absence on the personalities of adolescent girls, comparing daughters from intact families, daughters whose parents were divorced, and those whose fathers had died.

One of Hetherington's most significant findings was a *delayed* reaction by girls to father loss. Boys seemed to experience emotional upheavals earlier, which dissipated sooner. Not so girls, whose quiescent pain erupted in adolescence. For these girls men were not only "other" but were also the imagined source either of rescue or of rejection.

All the girls in Hetherington's study were less comfortable talking with male interviewers and made less eye contact—perhaps because they were teenagers—than with female interviewers. But their behavior with boys and men showed sharp differences, depending on the quality of their ties to their fathers.

Girls from divorced families tended to be seductive or assertive with male interviewers. They craved male attention, which they sought by hanging around boys' games or the stag line at dances.

The girls whose fathers had died were extremely anxious and shy with male interviewers, and they tended to avoid boys altogether.

Those girls from intact homes were the least uncomfortable with male interviewers and, of the three groups, were the least awkward with boys.

I interviewed Dr. Hetherington to find out if these twenty-year-old findings still hold up, especially in light of her subsequent studies of the girls. "Absolutely," she replied, adding,

> We followed these kids into their marriages. They tended to marry the images of their fathers. Daughters of widows often married people who were, one of the interviewers commented, "repulsively straight"—good providers, very traditional. Our divorce girls tended to be sexually active early, to marry people with drug and alcohol problems, and to be pregnant when they got married. When girls brought up with no warm, supportive male around venture out into heterosexual relationships, there's more anxiety, because it's a new experience for them. It's like encountering your first aardvark and saying, "What is this strange creature? How am I to re-

spond to him? How is he to respond to me?" Whereas girls from mother-headed households who have close relationships with, say, grandfathers or uncles or brothers, are less likely to feel that way.

Most studies of father absence focus on divorce or death. But I have found in my sample as many daughters from intact families who experience "father hunger" as those whose fathers abandoned them or who saw them only on visitation day.

Says therapist Ronald Gaudia, who has treated a large number and variety of men in his thirty-year practice, "The concept of 'father absence' is misused. The guy who isn't involved in the family when he's home, who says, 'Ask your mother,' is 'absent.' "

Dr. Hetherington concurs:

It isn't just the physical presence of the father that matters—it's his engagement and involvement. An emotionally remote or rejecting or actively punitive father leads to girls' feeling pretty apprehensive around men.

Paternal neglect, even in intact families, can have a shattering effect on how daughters—even those with loving mothers—feel about men. Says Karen, thirty-eight,

My father would work six days a week, and on the seventh order us to help our mother with the housework. I'd think, "Who are you to tell us what to do? You're just a visitor here." My mother never complained about how little she saw of my father and always encouraged us to love him. Still, the message I got was her dissatisfaction about being tied to the house and kids while Daddy got to be the king everyone waited on.

Many fathers are not just uninvolved; what's striking is that their daughters are simply not a priority. This became abundantly clear when I interviewed a leading figure in the men's consciousness-raising movement. With an infectious and charming zeal he proudly declared that conferences of feminist men are, at last, putting on their agendas the enormous concern fathers have about their ability to be good parents—*to sons.*

When I asked, "What about the daughters?" he was stymied. After a long pause he replied, "That's a good question."

When fathers *are* lovingly involved with their daughters from birth, the daughters reap the benefits all their lives. Daughters who had fathers they could count on are the most likely to be drawn to men who treat them well, to see their lovers as dependable people who won't suddenly disappear, and to be consistently orgasmic.

But the less involved the father, the more vulnerable the daughter is to feelings that she's "just a girl"; to a sense that she deserves rejection or exploitation; to an inability to experience sexual release; and to unaccountable bouts of depression. Even when Mom and Dad are still together.

In a 1987 study of college-age women and their fathers—all from intact families—it was found that those daughters most likely to become depressed had fathers who frequently were insensitive, unaffectionate, and unavailable. These young women often had trouble in their relationships and felt a keen sense of unworthiness and guilt.

The psychological absence of fathers can be nearly as devastating as physical absence. When fathers are alive but not a predictable presence actively participating in their daughters' lives, the relationship becomes a permanent "maybe."

Five Degrees of Separation

Which is not to say that *all* the fathers of the women I interviewed were distant. Many were very much a part of their daughters' lives. What was of significance, however, was the *kind* of paternal participation.

Some fathers were eager and loving and concerned parents to their daughters. Others hovered over their daughters in a kind of parody of excessive maternality. Still others were daunting in their constant demands and punishments, or terrifying in their seductiveness. Whatever the degree or kind of involvement, these fathers were a minority.

The majority of fathers were, *or seemed to be,* in one way or another either shadowy figures or indifferent to their daughters.

According to the women I interviewed, there were five variations of this paternal distance:

- Work priority
- Emotional absence
- Physical absence
- Favoritism toward sons
- Maternal interference

Work Priority. The most common lament among daughters was that their fathers rarely seemed to be at home. Even those who were utterly devoted to their fathers remarked on how much time was eaten up by their fathers' job. In some cases work overload was an unavoidable consequence of economic need (most mothers were housewives); in others it was a matter of career priority.

Said Roberta, thirty-nine, whose father was an electrician,

> I wish he'd been around more often; he wishes it too. But he had a family to support and didn't want my mom to work. The only thing my parents fought about was money—there never seemed to be enough to pay the bills. So I just didn't see him much. Except weekends. That's when we'd go to the beach or the zoo. Weekends with Dad were the best—only he worked Saturdays too.

Emotional Absence. Even when fathers worked regular hours, many were a silent presence at home. These fathers were roused for damage control—to shovel snow, remove the carcasses of dead mice, negotiate parking tickets and flat tires, talk tough to the car mechanic who overcharged Mom.

But day-to-day conversation with kids, especially daughters, was in short supply. Even otherwise gregarious fathers would dummy up at home.

Said Edna, twenty-seven,

> My father was Mr. Nice Guy at the department store where he worked—everybody loved him. But at home he was a nonperson. He just wasn't a talker. You could never have a real conversation with him. When I'd ask him a question, he'd say, "Go ask your mother." Outside the house he was always the first with a joke; inside it was like he wasn't there. People would never believe me when I'd tell them that. They'd say, "What do you mean? He's *great*!"

Physical Absence. A number of women had fathers who simply were gone, either because of choice—through divorce, desertion, or suicide—or because of chance—as in death by accident or due to illness. Whatever was the cause of their fathers' defection, all these daughters felt that any chance for getting Daddy's attention and approval was gone for good. Sadly they usually were right.

In the case of divorce an estimated 90 percent of children are in the custody of their mothers, which, admittedly, puts fathers at a considerable disadvantage at the outset. But as the postdivorce years grind on, these fathers see less and less of their children; up to half have no regularly scheduled visits with their children. Half of these children have never been in their fathers' home, and 42 percent haven't seen their fathers in a year. And, as was noted earlier, fathers who do visit tend to do so more for sons, and for a longer amount of time, than for daughters.

Contrast this with noncustodial mothers, who see their children at a significantly higher frequency. Only 7 percent of children living apart from their mothers have not seen their mothers in the previous year; and 58 percent sleep over at their mothers' house at least once a month.

Some daughters were simply abandoned by their fathers. Elaine, thirty-seven, whose parents divorced when she was an infant, was told by her mother that her father had died when she was a baby. When, two decades later, a distant cousin violated the "family secret" and inadvertently tipped Elaine off that he was, in fact, still alive, Elaine tracked him down, after months of detective work. Of their reunion, she says,

> I asked why he never tried to get in touch with me. He claimed he had sent letters that were never given to me. Then I said, "Well, you could have just shown up." He replied, "I didn't want to rock the boat. I figured you were happy, why spring this on you?" I never got a satisfying answer out of him. Do I forgive him? What's to forgive? I don't have the emotional commitment to him that forgiveness requires. He's my biological father. That's it.

But daughters whose fathers died had a very different response to their "abandonment." Daddy often got enshrined in their memories, sealed in a psychic compartment of wistful, adoring loss.

Says Carly, thirty-six, whose father died when she was four,

I know he loved me. I'm sure of it. I spend a lot of time looking at old photo albums, and he seems like such a nice guy. I can tell from the pictures of me sitting on his lap that he was a lot of fun, that he was good to me.

Favoritism Toward Sons. Many women told me that they were unimportant to their fathers because, as one put it, "boys are better." They were, by biological definition, second-rate.

One woman, a high academic achiever, said,

I was always afraid to bring home prizes from school, because my father thought it would hurt my brother to have a sister outdo him. Consequently I never got compliments. Dad always said that praising me would discourage my brother. So my brother was always coddled—by all of us. I figured it was my job too.

Said another woman,

The rules in my family were relaxed for my brother. When it came to dating, he could sleep around, I couldn't. My family is Jewish, yet it was okay if he went out with non-Jewish girls. I once had a date with a Catholic, and my father flipped out. I resented the double standard—but that's just the way it was.

Maternal Interference. The final reason many fathers are at an emotional remove from daughters is that—compared to women— they simply aren't trained in parenting and often are terrified by their own ignorance.

If fathers elect to be backseat parents, often it's because their wives *prefer it that way.* One study found that up to *80 percent* of mothers do not want their husbands to be more involved with the children, for reasons that will be explored in Chapter 3.

Paternal reticence results in the *indirect* influence fathers have on their daughters—that is, through their *direct* influence on mothers. The relative gains and losses of this secondhand fathering depend on whether or not the mother is encouraged and admired or denigrated by her husband.

In view of all this paternal distance I was surprised by the daughters' extraordinary fairness—their byzantine struggles to justify their fathers' absence or neglect, their fathers' silence or anger, even their cruelty. One reason came from Elaine, whose father abandoned her when she was born and whom she found when she was grown.

"Did you ever say to him, 'I'm furious with you for leaving and never looking back'?" I asked.

"No," she replied. "If I expressed my anger—if I even admitted it to myself—I wouldn't have a father at all."

The Idealization of Fathers

Whether they had fathers who defected, or who were merely silent partners in the family, most daughters shared a stunning protectiveness, a tendency to excuse their fathers' remoteness or to idealize them beyond all proportion of the facts of their childhoods, a phenomenon writer Letty Cottin Pogrebin calls Teflon fathers.

Why does Daddy—much more often than Mom—get forgiven by daughters? Why this search for silver linings in so cloudy a relationship? Dr. Frank Pittman gave me the beginning of an explanation by saying, "We forgive fathers almost anything—once they leave. When they're *really* around, there's no idealization."

A more detailed understanding comes from Dr. Ernst L. Abelin, who, drawing on the work of Margaret Mahler, describes the concept of "refueling": a child's need to have sufficient emotional "fuel" to toddle, and later, walk, farther and farther from the comforting parental embrace. It is from the parent who is *most* absent that the child needs the most "refueling." "The longer the absence," Abelin writes, "the greater the need for [this] refueling."

Since it is fathers, much more than mothers, who are absent, it is not surprising that children often seem to prefer their fathers, because they so desperately crave Dad's longed-for, reassuring presence. In the delicate balance of a child's emotional negotiation, it makes perfect sense to impart to fathers heroic qualities. Surely, they think, Daddy would be here if he could; he must be doing something *very* important out there.

Some sons express their need for a father's refueling by vowing to become just like Daddy when they grow up, even if such vows are alien to their own talents and ambitions. And, in extreme cases, they express it by becoming transsexuals—their desperate "solution" to father absence is to decide not to imitate their fathers *at all.*

Some daughters express their father hunger in adolescence by becoming "boy crazy," or, in adulthood, by being drawn to men who are just like Dad. Or by avoiding men altogether. Or by believing no man can possibly live up to their vision of Dad.

And some daughters express it by starving. Father absence has been implicated in anorexia nervosa, in which daughters may exhibit father hunger by literally starving themselves.

The psychological mechanisms for coping with emotional loss, which seem to be tailor-made for daughters, include the following:

Identification with the Aggressor. This emotional defense against psychic pain is so ingrained in women that it's almost automatic.

Most people can recall schoolyard confrontations with bullies. Boys were expected to deal with them by standing their ground and slugging it out, even, as one man told me, "if you knew you were going to get your head bashed in. You had to show you could take it, and you'd *die* rather than cry."

But for girls the surest and safest way to avoid being picked on or terrorized is *to get the bully to like you.*

Here is an example of the imbalance of power and physical strength between boys and girls, men and women. If boys are bigger and stronger than girls, you can guess who's going to choose flattery or tears over flight or fight.

Girls identify with powerful males with uncanny ingenuity. They do it in childhood either by cozying up to them ("What muscles!"), or by looking for flaws ("I hear he wets his bed at night"). Only rarely do they try to be as tough as boys, with—given their relatively greater physical weakness—predictable results.

The False Self. Girls are also astonishingly adept at figuring out what their parents expect of them, and delivering it. If Daddy wants his little girl to be demure, or obedient, or more like a boy, or his biggest fan, the daughter will find ways to accommodate him.

To fail to please Daddy puts girls in terrible peril: "I need my daddy's protection, and since he's so rugged and wise and I'm so little, he must know what's best for me. He might even harm me if I don't do what he asks—or, worst of all, he might leave." Therefore, the little girl reasons, what she's feeling deep in the pit of her stomach—that he's unfair, or mean, or neglectful, or maybe, *maybe,* too friendly—must be very, very wrong.

This brilliant, albeit costly, logic, is what psychologist D. W. Winnicott calls "the false-self personality" at work.

Mothers and fathers all impart to their children the ground rules of acceptability. And children, in a kind of emotional juggling act, try to find ways to please them *both,* stifling their own talents, their own gut reactions, their own awareness of what is true and right and just.

Psychologist Alice Miller describes this complex survival mechanism in terms of mothers, but it applies equally to fathers:

> [Children develop] the art of not experiencing feelings, for a child can only experience his feelings when there is somebody there who accepts him fully, understands and supports him. If that is missing, if the child must risk losing the mother's love or that of her substitute, then he cannot experience these feelings secretly "just for himself" but fails to experience them at all.

Thus little girls whose fathers are remote or absent or abusive suppress their *true selves.* They bury their instincts under layers of denial, like icing on a decaying cake. They put a pretty face on their own pain.

If, for example, Daddy scares them, the safest recourse is to become "all girl"—uncomplaining, yielding, adoring, proud to have so masterful a guardian who might, in a macho-challenging pinch, come to their aid.

Anything to avoid seeing Daddy as he is: someone who is *accountable.* Someone who either has not sufficiently been there for them or cannot express love. Or someone who distorts love—or is incapable even of feeling it.

The adult legacy of the false self can be seen in women who lay low when their partners are on a tear, or who believe they can't survive without them. The false self is at work, too, in women who assume *they* are responsible for setting off a partner's dark mood or temper or addiction or physical brutality—all of which they believe can be offset by redoubling their efforts to please.

The Female "Talent" for Understanding. The final reason daughters idealize their fathers is because *it is their training* to read between the silences, to interpret the dark moods, to flesh out the unspoken feelings of men. Being understanding of one's father is a daughter's labor of love.

By compensating for Daddy's absence in this way, a girl keeps him close, if only in her head. But what's kept "close" is the fantastic image, not the real, human, father. To see Daddy's flaws is to deidealize him. And to lose an idealized daddy is to jeopardize not only his tenuous, piecemeal love and protection but also one's last court of appeal if the relationship with Mommy falls apart.

Perhaps the greatest price of this relentless, insidious "understanding," says Dr. Ellen M. Berman, is that it becomes a self-fulfilling prophecy that echoes generation after generation:

> Many women perpetuate the idea that they are responsible for everything, and let men off the hook by protecting them emotionally.
>
> Part of the job of therapists is to put the responsibility back where it belongs. It's not enough for women to be "understanding." And it's not enough for men to be "sensitive." Having men get in touch with their feelings is not a substitute for having them understand their real power in the world. You can get in touch with all your feelings and still tell your wife or grown child what to do and insist that your word is law.

Daughters who fail to address their fathers' absences stockpile their disappointment, keeping it under emotional lock and key until they are romantically involved. Then they either find a reprise of Dad in the distant lover or present their partner with an unconscious laundry list of losses to be redressed. And when they have children, they attempt to make up for their "lost" fathers by asking too much of the next generation as well.

The unexamined father-daughter relationship explodes on safer battlefields: Lovers and husbands can be confronted or got rid of or replaced, children can be dominated—not so the idealized, unaccountable Dad.

Obviously fathers have been set up for failure by a social system that insists that "real men" are invulnerable, and by an economic system that rewards men more than women, making the financial burden primarily the father's.

It wasn't always that way.

A Brief History of Fatherhood

There was a time when mothers and fathers were *both* home with the children. That was when home and workplace were one and the same: the agricultural community. According to Philippe Ariès and other historians, throughout most of recorded history children and adults were—save for size—considered to be indistinguishable from one another.

In a sense they were social peers. Almost all were illiterate, and all were needed for the family to survive. There weren't the family niceties we take for granted today—separate bedrooms, children's toys and books, and televised childrearing gurus. Parents, and children who were old enough to wield a tool, toiled and played together in the fields or in the house, usually in one, all-purpose room.

But fathers—given the brawn required to roam the horizon for big game and to protect their mates and children—were *always* the head of the household. For much of history fathers had the power of life and death over their families—and, in the case of divorce, automatic custody of their children.

In ancient times infanticide, especially the killing of girls, was common. So, too, in Greece and Rome, was the paternal right to sell children, or to fondle their genitals, or even to sodomize them. Prepubertal children were thought to be indifferent to sexual stimulation.

Children were expendable, economic commodities, right through the Middle Ages and beyond. Child labor wasn't eliminated even in the United States until the late 1930s.

Part of this behavior, which today we consider horrifying, can be traced to the high incidence of infant mortality prior to modern medicine. As Ariès puts it,

> The little thing which had disappeared so soon in life was not worthy of remembrance: there were far too many children whose survival was problematical. . . . People could not allow themselves to become too attached to something that was regarded as a probable loss.

By the seventeenth century literacy and the influence of the church saw changes—although not necessarily a reduction in patriarchal authority—in fatherhood. Father knew best on all matters public and private, and brought his authority with him to the New World.

Indeed it wasn't until the late nineteenth century that divorced American women were allowed to gain custody of their children— and then only if a judge considered them morally and economically worthy. As for financial support of their children, noncustodial fathers were not required to pay *any* until the 1920s.

Sociologist Joseph Pleck has seen American fatherhood go through four historical phases—from the "moral teacher" of early Puritan and Colonial times, to the "breadwinner" of the Industrial Revolution, to the "sex-role" model of post–World War II, to the alleged "new, nurturant father" of today.

But of the four periods it was the flight by men from the land, or the homes in which they traded, to the factory in the late nineteenth century that had the most polarizing effect on parenting. The Industrial Revolution changed forever the face of the family, as fathers repaired to the centers of commerce and mothers remained by the hearth, isolated with their children from the outside world and all its "corrupting" influences.

Women served their industrializing nation in two ways: first, by becoming the guardians of their children's God-fearing moral purity and sense of duty; and second, by providing for their husbands sanctuary in which men could decompress and be recharged for their wage-earning rigors in the cold, cruel world of work.

As Barbara Ehrenreich has pointed out, family was now the last frontier of a man's *real* power. Here, at least, he could assert his authority in ways he could not as a wage earner, toiling in mindless or back-breaking labor for someone else, his job subject to the mood of a boss or the vagaries of the marketplace. At home he could reign, if not rule.

The value of a man—his social definition—was not his paternity but his *work,* measured in money. And if work is all, in terms of masculine self-regard, what possible currency could *daughters* have for fathers? What could be the value of a child who could neither be taken into his business or trade nor carry on his name?

Unless, in the most perverted cases, she were to function as a "little wife." The power imbalance within the family is *the key factor* in the incestuous abuse of daughters. Virtually all authorities on incest agree that father as insensitive patriarch, as unemotional family overseer, is *the single greatest cause of sexual abuse by fathers of their daughters.* One authority put it this way: "As long as fathers rule but do not nurture, as long as mothers nurture but do not rule, the conditions favoring the development of father-daughter incest will prevail."

A culture that measures a man according to his economic and physical viability, rather than his humanity, will write laws and form family policies that ignore mothers and children. It will endorse father as silent partner—indeed, making this the norm.

The twentieth-century version of that silence has been quantified by researchers who study how fathers interact in the family today. And from the looks of it, the "new, nurturant father" is but a blip on the sociological screen.

Dr. Michael E. Lamb divides parental behavior into three categories:

Engagement: one-on-one conversation, or play, or assistance, say, with a school project.

Accessibility: being around, if only in front of the TV, in case a child needs or asks for attention.

Responsibility: the overall job of seeing to it that the child's basic needs—medical, social, academic, nutritional, safety, general welfare, and care—are met; the administration of parental obligations.

According to Lamb, when fathers are employed and mothers are housewives, fathers spend approximately a quarter as much time as mothers in "engagement" and a third as much in "accessibility." In two-career families fathers are about a third as "engaged" and two thirds as "accessible" to children as mothers.

But when it comes to "responsibility," *almost all mothers—working or not—bear this burden alone.* And when Dad *is* around, it is not so much for caretaking—Mommy's job—as it is for play or discipline.

"Like prisoners who 'do time' in prison," writes sociologist Ralph La Rossa, "many fathers see themselves as 'doing time' with their children."

Contrary to popular opinion, it is the blue-collar father—rather than the affluent, ostensibly nurturant white-collar father—who does the most "time," or, at least, is the more accessible to children.

Much has been written recently about the current trend toward parental androgyny, about "sensitive," "nonsexist" fathers. But recent studies indicate that while the egalitarian, college-educated, feminist male may *talk* a good "nurturant, nonsexist" game, in fact, he may not really *believe* it.

Of this dichotomy Dr. Ross D. Parke says,

> There are interesting discrepancies between what a father says—his attitude—and what he does—his involvement. On one side you've got middle-class and higher-income men espousing more liberal attitudes toward the importance of father involvement and nurturance who put in sixty-hour work weeks. On the other side are the lower-class men in jobs with set hours, set vacations, who don't bring work home with them, who have the more macho, football-playing, hard-drinking kind of image. Yet there are lots of lower-class men, particularly now that their wives are also working, who put in more time than the upper-class men.

One of the men I interviewed—a forty-nine-year-old surgeon whose kids are grown—corroborated Dr. Parke's observation by saying,

> I always thought of myself as "Dr. Sensitivity." One day I was bragging to my wife about having been such a doting father when they were little, and she said, "What are you talking about? You were going to school. You were building a practice. You weren't around a hell of a lot." I don't have a real clear recollection of that part of it. Isn't that interesting?

There's no question that being a father today is fraught with double-binds and mixed messages. But withal, quantitatively speaking, most fathers are not as involved with or available to their children as were the fathers of long ago.

Fathers Reply

This sounds like a bad rap for *all* fathers, who are caught between an emotional rock and a cultural hard place. When men attempt to be more nurturing, they often draw on dwindling or even empty reserves, repeating what they know *from their own fathers.*

Said a fifty-five-year-old father,

> Every man hears his father's voice coming out of his mouth
> from time to time. I find myself saying things to my kids that
> my father said to me, laying down the law. And every time, I
> have this feeling that I've heard this stuff before. My father
> was the autocrat of the dinner table. What I knew about fa-
> thering, I learned from him.

And, in attempting to reverse the past, to become more nurturing, fathers have little support from other men, or the corporation,
or in many cases their wives—and *especially* not from the culture
that spawned them.

Fred, sixty-eight, recalls that when he was a boy, he was unathletic, easily given to tears, and bookish. He later became a speech
writer for a corporate CEO and, on his own time, a novelist. His
early emotionality was galvanized into dry-eyed "manliness" by
one experience alone: the army.

Of his four-year, World War II military service he says,

> It was the cult of masculinity. You weren't allowed even the
> most superficial kinds of feelings or you'd get nailed—a ser-
> geant's whim could land you in the stockade.
>
> That the function of the army is to degrade you is best
> summed up by this fact: They make you take a crap in the
> presence of a dozen other guys. Even in the bathroom there
> isn't a shred of dignity or privacy. So you learn to shut every-
> thing off.

The cost of American masculinity is high, and its male casualties
often become silent to the world around them and deaf to their
own inner voices. Only in middle age do they begin to count their
emotional losses.

Indeed, many fathers who today are in their fifties, sixties, and
seventies express deep and aching regrets that they were not different kinds of parents when their children were small, that when
their children phone home, they ask for Mom.

All the over-fifty fathers I interviewed expressed such rueful
second thoughts. "The men who are *grandfathers* should be the
fathers," one sixty-two-year-old man said. "Grandpas get to do it
right with their grandchildren."

Many fathers *are* aware of their emotional and physical absences—an awareness that, they often admit, comes very late in the game. "It's like Alzheimer's," one father joked, adding,

> People who have it don't know it. Do I wish I had it to do over? *Oh,* would I be different. *God, yes.* I wish I'd talked with my kids more when they were little. I wish I hadn't been so caught up in my work. I did what I thought I was supposed to do, and now my kids say, "Dad, you were never home, and we never knew what you were thinking when you were." Men weren't allowed to show their feelings. It never occurred to me to tell them how I felt deep down inside—it just never did. I didn't realize that I'd been shortchanged by the culture— being the heroic provider—until it was too late.

A Word About Stepfathers. Although the stepfather-stepdaughter relationship will be explored in subsequent chapters, since there are thirteen million stepfathers in the United States who are "silent partners" almost by definition, they deserve mention here.

Many stepfathers are unsung family heroes, frequently picking up the financial slack of biological fathers who pay little or no child support. Often they valiantly try to pinch-hit for fathers who defect. If stepfathers often wind up as silent partners, in many cases one can hardly blame them.

For even the most nurturing, devoted, loving stepfather has, with a stepdaughter, an uphill battle. The relationship can test the mettle of the sturdiest remarriage, the sanity of the most circumspect husband.

As one man who has been a stepfather to a stepdaughter for fourteen years said with a chuckle, "With her, I always ranked third in the family—right after my wife and the dog. Until we got a hamster—then I dropped to fourth place." His wife nodded in sympathetic agreement.

With stepsons the picture is a little brighter. According to studies conducted by Dr. Hetherington, mothers and sons following divorce frequently have acrimonious relationships, and the addition of an interested, warm stepfather can be a welcome change for them both.

But daughters, especially between the ages of seven and eleven, often have little love for their stepfathers, who are seen as the enemy of the intense mother-daughter tie. In fact the happier the remarriage, the more conflict between the daughter and the couple.

In contrast teenage stepdaughters often fare better when Mom remarries, especially if the marriage is happy. One reason may be that these daughters are already separating from their mothers, and the mothers' happiness makes this transition easier. It is also likely that if stepfather is crazy about Mom, the daughter does not have to worry about possible sexual complications with him.

All the stepfathers I interviewed corroborated this research. Said David, forty-nine, who has been happily married for two years to a woman with three daughters—now ages thirteen, seventeen, and twenty—from a previous marriage,

> The two oldest girls introduce me as their stepfather. The youngest says, "This is my mother's husband." At home she treats me like I'm not there. When I've tried to initiate conversations, she gives me staccato, one-word answers. When I've offered to take her to a movie or out for a pizza, her answer is always a curt no. With the other girls it's a lot better.

Stepfathers are very often the losers in the initial stages of remarriage. For if Dad is gone, why would a daughter invest in his substitute, who might also leave and who might take Mom with him?

In spite of all this disquieting research, Dr. Hetherington has also found that, difficult as stepfathering can be, children are better off in a harmonious remarriage than they are in the pressure cooker of a hostile first marriage. Time is on the side of the stepfather who can ride out the rocky first years.

As for the stepdaughters I interviewed, especially those with cold or distant biological fathers and whose mothers did better the second time around, many said that eventually they formed affectionate friendships with their stepfathers.

Breaking the Silence

The bad news about paternal regrets is that in some cases it may indeed be too late to repair the father-daughter relationship.

The *good* news is that by talking about these issues, many fathers and daughters are able to make up for all that lost time. As we know, it is in a man's advancing years that he may become aware of the implications of his earlier emotional retreat. Several therapists, in fact, told me that male intimacy with children is a *developmental* issue—that by midlife, men can give peace and love a chance.

Says psychiatrist Willard Gaylin, president of the Hastings Center and author of *Rediscovering Love,*

> It's not an easy thing to discover paternity. Fathers become aware—often too late—that there was a deficiency in their capacity for, or commitment to, love. As a result, when men achieve the fruits of their material success, they often become aware of an emptiness—an incompleteness—in their lives; the hollowness of having, but not *raising,* children, of not making true commitments to them. Which, sadly, does not mean that they weren't capable of it.

The emotional cost to fathers of that "deficiency" may in some ways be as great as the cost to their children. Denying themselves the day-to-day pleasures of seeing their children mature, and denied the concomitant pain that leads to emotional seasoning, fathers do not, as much as mothers, profit from this wondrous synergy.

It may be that in raising children women have matured in a way that men, playing a less pivotal role in the family, have not—most women do not have the arguable luxury of waiting to "develop" the ability to be intimate with their children.

Some researchers have made the case that a father's emotional distance has benefits in terms of a girl's gender identity—that is, by being less available the father encourages his daughter to identify with her mother—an argument that elevates paternal silence to a psychological virtue.

Seen in this rosy light, it is fathers, as exemplars of the "outside" world, who provide the transitional relationship between a mother's loving, possibly suffocating, embrace and the child's move into independence.

In my view that theory is akin to saying you don't have to go outside the family to be rejected, because you can get it at home. To justify a father's emotional distance as character building flies in the face of everything we know about love, about self-confidence, about family as source of inner peace in a chaotic world.

Not one of the adult daughters—or sons, for that matter—whose fathers were emotionally unavailable could find a single good thing to say on behalf of paternal distance, no matter how they felt about their mothers.

Surely fathers can provide lessons on the importance of independence for their children and still be integral parts of the emotional family scene. After all, a great many working mothers are doing just that every day.

And the well-loved daughters of available fathers know the difference. For there have always been fathers who *have chosen* and who *choose* not to be silent partners within their families.

These fathers turn down jobs that would uproot their families or would put them on the road for weeks at a stretch. Some gamely endure jibes from their buddies when they elect to be their children's primary caretakers while their wives pursue careers. Others make it a point to be on deck for their children, even if it means leaving the office early or in the middle of the day. Still others actively seek to change the corporate and governmental policies that ignore the reality of children and working parenthood.

But these fathers are a minority. The fact remains that the majority of fathers *do* withdraw from their children more than mothers, and they *do* withdraw more from their daughters than their sons, especially as daughters approach adolescence. *That fact alone accounts not so much for a daughter's ability to relate to her mother as it does her inability to relate to "available" men.*

The daughters of distant fathers, when they're little, don't know about biology and cultural bias and incest taboos and gender role and economic downturns and all the buzz words of sociological, anthropological and psychological mitigation. All they know is that Daddy isn't there as much as Mommy, and when he is, it's usually *with* Mommy. Daddy isn't available just to chat—to ask, "Did you have a good day or a bad day, and why?"—as much as Mommy. Daddy isn't accessible to demonstrate both the good and the bad sides of human behavior as much as Mommy. Daddy isn't responsible for a visit to the dentist or for a talk with a difficult teacher as much as Mommy.

Daddy is simply the silent partner. That makes Mommy's job—for parents and children alike—a very mixed blessing indeed.

3

vvvvvvv

The "Other" Woman (Mom)

For most of my life I thought the reason my father and I had no relationship was because he just didn't care. But now I realize a lot of it's because of my mother. I've been trying to get closer to my dad, and every so often I'll call and ask to speak to him. My mom will suddenly become very distant with me. It's true that he's the silent type, but she didn't help. She kept me away from him. She made sure we had nothing. Funny—I never picked up on that before.

—JANICE, THIRTY-FOUR

Of all the haunting moments of motherhood, few rank with hearing your own words come out of your daughter's mouth.

When my daughter, Jenny, was eighteen, I observed her sitting at my desk, her feet propped up, the telephone cradled against her shoulder, dispensing advice to a chum whose boyfriend had lately throttled back his hot romantic pursuit.

"Well," Jenny drawled in tones so cool, so certain, *so familiar* that I winced, "you should just become unavailable for a while. You're too easy. Men like a challenge, and all you do is sit and wait for him to call."

What stunned me was not simply that this counsel was mortifying evidence of a teenage mentality—mine: I had once said those very words to her. Rather it was the realization that Jenny was doing *exactly* what my mother, and her mother before her, and all the mothers I have known since have always done: *interpreting a man.*

One of the largely unproductive chores of maternity is helping daughters figure out what Daddy is all about, rather than letting daughters experience Daddy for themselves. If men are mysterious to women, not the least reason is because mothers are the self-appointed code breakers of fathers' cryptic messages, an expertise that, at best, is so much guesswork.

For good or ill, mothers are the translators of men.

Most of the women I interviewed recalled some version of their mothers' rubrics about men when they were growing up.

This, from Elizabeth, twenty-six:

> My mother always said, "Men are a different species. They have their own way of seeing life that talking can't resolve. The best thing to do if they really get on your nerves is to go to Bloomingdale's and have yogurt."

And this, from Arlene, thirty-nine:

> My mother's big message to me was this: "Men are wonderful, but basically, they're babies. Women are much smarter than men. We know everything, we can handle everything. So the best way to handle your father is to let him think he's making all the decisions—and then do what you want."

What's going on here? How is it that mothers, rather than *fathers themselves,* are the arbiters of men to their daughters?

The answer is rooted in family politics.

Trade-offs

In the juggling act of working motherhood, women are doing double duty, a singularly unsung and frequently unrewarding feat. Compared with men, they are denied commensurate income and respect for equal work; they also are denied an equal shouldering of domestic and parenting responsibilities on their husbands' parts.

Add to this imbalance the fact that motherhood is a ghettoizing experience. At the turn of the century, for instance, some 90 percent of households included at least three other adults—an aunt, uncle, or grandparent. Today this is hardly the case: Whether married or single, when it comes to parenting, most mothers go it alone.

Women have learned the language of power, an add-on to their emotional fluency and a skill required for the financial survival of the family—but the cultural rewards for their twin efforts are slim indeed.

For their part most men have *not,* correspondingly, had much incentive to "add on" to their skills a talent for love. They already have cultural status and power, the trade-off for being relative strangers to their children. And in view of the object lesson of working mothers' struggles, it's a trade-off they are loath to relinquish.

What's a mother to do? How is she to wrest from these inequities any sense of personal value? By drawing on the one sure source of power she *does* have:

Stepping into the void of her silent partner and filling it up with herself.

And the greatest weapon in her domestic arsenal, for reasons that will be explored, is what she tells her daughter about Daddy.

Not that sons don't *also* get Mom's rendition of Dad and of men in general. Mothers who have both boys and girls often find sons a whole lot easier and less complicated than their daughters. Hence boys are frequently treated by their mothers as though they were crown princes.

Just ask Jeff, a forty-two-year-old newspaper tycoon:

> My mother was a fabulous mother to me, but not to my sister. I was her favorite—she considered everything I did to be perfect. So naturally my sister's a colossal underachiever. Today I feel guilty about my mother's obvious favoritism. When I was a kid, of course, I loved it.

But some mothers can make sons feel as though they are anything but sainted. Researchers have observed a version of maternal sexism (they call it "gender socialization") in the behavior of mothers toward infant boys: The more their little sons cry, the *less* comfort mothers offer, whereas they are much more responsive to a daughter's tears. This behavior may be a mother's way of "toughening up" her son, but the message he may get is that Mom takes a dim view of his sorrow, or at least the *expression* of it.

And some mothers, because of a deep and abiding dislike for men, will go one better—they'll treat their sons as though they were intrinsically damaged goods by virtue of gender alone. As Ron, thirty-eight, put it,

> I rarely initiate affection with my daughter. If she says, "Daddy, I need a hug," I can really get into it—she says I'm the best hugger in the world. But I wait to be invited, which goes back to my childhood. The worst insult my mother could give me was to say, "You're just like your father," because she thought he was disgusting. She even said, "Men's bodies are ugly." I grew up believing that women would find me repulsive. I got over it, at least with my wife. But when I'm introduced to a woman, I still think, Should I shake hands? Will she think I'm intrusive? I always have to make sure I'm welcome.

But as much as mothers may have a laudatory or corrosive impact on their sons' self-concept, sons are still the ultimate domain of their fathers.

So daughters are a mother's primary parental turf. Mothers have a particular and *more* tenacious influence on their daughters than their sons: Indeed of all the pairings within the family mother/daughter is the most intense and most mutually dependent.

A daughter is a mother's gender partner, her closest ally in the family confederacy, an extension of her self. And mothers are their daughters' role model, their biological and emotional road map, the arbiter of all their relationships.

Consequently daughters will turn to their mothers for all kinds of permissions—including, sometimes, the license to love Daddy.

Unlike the mother-son relationship, a daughter's relationship with her mother is something akin to Bungee diving. She can stake her claim in the outside world in what *looks* like total autonomy— in some cases, even "divorce" her mother in a fiery exit from the family—but there is an invisible emotional cord that snaps her back. For always there is the memory of mother whose judgments are so completely absorbed into the daughter's identity that she may wonder where Mom leaves off and she begins.

Those memories and long-ago opinions are the prism through which a daughter views the world: Mother-daughter intimacy, or disaffection, is the fertile ground in which a daughter's sense of self in relationship to others begins to grow.

For all these reasons mother is a powerful moderator of the father-daughter connection. This maternal influence—sometimes extremely reassuring, at other times extraordinarily damaging— shows up in four key ways:

- Maternal gatekeeping
- Rivalry for dad's affection
- Rivalry for daughter's affection
- Maternal abdication

Maternal Gatekeeping

Of all the current debates about maternity, perhaps the most hotly disputed is whether or not there is a "maternal instinct"— the classic and compelling male rationale for banishing mothers to the home and for excusing themselves from paternal involvement.

Clarice Kestenbaum, M.D., director of training in the Division of Child and Adolescent Psychiatry at the Columbia University College of Physicians and Surgeons, has researched this question, among others, for twenty-five years. She believes it's nearly impossible to separate "nurture" from "nature" in mothering. Nevertheless her research suggests that there may in fact be a biological determinant to the fierce attachment most mothers have with their babies.

To illustrate this premise, she videotaped career women in advanced pregnancy patting their swollen bellies and saying, "This child won't change my life much" and videotaped them again after giving birth. And what she saw, she says, was this:

> Suddenly the baby becomes the most important creature in the world, more than the husband or anyone. The attachment is *instantaneous.* She would *die* for her baby. It's the most amazing phenomenon, and it shocks every medical student class that witnesses it.

Given this immediate attachment and protectiveness—which, Dr. Kestenbaum says, does not occur as quickly with mothers who adopt—even the biological father may in some primitive, primeval sense be perceived as a predator. Indeed some researchers believe fathers should be in the delivery room for two reasons: not just to boost the mother's morale but also to be on hand to hold the baby immediately after birth, thereby bolstering the mother's *trust.*

Postpartum, and assuming that her marriage—if she is married —is stable and loving, the mother will gladly welcome the father's participation. For what greater tangible proof of a couple's mutual affection and esteem can there be? What greater joy than to widen their embrace to include this living, breathing result of their love?

Still, mother is the primary parent in a child's infancy. And her attitude toward Dad is apparent to little girls from the first year of life, an attitude that is tailored by the quality of her marriage, her views of men, and the health of her self-esteem.

Balancing Acts. In the normal course of events a daughter follows her mother's example of how to behave with a man. And if it is obvious that the mother is loved by the father, the daughter concludes that Mom is very good at attracting, and keeping, a man —hence, worth imitating. Thus daughters observe their mothers' pleasing ways, and themselves try to become similarly pleasing to Daddy. The well-loved, secure wife has no trouble allowing her daughter to share Daddy's love.

To continue this ideal scenario, a father is available to help his daughter balance both her love and her anger toward her mother, to moderate the inevitable emotional extremes in the intense mother-daughter equation. With Daddy's steadying influence daughters can learn to be comfortable with healthy anger, rather than feeling that they must be eternal good girls who must at all costs conceal it.

At the same time the father can help the mother loosen her maternal grip. He can intervene if Mom is too emotionally invested in the child, or too harsh, by temporarily siding with the daughter, at the same time providing the boundaries of rage— acknowledging the child's feelings but setting limits on their expression.

"The only time my father ever got really angry," one woman told me, "was when I was rude to my mother. *That* he would never permit. I could disagree with her, but never could I be insulting or disrespectful."

Many fathers are the "objective party" in inevitable mother-daughter skirmishes, sometimes in hilarious, unexpected ways. One woman told me that when she was eighteen, she accidentally became pregnant, and her mother, in a fit of frightened tears, didn't know how she was going to break the terrible news to the daughter's father. As it happened, the daughter had just bought a secondhand car with a bank loan her father had cosigned.

When her father found out about the unwanted pregnancy, rather than accuse his daughter of moral decadence, he said, "You stupid kid! If you have a baby to support, *how will you make your car payments?"* And, indeed, it was the father, not the mother, who accompanied his daughter to the doctor when she decided to terminate the pregnancy.

Fathers also temper the mother who thinks everything requires interminable, belabored discussion and emotional dissection. Said the daughter of a female psychiatrist,

> Whenever I was in desperate straits, my mother made it worse by *dealing with it;* it was a relief to have my father either make a joke or say, "Oh, come on, it's going to be fine." Daddy was able to reduce troubles to their essentials.

The normal family triangle, then, provides the daughter with a stage upon which to rehearse her separate identity. When the parents' marriage is relatively free of conflict, the daughter can go from one parent to the other for an emotional safety valve, to let off steam. Having equal, unambivalent access to both parents—and spared their competition for her loyalty—she can then concentrate not so much on dual allegiance as on simply growing up.

In an important study of twenty-five extremely successful women, virtually all of them came from such households. The mothers were warm and nurturing, and the fathers believed that being "feminine" and being "successful" were not mutually exclusive. (Of course the fact that there were no sons in these families was a variable of *immeasurable* significance.) The fathers encouraged their daughters to be risk takers, and the mothers, although raised in a culture that frowned on female ambition, did not discourage it.

While the daughters did not want to replicate their mothers' traditional "female" model of home-based femininity, they were not considered by their mothers to be traitors for taking a nontraditional route—becoming ambitious in the working world and postponing marriage.

Most important these daughters "did not see themselves as having to compete with their mothers for their fathers' affection." Indeed fathers were seen as loving by both mother and daughter.

When a daughter is allowed to love *both* parents, the family triangle does not become a three-way stretch.

This ideal picture, however, does not characterize most families, for a variety of reasons—including the ambivalence many mothers feel about sharing their maternal influence, even in a two-career marriage.

While some research indicates the willingness—even urgency—of employed mothers to have husbands assume more parental responsibilities, other studies show an opposite trend: The mother, feeling guilty about her own absence, redoubles her maternal importance in the "quality time" that is the residue of the working day. In effect fathers are "crowded out" by that guilty compensation.

The intractibility of "maternal gatekeeping" has puzzled researchers, including Dr. Ross D. Parke, who has studied fathers for over two decades and seen gatekeeping continue to be evident, even in the wake of women's liberation. He says,

> Many mothers say they want fathers to be more involved. But they don't want to give up their own sense of control over the domain of caregiving. They're struggling not to give up the things that historically and culturally are part of their identities and at the same trying to gain other things in terms of equal cultural status. They're trying to balance the new pieces with the important and cherished old pieces.

Norman, forty, ought to know. He is by any measure a "modern, nonsexist" father: He and his wife are both members of the National Organization for Women. Even so, there are limits to how involved his wife will allow him to be in the parenting of their two young sons. He says,

> Sometimes my wife complains that she's overwhelmed with work and just can't take one of the kids, for example, to a piano lesson. I'll offer to do it for her, and then she'll say, "No, I'll do it." We have to negotiate how much I trespass into that mother role—it's not given up easily.

Another father, the happily married veteran of many parenting workshops, is aware of his wife's mixed maternal emotions: On the one hand, she encourages his desire to be an active participant in the rearing of Carolyn, their seven-year-old daughter; on the other, she also subtly sabotages it. Says the father,

> My wife usually puts Carolyn to bed at night and then calls me in to tuck her in. One night Carolyn started telling me all about her school day, and my wife said, "She's got to go to sleep now." But Carolyn wanted me to stay. So we kept on talking and laughing. My wife came back in and said, "If Carolyn can't get up in the morning, it will be your fault." My daughter and I had formed an alliance, and my wife felt excluded.

But in other cases, where the marriage is not solid, the mother's sabotage is anything but subtle.

Stanley, the forty-six-year-old father of a ten-year-old daughter, Hillary, has been married to Sarah for fifteen years. An ongoing source of conflict for the couple is Sarah's perception of Stanley as a "militant" father and his feeling that she "interferes" with his parenting. Says Stanley,

> Sarah is always setting me up, and then jumping in the middle. She'll ask me to tell Hillary to stop watching TV and finish her homework, and then when I do, she'll say, "Oh, be a sport, let her finish her program." Recently I realized that I'd never been alone with Hillary. So I took her fishing for the weekend, just the two of us. It was heaven—no arguments, no disagreements, just hanging out together. That was a revelation to me: My wife and I have never had a vacation with Hillary that the three of us didn't constantly fight.

Ghosts in the Nursery. As these examples illustrate, there is more to the family triangle than just its parts. Because at the moment a woman gives birth, the ghosts of her past become equal players in her maternity. In fact one of the most important indicators of how great a role fathers play in the family is the mother's relationship with her *own* father.

Says Jean, forty-two,

> When my daughter was born, my husband took one look at her and decided she was the most wonderful thing that was ever created in the history of the world. There have been

times when his adoration of her has given me pause. Once when she was nine, they took a walk together, and I was envious. I thought, "This is the way it should be, what's the matter with you?" I realized it wasn't because I wanted to go with them that I was jealous—it was because I never had that with my own father.

And if, in the bargain, a mother always felt that she could never do enough to please her *mother,* she views the female child of her flesh as her chance to redress all the losses of her own childhood. She looks at her daughter and *sees herself.*

The daughter can become the mother's opportunity either to make up for the past and right previous wrongs or to exact retribution for her losses. The mother's own experience of the long-ago family serves as an overlay to her mothering: Past and present are inextricably intertwined.

And since mother has the biological and cultural advantage over her husband, she is in an extremely influential position to determine how her daughter will respond to Daddy. For if the father needs his wife's "permission" to become involved with his daughter, so, as we have seen, does the daughter need maternal permission to have a relationship with her father.

As Simone de Beauvoir caustically put it, "One of the curses that weigh heavily upon women . . . is to be left in women's hands during childhood." Mother will, in general, determine who does and who does not get past the protective "gate" of her emotional and biological primacy.

That primacy contains within it an inherent contradiction. As one researcher noted, mothers are perceived by children as powerful in their *mothering;* but as *wives,* who are emotionally and/or financially dependent on their husbands, they are often perceived as weak.

Maternal supremacy also contains within it the seeds of potential failure. For if mothers are the emotional gatekeepers, they are also the targets for blame when the kids turn out badly. Hence most fathers are, by cultural definition, absolved from accountability.

Mothers contribute to that paternal absolution in one important and devastating way: by making excuses for the emotional and physical absence of fathers, thereby encouraging their daughters' idealization of them.

Covering Up for Daddy. Time after time in my interviews with daughters they quoted their mothers' misguided excuses for their fathers' behavior: "He was unfaithful because he was always looking for mother figures," or "He can't help himself when it comes to getting drunk—his father used to beat him," or "He works so hard for his family that there's nothing left over at the end of the day. He's doing it all for you."

Maternal gatekeeping does not have a whole lot to recommend it, because it robs a daughter of her ability really to know her father. It traps her in a kind of limbo, somewhere between the truth and the dream, the reality and the idealization. It forces her to find disparate ways to accommodate *two* masters. And it is in the wish by a daughter *to please both her parents* that the family triangle can become an emotional tinderbox.

Rivalry for Dad's Affection

The second way a mother influences the father-daughter relationship has to do with the fact that mothers and daughters are of the same sex. That gender partnership can strain their bond. After all, a daughter is *another woman.* Indeed, she is *the* "other woman."

Do fathers feel the same way about the mother-son connection? Are sons the "other man"? Freud certainly thought so. But, on the whole, fathers are less concerned about a mother's partiality toward a son than her possibly "sissifying" him.

Instead father-son competition moves to a wider stage: sports, or the marketplace, or, yes, *other* women.

In the sporting arena fathers and sons often joust for physical supremacy. "You should see my son and husband playing basketball," says Carol, chuckling. "My son says, 'Okay, old man, let's see if you can cut it,' and my husband kills himself trying to outshoot him one-on-one. Someday he's going to land in the coronary unit, all because he can't bear it if his son beats him."

As for work many fathers feel ambivalent about their sons' success. While some long to see their sons outstrip them in money and prestige—and even pressure them hard to do so—others undermine their sons' ambition. One way they do it is by taking the son into a family business so that the paternal hierarchy is maintained. As long as Dad is still in harness, his son will never take over the metaphorical or actual store.

In terms of sexual rivalry there are those narcissistic fathers who compete with their sons for women *outside* the family. As one man told me,

> My father taught me that women were either morally noble and pure or they were whores. Frankly I've come to believe he thought they were *all* whores. One time we were at a restaurant, and our waitress was young and had a fantastic body. I made the mistake of telling him that I wanted to ask her out, because suddenly he made a pass at her himself. It was one of the many occasions when he got between me and a girl. I wasn't competing with him—he was competing with me.

Mothers *also* compete with their daughters in similar ways—denigrating a daughter's job promotions, tweaking her about her weight, even flirting with her boyfriends. But the most dramatic rivalry between mother and daughter occurs within the family itself.

Since professional competitiveness has traditionally been considered "unfeminine," the only safe horse race for women is the *personal:* specifically, jockeying for a man's attentions. And while this was truer of prior generations than the current "liberated" one, it still finds its expression in the family triangle.

For as fiercely as Mom may protect her children, she often just as vigorously protects her marriage. A mother wants to be first in the hearts of her children, but she also wants her husband's unconditional and undivided supportiveness and love.

It is because of her mother/wife territoriality that love between daughter and father can sometimes be risky. For if daughter is the extension of the mother's fondest dreams and best hopes, she is *also*—if those dreams are realized—a serious threat to her mother's domestic power base and self-esteem.

This is poignantly true of the mothers of the baby-boomers. The vibrant, *young* daughter with unlimited options—career, sexual freedom, postponed marriage, combined work and motherhood—is a painful reminder to mother of all the choices that were denied women of her generation. Making matters worse, nowhere is the culture crueler than to women who are now over fifty, women who were raised with but one mandate: to marry and raise kids.

Hence to see their daughters idealize their fathers and *also* to be condemned for being "just a housewife" is to be doubly threatened.

No wonder these mothers and daughters are pitted against one another. No wonder they joust for Daddy's love. Especially if the father is less than attentive to his wife. For then the aggrieved, or neglected, or narcissistic wife will see the daughter's love for her father—and his for the daughter—as a stake in the marital heart.

So it is that some mothers, in their craving for their husbands' undivided attention, will express their jealousy, *often stoked by their husbands,* with sarcasm. Says Nancy, thirty-six,

> My father always called me "Mrs. Campbell," and that did *not* sit well with the *real* "Mrs. Campbell"—my mother. She'd say to me, "You're his own flesh, I'm the impostor." And if ever my father defended me, she'd say to him, "Go ahead, take her side. She's your 'wife.'"

Other mothers express envy with uncontrolled rage, occasionally fueled by either paranoia or substance abuse or both. Says Rona, forty-three, of her alcoholic mother,

> She'd say, "If your father really loved you, he'd spend more time with you." Or, "Don't let your father see any signs of your period, because he'll think you're soiled. Keep yourself completely clean." Or, "Don't ever cry in front of your father. He hates it when women cry." I was always fed this antifather material, which made me adore him even more. He was nice to me. He didn't smack me. He didn't lock me in my room the way she did.

The daughters of such mothers suffer emotional abuse—as devastating, if not more so, as physical abuse. And in their deprivation they remain bound to their mothers by careening between two extremes of emotional enmeshment: rage and regression, fear and neediness.

The irony is that their fathers often come off as victims. For the "innocent" father is frequently a coconspirator in the mother's venom. As Brandt F. Steele, an authority on child maltreatment, has noted,

> We rarely see abuse by one spouse that is not either consciously or unconsciously condoned and tolerated, if not actually abetted by the other spouse. We have known fathers who, while complaining of a wife's abusive attacks, are unconsciously doing everything to stimulate her attacks, and who begin to be abusive themselves if the wife stops her maltreatment.

As Rona, to her horror, discovered in therapy when she was grown. She says,

> My father *knew* my mother was beating me. It took me *years* to figure out that by not standing up to her, he was really encouraging it. He got to be the good guy. I *had* to see him that way. I was desperate.

Rivalry for Daughter's Affection

The third way mothers influence the father-daughter relationship is the flip side of mother-daughter rivalry. In this case the mother *competes with father* for the daughter's allegiance. This can happen when a mother seeks, in her daughter, the mothering she never had. By vying with Dad for her daughter's love, not only is their relationship imperiled, so, too, is the healthy father-daughter connection. Now father and daughter are sometimes thrown together, like shipwrecked lifeboat passengers. Says Kelly, forty-six,

> My mother discouraged my relationship with my father because she wanted me all to herself. He consciously tried not to compete when my mother was around. Whenever I'd ask him something, he'd say, "Go ask the boss." My mother bad-mouthed my father from the day I was born, although he never said a critical word about her. He and I were like two little squirts, protecting ourselves. We were on each other's side. We were really more like siblings than father and child.

In other cases a mother uses the daughter to compensate for her rocky marriage. Here the daughter is elevated to her mother's partner, a rank that may fill the daughter with a giddy sense of importance but that denies her not only her father but also her childhood.

Marilyn, fifty-one, understood the term *maternal gatekeeping* immediately. She said,

> My earliest memories of my father are that he was very loving, very available, all the good things—until I was six. After that our relationship was just rotten. That's when my mother really took over. I became Mommy's girl in cahoots against him. She made me her ally because she was so angry with him, and I was supposed to be angry with him too. And I was. I was a very, very good girl. Without her telling me in so many words, I knew exactly what I was supposed to do.

In her study of adult daughters and their mothers, Lucy Rose Fischer, Ph.D., found that when they were too "invested"—that is, mutually dependent and symbiotic, forming an unhealthy best friendship—often it was because they had formed a "tight . . . *alliance against the father.*" In half the cases the fathers were alcoholics or "otherwise irrational." Winning Mom's undivided attention—even for understandable reasons—overloads the relationship. This mother-daughter "alliance" is one for which the daughter will dearly pay.

For example a mother may inappropriately take a daughter into her confidence about her marital unhappiness. Says Willa, twenty-six,

> When I was fourteen, my mother said, "Daddy and I haven't had sex in six months." This was not news I was pining to hear. But I was like the parent in the family, always advising my mother about Daddy. I didn't want that responsibility, but it was handed to me at a very early age.

Nowhere is the phenomenon of maternal neediness more prevalent than in the case of divorce. Given the fact that most children of divorce reside with their mothers, the daughter will have little option but to take her filial cue from her mother.

Without a father, except in the most sporadic sense, the daughter is severely hobbled in her attempts to find her separate identity. Without a father it is inevitable not only that the mother-daughter relationship is in danger of overheating but also that the father's influence can be either enhanced or frayed.

A mother's ability to give her daughter permission to maintain dual allegiance is severely tested when her marriage dissolves. Because of the acrimony that accompanies most divorces, such permission is extraordinary. Still, some mothers are able to pull it off. Says Diane, forty-six, whose parents divorced when she was seven,

> When my parents split up, my father moved to another state. But my mother kept him alive for me. She said, "Don't ever think he left you—he left me. It wasn't about you." Three years later he moved back and wrote to me saying he wanted to reestablish our relationship. I asked my mother what I should do; I was afraid that if I saw him, she'd think I was betraying her, and she knew it. She said, "Don't worry about my feelings. I took care of them long ago. He's your father. It's important for you to make up your own mind about him." So I did. I found out he's vain, he's selfish, he's immature. But at least I found out for myself.

None of which is to recommend that mothers shield their children from the reality of a father who utterly betrays his children. As we have seen, some mothers "cover" for fathers by saying "He really loves you" when the evidence is categorically otherwise: He failed to stay in touch with his children, or he used them to hurt their mother. He provided no financial support, or he battered his family. He was addicted to drugs or alcohol, or he gambled away the family's assets.

It is critical that children be allowed to express their sadness or rage at the father who does such things; it is vital for them to mourn the family earthquake of divorce and father loss.

So it is that sometimes a mother has to give her child permission temporarily to hate her father. Anger is the first step toward emotional healing. And until the child becomes angry, she will put the "blame"—the *accountability*—anyplace except where it belongs.

The daughter who has not been allowed to claim her own pain, or to believe the evidence of her own eyes and senses, can only conclude one of two things: that Mom drove Daddy to defect, or that she herself did.

But daughters can reach the *same* conclusion when mothers go to the opposite extreme. Some mothers, embittered by the divorce, *force* their children—especially their daughters—to hate the father, who may have committed none of these atrocities, and to take his place.

In her fifteen-year study of sixty divorced, middle-class families, Judith S. Wallerstein, Ph.D., found that girls assume far too much responsibility for their mothers' happiness, that in fact the intimacy between them is a caricature of the healthy mother-daughter attachment in harmonious, intact families.

Here the generations often reverse: Daughter becomes the mother, and mother, in her struggles to regain her self-confidence, or to wreak revenge, becomes the needy child. And since the daughter is acutely aware that her survival depends on the allegiance of the remaining parent, she may reasonably deduce that she must jettison all traces of love for her father. And if the father drops out of the picture altogether, the daughter's allegiance may feel like a matter of life or death.

Thus the daughter makes this terrible bargain: *I will love and help and defend my mother to make sure she, too, won't leave me.*

Such a daughter may distort her perceptions of her divorced parents so that Mom becomes always right and Dad becomes always wrong. Here, again, she may possess a heady authority that has disastrous consequences: By becoming Mommy's quintessentially good girl, protector, and best friend, the daughter deliberately demolishes her own needs. The tragedy of her bargain is that she drives underground her rage toward the mother for putting her in this untenable generational leadership. Instead she trains her angry sights on Dad—or herself.

The daughter is trapped within a terrible dilemma: On the one hand there is the tragic mother, the woman upon whom the daughter patterns herself—but who could not keep a man. On the other hand, there is this wretched, clinging woman upon whom the daughter's very existence depends.

Because of her loyalty conflicts she may fear or even sabotage success in the workplace or in love rather than risk winning where her mother so obviously lost.

Writes Dr. Wallerstein,

> *I have found that the quality of the mother-child relationship is the single most critical factor in determining how children feel*

about themselves in the postdivorce decade and how well they function in the various domains of their lives. [Italics in original.]

The ultimate danger of the symbiotic mother-daughter attachment is that eventually it may collapse under its own weight. For when the mother is so injured that she cannot right the reversal of parental authority, she may eventually lose the love and trust of her children.

Ten years after the divorce one third of the good mother-daughter relationships in Wallerstein's sample had deteriorated.

But it isn't divorce per se that can shatter parent-child relationships. According to Dr. E. Mavis Hetherington, other variables, including age, the number of other children and their birth rank, innate resiliency and temperament, and the existence of outside emotional and financial supports, *also* play a part in the daughter's adjustment to divorce.

To take one example, 43 percent of divorced custodial mothers have annual incomes of less than $10,000. Extreme poverty and single parenthood do nothing to improve a divorced mother's, or a child's, equanimity.

Dr. Hetherington paints a picture of the postdivorce family that is different from Dr. Wallerstein's. In her longitudinal studies of divorce, she included—as controls—data about the daughters of deceased fathers as well as about daughters from intact families. I asked her to describe how the parent-child relationship is affected by divorce. She said,

> On the average, kids who have gone through a divorce are worse off than kids who haven't. But it's a very small group whose behavior is more deviant than those in two-parent families. Kids in a well-functioning single-parent household are a heck of a lot better off than in a conflict-ridden two-parent household. Kids from divorced families have a slightly higher chance of divorcing in their own marriages, but it's a small effect. There is a subgroup who show very long-term disruptive effects, but by three years after divorce, most kids are doing pretty well. If you have a firm but loving mother who isn't putting down men in general, those kids can do well. It's obvious that all girls in divorced families don't hate men. One

loving, competent, concerned adult is often the key to kids' weathering terrible, terrible situations.

Even when that "one loving, concerned adult" is the healthy, unvengeful mother, she will still have her work cut out for her.

Especially when Daddy dies.

Keeping Daddy's Memory Alive. Mothers whose husbands die, compared with their divorced counterparts, have a relatively easier time of it, which doesn't mean it's *easy*. While the widow must grieve and realign her sudden and unbidden role as single mother, at the same time she must try to keep Daddy's memory alive for the sake of her children's psychological health.

It is a tragic double bind: She is angry at her husband for leaving her in this terrible fix, even though—unless he committed suicide —he didn't *choose* to leave. Her children can become both burdens and essential to her emotional recovery.

In her book *Father Loss: Daughters Discuss the Man That Got Away,* Elyce Wakerman, whose father died when she was three, eloquently describes the consequences of the permanent loss of Dad. One way widows hamper their children, she writes, is in not allowing those children to express their grief, to acknowledge their loss—unlike children of divorce, who often are forced again and again into an awareness of their fathers' absence and neglect. In Wakerman's study most of the daughters whose fathers died when they were young were not encouraged to mourn.

This phenomenon was corroborated by many of the fatherless daughters I interviewed. As one woman, whose father died when she was five, said, "Nobody bothered to tell me my father had died. My mother never discussed him. He just didn't come home. My aunt finally told me. I was left with the feeling that one day he'd come back."

But other fatherless daughters *were* allowed by their mothers to grieve; their mothers gave them the gift of finality. These daughters never doubted themselves the way daughters of divorce do— but often they shared *another* lingering problem: Daddy, and his exalted memory, were frozen in time.

When a father dies before the daughter has completed the normal progression of dethroning him and learning to accept him as a whole human being, she isn't sure she has "permission" to love another man. One such woman, whose much-decorated father died during World War II, says,

My mother was wonderful. She showed me pictures of Daddy and told me how much he loved me. She wanted me to remember that we were the most important people in his life. The only problem is that he was described in such heroic terms that I remained loyal to his memory in the most bizarre way: I kept being attracted to men who would not eclipse him. She never discussed his flaws or put him in any kind of realistic perspective. It wasn't until I was forty that I allowed myself to be truly loved by another wonderful man—thanks to five years of therapy.

If the daughter idealizes the dead father, it is in no small degree due to the *mother's* idealization. When the mother copes with this "rejection" by deifying him, she herself cannot invite memories of his flawed, mortal being. Here again the daughter is not allowed to see her father as human, with good qualities *and* bad, but only as a saint. She will keep Daddy alive as the only man worth loving and discard or severely test the rest. And if she is afraid to push angrily against her mother, the surviving parent, in the normal process of adolescent separation, she may transfer her rebellion to all the men who can never measure up to her father's unsullied ghost.

Still, try as she might, the widow will not be entirely spared her children's rage and grief at having lost their father. As the only parent who must be both mother *and* father, she is the lightning rod for their fears, which are piled on top of her own.

Which is one more reason why being a mother is not for the faint-hearted. And for some mothers, whether or not their husbands are still in the family picture, the task is simply beyond them.

Maternal Abdication: When Mothers Don't Mother at All

Perhaps the most damaging way a mother can influence the father-daughter relationship is by abdicating her role *entirely,* thereby allowing her husband to become far *too* important.

Sometimes the mother is so passive, so defeated, or so dependent, that the daughter becomes her sexual surrogate.

What we are talking about, of course, is incest.

Although fathers, by virtue of physical strength, are able to tyrannize mothers as well as children—a subject that will be explored in greater detail in Chapter 8—most studies on sexual abuse agree that *both* parents play a role in a father's sexual exploitation of a daughter.

If the daughter who is abused by her father is to turn to anyone for help, it will be her mother. And if her mother denies the reality of the daughter's experience—*which is usually the case*—the daughter will feel hideously betrayed not once but *twice:* first by a mother who failed to protect or even believe her, and second by a father who took grotesque advantage of the mother's abdication. For a daughter the more acute betrayal is *the mother's,* the person she tries hardest to please, tries hardest to emulate.

For this reason it is the mother for whom the incestuously abused daughter often holds the greatest contempt. As one such daughter, who at eleven was forced by her father to bathe only in his presence, put it,

> When I told my mother, she became very angry with me. She said that I had always been too flirtatious with him. She called me "voluptuous," a word I didn't understand. So I looked it up, and when I read the definition, I cried and cried.

The ultimate maternal abdication, of course, is when a *mother* dies. It's useful to examine what happens to the father-daughter relationship in this instance, because it puts into dramatic perspective the pivotal role mothers play in it. Once mother is entirely removed from the equation, a daughter is set adrift in a twilight zone of emotional and identity confusion.

Remembering Mama. In this instance it falls to Dad to keep Mom's memory alive and also somehow to be her surrogate.

Since most mothers of the daughters described in this book were raised to do the childrearing and fathers to be the disciplining breadwinners, the widower was at a double loss when his wife died. Not only did he lose his life's partner and parental mediator, he also had to call upon skills he may never have been allowed to *recognize,* let alone honor or employ.

Says Ruth, twenty-nine, whose mother died when she was twelve,

> My mother was the nurturer, the steadying influence. My dad kept tabs on us kids by asking her, "How are they doing?" Once she died, he still did that; he'd ask my *older sister*—who

was away at college—how I was doing. My dad's a wonderful person, but he did not handle that first year well. A more observant father would have found a woman to help me through it—an aunt, a female friend of the family. I had no one to help me pick out bras, to go buy sanitary napkins. And I couldn't say, "Dad, I have this vaginal itch—what should I do?" My father was very uptight, and without Mommy it was very difficult. The thing I'm most terrified of today is becoming a wife and mother.

If it was "difficult" for Ruth to lose her mother, it was life-threatening for Lisa, whose overprotective mother died when she was ten, leaving her in the hands of her alcoholic father. Lisa, now thirty, recalls,

One night when I was about twelve, he said in a drunken stupor, "I've been a sexless man for four years, so you'd better watch out." He never actually touched me. But from that time on I always slept with coat hangers on my door so if he ever tried to come in, I'd hear them jangle. Had my mother lived, she would have killed him if he ever harmed me.

A Word About Stepmothers

Since 80 percent of divorced fathers remarry one or more times, stepmothers can play an important role in a daughter's life. Being the instant parent to someone else's kids is, to put it mildly, a disquieting experience. But in general the stepmother/stepdaughter tie is less emotionally loaded than that between stepfathers and stepdaughters. And since divorced fathers often are only sporadic figures in their daughters' lives, so, too, are stepmothers.

Judith Wallerstein found in her study that most stepmothers get along relatively well with stepchildren. In fact the only children in her sample who had stepmother problems were those whose fathers' new families did not welcome them.

In some cases a loving stepmother can be a psychological salvation for a daughter. Samantha at the age of six was awarded to her brutal mother's custody. There she remained, even though through the years she repeatedly begged her father and his new wife—whom she deeply loved—to let her live with them.

Part of the problem was that Samantha was unable to tell her father that her mother beat her; she was terrified of her mother's retaliation. So her father did not have sufficient grounds to mount a legal offense—and it is entirely problematic, given the legal pattern of custodial motherhood, whether he would have won.

By the time she was twelve, however, few judges would have insisted that she remain with a biological mother she both feared and despised. Thus her father was able to gain her custody.

"The day I came to live with my father," says Samantha, now thirty, "is the day that my life really began. My stepmother was everything my mother was not—loving, interested, loyal, concerned. I can talk to her about anything. I'd be dead now if it weren't for her. I'm absolutely certain that had my father not gotten me when he did, I would have killed myself."

In other cases, however, the stepmother is yet another rival for Daddy's love. And because the daughter has no ambivalent biological tie to her, the stepmother can easily be scapegoated.

Hence many daughters are anything but sanguine about their fathers' new wife. The "wicked" stepmother is a useful foil: She keeps the daughter from hating *either* of her parents. As one woman, whose mother died when she was twelve, put it, "When my father married my stepmother, I could let him off the hook by blaming *her* for our distant relationship." Stepmother becomes the repository of all the daughter's mixed emotions about her biological parents.

One additional factor can poison the daughter/remarried-father relationship: the age of both new wife and daughter at the time of remarriage. The most explosive combination is when an adolescent daughter's father marries a woman who is practically the daughter's age.

Says Dr. Kestenbaum,

> Now the father hasn't just betrayed the mother, he's betrayed the daughter. The young wife isn't a mother substitute, she's a *daughter* substitute. Teenage daughters recognize it, and often won't speak to their fathers for years.

The generational distance between father and daughter is suddenly removed; now stepmother cannot possibly be any form of "mother." Chronologically and biologically she is simply "rival."

The Price of Divided Loyalties

Blaming Mom for everything—including the distant father-daughter relationship—is a cultural pastime. There is no question that fathers often abdicate their parenting responsibilities, doing terrible harm to their children that is sometimes irreparable. And there is no question that by forcing women to find social value in the narrow aperture of family, they are at a huge disadvantage, because they are given so little cultural, matrimonial, and—in the case of divorce—financial support in the parenting process.

Nevertheless the fact remains that most mothers *are* the primary caregivers, the arbiter of their children's parental allegiance, the keepers of the maternal gate. And, unfair as the division of emotional labor within the family—the de facto source of maternal power—may be, the mother's role, while unsung and much maligned, is one that she herself does not always readily share.

Hence, just as fathers must be held accountable, so, too, must mothers, if there is to be any solution to this family conundrum. For in the amalgam of parental influences on a daughter's identity —which sometimes hangs in the balance—we see the residue of her divided loyalties in her choice of romantic partners.

While many women select men who in some way resemble Dad, how they relate to them—how they *behave toward a man*—calls up their early recollection of their parents' marriage. And if it was conflicted or hostile or terminated, the daughter will, in her relationships with men, seek to pick up the disparate pieces.

She may choose a lover who is a mother substitute, or a lover who is a father substitute, or a combination of both: a man *like her father* to whom she behaves *like her mother.* By being true to both parents in this way, she can set herself up for romantic loss. Thus do a daughter's divided loyalties toward parents who failed her haunt her adult life—and her future children's lives.

But thus also do the *undivided* loyalties of the daughter who has been well loved by both mother and father—whether or not their own marriage survived—pave the way for her to make healthy romantic choices.

It helps enormously to have had a loving mother. Mothers can give their daughters permission to love their fathers. Mothers can help their daughters feel good about becoming mothers. Mothers can help daughters learn the value of openness and female friendship, especially when times are bad.

A mother can make up for many things—but she cannot replace the father when it comes to how her daughter feels about herself in her intimate connections with men.

In a daughter's interaction with a *lover,* in her sexual responsiveness and capacity to trust a man, there the mother cannot help, no matter how much wise counsel she may give or how much she roots for father-daughter affection.

In matters of the adult daughter's romantic, heterosexual heart, the critical piece, still, is this:

Whether or not her father was lovingly involved in her life.

PART TWO

Fathers: Templates for Future Attachments

4

The Good-Enough Father

Family always came first for my father. When I was little, he would drive me to school every morning on his way to work. The day I started kindergarten, I was terrified—I took his hat so he couldn't leave. He peered through a glass door, waving and smiling every time I looked up at him. Finally I started playing with the other kids and let go of the hat. He did that for five days in a row, until I wasn't afraid anymore and he could just drop me off. He never got annoyed, not once. That's my daddy.

—MILLY, FORTY-THREE

A couple of years ago my husband and I attended the June wedding of Angela, the daughter of close friends of ours. Two hundred guests sat on delicate white chairs, arranged on a velvet country-club lawn; the sun hung low in the sky, spreading a pink glow over the idyllic garden setting. A string quartet played Mozart as we waited for the ceremony to begin on this perfect spring evening.

But something was decidedly imperfect: The wedding had been scheduled for four-thirty, and now it was nearly five o'clock.

Inside the clubhouse a drama was unfolding. Angela, in a profusion of white tulle and organdy, was hysterical: "I can't go through with it!" she wailed. A clutch of five bridesmaids stared at her in fidgety silence. The mother of the bride, ashen, looked as though she had been struck.

Suddenly Tom, the father of the bride, strode into the center of this tableau, gripped his daughter by the shoulders, and said firmly, "Stop crying for a second while I say something." The bride's sobs shuddered to a halt.

"Let's make a deal," he calmly continued. "You'll go through with the ceremony, and tomorrow, if that's what you want, we'll have the marriage annulled. Consider this just a terrific party. Okay?" Sniffling, she nodded her assent.

Minutes later the bridesmaids filed outdoors to the strains of "The Wedding March," followed by Tom, smiling and nodding to the guests as though nothing were amiss, supporting his trembling daughter by the arm. The wedding went off without a hitch, and the bridal couple held each other in a long, passionate embrace.

"It was my father's finest hour," Angela told me three weeks later, suntanned and beaming, having just returned from her honeymoon with the husband she clearly adored. She continued,

> I just freaked out from exhaustion. My father didn't try to talk me out of my panic, he didn't threaten, he didn't judge me. He just let me know that he loved me and that he'd back me up no matter what I decided. It was the *primo* moment of life with Daddy.

"Daddy." The word evokes celluloid images of ideal paternity: Spencer Tracy in *Father of the Bride,* sadly watching his newly married daughter drive away and murmuring, "I didn't have a chance to say good-bye." Fredric March, in *The Best Years of Our Lives,* wisely counseling his daughter about her star-crossed love affair. Ben Kingsley in *Silas Marner,* single-handedly and against all odds devoting his life to his adored little girl.

"Dad" is what most sons call their fathers; "Daddy" is the term of endearment—even homage—of daughters. Says psychiatrist Frank Pittman, "When it comes to little girls, God the father has nothing on father, the god. It's an awesome responsibility."

Many of the women I interviewed could cite isolated moments when their fathers came through in crises, making them sound awesome indeed: Doting fathers could summon a cheery word in the darkest night; remote fathers could be counted upon for sound advice; domineering fathers could be relied upon for a show of protective force; even some rejecting fathers could turn up, like Robin Hood, for an unexpected good deed.

But "good-enough" fathers are more than periodic, foul-weather heroes. For them fatherhood is more than mere paternity and sporadic rescue; rather it is a continuum of dependability, of involvement and interest over the course of their daughters' lives.

The good father does not have to be *perfect*. Rather, he has to be good *enough* to help his daughter to become a woman who is reasonably self-confident, self-sufficient, and free of crippling self-doubt, and to feel at ease in the company of men.

What does it take to be a good-enough father? And how is he different from the "bad" father?

To understand, it's useful to examine the forces that shape a father, both before and after he hears these fateful words "We're going to have a baby."

Fatherhood has four key components:

- The father's cultural roots
- The father's emotional history
- The father's temperament
- The seasons of a father's life

The Father's Cultural Roots

It is virtually impossible to assess any human relationship apart from the cultural backgrounds of the people involved. While the notion of a national or ethnic character is sometimes dismissed as overgeneralization or politically incorrect stereotyping, culture cannot be discounted.

For example, Mikiko, twenty-three, was born in Japan and, with her parents, grandparents, and older sisters, moved to the United States when she was nine. Her parents brought with them their traditions: At dinner no one could eat until the grandfather had picked up a spoon or other eating implement; her older sisters' marriages were arranged by her parents; the children could not speak to their elders unless spoken to.

But Mikiko spent too many of her formative years in California to avoid being significantly westernized, particularly by her school friends and their parents. Indeed in time she became an expatriate within her own family, especially with regard to her father.

When she entered adolescence and began to show signs of independence, he felt dishonored and reacted like a man betrayed. At fourteen she impulsively dyed her hair and he slapped her for not having asked his permission. Once, she said she was going to a party, and he locked her in her room. Finally, at seventeen, she ran away from home and worked her way through college. She hasn't seen her family for five years—although she talks by telephone to her mother from time to time.

Mikiko's father was exerting what he considered to be his absolute, ancestral, patriarchal right. That's how he was raised, and, by God, that's how his daughters were going to be raised—in spite of shopping malls, school sex education, television influences, women's liberation.

Such cultural clashes can occur even in families that proudly claim generations of citizenship. Customs of the past are handed down from parent to child like heirlooms, only slightly worn by the passage of time, and heaven help the child who violates them.

The Father's Emotional History

Fatherhood has been variously described as a "hobby," a "by-product of nature," even as "unnecessary." Which raises this question: Is there in fathers an equivalent of the alleged "maternal instinct"—an intrinsic, basic drive to nurture and protect one's young?

One researcher suggests that there is, but—unlike motherhood—it is defined more by *doing* than creating, more by practical function than by emotional form. Other researchers suggest that the father instinct is simply the man's wish for immortality through his children, especially his sons.

Still others believe that if there is a paternal instinct, it is contingent—that is, *bound up in the individual father's capacity for intimacy with his wife.* That capacity is spawned in his childhood.

To find out how expectant fathers feel about themselves and their impending parental role, Dr. James M. Herzog conducted a retrospective study of 103 first-time fathers of premature babies. He grouped the men into three categories, defined by the degree to which they were in touch with their feelings during their wives' pregnancies: "most attuned," "less well attuned," and "least well attuned."

During the first trimester many men thought of their paternal value in sexual terms. The most attuned fathers, for example, often had fantasies that sexual intercourse in some way "refertilized" the fetus. These fantasies were echoes of the physical intimacy and tenderness the men had experienced with their mothers when they were infants.

Sex for the least well-attuned men, however, was for personal satisfaction and reassurance rather than to "nurture" wife and fetus; many of these men wanted more sex with their wives—some were insatiable.

In the second trimester there was a significant shift in how all three groups of men felt about themselves. The most-attuned men became extremely introspective, worrying whether they would be good-enough fathers. They felt an urgent need to clear their emotional decks, to settle old scores with their *own* fathers. These men wanted to resolve whatever losses there may have been, to glean from the relationship anything that was good and use it as a kind of beacon. Dealing with their "father hunger" in this way made it possible for them to become more empathetic to their wives and better able to address upcoming fatherhood.

With the other two groups, however, there was little or no such resolution. In many cases there was no father to whom the men could turn—a large percentage of them had fathers who had been absent for much or all of their early childhoods.

The men who were unable or unwilling to reach a rapprochement with their fathers had the most difficulty adjusting to the idea of fatherhood. They were most likely to recoil from their own feelings, their "maternal," nurturant sides, and to be emotionally detached from their wives' pregnancies.

Instead they became obsessed with their own masculinity. Many of them had affairs. They became obsessed, too, with the sex of their unborn children. While two thirds of the most-attuned group hoped for sons, in the other two groups that figure rose to nearly *100 percent.*

As childbirth neared, the most-attuned fathers were acutely aware both of their inner emotional lives and of their need to provide for the child. And when the child was born, the miracle of the birth process filled them with awe and tenderness for their wives, which increased their "attunement." These men were able to "parent" both mother and premature child.

Childbirth affected the less- and least-well-attuned fathers quite differently: Suddenly they were no longer emotionally detached from their babies. Instead they became *riveted* on their newborns, whom they saw as a potential source of unqualified devotion.

However, childbirth did not bring these men closer to their wives. Rather the mothers were seen as rivals for the babies' affection. Paternity did not inspire nurturing in these fathers—instead it stoked their neediness.

The most significant finding in Dr. Herzog's study was this: *The greater the father's hunger for his own father, the less able he is to participate in expectant fatherhood.* As Herzog writes, "If you are always searching for a father, it may interfere with your ability to become one."

Another study confirmed these findings and added to them. Expectant fathers revealed to investigators a number of fears that, they said, they had been encouraged to keep to themselves, to avoid agitating their wives. Many of the men felt that nurses and doctors disapproved of their presence in examining and delivery rooms and discounted their concerns, concentrating only on the mother.

And so the men suffered a number of anxieties in relative silence. Many were afraid they wouldn't be up to the task of fatherhood. Some were frightened they'd pass out in the delivery room. Others were terrified that something dire would happen to either their wives or their newborns or that they'd be replaced by the babies in their wives' affection.

What made these concerns doubly intense was *the paucity of close family ties and friendships* in the fathers' lives.

As these and other studies make clear, in too many ways fathers feel isolated from parenting. This sense of isolation, with its attendant anxieties, can be seen as cracks in the rigid roles into which men are culturally contained. These cracks can deepen throughout the paternal process, as we shall see later in this chapter.

But, as the Herzog study illustrates, feelings of parental redundancy also reflect a man's childhood: his emotional history is the archive on which he draws to guide his own parenting. If a father has not sorted out the conflicts he had with his own parents, those conflicts may be recapitulated when he becomes a father—beginning with gender preference, his wish for either sons or daughters.

Preference for Sons. Many men prefer sons because of the Oedipal triangle of their own childhoods: A son's need to identify with his father can make a relationship with *any* member of the opposite sex problematic, including future daughters.

Obviously fathers can identify more easily with sons than daughters. After all, they share the same biological equipment. So strong is this identification that some fathers think of a daughter as *physi-*

cally incomplete, "simply because she is not male," as one researcher put it.

Moreover a son is an opportunity for a father to *improve* on the original model, to enjoy vicariously through his son the realization of his dreams for himself, to redress the losses of his own life. Such fathers may think, "Well, since I didn't get everything I wanted, I'll see to it that my son *does.*"

Sometimes, though, a man's desire to have sons is far more urgent and runs considerably deeper than mere identification with all things male. Sometimes it is the result of his hatred of his mother.

Neil, thirty-nine, grew up with a workaholic father and a mother who was alternately violent and suicidal; Neil never knew from one day to the next whether she'd attack him or herself. So when his daughter was born, he was bitterly disappointed. He says,

> I'm much harder on my daughter than my son. I think it's because I've got a lot of underlying hostility toward women stemming from my childhood. I'm very controlling with her. She and I have gone head-to-head ever since she was born. She triggers something in me my son doesn't.

Preference for Daughters. Other fathers prefer having daughters, in part because in some ways there's less at stake: If a daughter turns out badly, the father can always point an accusing finger at her gender role model—the mother.

But some fathers pray for daughters, often because they had horrific relationships with their fathers.

Charles, forty-six, was raised by a passive mother who lived in the shadow of his father, a swaggering back slapper who wanted his son to be "like his old man"—a jock, a "regular guy." Tragically, when Charles was six, he contracted a mild form of polio, rendering sports out of the question. From then on his father virtually ignored him.

When Charles was grown and his wife told him she was pregnant with their first child, he was concerned about his ability to set a "proper example of masculinity" for a son:

> I was terrified of having a boy. I was a monumental disappointment to my father and didn't even remotely fit the ma-

cho stereotype. But then, mercifully, my wife had a girl. Having a daughter just made all those issues go away.

Other fathers prefer girls because they felt tender and warm about their own mothers and wanted to replicate those feelings with a daughter.

Matt, fifty-one, was ecstatic when his daughter was born, not the least reason being that his father had died when he was young, and he was unusually close to his mother.

> I *much* preferred a girl. Maybe it's because I prefer women to men. There's something missing from most guys. You can't get past some kind of barrier. My mother was strong as hell, but always loving. So when my daughter was born, I said, "Thank you, God."

But the relief in having a girl can also stem from a man's need to dominate: Daughters, more than sons, *can be controlled*—or so many fathers believe. Men who had volatile relationships with their fathers sometimes seek retribution from the child they believe is least likely to defy them—the sweet, compliant little girl—a fantasy that may backfire. Says Henry, forty-two,

> I thought having a girl would be a cinch, and it wasn't. When she disagrees with me, it's like a knife in my heart. She's definitely not submissive, all the things I thought she'd be—she's got a mind of her own.

The Father's Temperament

As this example illustrates, another component of how a father feels about fatherhood relates to whether or not he finds a daughter or son to be his kind of people.

Sam has a daughter, twenty-eight, and a son, twenty-six; his experience with both has shattered all his preconceptions about gender:

> I always thought that fathers and sons are closer than fathers and daughters, and it's turned out to be quite the opposite. I have conversations with my son that are totally different from

those with my daughter. He's very sensitive, easily hurt, more like his mother. But my daughter is *just like me.* She has followed my pattern of behavior *exactly.* She's burning with ambition, a political animal, always working the angles. The difference between my kids continues to amaze me.

It cannot be overestimated how important a role temperament plays in the parent-child relationship. Drs. Stella Chess and Alexander Thomas, in their studies of temperament in children, have noted that one can find psychopathology in children of "good parents," and healthy children whose parents are on the fringes of emotional stability. The variable is often the innate personalities of parent and child and how well they "fit" together.

The researchers isolated a range of temperamental characteristics that show up in early infancy, including activity level, distractibility, and attention span. These characteristics, they found, coalesce into three distinct temperamental constellations: the Easy Child, the Difficult Child, and the Slow-to-Warm-Up Child.

Imagine how the relationship between an exacting father and an "easy child" will compare, say, to the same father's relationship with a "difficult" or "slow-to-warm-up" child. When parent and child are temperamentally out of sync, they do not read each other's signals; it's as though they're from different galaxies.

Thus "goodness of fit" is a crucial element of the father-daughter relationship—which the good-enough father understands.

Marital Role-Reversal. A tangent of "fit" has to do with the marital partnership. Sometimes the temperamental differences between mother and father can result in the father taking on the more nurturing role with their children. Of all the stereotypes of parenthood, one of the most destructive is the assumption that *all* mothers are cut out for a Donna Reed kind of maternal love and that fathers are biologically incapable of it.

Some women are temperamentally better suited for the traditional *father* role, and some fathers are happier being full-time nurturers. Approximately 2 percent of married American fathers are stay-at-home dads. Says one of them, Gene, forty, the primary caretaker of his and his wife's two young children,

I'm much more a Mediterranean personality, warm and effusive, and my wife is much more the Scandinavian personality. She relates in a cerebral, practical way. At first it was a real problem, because she got stuck with full-time mothering when she really should have been out there working. I didn't have any of the conflict she had about being the primary parent. Recently we decided to try an experiment; I'd take a leave of absence from my company so that she could have her shot. And I love it. I may never go back.

A study of Australian fathers who are full-time caregivers showed that such "untraditional" parenting has a remarkable effect on children. These fathers were far less stereotypic in the ways they played with their children, able to be both "football coach" and "storyteller" to their kids. A study of the children of American primary caregiving fathers found that the children felt a greater sense that they were in control of their fate, and scored higher on verbal ability, than those raised traditionally.

In another study children of single fathers rated their fathers as *"more nurturing than children from two-parent families rated either parent"* (emphasis added). These fathers were actively involved with their children prior to divorce and afterward made a concerted effort to be better parents by seeking counseling and reading books about childrearing, just as many mothers have traditionally done.

But "goodness of fit" is not static; it can be enhanced or strained by a number of factors, *especially* the father's own emotional evolution in the ebb and flow of his adult life.

The Seasons of a Father's Life

The final component of fatherhood is this very fluidity—one is not the same parent at forty-five that one was at twenty-five. Personalities and emotional rhythms are buffeted not simply by internal forces but by external pressures as well: an economic slump, the death of a spouse, sudden illness—all sharpen or soften the contours of our lives.

In addition there are key, predictable events in a man's life that can lead to painful change. In his book *Seasons of a Man's Life,* Daniel J. Levinson described a study he and his colleagues conducted of forty men from a variety of socioeconomic backgrounds. He wanted to understand the psychological changes that occur in adult men.

Dr. Levinson discovered that certain life "crises," common to most men, can lead to psychological growth: the beginning of a career; marriage; the birth of a child; the midlife awareness of a shrinking future; the marriage of children and births of grandchildren; the deaths of one's own parents.

Children, of course, also go through their own predictable developmental "crises"—for example, being toilet trained, starting school, adjusting to puberty. And when the father's crises coincide with a child's—a collision of what psychiatrist William S. Appleton calls "the double life-cycle perspective"—they can set off tremors within the family.

When, for example, a three-year-old daughter is wrestling with Oedipal issues, breaking away from Mom and turning toward Dad in order to carve out her separate identity, the father may be concentrating on building a career.

And when in adolescence, the daughter again turns to Dad, this time as the last sentry before she crosses the emotional frontier into adulthood, seeking from him an emotional visa to her independence, it may be just at the point when he is flattened by a full-scale midlife crisis.

Middle age is a period when a man, for the first time, may be plumbing his "feminine" side—the part that cries easily at movies, that needs to hold tenderly and to be held by the people he most loves, the part that is aware of his emotional losses. In a way he may be making room for the daddy he never was, the daddy he now longs to be—and the daddy he may never have had. He may regress and go through a kind of adolescent trashing of all his relationships and values.

At the same time he may have an anguished sense of unfinished career business: Did I do everything I set out to do? Which of my dreams came true and which did not? Am I over the hill? Is a young firebrand gunning for my job?

Confusing matters even *more,* his wife may be making midcourse corrections of her own—getting in touch with her "masculine" side, trying to wrest from the world the goodies she may have postponed in the long hiatus of childrearing, filling the emptying nest with her own career goals.

And what of the adolescent daughter caught in the middle of these parental upheavals? For one thing, since her mother was probably always intimately involved in her life, the daughter, now trying to break away, may be downright *thrilled* to have her off her back. Moreover she may *never* have had an intimate attachment with her father, lacking what Dr. Appleton calls the "oasis" period of young childhood when many fathers and daughters have a special, adoring relationship.

Daddy may always have been too busy for her. So the timing of his sudden emotionality—his becoming too much like Mom—may be annoying, even suffocating, an altogether startling and unwelcome turn of events.

Daddy Dethroned. One of the tasks of adolescence is to pull one's parents from their pedestals, to deidealize them so that the child can begin preparing psychologically for eventual leave-taking. Dethroning Mom and Dad paves the way for a realistic adult child-parent friendship—*depending on how the parents respond.*

Some fathers fall from their children's esteem with less grace than others. The middle-aged father, thrashing around with all his midlife doubts and dwindling physical reserves, may suddenly and inexplicably begin lashing out: first, at his wife, who already knows all his physical and psychic flaws; and then at his children for discovering them. He may, as one researcher noted, angrily put his son in his generational place, punishing him for misdemeanors the father perceives as crimes; he may pick fights with his daughter or her boyfriends, who are, he feels, threatening his place in her heart.

Seeing Daddy behave in these confusing ways is not a pretty sight; suddenly, or so it seems, he is something less than heroic to his children.

And fathers know it.

One of the few times the fathers I interviewed wept was when they recalled the termination of their tenure as their daughters' heroes. Even some of the most outwardly posturing and stalwart fathers crumpled with self-reproach when relating, in husky voices, the first, terrible time they caused their little girls to look at them with fear or embarrassment or disgust.

The most painful dethronements occurred during the men's midlife crises.

A decade ago, Patrick, now fifty-five, was at a professional and personal Rubicon: The corporation for which he worked was trimming its payroll, and his high-paying job hung in the balance. His wife had begun a career in real estate, and Gena, his sixteen-year-old daughter, was becoming more and more independent.

Patrick panicked: Suddenly he had control over nothing, was *needed* for nothing. Of that period he says,

> I was just a working stiff who paid the bills and who no one wanted. I thought, "Fuck it." I packed a bag and took off. I couldn't believe how easy it was to leave my family, everything I'd spent my entire life working for.

Patrick had an extramarital affair, but kept up telephone contact with his wife and daughter. His wife decided to make no ultimatums and instead began assessing, in therapy, her part in her husband's emotional derailment. Gena didn't know *what* to make of her father and was furious with him for causing her and her mother so much pain.

After two months Patrick ended his affair and, suffused with contrition, came home. At his wife's insistence they saw a marriage counselor. But, he says, he still had "some explaining to do" with Gena. He recalls,

> I apologized profusely. I admitted I was far from perfect. She saw me cry for the first time. It scared her to find out that Daddy didn't have all the answers. But she also saw me become a better person. I think she's forgiven me; we're certainly very, very close today. My marriage is stronger than it ever was. But I took a lot of people down with me and caused a lot of grief. I don't recommend it.

Sometimes Daddy's midlife crisis does not take the form of an affair; it takes the form of a kind of emotional implosion, a psychological cave-in that results either in depression or a nervous breakdown.

That's what happened to Roger, sixty, whose childhood had been a series of gothic horrors, memories of which he tried to escape by sheer velocity. He raced through college, married at twenty-three and immediately began a family, and plunged into a career on Wall Street, leaving the emotional chores of parenting his daughter to his wife.

For most of his adult life the momentum of his work hurtled him far from his psychic demons. Enforced early retirement allowed him belatedly to become aware of them, rather like a sonic boom. Now he had nothing but time to examine the unavoidable day-to-day reality of his brittle sense of self-worth. It was more than he could bear.

The crisis came the day Roger seriously considered murdering his wife, a gentle woman whom he cherished. "I can only say that I went crazy," he said, his voice breaking as he recalled his emotional hell:

> I had what the shrinks call a "psychotic episode." Retirement brought up my childhood fear of being dependent, the same feeling I had as a kid with my mother, who was dangerously abusive. I vividly remember being terrified that she'd kill me, and there wasn't a thing I could do about it. I was completely at her mercy. My father never knew—I just couldn't talk to him. He wouldn't have believed me anyhow; he always sided with her.

Galvanized by his homicidal rage, Roger immediately went into intensive therapy. And, like Dan, his emotional crack-up and slow but steady recovery ultimately improved his family ties.

But with his daughter the benefits were bittersweet: Seeing her father so possessed, so out of control, made him suddenly and wrenchingly real—and frightening.

Today father and daughter are a work in progress. They have a tentative, careful attachment that is based on a recognition of what they never had, and the truth of what they do have. They are in the process of repairing their relationship. Says Roger,

> Recently we had a major breakthrough. She said, "Maybe I'm not exactly the daughter you wanted." I took a deep breath and replied, "Perhaps not. God knows I'm not the father you bargained for either. But you're my daughter, and I'm your father, and I love you very, very much."

Daughter Dethroned. If Daddy must be dethroned for a daughter to begin to accept him as merely mortal, so, too, must a father give up the idea that his daughter will forever be his worshiping little girl—a process that can be peaceful or, more often than not, turbulent.

For just as daughters often have trouble separating from their parents, so, too, do some fathers have a hard time letting their children—especially their daughters—go. As Dr. Appleton points out, the father who does not want to see his daughter grow up—defying him, making her own rules, having a sex life—longs to recapture the oasis period of her early childhood when she saw him as perfect. And when she shatters his fantasy by becoming more adult, he may be devastated.

One father described for me the *exact moment* his daughter fell from grace:

> At her high school graduation, she introduced me to a young man, and when she said, "This is my father," the guy's jaw dropped, as though I had caught him red-handed. It was obvious he had slept with her. I thought, "What a waste. She's not such a quality kid after all." It was very traumatic for me.

Off-Season Fatherhood. Some fathers sidestep this collision of tandem developmental changes altogether by having children after their midlife storms have passed, often in second marriages. This "seasoning" can be wondrous both for father and child. Says Ted, fifty-eight, who has a three-year-old daughter,

> There are times with her that are transcendant, when I realize this is what counts—that she will only be three for one year, so I'd better play with her or talk to her now. And again when she's four, and five. And every year. I'm smarter than I used to be. I may be a little creakier, but I'm *absolutely clear* about my priorities as a father.

Unfinished Emotional Business. Still, most fathers have children in their younger years, and conflicts are often unavoidable as they struggle along parallel paths toward maturity and inner peace. If father and daughter can manage to cross the finish line of her emancipation together—she accepting Daddy's flaws, he viewing hers as opportunities for her to learn and grow—the ups and downs of their relationship and mutual growth can prepare her for the ambiguities of life. The example of the father weathering his emotional seasons can help the daughter weather her own.

With this caveat: As similar as these evolving life cycles are, father and child are *not* alike in one crucial way. He is of the senior generation, tempered, at least theoretically, by time. He is a veteran of life's battles, and she is a rookie.

Although Daddy's dethronement is essential for the daughter to separate from him, how that deidealization occurs varies widely. Daddy's flaws can be violently imposed, or they can be gradually discovered.

For while many men go through a midlife hurricane, *many others do not.* The midlife crisis is nothing if not a symptom that a father's unresolved issues have reached the flashpoint. This "crisis" is not an immutable fact of every man's life—only for the man who has ignored or denied his conflicts and kept them under wraps.

It is inevitable that these buried conflicts will eventually break out into the open. And children deserve a better version of separation than a crash course in Daddy's unfinished emotional business. Fathers have *choices* in how they parent, in how willing they are to listen to their inner voices, in how able they are to express their emotional needs in appropriate ways. And if they have trouble in these areas, they have options about what to do about it.

There are those fathers who are able to keep their inner, loving capacities alive, in spite of cultural and psychological temptations to deny them. There are those fathers who get help in resolving their conflicts so that they do not destroy their relationships with their kids. These fathers may from time to time be unhinged by misfortune or psychic turmoil, but as *parents* they do not bail out.

It is against this background of cultural, emotional, and seasonal history that the definitions of "good" and "bad" fathers emerge. For the question is not *that* a man experienced personal tragedy or horrendous deprivations—many people have. What matters is how he *deals* with life's blows and whether or not he allows them to serve as justification for inadequate fathering.

Bad Daddy

When it comes to evil, there are no gray areas. Fathers who abuse their children by battering or starving or raping them automatically relinquish any entitlement to mitigation or sympathy. They commit the unpardonable moral offense of betraying their children. It matters not what their own histories were; millions of people with childhood horror stories to tell do not repeat them with their own children.

Still, it's hard to escape the reality that ours is not a child-oriented culture. Child maltreatment is on the rise: The number of reported cases of all child abuse and neglect rose *223 percent* between 1976 and 1986.

The sanctity of the home often virtually overrules moral law. Any outside interference with parental authority is almost as socially taboo—some would argue that it is more so—as abusing a child in the first place. The prevention of child maltreatment takes second place to the possibility that a parent will be falsely accused of child abuse.

Nevertheless there are unwritten rules that govern the treatment of children. Most people would agree, for example, when seeing a parent bellow at a toddler or slap a ten-year-old, that they are not witnessing anything even remotely resembling a fair fight. Most people would agree that physically or sexually assaulting a child is very, very wrong.

But when it comes to emotional abuse—the kind that leaves no physical scars—our notion of parental "badness" takes on ambiguous moral hues. Does psychological maltreatment *really* compare in psychic damage, say, to cigarette burns on a baby's skin?

The answer is that it does. Psychological abuse is at the heart of *all* maltreatment—and emotional wounds, which don't show, may never heal if they are left unexamined and untreated.

In these and other ways many fathers do in fact abuse their daughters, as we shall see in subsequent chapters.

But "good fathers" do exist—if not in the numbers one would wish. Studies of the father-daughter relationship estimate that from 20 to 39 percent of fathers are "good"—that is, able to walk the thin line between too much closeness and too much distance.

Good Daddy

Good fathers have one or more of the following characteristics:

Androgyny. One of the components of being an effective father is a willingness to listen to his own instincts and code of ethics and act upon them, rather than feeling he must adhere to a cultural definition of what is "appropriate" fathering. Says therapist Ronald Gaudia,

> To be a good person, sometimes you must go against the culture. How many times do you hear about a man killing

another man for making a move on his girlfriend? The guy will say, "That's my macho culture, you're not supposed to insult my woman." To which I say, "Don't tell me the culture made you do it. I'm sick of that one." The "culture" is no excuse for irresponsible behavior.

Good parenting has been defined as the ability to "borrow" certain qualities from the opposite sex. For instance some men take to the parenting role more easily than others because they were close to their mothers and feel comfortable following the maternal example. In fact a study of divorced custodial fathers found that they had been far closer to their mothers than they were to their own fathers.

The good father, then, identifies with the nurturing mother. He is not obsessed with his masculinity; rather he is at ease with his "feminine" side.

Studies of homophobia show that one reason so many men— and relatively so few women—are hostile toward gay men is because they perceive gays as "feminine" and fear their own "femininity." Hence, said one researcher, "the more feminine a gay man appears, the more hostility he evokes in other men."

Since good fathers aren't so insecure about their sexuality, they aren't preoccupied with the gender division of parental labor. Androgynous fathers are involved with their babies from the start, smiling, holding and talking to them more than fathers who characterize themselves as traditionally "masculine." Their children reap the benefits of Dad's warmth and flexibility, including academically; androgynous fathers do not have preconceptions, say, that boys alone excel in science and girls alone are good at English. Rather they encourage their children's gender-neutral talents.

Moreover, androgynous fathers are least likely to sexually abuse their daughters, both because of their early and ongoing paternal involvement *and* because of their capacity to identify with their daughters.

Generational Authority. The second component of good fathering is the father's ability to adjust to his daughter's possibly different temperament and opposing opinions without feeling betrayed or becoming childlike himself. He knows he is the adult and can respect the generational differences between them, at the same time maintaining his generational authority.

While monitoring a daughter's expression of feelings and ideas —that is, by not tolerating rudeness—the good father does not insist that his opinion prevail. Says Lorraine, thirty-eight,

> My father would talk to me very intelligently and never say, "You're stupid for thinking that." He would listen to everything I had to say, and then if he disagreed, he'd tell me why. But he never tried to talk me out of the way I felt or what I thought.

The Good Daddy is mature enough to be aware of his overreactions—to take an emotional beat if he finds himself becoming unreasonably exercised and figure out what's *really* going on.

For example, when Andy's daughter, Robin, was fifteen, she asked him to help her with a writing assignment. He offered a variety of suggestions. She kept insisting, "I can't *do* it." Says Andy,

> I started to get really angry. But all of a sudden I remembered that's what my father used to do—if I resisted his advice, he'd storm out of the room. I realized that you can't be much help to someone if you're critical of their inability to grasp an idea. I learned something; her way of dealing with the world is first to panic, then to listen. Now our homework sessions go much more smoothly.

The good father draws on his emotional and chronological seniority to hold a steady course during his daughter's emotional heavy weather. While she sees life up close—vivid, immediate, raw —he sees it from the distance of generational perspective.

That perspective, coupled with his androgyny, makes it possible for him to treat each of his children as unique individuals, precluding many of the sibling hostilities that result from parental favoritism, as we shall see in Part Three.

Desexualizing the Relationship. The good father's maturity helps him adjust to his daughter's sexual changes as well. He remembers he is the adult male figure in her life, rather than seeing her as a peer—as in "lover"—or as though she were a surrogate parent.

During her infancy and early childhood he is affectionate,

tender, playful, all the while allowing her to take reasonable risks —just as he would a son.

As she enters preadolescence, the Good Daddy reframes their intimacy. Long gone are the days when he bathed her. Now he gently discourages behavior such as nudity, which might sexually stimulate either of them. And if his daughter is flirtatious, he does not allow her behavior to throw him off his parental course, nor does he ricochet away from her.

This tumultuous period tests the mettle of even the most circumspect fathers. Says psychiatrist Marianne Goodman, "The best of fathers have trouble coming to terms with their little girl's increasing sexuality and growing into adulthood."

Albert, forty-eight, grew up in a household of bewildering chaos. Both his parents were alcoholics who alternately neglected and denigrated him. In adulthood he married a loving woman who helped him overcome his anxieties about his masculinity.

But when his wife got pregnant, Albert realized that the malevolent messages of his childhood could easily eclipse his good paternal intentions, so he went into therapy as a preventive measure. Consequently when their daughter, Hope, began to emerge from childhood, he was able to shift gears.

The day Hope turned twelve, her mother bought her a training bra. Of that momentous day Albert says,

> My wife and I were getting ready for bed, and I heard a knock on the door. I opened it, and there was Hope in her panties and her training bra. She put her fingers to her heart and said, "Daddy, look." And I said, "Oh, honey, you look so nice."
>
> I was aware that she was a sexual creature. It's difficult for fathers—it may be your daughter, but let's face it, it's a young, female body. Still, I'd been through enough confusion in my childhood to know what confusion was all about. So I wasn't going to cover my eyes and run away, but I wasn't going to deny my own feelings either. I just played it right down the middle. I was damn clear about it, and I think I handled it pretty well.

According to Dr. Judith S. Kestenberg, one reason the daughter's puberty often jolts fathers is because men are generally less prepared for physical changes than are women. Most mothers talk with prepubertal daughters about the day when they'll begin to menstruate, laying in a supply of sanitary napkins. Boys do not generally get such anticipatory consciousness-raising because they do not require special equipment—and, of course, they can't become pregnant; daughters *must* be made aware of the consequences of their bodily changes.

Still, the good father who has been an active participant in his daughter's life will see changes coming; because he has put in so much parental time, the changes do not ambush him.

Most fathers react to their daughters' bodily transformation by respecting their privacy. Fathers, even more than mothers, knock on the daughters' bedroom door before entering. But good fathers adjust to their daughters' puberty with particular sensitivity, involvement, and even inventiveness.

A few fathers told me, for example, that they *celebrated* their daughters' first menstrual period, wanting it to be a "family event" rather than a secret between mother and daughter. One father bought his daughter a special purse in which to carry her tampons. Another father hosted a ceremonial dinner:

> Her mother and I thought of our daughter's menarche as a rite of passage, like a Bat Mitzvah, and I wanted to be included. So I bought her a little gold necklace. We took her out to a fancy restaurant. I handed her the gift, and said, "Congratulations. Today you are a woman."

Without violating their generational authority and healthy emotional distance, good fathers assist their daughters' emerging womanliness in another way—by providing an opportunity for daughters to "practice" for their future romantic attachments.

Several of the fathers I interviewed talked delightedly about their occasional "dates" with their daughters—say, when Mom was working late or during solo visits to their daughters at college. These fathers expressed the singular pleasure in the private joke they and their daughters shared when walking into a room together and watching people's reactions. Says David, fifty-seven,

> Once when my daughter was around seventeen, I took her out for dinner. She was dressed to the nines, looking gorgeous. All these people turned around. They looked at her, then looked at me, trying to figure out what the relationship

was. So I started to flirt with her, holding her hand, smiling at her. She got a huge kick out of the charade. She thought it was hysterical that everyone thought I was just a dirty old man.

Such occasions give the daughter a sense of her womanly self; they also give her the protection of an escort who is her loving parent, a man who will make no inappropriate demands upon her, as well as the experience of a man's respect.

But the father's adjustment to his daughter's sexual maturity is not without some pain on both sides. As the father reframes their relationship, his daughter may be dismayed by his altered state, perceiving it as lack of love. Good fathers explain their behavior. Says Evan, forty,

> There was a time when my daughter was around fourteen that she walked around the house nude. I just said, "Look, I'm not comfortable when you do that. Please put on a robe." I set the tone as much for myself as for her.

In renegotiating the relationship, the good father collaborates, according to one researcher, with his daughter. He becomes instrumental in her passage to independence, encouraging her goals, supporting her strivings, and becoming involved in them. In this way the father-daughter connection remains strong, but with a different caste. Since a father's physical affection, such as back scratching, can be perceived as sensuousness by the daughter and so is no longer appropriate, now it is replaced by his mentorship.

The father who maintains this affectionate distance remains secure in the knowledge that these and other changes are necessary. Thus he is able to let his daughter go, having prepared her for her leave-taking. His gradual detachment—without emotional defection—helps her become an adult, with all the evolving memories of her loving daddy stored in the scrapbook of her mind.

Detriangling. A final ingredient in good fathering is the father's ability both to be supportive of his wife, to reduce possible mother-daughter jealousy, and to keep his daughter from being caught in the cross-fire of marital skirmishes.

This is called "detriangling," the family-therapy term for staying out of the middle. The ideal setting for detriangling is the harmonious marriage. Assuming that the husband and wife love each other and want to remain married, the good father takes both his own emotional pulse *and* his wife's.

Ralph and his wife of twenty-six years have reached a depth of understanding and mutual respect in spite of their great temperamental differences—he has always been the more emotional and nurturing parent, his wife the more detached and pragmatic. He and his daughter, Holly, his temperamental twin, are extremely close. Says Ralph,

> Once my wife asked me, "How come she can talk to you and she can't talk to me?" I took that as a signal that she felt left out. So I made a real point of keeping her up-to-date on anything Holly told me. I never wanted her to feel that Holly and I were ganging up on her or forming a conspiracy. My daughter knew that anything she told me, I would tell her mother. And when they had a disagreement, I stayed out of it; I didn't choose up sides.

Detriangling is extremely difficult if parents are divorced. But good fathers do not allow themselves to be goaded either by vengeful ex-wives or by their daughters' ambivalences. Some daughters of divorce test their fathers' loyalty to them; others attack their fathers out of allegiance to their mothers.

Good fathers hang in with these daughters, deflecting emotional flack and steadfastly remaining in their daughters' lives. They know that one day the daughter will be an adult, able to form her own conclusions. And in most cases, unless the mother has caused horrendous psychological damage to the daughter, good fathers and their daughters end up as loving friends.

One of the best definitions of "Good Daddies" came from Dr. Marlin S. Potash:

> A good father loves his daughter with no strings attached. He is available. He is both strong and tender. Being big and strong doesn't mean being separate from one's feelings; to the contrary, it means being very much in touch with them. Women who experienced fathers like that know that a strong man can cry, and that a man who can cry can also be very strong.

Many good fathers follow the example of their own parents, who treated them with kindness. And if they did not have happy childhoods, good fathers make it their first priority to *unlearn* the painful lessons of the past.

Good fathering, then, is a lifelong, adaptive process that requires androgyny, self-awareness, maturity, and introspection.

Is it *easy*? No. Do good fathers get through it without making mistakes? Never. Do they have regrets? Always.

But the *good-enough* father can acknowledge to himself, and to his daughter, when he's erred and make the necessary changes in his behavior. He can describe his own fears and mistakes, rather than struggle to be the unblemished hero. He can give her the gift of his own vulnerability and doubts, sharing what he has done about them. He can be *real*.

The good-enough father is not simply a knight in shining armor galloping to the occasional rescue; he is there through good times and bad, insisting on and delighting in his paternity every pleasurable and painful step of the way.

Most of all the good-enough father is *familiar*. And because he is, he does not become the "other," the "occasional," a mythical, idealized, or vilified mystery man. Rather he is a man of human scale, sometimes good, sometimes not so good, but altogether good enough—the best possible template for his daughter's future romantic attachments.

Finding Our Fathers

As we shall see in the next five chapters, some fathers—depending on their temperaments and histories and emotional wiring and marriages—come closer to this ideal than others.

The behavioral constellations of fathers cluster into general patterns, with extremes of "good" and "bad" fathering. Some of these categories overlap; others apply to one stage of a daughter's life, only to change when she hits adolescence or as the father evolves and ages.

But in general there is a central theme in the father's personality, a core to his character that influences and shapes his daughter over their lifetime together:

The Doting Father, who wants to be the adoring center of her life.

The Distant Father, who is a passive or silent presence within the family.

The Demanding Father, who dominates through rules, rigidity, or violence.

The Seductive Father, who puts his love on a suggestive or erotic basis.

The Absent Father, who seldom sees his daughter, or abandons her, or who dies.

Most daughters don't know their fathers very well. The purpose of the next five chapters is to help daughters begin to discover what formed their fathers—to gain some perspective on why their fathers behaved as they did. The goal is to separate fact from fiction, motivation from intent, accountability from blame.

In the process women can start to acquire a balanced assessment of what their fathers were able to give them, what they could not give, and why—the first, crucial step in understanding the patterns in their relationships with men.

5

▼▼▼▼▼▼▼

The Doting Father

One of my earliest memories of my father was when I was four. I woke up in the middle of the night and saw these scary shapes on my window shade and screamed, "Daddy! Daddy!" He rushed in, sat on the edge of my bed, and explained that it was just the streetlight playing tricks and that everything was all right. He stayed with me until I fell back to sleep. I remember thinking, "When I grow up, will I ever find a man as sweet and good and kind as my daddy?" So far, I haven't.

—CAROLE, THIRTY

The doting father is every daughter's ideal. This is the daddy whose patient reassurances banish the apparitions of the night, whose pockets bulge with treasures when he comes home from a business trip; the daddy who lets his little girl keep him company when he's shaving, lathering his face and hers, and into whose arms she rushes at the end of the day.

This is the daddy who makes everything all right.

Daughters who had fathers like that have a huge advantage: They got Daddy's adoration *on time*—that is, when they were young and dependent and trusting, and their identities were first taking shape.

Daughters *need* paternal adoration when they're little; it shields them from the wrath of a vengeful teacher, the sting of a playmate's cruelty. It helps them to face the outside world with their fathers' voice in their heads saying, "You'll always be safe, always be cherished." Daddy's unconditional love gives a daughter confidence and courage and a special edge on life, a particular head start.

Says Dr. Clarice Kestenbaum,

> I've always believed that everything that makes a woman feel feminine and appreciated and loved by a man comes from that adoration that the loving father gives his very young daughter. There's something in what fathers do—they love their little girls, there's never been a girl like this. Few mothers beam at a little girl the way a father does.

Which can be very, very good news. Or bad.

Bad news? How can there possibly be too much paternal love? How can being an adored daughter be anything but a celestial gift?

Because doting fathers may make it extremely difficult for their daughters to grow up and lead their own independent lives.

The dark side of doting fatherhood is hard to acknowledge, harder still to recognize. Women whose fathers didn't even *notice,* let alone cherish them, can't *imagine* that there could be a downside to paternal devotion. Nor can beloved daughters themselves.

Adored daughters have difficulty seeing their fathers' tender mercies as harmful because it feels like the ultimate disloyalty. Moreover to see Daddy as life-sized, instead of a gentle, romanticized giant, is to jeopardize the wondrous feeling that he can put to rights anything that goes wrong.

Idealizing Daddy is grand when you're five; it's crippling when you're twenty-five or thirty-five. For if you still believe in Daddy's miracles, you may not believe that you can make your own dreams come true. Worse, you may not even be able to formulate them without his guidance.

Little children require their parents' unqualified love in order to survive and to feel secure. Very soon, however, they need a tempered version of that devotion—parents who can give them the freedom to fail or feel sorrow or taste frustration, to fully experience their own pain and pleasure and learn from them. Therapists call this phenomenon "ownership."

Doting fathers are able to do the first part—glorifying their daughters—extremely well. But they have trouble with the second part—letting their daughters go, allowing them to "own" both their victories *and* their setbacks. They want to be indispensable forever.

And so, in the name of love, they deny their daughters the

consequences of their wrong turns, bailing them out of every conceivable scrape, satisfying their every whim.

Their daughters have only to wish for a new stereo, and it suddenly appears; they have only to suggest that there's a problem at school, and Daddy is on the phone with the principal; they have only to hint that they dislike a chore, and Daddy will get someone else to do it; they have only to mention that they're short on cash, and Daddy will peel off a twenty-dollar bill.

The one gift these fathers dare not give their daughters is the gift of self-reliance, because they cannot bear to be separated from them. Losing their little girls' adoration, even temporarily—as we shall see later in this chapter—is to lose a huge part of themselves. In many ways the doting father is as dependent on his daughter's love as she is on his.

Such fathers can become Bad Daddies in either of two ways: by *infantilizing* their daughters, beguiling them into lifelong dependency; or by *parentifying* them, flattering their daughters into giving them a maternal kind of love.

"I have seen many more women tied to fathers who are too kind, generous, helpful, and charming," writes Dr. William Appleton, "than I have seen cut off by uncaring, abusive ones."

There's an enormous price to be paid by daughters for the special favor of their doting fathers: Sometimes it's the disintegration of the mother-daughter relationship; sometimes it's the unraveling of a sibling relationship; and sometimes it's the loss of the daughter's separate identity.

Chains of Love

Victor, fifty-one, an elementary school teacher, always made his children—Gil, twenty-seven, and Ann, twenty-four—his first priority when they were little; indeed he was their primary caregiver. His availability to them was in part due to his wife's demanding career—she's a physical therapist with a large practice—and to his more flexible work schedule. It fell to Victor to do most of the shopping, meal planning, and day-to-day parental clucking, which suited his nurturing inclinations—toward his daughter, at least.

Victor, a dashing, outspoken man, was extremely strict with his son when he was a child. But, he says with an unabashed grin, he's always been "a sucker for my daughter. She can twist me around her little finger."

To illustrate his unapologetic favoritism, Victor tells me an anecdote, midway through which he struggles for composure:

> One night when Ann was around two, we were all sitting at the dinner table. I was not in the best of moods, and my son was horsing around. I yelled at him to settle down. Then little Annie piped up about something and I shouted, "And that'll be enough from you, too!" I'll never forget it . . . her face had this little smile . . . it was so awful . . . tinged with bewilderment. It's the only time I ever disciplined her. It *killed* me to see that look. She's always been the apple of my eye. I'm still her fawning father.

Such paternal sheltering of girls, says family therapist Dr. Augustus Y. Napier, is the cultural norm. In his book *The Fragile Bond* he notes that the daughters of such fathers are taught that they need "special help and protection," which serves to keep them eternal ingenues.

No one "protects" the way a doting father does. Mothers can hover, but fathers can back up their devotion with a fearsome authority. Says Ed, fifty-eight,

> One day when my daughter was around twelve, she was in the backyard, roughhousing with her boyfriend. And I almost did a terrible thing: I ran outside, grabbed him by the throat with one hand, and leaned him up against a tree. Had I not gotten a hold of myself, I would have ripped him apart. I realized I was overreacting—they were just having fun. So I put him down and said, "Boys aren't supposed to wrestle with girls."
>
> But my daughter got the message: You don't mess with Daddy's little girl without Daddy getting very unhappy.

At times, however, a doting father's protectiveness borders on burlesque. Madeline, twenty-eight, recalls with a mixture of glee and chagrin the time when she was seventeen and came home a half hour late from a blind date:

> It was a sweltering July night, and my dad was up on the roof of our apartment building looking down on the streets, watch-

ing for me. When I finally strolled up the block with my date, my dad came racing down the five flights of stairs and burst out onto the front stoop. Gasping for breath, his face wild with worry, he stood there *wearing nothing but his shorts.* I turned to my date and said, "I'd like you to meet my father."

And no one *possesses* like a doting father, especially in a daughter's teenage years.

Ellie vividly remembers the *one* time her normally gentle and soft-spoken father lost his temper: As in Madeline's case, it was when she came home late from a date.

My boyfriend and I were sitting in the car in the driveway of my house, just talking. It was around midnight; technically I was home on time. I came in the house a couple of hours later. The next morning my dad screamed, "You *tramp!* If you're so oversexed, why don't you just hang pictures of naked men all over your room!"

Sometimes, however, the doting father's vigilance takes a sinister turn. As one researcher put it, "Occasionally, the selfsame father who has behaved well toward his daughter prior to her adolescence becomes possessive, untrusting, and pernicious during her adolescence . . . [inspecting the] daughter's panties for telltale signs of sexual secretions."

Doting fathers try to hang on to their daughters for as long as possible, keeping them in their adoring place in a variety of ways.

Girls Must Be Girls

Some fathers, particularly those raised in very traditional, blue-collar families, expect their daughters to be homespun, chaste, interested only in things "feminine." These are men for whom most feminist values are a world away—tolerable, perhaps, on the job, but unacceptable at home. Many of these fathers are from tightly knit families, never straying far from the metaphorical or literal neighborhoods of their youths, marrying young and choosing brides who share their mores.

Richard, thirty-six, is the dutiful firstborn son of immigrant Romanian parents, whom he visits every Sunday. He and his wife have two children—Susan, twelve, and Anthony, nine. Of his relationship with his daughter, Richard says, beaming,

> She's my little princess. She's always adored me. I'm much more protective of her than my son. I figure he's going to be a man soon, and he's got to be able to handle all kinds of problems. But girls should be sheltered. I never wanted her to do things that might hurt her, like running too fast. I wanted her to be a little lady, the old-fashioned type. And she is.

To help pay the bills, Richard works two jobs—by day he's a plumber and by night a gas station attendant. He gets in "bonding time" with his son by letting him help out at the garage on weekends. Susan has begged to be allowed to work there, too, but Richard is adamant: "That's no place for a girl. She'd get all dirty. Anyhow, she's too small."

Anthony seems to be a fairly typical little boy—playing outdoors with his pals, involved in team sports—a blithe imitation of his affable father. But Susan has what the school guidance counselor calls interpersonal difficulties. She has few friends; she hangs around the house watching television and stuffing herself with junk food; she's afraid to ride a bicycle or venture too far from home. Richard is stymied by her fearfulness, forgetting that *this* is the child who wasn't allowed to run too fast, or too far, because she might "get hurt."

Middle- and upper-middle-class fathers, in their anxieties about their girls, can instill the same kinds of fears. A lawyer I interviewed said with a self-deprecating snort that he's "Mr. Mom" in his family. With great reluctance he gave his eleven-year-old daughter permission to play baseball, but with this proviso: She had to wear a helmet during the entire game, and not just at bat. Not surprisingly she gave up the sport because she was the only member of the team made to wear the unflattering headgear full-time.

Such fathers, Dr. Henry Biller writes, "shower" their daughters with "love and tenderness"—or money, or clothes, or new cars—but only "when she acts passive, helpless, and/or femininely seductive." Their daughters understand, if only subconsciously, the mandate implied by their fathers' loving-kindness: Don't aim too high or too far from Daddy. Be a lady. A *little* lady.

Tender Trap

Another way some doting fathers keep their daughters hearthbound is by making the homefront so inviting, so full of love and companionship and collective activity, that there's no earthly reason to leave it.

To borrow from football coach Vince Lombardi, family isn't simply everything to these fathers, *it's the only thing.* In the most benign and almost imperceptible way, they unwittingly fall into a category of emotional maltreatment as defined by Dr. James Garbarino—"isolation": They wrap the daughter within a web of extended family that minimizes or deprives her of any outside influences.

Most of these fathers are doing what comes naturally: replicating their own childhoods. In general they are married to women who either had similar childhoods and are equally enmeshed with their children or, more often, are relieved to have their husbands take on the burden of primary parenthood.

With only an occasional complaint, these wives do not mind that virtually every family outing, every vacation, includes the kids. A couple of the doting fathers I interviewed did admit that to keep their wives happy, once in a while they'll take a trip with them alone. Even then, they say, they call home at least twice a day, just to make sure the kids are okay.

Such was the emotional climate in which Arnold, fifty-four, raised Carole, quoted at the beginning of this chapter, and her two brothers. Both Arnold and his wife were extraordinarily close to their own parents. Arnold still has breakfast with his mother and father, who live next door, each morning. Cousins, aunts, and uncles on both sides of the family have been one another's best friends, roommates, and business partners for three generations.

Arnold's sons have families of their own and live in other parts of the country. But Carole lives two blocks away, in a condominium he bought for her. The minute she comes home from work or a date, she calls her father, because she knows how much he worries about her living alone. She spends part of every weekend with her parents. Carole has been pulled into a comforting paternal embrace from which there is little incentive to break free. Apart from sex, her father gives her everything she could want from a man.

Choosing Up Sides

One consequence of doting fatherhood is that it can cause enormous resentment among siblings who fall outside the spotlight of Daddy's favoritism toward a daughter. The intensity of his single-focus love is so great that it leaves little for the other children to share; his emotional quota has been filled.

For parents to each have a favorite child is not uncommon. As we know, there's often an unconscious division of filial spoils. Sometimes this pairing off of parent and child is the inevitable attraction of temperamental sameness. More often, however, it's the result of the parents' unresolved emotional ambivalences spawned in their families of origin.

Splitting. The choosing of one child for a special relationship is a version of "splitting," the psychological term for the mechanism by which a very young child makes sense of both the good and the bad qualities in parents.

Children begin life by perceiving parents as perfect. And if a parent behaves imperfectly—through either anger or coldness—the child "splits" up the parent into *two* parents: The good one and the bad one. With maturity both images blend together; by late adolescence children begin to accept their mothers and fathers as composites of strengths and weaknesses, rather than as wholly separate, unambiguous images.

Unless, of course, the parent is so possessive or rejecting or brutal or seductive that the child remains emotionally sidetracked. The blending of images does *not* occur, and the child, as she gets older, may then "split" each of her parents into separate representatives of virtue and evil. One parent becomes *all* good, and the other becomes *all* bad. So, too, does this child see himself or herself as either all good or all bad—that is, the unintegrated, other half gets denied.

Parental favoritism is a form of splitting. One child becomes the "good," favored child, reflecting the parent's perception of his or her own goodness; another child becomes the "bad one," a projection of the parent's unconscious, disavowed, troubling side. Included in this latter category is the child who reminds the parent of a favored sibling from the parent's past. The child is made to pay for this ancient favoritism, to do penance for the parent's having been scapegoated or rejected.

Favored and unfavored children often live out the legacies of their parents' unexamined childhoods, their parents' inability to accept and "own" *all* aspects of their emotional histories.

Thus splitting infects one's parenting as much as it does one's own childhood.

"Replacement Child." Occasionally, being Daddy's darling can occur because the daughter has "replaced" an older child who failed to meet his expectations of devotion or achievement or who has already been staked out for favoritism by the mother.

This trickle-down paternal partisanship can also occur when an older child has died. That's what happened to Michelle, forty-nine, a family-court judge in a large midwestern city. She was the second of her parents' three children. The first, Michael, died of leukemia four years before she was born, and it was for him that she was named. Michelle has a sister, Carrie, who is two years younger than she is.

Michelle's father was a justice of the peace in the small town where she grew up. "I absolutely *adored* him," she says. "He was an *enormous* influence on my life."

It is no accident that she went into jurisprudence. Her father used to let her observe him in his courtroom. He urged her to attend law school, which, because he was raised during the Depression, he had never been able to afford for himself. He spent countless hours with her, reading Shakespeare, choreographing her courses, grooming her for greatness.

The veteran of many years of analysis, Michelle understands all the psychological underpinnings of her life's work and choices. She says,

> My whole work ethic is absolutely his: I could only be the lawyer he wanted me to be. I originally planned to become a criminal prosecutor. He thought that branch of law was too dangerous for a woman and talked me into domestic law instead. It was clear, however, that I was to take Michael's place. Every Sunday Dad would go down to the basement, open an old file cabinet, and take out the portrait of my dead brother, the son who was to fulfill all my father's dreams. In therapy I had to resolve my trying to live up to a ghost. But what was left after working through all his expectations, all my desires to make up for the son he lost, was just the love we felt for each other.

The same cannot be said for Michelle's younger sister. Since Daddy was "taken," and since he put all his energies into Michelle, virtually shutting Carrie out, Carrie had no choice but to ally herself with her mother, a demure, rather passive housewife. While Michelle's closeness to her father was a reflection of their similar high energy and fierce intelligence—a perfect "fit" of interests and temperaments—he was not sophisticated enough to understand how much their intimacy would cost his other child.

Michelle has had enough therapy to be able to "own" her accomplishments—to enjoy them for herself, rather than as the tariff of Daddy's love. But for Carrie, following her mother's lackluster, limiting example—the residue of her father's favoritism—has left her with a lingering bitterness. Today the sisters, who seldom see each other, are the living legacies of their father's lopsided love.

Three's a Crowd

Perhaps the most damaging consequence of being Daddy's darling is that it can undermine the daughter's relationship with her mother. Doting fathers often become substitute mothers, corroding the daughter's ability to connect with her actual mother.

"I was my father's pride and joy," says Olivia, twenty-nine. "And he was mine." She continues,

> I can't even tell you much about my mother, because she was just amorphous. She took care of the house, but was very much in the background. They never fought. They never had much of anything, really. My father would be very likely to kiss me good night and pat my mother on the head when he went to bed. He was so much more important to me than my mother. I feel very guilty saying that, but it's true. I wish she and I could have had a closer relationship.

Such fathers push mothers to the periphery of their daughters' lives, making themselves the "good" parent to the mothers' "bad."

Frequently a father's devotion to his daughter has the bizarre effect of keeping a foundering marriage afloat. This is an example of "triangling," wherein unhappiness in a relationship is dispersed by asking a third person to absorb it. Since children are emotional blotters, they are easily drawn into the marital fray.

Here's how it works. In the family, according to Dr. Michael
Kerr of Georgetown University, there can be an uneven balance
between the "togetherness" force and the "individuality" force—
too much of the former in one parent, too much of the latter in
the other.

So it is that some doting fathers, with their blurred emotional
boundaries, are married to women—a surprising number of whom
are older than the men—who are their temperamental opposites.
These women tend to be aloof, providing ballast for the gusts of
their husbands' impulses and passions and playing "bad cop" to
their husbands' "good cop" with the children.

It is a curious and ingenious bargain: These men get their wives
to do the distancing, or enforcing, or expressing of anger that the
men are unable to do themselves. At the same time the men do
the "emoting" for their wives.

Into this equation the favored daughter is sometimes "trian-
gled." She is called upon to supply for the father the love he
believes he does not inspire in his wife, to "fix" the marital relationship. This triangling has almost nothing to do with the daughter.

Thus the overall "balance" in the family is divided among its
members: Daddy gets an adoring ally, aloof Mom gets an excuse
to be estranged from both the daughter *and* her husband, and
daughter gets Daddy all to herself.

But at great cost to the daughter.

A number of women described for me their doting fathers' favoritism with a guilty sense of complicity, as though theirs were
adulterous relationships. But many of these daughters were set up
for their mothers' displeasure; their fathers stoked maternal jealousy by making it obvious that they preferred the daughters' company.

Charlotte, forty-one, is her parents' only child. Her mother, a
novelist, is a beautiful and lionized member of San Francisco's
monied social set. Charlotte, a social worker, is, if anything, even
more beautiful than her extremely vain mother and has been her
father's darling since the day she was born. "My mother and I
don't see each other, by mutual consent," she says with a baleful
sigh. "She confessed to me when I was a child that because she
wanted a son, she couldn't love me."

But her father *did* want a girl and *did* love her—with such obsessiveness that her mother retaliated by shipping her out to boarding schools and summer camps beginning at the age of ten.

Through the years Charlotte and her father have had a special, loving connection, but always separate from her mother. They speak on the phone daily, usually from their respective offices. They have dinner at a restaurant once a week. And although her father pays lip service to his wife's insecurities, begging Charlotte to pay more attention to her, he makes little effort to assuage those insecurities himself.

While he has good reason to complain about his wife's self-centeredness, to say nothing of her abusiveness toward Charlotte, he does not attempt to work out his own contribution to their marital friction. The time he does spend with his wife is either filled with brooding silence or punctuated with fights about Charlotte—the "ungrateful" child, according to the mother; the "unappreciated" child, according to the father.

Theirs is a perfect marriage: Each has found in the other a reason to rage, and Charlotte is the hostage of their symbiotic misery.

The Roots of Doting Fatherhood

Being Daddy's girl may be filled with countless delights, but it also can be honeycombed with hidden paternal agendas.

In reviewing the histories of the doting fathers I interviewed, certain similarities emerged. One overwhelming reason for their heavy emotional investment in daughters was a certain androgyny, traceable to their childhoods.

When most of these fathers were growing up, they did not fit the stereotype of the all-American boy: the athletic, macho member of an all-male pack. A few of them participated in sports, but only those that didn't require heft, such as swimming or track, or through auxiliary support, such as basketball equipment management.

But the vast majority of doting fathers were wholly unathletic. Either they were singularly uncoordinated, or small for their size, or overweight, or more at home in a library than a stadium.

It is impossible to exaggerate the role sports played in the shaping of American men who grew up in the 1930s, 1940s, and 1950s, and the emotional and social consequences to those who didn't take part in them. For it was the one activity in which they were allowed to show affection for one another without being accused of homosexuality.

Research shows that American men and women are programmed differently regarding physical contact. Fathers tend to touch their children only in play, whereas mothers touch for grooming and comforting. For sons, then, nonsexual touch can create anxiety, because men aren't supposed to need comfort, hence friendly touch feels threatening.

Except in sports. There it *is* okay for men to touch each other in a loving way and to be intimate. Closeness and camaraderie between unrelated men can be seen in packs—on the playground, or in the locker room, or around a campfire, or hip deep in a trout stream—but rarely in quiet, self-revealing, conversational pairs.

One has only to watch a football game, where players routinely pat each other on the butt or kiss or crush each other in a victorious embrace, to see the socially acceptable version of male-to-male, nonhomosexual love, American style.

Says Dr. Frank Pittman,

> A masculine way of being together usually involves being physical rather than being verbal. Men can overcome their homophobia in public, through sports, but in private, companionship has to take the form of competition and one-upmanship. Then they show each other love by insulting and teasing each other.

This gender-tailored affection applies to the father-son relationship as well. And for most doting fathers these male arenas for safe, paternal love were missing when they were growing up.

"Sickly" Sons. A surprising number of the doting fathers I interviewed had a variety of chronic illnesses or physical handicaps in childhood. One man had a club foot; another had polio; a third had terrible asthma.

Because these men were housebound for long stretches in their youths, they did not have the more typical boyhoods of their peers. Rather they watched their buddies or brothers play stickball on city streets or basketball on suburban driveways.

For most of these men their ailments had a disastrous effect on their relationships with their fathers. For one thing illness put them in the uninterrupted company of their mothers. For another their fathers either worked long hours, or were present in the most passive way, or felt shortchanged by having sons who were perceived as almost-girls, with whom sporting companionship was out of the question.

As a result mother-son intimacy was almost hermetically sealed.

In many ways the mothers' influence was all to the good: These men had the full measure of maternal devotion, which contributed to men's familiarity with women and all things "feminine," including being aware of and talking about feelings.

In other ways, however, confinement to Mom was harmful in her huge and disproportionate effect on their personalities, especially if the sons were expected to make up for their fathers' marital neglect. As psychiatrist Stanley H. Cath has written of sons whose parents have divorced,

> Mother may often remind her child that, in contrast to his father, she has "stuck by him." This may add to the burden of guilt he may feel for . . . having "won the oedipal struggle." Too often boys raised in such atmospheres become "mother's sons" with problems centering on masculinity [and] potency.

The same can be said of sons whose fathers are silent partners in the intact family. A sickly son is an easy target for a lonely mother's frustrations. These sons were either their mothers' "little husbands," feeling compelled to side with their mothers in domestic disputes, or they were trapped by their mothers' bitterness.

If a neglected wife has no separate life of her own—and most women of the senior generation did not—an unrobust son can be both a painful reminder of her emotionally absent husband and a disappointment in his inability to "be a man," strong enough to take care of her. Her maternity may be a study in extremes—at times smothering, at other times hostile.

Arthur, forty-nine, grew up in such airless circumstances. As a child he had osteomyelitis, an infection of the bone marrow, which in the 1940s frequently resulted in leg amputations. Arthur survived with his leg intact, but five surgeries kept him in almost constant contact with his mother, a woman of extraordinary narcissism and neediness.

During those years his father, a salesman, was frequently on the road and not available to siphon off his wife's urgent and demanding devotion to their son, nor to spell her from Arthur's almost total physical dependence. When the father *was* home, he could not disguise his disgust at his son's being a "wimp" and paid almost no attention to him.

When Arthur grew up and became a father himself, the legacies of his childhood spilled over into his relationships with his children—Nancy, twenty-two, and Will, twenty.

With Nancy he recaptured the closeness he once had with his mother, at the same time reframing it: His daughter adores him and gives him the unsullied tenderness his unhappy mother could not. "I'm the only guy I know who has a maternal instinct," he says, chuckling. "I even shop with my daughter more than my wife does. I'm the one who told her about birth control."

But with his son Arthur was particularly hostile and, on occasion, even physically violent. He once beat his son with a broom handle for disobeying him. Will, in his physical perfection—he was a high school football star—is everything his father could never be; hence, he is the repository of Arthur's unresolved, impotent childhood and paternal rage.

"Sainted Sons." Another feature doting fathers share is that many of them were the firstborn, undisputed favorites of their mothers. Like the sickly sons, most were unathletic and had fathers who were too busy for companionship. Even if these sons had love-hate relationships with their mothers, it was the mothers more than the fathers who provided the most profound influence on their lives.

For Hank, thirty-eight, being his mother's cherished, only child, probably saved his life. Hank learned how to become a "man" the hard way: by defending himself from his alcoholic father's punches —which once put Hank in the hospital for three months—and by trying to protect his mother. As an adolescent, he spent most of his time either in detention in school, or playing hooky, or proving himself in gang rumbles.

It was his mother who taught Hank that there were ways to communicate with people other than slugging it out. "I was good at fighting," he says sheepishly, "but I always had a meek side, which comes from my mother. If I really hurt someone in a brawl, I'd go visit him the next day and apologize. I just didn't have what fighters call 'heart'—the killer instinct."

Today Hank has an obsessive love for his five-year-old daughter, forged in the crucible of a childhood in which his mother was the only saving grace. His gentle spirit has an outlet at last with his little girl. He says,

> I love playing with her, pretending with her. There are so many things I see with her that the fathers I know never notice with their daughters. Little things. Like how girls comb their hair, how they try to ice-skate, how they look at you, how they laugh. My biggest fear is that something will happen to her. I wake up in the middle of the night in a cold sweat thinking about it. I want her to stay little forever. If anyone hurt her, I wouldn't just kill him—I'd wipe out his whole family.

For all these reasons doting fathers were "programmed" more for maternity than for paternity. Many of them are in the helping professions, working as doctors, therapists, teachers, or volunteering in such organizations as Big Brothers.

Nurturance was a predictable and permanent fixture in their psyches. It was inevitable that these men would tend to identify more with their mothers than with their fathers, more with their daughters than with their sons. Even when these men had ambivalent or angry feelings toward their mothers, because they spent so much time with their mothers maternal *behavior* was woven into their own emotional wiring.

But they paid a heavy price for their sensitivity—unless their fathers were also of the sensitive, androgynous sort. Many of them were conflicted about their own sexual and "masculine" identities.

And virtually all of them felt a lifelong hunger for their fathers.

One way to look at paternal indulgence of daughters is to see it as evidence of that "father hunger." As Dr. Napier writes,

> Parents who infantilize their children often got little support themselves as children . . . it is this deprived "inner child" which they project onto their literal child. In overhelping their child, they are indirectly attempting to meet their own needs . . . [and] establish habitual dependency in the child.

And the child they usually "overhelp" is a girl. While being "maternal" was second nature to doting fathers, its devaluation in a world that expected men to behave one way and women another tended to overload the father-daughter relationship, for frequently it was their sole source of gentle intimacy.

Many of these "sensitive," doting fathers were concerned that their own sons not be sissies, not be like them. And so they turned to *daughters*—the "understanding," "tender" gender—to redress their childhood losses in a socially acceptable way.

For the father who was deprived of sufficient affection from his own father, and suffocated by too much maternal attention, the favored daughter may be either the tender "father" he never had or the mother he *did* have, the one who made him the center of her life.

So it is that for many doting fathers their daughters' emancipation is excruciating.

The Legacies of Doting Fatherhood

A doting father is not simply surprised when his little girl grows up, he is *crushed*. His love may have an invisible price tag that sounds a shrill alarm when she edges toward independence, planting the notion that without his vigilant ardor she can never feel safe. He will always be there for her—*as long as she still worships him, still turns only to him for solace and wisdom.*

And when she does not, when she finds substitutes in her teachers or friends' fathers or boyfriends or even herself, the devoted daddy may be as grief-stricken as though he were a rejected lover —as, in a sense, he is.

Psychologist Carl Hindy conducted a study contrasting the patterns of parent-child love with the same patterns in the child's adult love life. He found that "anxiously attached" men fear rejection and extort love from their partners, trying to be reassured of their lovability. It is this "extortion" that can be at work in many doting fathers with their daughters.

Such neediness can be seen as a basic narcissism that is at the heart of the doting father's paternity. In *The Culture of Narcissisim* Christopher Lasch makes the following observation of mothers who are enmeshing hoverers, but he could easily be writing of doting fathers:

> Because she so often sees the child as an extension of herself . . . [by] treating the child as an "exclusive possession,"

she encourages an exaggerated sense of his own importance; at the same time she makes it difficult for him to acknowledge his disappointment in her shortcomings.

If the doting father is unable to sort out his dependence on his daughter, he may be unable to release her from her dependence on him, or her ambivalence about him.

New York psychoanalyst Dr. Robert Akeret knows firsthand the anguish of being loved and left by an adoring daughter. He says,

> I remember the first time my oldest daughter went away to school. I'd go into her room at night, and the tears would just flow, because I missed her so terribly. It was a really powerful wrench. But it was also the beginning of the process of letting go.

In Dr. Akeret's case, by working through his feelings and by helping his daughter move into independence, he got a bonus: The man she eventually married became, in a sense, the son he never had.

My Heart Belongs to Daddy. But many doting fathers can't say good-bye. They are unable to achieve the delicate balance between too much love and too little. And when the daughter emigrates to the outside world and outside relationships, there is no mistaking the adoring fathers' bereavement. Sometimes it is expressed through guilt-inducing entreaties to visit or call home more often, usually in the mother's name. More often it takes the form of undermining the daughter's self-confidence, or withholding adoration.

George, forty-eight, was by any measure a superb father to his daughter, Marion, taking an interest in her life, helping her with her schoolwork, cheering her victories, and providing solace in her defeats. Until she got engaged. Then he began to retreat—neither calling his daughter nor returning her calls—with such suddenness that she was stunned.

"I asked my mother why Daddy was being so cold," she told me. "She said that he's preparing himself emotionally for my marriage."

What often happens in such cases—unless father and daughter talk it out, as Marion and her father did—is that the daughter may be unable to transfer her love for her doting father to another man. In a sense she can never grow up.

When the daughter leaves the family scene, the doting father is suddenly brought face-to-face with the imbalance and extremes of his marriage. Without a daughter to buffer their connection, the differences between them can seem insurmountable.

The daughter's leave-taking can be an opportunity for such couples finally to come to terms with their difficulties. But the doting father may not be able to manage such a marital rapprochement, because, as Dr. Kerr puts it, he is addicted to his daughter's love. To lose it is like having his supply of "drugs" dry up; he goes into a kind of shock, suffering emotional withdrawal pains, and may do everything in his power to get her back.

Thus the adored daughter may be tugged by conflicting enticements: afraid to leave her loving daddy and afraid not to.

When Adored Daughters Can't Love. Another consequence of doting fatherhood is that while the indulged daughter may know what it's like to *be* loved, she may not know how *to* love. In particular she may have difficulty developing the capacity to feel anyone's joy or discomfort but her own.

Recent research into the mechanics of empathy have turned up the startling conclusion that parental love is not enough in order for children to become compassionate. It has long been thought that the key to empathy is the mother-child connection—that if a mother is loving and nurturing, the child will learn by her compassionate example. But new studies suggest that it is the involvement of the *father* that is the most important variable in the development of empathy in children—in particular, his ability to be both warm *and* to set limits on unacceptable behavior.

As Dr. Nancy Eisenberg of Arizona State University told a reporter,

> Warmth alone is not enough to develop empathy. In fact, warmth alone can encourage selfishness in a child. . . . Parents who set certain emotional limits have children who help. These limits are taught at moments when a child slams the door in anger or stares at someone who is crippled, and parents let the child know that won't be tolerated.

These studies demonstrate that to be truly compassionate involves two steps: first, the awareness of the suffering of others;

second, the ability to put one's own sympathetic distress aside and take some action.

But without that limit-setting the daughter may remain mired only in the feeling stage—that is, her *own* feelings. If her doting father never set such limits—if his love was *too* unconditional—she may become a woman who, like him, is "addicted to love." Any man who cannot adore her unqualifiedly, as her father once did, may be perceived as someone who does not love her *at all.*

The daughter who is her father's indulged "little princess" may spend the rest of her life stamping her foot when she doesn't get her way, or pulling away when a love affair hits rough waters, or becoming a fair-weather friend who detaches when a chum asks too much of her.

Such an unappeased appetite for attention can result in her exhausting her sources of love. Her friends may tire of her being more taker than giver; her lovers may weary of her endless requirements of devotion and attention and reassurance.

The daughter who got more love than she ever bargained for may grow up to become the adult for whom there is never enough love: a true narcissist. She may never understand that it was Daddy—the man who was so doting, so devoted, so eager to please—who never gave her the most important lesson of all: To receive love, one must also give.

Profile of a Doting Father

Most of the fathers I interviewed for this book were strangers to me, and the usual place for meetings was a restaurant. But Peter, the husband of my former college roommate, Susan, is an old friend. I asked him to come to my house on a still summer morning, sweetening the deal with the promise of fresh bagels and lox, his favorite.

Peter, fifty-nine, is an extraordinarily charming man whose earthbound, unflappable wife anchors his impulsive, romantic personality. In fact, he says, if it weren't for Susan, he'd probably be in a mental institution.

Five years ago his firstborn child, Sharon, died in a boating accident at the age of twenty-four, and since then, Peter has been locked in a grief so deep that even to touch the subject is to create an emotional hemorrhage. Since then he hasn't been able to dis-

cuss Sharon with anyone outside the family—and rarely, except
for his wife, with anyone in it, not even his surviving daughter,
Allison.

But when I called to ask him if he'd be willing to talk about both
girls for this book, he thought he'd risk it.

"I guess it's time," Peter says, sinking into a chair on my porch.
Leaving his breakfast untouched, he lights up the first of what will
become a pack of cigarettes during our two-hour talk.

Peter grew up in the hardscrabble hills of West Virginia, where
his father was a miner. "You know the father in *The Brothers
Karamazov*?" he says. "My father was like that." Peter's father
didn't beat him. But when he was drunk, which was always on
payday, he'd shove Peter's mother across the room or cuff her if
dinner was late.

"My mother was the epitome of devotion in a world of male
chauvinism," he says. "She understood her role and performed it
with a lot of love and physical labor, which took a very big toll. She
was a saint. I was always sure of her love; with my father, never."

Peter was the first person in his family ever to attend college.
Working by day and studying and attending classes by night, eventually he became an art director in an advertising agency. "My
father did not greet my education with any joy," Peter says. "It
meant I wasn't bringing home an income."

I ask him if he was a different kind of father to his own children.
He quickly replies,

> Oh, yes. I'd do anything for them. I spoiled them rotten. But
> when Sharon asked for a sports car, I drew the line. I felt it
> would be too great an indulgence. Still, it was all I could do
> not to give in, because it was my nature to be Santa Claus.
> Whenever I went away on business, I'd always bring the girls
> gifts, like jewelry or clothes. Sharon was the one who most
> appreciated them—she was so much fun, more feminine than
> her sister, just enchanting. She just made me melt.
>
> Looking back, what kills me is that if I had it to do all over
> again, I would have bought her that car.

He weeps uncontrollably, and I suggest we stop. He vigorously
shakes his head. His grief is so raw, so savage, that it's difficult to
imagine his sustaining it at this pitch for five years. At times he's
considered suicide, he says. His wife and remaining daughter have

managed to deal with their grief and let it go; Peter has not. Somehow he cannot release it, because to heal is to lose Sharon. He continues,

> Everything reminds me of Sharon: I'll see a bird, and it'll remind me of a kite, and the kite will take me to a string, and the string will take me back to Sharon. That happens in nanoseconds. She knew just how to get to me. One day when she was four, I raised my voice to her, and she looked me right in the eye and said, "You can't yell at your little blue-eyed angel." I went right down the tubes. I was always able to fix things for Sharon, to protect her. But her death was something I can't fix. I can't do anything about it. You can't imagine how helpless that makes me feel.

He retrieves a handkerchief from his hip pocket and blows his nose. He lights another cigarette.

I ask him to tell me more about his father. He hesitates, reluctant to dwell on that part of his past, unlike his openness about everyone else, and about himself. Finally he takes a deep breath and says,

> You know, I'm always judging myself as a father, but I have a hard time judging my own father. He really was a bastard. No one knows how rotten he was. No one. I guess I've always felt something I haven't been able to articulate until this minute: In a very real sense I didn't have a father. He was just a figure in the family—but he was not a father. When he died, I didn't feel a thing.
>
> It's funny. Sometimes I still think about him. On a fall day, usually on a Friday, when it's around sunset, when it's cold and the leaves are falling, I sometimes get a very depressed, melancholy feeling. Recently I tracked it down. Friday was payday, the day I didn't want to go home when I was a kid, because my father would be drunk and all hell would break loose. I would have given my right arm to have him teach me things. I never thought about the pain of that, I thought that's just the way it was.
>
> Suddenly it occurs to me that the reason I can't stop grieving for Sharon is because I never grieved for my father.

Peter has run out of cigarettes and says he has to get back home
—Allison is coming over for a visit.

I walk him outside to his car. He opens the door, steps inside,
and pauses.

"You know," he says, "I haven't visited Sharon's grave since the
funeral, and it's only a mile away. I'm supposed to design her
headstone, and I haven't been able to bring myself to do it. Maybe
I'll start. Maybe I'll draw up some preliminary plans."

He closes the door, starts the engine, and slowly drives away.

6

The Distant Father

My father could tune out an atom bomb. He would play the piano endlessly, no matter what was happening around him. My mother could be hysterical, screaming and yelling—saying her life was miserable and no one appreciates her and she's ready to kill herself—and he'd be totally oblivious. I had this vision that blood could be rising to the level of the keys, and my father would just keep right on playing the "Moonlight Sonata."

—DONNA, FORTY-FOUR

Of all the paternal styles described in this book, the distant father is the most common: the "strong, silent type" who was there in body but not necessarily in spirit, who fulfilled his marital and parental obligations by bringing home the bacon and who then walled himself behind a newspaper.

When this kind of father spoke, *his children listened;* and when he did not, they seldom questioned his silence, putting it down to a certain manliness, a lack of frivolousness.

In our culture male taciturnity is considered a virtue, a mark of true masculine grit. The American father is expected to maintain a certain laconic hegemony—to be, like the town sheriff of Western lore, a man of few words, loping tight-lipped through life, who, if driven actually to *talk,* is a force to be reckoned with.

Still, it's one thing for a father to possess a personality not given to garrulous instant intimacy, to be a man who chooses his few words wisely and well; it's quite another for a father to be *impersonal,* to barely punctuate his daughter's childhood.

Consider, for example, Natalie, who recalls with awe the time her reserved father proved himself in a moment of cherished, al-most lifesaving counsel. Twenty years ago, while home on spring vacation from college, she complained to her mother of nausea. Her mother—a high-strung woman given to hypochondria and histrionics—whisked her to the doctor, who quickly diagnosed the "illness": She was pregnant.

"It was the low point of my life," Natalie says.

> My mother drove me home, screaming, "How can you do this to me? What will I tell my friends? You've ruined my life!" I felt totally lost and abandoned. When we got to the house, she nodded her head toward my father, sobbed, *"You* tell him," and ran upstairs to have a breakdown.
>
> Mind you, my father wasn't one to contradict my mother, so I wasn't sure how he'd react. To my utter surprise he took my hand and said, "These things happen. It's not so bad. Babies are wonderful." It was *precisely* what I needed to hear: that I was a human being, that these things happen to human beings, and that it'd be all right.

In this case the taciturn father chose *exactly the right words* in a crisis. But for most daughters, the father of few words is, in fact, the father of *no* words. Says Claire, thirty-two,

> My dad was dependable—he was home every night for dinner and all that. But he was not there. It wasn't that he was cold or tense—he just wasn't there. I was a very affectionate child; I'd crawl all over him, hugging and kissing him. I just didn't get any feeling back. I could have been crawling on the furniture.

The narrative of the father-daughter relationship is missing when Daddy's words, however well chosen, are *too few.* Fathers who rise from their reticence only in emergencies, or who are merely white sound within the family, do not become whole in their daughters' perceptions.

Many of the daughters of distant fathers described them with adjectives of idealism or sympathy: "stoic," "repressed," "cau-tious," "laid-back," "browbeaten," "dignified."

These daughters were portraying two distinct breeds of paternal distance: *remote* and *passive.* On the smooth, seemingly imperturbable surface, these categories would appear to be interchangeable. In fact they are quite different.

The Remote Father

Psychiatrist Clarice Kestenbaum says that the remote version of "father absence" is legion among her female patients. "These men are there in the flesh," she says, "but don't understand their daughters or aren't involved with them. I have many, many cases like that. There's such a longing on the part of the daughters."

Some remote fathers are psychologically unavailable to their families, ducking behind what Dr. James Garbarino describes as "a barrier of silence." They don't intervene when their children are attacked by the mother or by siblings; even when told by teachers or spouses or therapists that their children are in trouble, they take no action; and when their children ask them for help, they do not react. They are, Dr. Garbarino tells us, simply oblivious to their children's needs for love, encouragement, and affection.

Paternal remoteness is not the same as a father's outright rejection. Rather it is a subtle and often unconscious spurning of *any* intimacy. What's curious is that these men do not want to *be* alone; instead they want to be *left* alone within the family context, to the enormous confusion of their wives and children.

What appears to be a remote father's indifference is often a vigorous attempt to keep his emotionality under cover, rather like a placid lake with mysterious demons lurking far beneath the surface. Most of these fathers are not devoid of feelings; what characterizes them is that they mute their passions, unable or unwilling to *express* their feelings.

In their guardedness remote fathers give new meaning to the word *denial*—they truly believe that they are doing their parental best and are stung by the suggestion that somehow they are lacking in concern for their children.

"Listen, I was *there*," the divorced father of two grown daughters told me testily. "Every weekend. Every Wednesday night for dinner. Two weeks every summer."

But when later I asked one of his daughters what "there" meant, she replied,

Oh, he was there all right. He adhered to my parents' separation agreement to the letter: Never a day late with child support. Never a second late picking us up. But when we got to his house, he'd park us in front of the television set, and he'd disappear into the basement to work in his shop. For *hours* he'd be woodworking. We could have been on fire, and I'm not sure he would have noticed.

Sometimes the remoteness of fathers reaches absurd proportions. One woman told me that her father was so lost in his inner world that he was blind to any external stimulation, any change in his surroundings, however unusual. She said, chuckling at the memory,

Once, while my mom was away visiting her parents, I brought home a stray dog. That dog lived with us for an entire week, shitting on the rug, yapping day and night, chewing on the furniture. *My father never noticed.* When my mother came home, she had a fit and made me get rid of it.

If remote fathers confuse their children, they make their wives *crazy.* These men tend to marry their temperamental opposites, women who are talkative, nervous, sociable, tearful, highly reactive to their husbands' brooding or absentmindedness or maddening ennui. The wives carry the emotional weight in their marriages, filling their husbands' silences with high spirits or high dudgeon.

At work, however, many remote fathers present quite a different mien, dividing their emotional lives between the public and the private, the professional and the personal. Occasionally the professional *is* the personal: On the job, at least, they are able to connect with people in a way that makes the fewest demands on them, choreographing the conditions of "love."

Some go into professions such as acting, or writing, or medicine —fields that would *imply* an understanding, or at least awareness, of human emotions.

One father, a chiropractor, had an adoring following of devoted patients. "He was very caring," says his daughter, Karen, forty-four. "He would call people from home to make sure they were all right; he was a healer in the best sense."

But with his family he was another person. He wanted, he declared, to be "left in peace." And by her own admission, Karen was a disturber of his peace: She and her mother constantly wrangled over the few crumbs of his attention that were available at the end of his draining day.

Says Karen,

> My father wanted me to be totally obedient to my mother in order to avoid conflict. I created a *lot* of conflict for him, because he was always being asked to mediate. The first thing he did when he came home at night was to turn on the radio and drown us out. He buried himself in the radio the way alcoholics bury themselves in drink.

Most remote fathers appear to be impervious to the domestic hurricanes that swirl around them. But some remote fathers will reach a point at which their simmering emotions break out, like a teakettle that bursts into angry song. In certain cases their eruptions are fueled by alcohol.

Arlene, twenty-nine, vividly remembers her alcoholic father's rare displays of temper:

> My father's way of coping was to go numb—but given enough booze, if he didn't pass out, he'd explode. We could tell from the way he drove his car into the driveway what kind of night it was going to be. We knew there was trouble when he took a long time getting into the house. My mother would start yelling at him, and once or twice he belted her. But with us kids he wasn't violent. He'd just get mean and nasty. We knew to stay out of his way.

Passive Fathers

Unlike remote fathers, the psychological distance of passive fathers is measured in their fearfulness, rather than repressed rage. By keeping a low profile within the family, they try to avoid becoming the target of anyone's anger. These fathers will pay almost any price for peace.

Like remote fathers, passive fathers tend to marry their temperamental opposites—only in this case, their wives are not so much volatile as steely, women who dominate the family with impossible expectations and eternal fault-finding. These women are what family therapists call "overfunctioners"—perfectionists who feel valued only when other people are dependent upon or controlled by them.

Ruth thinks of her father as the pathetic victim of a demanding, unpleasant wife:

> My mother never let him out of her sight. Sometimes she would scream at him, "You're so *stupid!*" He'd turn absolutely white; then he'd go into another room. He would never yell back. Never. He was very loyal and very devoted—he was just a good soul. But in a lot of ways he was frightened of the world—so unhappy, so insecure, so unaggressive. I didn't perceive him as a wimp; I perceived him as beleaguered.

Such men are "underfunctioners"—supremely lacking in confidence both at work and at home, and dependent upon others to be assertive for them.

Passive-aggressiveness is the psychological term for the behavior of many of these fathers. Such men are unable to plant their emotional feet and declare the things that bother them; rather they mount tiny rebellions that can barely be reckoned as aggression—making promises they don't keep, falling asleep at the dinner table, *avoiding* confrontations with words that say yes, and *provoking* confrontations with inaction that says no.

Sometimes a father's passive-aggressiveness becomes fodder for hilarious family legend. One woman told me that her mother gave up asking her father to help with domestic chores because he had a positive *genius* for bungling them:

> The last straw was the night my mother was standing at the sink washing and rinsing the dinner dishes; my dad's job was to dry them. She handed him a plate. He was idly chatting about his day and "accidentally" dropped the plate, apologizing profusely for his clumsiness. She handed him another plate, and that one slipped through his fingers too. She stopped giving him duties after that.

Protecting Daddy. If passive fathers bring out the beast in their wives, they bring out the tenderness in their daughters. Says Jessica, thirty-five,

I feel so protective of my dad. I don't know why—I guess I just felt there was this silent acknowlcdgment of me. I'm sure he loved me and was proud of me, although I don't recall his ever actually saying it. All I know is that I was the only one who supplied any companionship for him—we'd sit together and watch television for hours. The problem was that he wouldn't stand up to my mother. He just echoed whatever she told him. After she died, he said to me, "The whole time you were growing up and having all those fights with Mom, I was really on your side." I said, "Why didn't you say anything?" He said, "I didn't want to make any trouble."

The most dependent passive fathers can in extreme cases simply curl into themselves and, like a neglected infant, shut down emotionally and even deteriorate physically.

Daniel, sixty-seven, has always allowed his vivacious wife, Rose, to have the social and family limelight. It is Rose who is the life of every party, the organizer of bowling tournaments in the retirement community where they live. And it is Rose who grabs the phone from Daniel whenever their oldest daughter, Vera, calls home.

But recently, says Vera, her father's passivity seems to have taken a disturbing turn. Where once he was merely the bemused spectator to his wife's restless vanity—launching small insurrections, such as calling her "the chief," or pretending not to hear her—lately he seems to have begun doubting himself in a way that deeply distresses his daughter. Says Vera,

Once he retired and was with my mother twenty-four hours a day, he seemed to just give up. She's told him so often that he doesn't know what he's talking about that now he really believes it. My father is extremely well informed. But the other day he said, "I never know what to say in company. I feel so inarticulate." I replied, "That's not how I see you." He said, "Your mother is the storyteller in the family, not me." I said, "Dad, she's the one who gets all the practice." Now he's going deaf and won't get a hearing aid. I'm convinced it's his way of finally shutting her up.

The Closet Depressive. The price passive fathers pay for peace can be huge. It could be argued that many of them are depressed, if not clinically, then at least in terms of their downtrodden demeanor. In fact they may be the leading edge of a kind of epidemic of male melancholy, the psychological result of being emotional satellites to the family.

According to Ronald Taffel, Ph.D., director of Family and Couples Treatment Services in New York, many men are closet depressives—not just timid men but workaholics and tyrants as well. He writes,

> Whether the men passively disappear into the woodwork or shake the foundations of the house with their agitation, they share one characteristic—they cannot regulate their own moods . . . and they depend on their partners and children to do so for them.

Mood is as important an indicator of a man's emotional underpinnings as are "self-esteem" and "power," Dr. Taffel believes. And beneath the camouflage of outward behavior may be a profoundly despondent man who *requires* a family to fill in the blanks of his emotional ineptitude, a man who cannot survive without people who both love him and do the loving for him.

This interpretation is the underbelly of Daddy as Dagwood Bumstead—fathers who are laughably helpless, in danger of slowly starving to death when left alone for more than a day because they can't find the refrigerator.

Some passive men in their sixties, seventies, and eighties even call their wives Mother. As one therapist told me,

> I have a patient who flipped out because even when her children were grown, her husband still called her Mother. My own grandfather did it to my grandmother. One time she burst into tears and said, "I wish he would call me by my name."

Because most men of the senior generation were not trained to take care of themselves physically or emotionally and were taught not to disclose their feelings, they may be vulnerable to psychological and medical illness. As Dr. Taffel points out, since admitting to internal pain is to seem "unmanly," many men suffer in silence and become, in a sense, prisoners of other people's love and caretaking. The statistics regarding the numbers of men who die soon after their wives' deaths would corroborate this interpretation.

When Silence Is Sedition

Dr. Frank Pittman believes that at the heart of men's remoteness with women is a desperate fear of disappointing them. He writes,

> I don't think it off-the-wall to speculate that most of the problems between men and women are related to man's panic in the face of woman's anger. . . . If we are quite obsessed with our masculinity, we may ask our father, our priest, or all our friends how to deal with marriage, but completely refuse to talk with the woman, our ostensible partner. Protecting ourselves from her anger comes before learning how to make her happy.

Fear notwithstanding, distant fathers—whether remote or passive—are anything but powerless; even the most woebegone, "henpecked" husband is able to galvanize his family with his self-protective reticence.

Few behaviors are as effectively manipulative as silence, as can be observed in the reciprocal marital game known as pursuing and distancing. Says Dr. Ellen Berman,

> A very common pattern in couples is for the wife to be the pursuer and the man, who has been trained to be cool and may be very much afraid of women, to be distant. You've got a guy who feels helpless because he's not pleasing his wife, but who also feels that if he *does* try to please her, he's being "controlled." He sees the woman as this enormously powerful figure. The truth is she *also* is helpless, because even though he is afraid of her anger, she can't actually get him to do what she wants him to do.

Women are, in general, reared to be emotional pursuers. One has the image of a wife trotting from room to room after a distant spouse who won't tell her what's bothering him, a man who says,

"Nothing's wrong," or "Now's not the time," or who merely grunts.

It's not difficult to figure out who's really in charge here. As long as the husband keeps backing away, his wife will redouble her nagging, weeping, interrogating, cajoling, psychologizing, or ranting. In this emotional two-step the couple keeps circling the real issue: Neither one is taking responsibility for how they feel; rather they avoid examining their own emotions by *reacting* to one another.

None of this is lost on the daughter, who may be drafted by her distant father into helping him maintain the curiously intractable marital status quo.

"Don't Tell Your Mother." Several daughters said that their distant fathers formed secret alliances with them in the name of family harmony.

"My father adored me," one woman recalled, "but he was afraid of my mother." So he had to carefully pick his paternal moments; sometimes it was when her mother was out playing bridge. Other times it was when he invited his daughter to call him at his office—the only way, he claimed, that they could talk without his wife "butting in."

Some of these daughters in time acquire the perspective to see the *intent* behind these alliances: to shield Daddy from having to recognize his seditious role in the creation of family storms.

Clair, forty-two, couldn't *wait* for our interview because, she told me on the phone, "I've just had a huge breakthrough in my therapy." The minute she sat down at the restaurant where we'd agreed to meet, she leaned forward eagerly and said,

> Here's my theory about nagging bitch mothers: They're women whose husbands don't validate them. I used to view my father as an angel. Not anymore. He was the kind of person who couldn't confront anyone, so he'd do it indirectly; he'd egg on my mother by ignoring her. When she couldn't get a rise out of him, she'd become vicious to me—*and he never intervened.* My father *loved* it when my mother and I got into arguments. He'd tell me that he and I were two buddies, united against the witch. I realize now that he was letting me fight his battles for him.

So it is that distant fathers are not always blameless when their wives turn into harridans.

The Roots of Distant Fatherhood

Many of the fathers I interviewed acknowledged that they were indeed on the "distant" end of the emotional spectrum when it came to their family relationships—an inevitable legacy, it could be argued, of the cult of masculinity.

Paternal distance seems to have two sources—cultural and psychological.

Cultural Origins. It has been said that emotional distance is a uniquely American trait, inherent in the national and human character. Alexis de Tocqueville observed this trait some 160 years ago:

> [Americans] owe nothing to any man, they expect nothing from any man; they acquire the habit of always considering themselves as standing alone, and they are apt to imagine that their whole destiny is in their own hands. Thus . . . democracy . . . throws [a man] back forever upon himself alone, and threatens in the end to confine him entirely within the solitude of his own heart.

That stoicism lingers to this day. "My son and daughter perceive me as being uncaring, but it's not true," says Dave, fifty-eight. "I just have trouble showing it. I grew up in a family where showing your feelings just wasn't done. My father would make fun of me if I cried. I was always told it wasn't manly to wear my heart on my sleeve."

A certain emotional frostiness is the heritage of a culture that puts great stock in WASP values: One does not talk about money, sex, religion, and above all, one does not expose one's feelings. If a case can be made for the cultural contouring of personality, the Puritan ethic is the culprit in such rubrics as "Children should be seen and not heard" and "Never complain, never explain."

William, forty, the only son of a father who was inordinately proud of his *Mayflower* roots, speaks to that cultural chilliness:

> I was smarter than my father was, but he intimidated me. He would return my letters to him with corrections in the mar-

gins. He would pontificate endlessly. I was determined not to be like him—that was the guiding concept. I knew how *not* to be a parent. Where I fell down was I didn't know how to *be* a parent. I was likely to sulk rather than really get into issues with my daughter; it was a real war of nerves between us.

Psychological Origins. However widespread paternal distance may be, it is solidified by the psychological climate in a man's childhood.

Most distant fathers grew up in families where the mother, rather than the father, took center stage and the father was a bit player. They described their mothers as intrusive, judgmental, and extraordinarily demanding.

One man said it was his mother who taught him to keep his emotions under wraps:

> I was a pretty sensitive kid. Even as a teenager I could be moved to tears. When our cat died, I wept uncontrollably. My mother said, "C'mon, pull yourself together. It's just a cat." She was a tough customer. So I learned to discipline myself; I learned not to cry. To this day there are parts of me that are simply not accessible.
>
> I just started therapy. I'm trying to learn how to feel again.

What propelled him into treatment was the harrowing effect his remoteness had on his sixteen-year-old daughter. Six months ago she attempted suicide by swallowing a bottle of tranquilizers. "I was wrecked," he says in a nearly inaudible voice, "but I realize now that I wasn't wrecked enough. I didn't feel enough. I think she thinks I just didn't care. We practically never talked about it, which is a way of saying I pretended it never happened."

Some researchers see this kind of paternal detachment as a reaction against the domineering or too seductive mother, coupled with a father who was emotionally absent. The psychological term for this dynamic is the *reengulfing mother.*

Thus, for many men, love for a woman is commingled with anxiety—a disastrous Catch-22 that can cost them their sense of empathy and sometimes even their humanity—and that can have a damaging impact on their fathering of daughters.

As Dr. Pittman explained it, "Men affirm their masculinity in two ways: first, by having women respond to them sexually; and second, by escaping women, making sure a woman doesn't get control of them." Thus, sex must not carry with it the risky entanglement of real intimacy.

Clearly sons would not be so terrified of intimacy—of the "reengulfing mother"—if their *fathers* played larger roles in their lives, providing the example of masculine tenderness. As it is, many fathers are simply strangers to their sons.

I asked therapist Ronald Gaudia to describe the single most important reason his male patients seek treatment. He replied,

> Most of them had absentee fathers, and not necessarily because their fathers worked around the clock. I ask these guys, "Who was your father?" and they say, "I don't know." That's trouble. If the guy says, "he was a no-good bastard," it ain't good, but it's better than "I don't know." If there's a nonentity there, you don't know anything about yourself except "I don't know."

The Legacies of Paternal Distance

If sex is the only acceptable way a man can achieve intimacy with women—and if a man has not been trained by his father to be close to women in a nonsexual, non-"engulfing" way—his daughter presents a terrible dilemma: As long as she is little, not yet womanly, a father's sexual and emotional ambivalences are kept at bay. But once she begins to develop, her body complicates matters for him.

According to research and interviews with social scientists, *the overriding reason for a father's emotional detachment from a daughter is his unconscious fear of being sexually attracted to her.* Where other fathers might sublimate this fear into indulgence, or rigidity, or rage, the distant father *denies* it with such vigor that he can find no halfway measure between love and lust. It is easier to push his daughter away than to risk the only way he knows how to connect with a female: sexually.

Of course his daughter doesn't know anything of his psychological turmoil. All she knows is that he seems to be mad at her all the time. All she knows is that it's hard to figure out *what,* if *anything,* will please him. All she knows is that his presence is so inscrutable, so imponderable, so periodic, that she must figuratively stand on her head to get him even to notice her.

Daddy's affectionate approval is the prize for which the daughter must feverishly toil, providing she can find the key—the terribly good or extremely bad behavior that will get him to put down his newspaper. And when she cannot, she believes that it must have something to do with her; it must be that she is not worth loving.

By assuming responsibility for her father's emotional absence, she fills in the blanks of his inattentiveness with fantasies of how he would be if she *were* more lovable. Self-blame gives the illusion of control; it is far more preferable to think she is not "good enough" than to imagine that there is no feeling from her father at all, no possibility of ever gaining his love.

But while self-blame "solves" one problem, it creates another: If she is unacceptable to her own father, she may wonder how any man will ever come to love her.

The emotional consequences to daughters of distant fathers are myriad—and can be devastating.

One, as has been discussed, is anorexia nervosa. Many authorities on eating disorders view a father's sexual discomfort with his daughter as causal in this pathological response to his emotional distance. "With true anorexia," says Dr. Kestenbaum, "many girls have a distorted body image in a wish either to be Daddy's adored boy or to be the asexual person without breasts that Daddy used to love."

Says Alicia, fifty, who is still struggling with her anorexia,

> When I was a kid, I felt that if I were a boy, my dad would like me. So I tried to have the body of a boy. I knew that boys liked baseball, so I'd go to ball games with him as a way to get close. I could never get him to talk to me—except at ball games. My anorexia was a denial of my own sexuality so that I could get my father to love me. I can't believe how much of my life has been involved in trying to please him.

Another consequence is that daughters may, in adulthood, look for a man who, as Dr. Kestenbaum puts it, "doesn't notice you, doesn't look at you, doesn't see you." Emotionally distant fathers are a constant disappearing act in the hearts of their daughters, who do not get the full experience of the first man in their lives.

Rather they get only glimpses of the shadow he leaves in his psychological and physical retreat. And when these daughters enter into romantic relationships, it is the disappearing shadow, and not the whole man, to which they often respond.

A third consequence for daughters is that sex with a man becomes a double bind. Says Dr. Marianne Goodman,

> If a father is sexually uptight, he transmits anxiety to his daughter. He doesn't want her to sit on his lap, he isn't comfortable hugging her—which makes the daughter feel unconsciously that it is "wrong" or uncomfortable to be demonstrative in a physical way with a man. If being a good girl means not being physical, the result is a daughter's sexual inhibition and repression.

In a sense these daughters are the fulfilled prophecies of their fathers' own confusion and ambivalence. In an attempt to be eternally good, "acceptable" girls, some daughters may relegate eroticism to the safe, forbidden zone of empty or inappropriate affairs, in which they can respond without shame. They may plunge into anonymous sex with a zealous detachment, able to become erotically satisfied only when love is not at stake, only when there is nothing to lose.

But many more daughters of distant fathers are unable to reach orgasm, or achieve it with consistency, with *any* man. Indeed these daughters have the most trouble in bed: for them, affection and arousal are synonymous with rejection.

As Dr. Seymour Fisher writes,

> The greater a woman's difficulty in reaching orgasm, the more likely she is to be concerned about the lack of dependability of love objects. She is concerned about how transitory relationships are and how easily loved ones can be lost.

A final consequence of distant fathering is that his daughter may become a lesbian. According to research on sex roles, inadequate fathering is more of a factor in the development of female homosexuality than inadequate mothering. With another woman, the lesbian often believes, she may stand a better chance of having both her sexual *and* her emotional needs met, because love need not be equated with lust. Said one lesbian,

My lover has no trouble being nurturing without sex. What I treasure is that most of our relationship is not about sex. It's about two people growing together and creating a life together and being there for each other. Touch and making love don't have to mean sex. We can go out for dinner or take a long walk and just talk, and I can feel a glow that's like we just made love. So in that sense I feel like we make love all the time. With her I know I'm never going to be emotionally abandoned. It's the greatest gift.

Distant fathers, in retreating from emotional involvement with their children, create in them a poignant and profound longing for paternal affection. When these fathers remain sequestered behind their emotional barriers, they become strangers both to their families and to themselves—unaware of their role in their children's "father hunger" and their wives' frustrated pursuit, and blind to their complicity in their own isolation.

Thus the distant father tyrannizes his family through an endless, unyielding silence that speaks louder than words—a silence that leaves a gaping hole in his children's lives.

Profile of a Distant Father

When Howard called me at the suggestion of a mutual friend, we discovered to our delight that we had met before; some twenty-five years earlier we had both worked on a New York news magazine. He was a young editorial assistant who exuded a quiet self-assurance: tall, lithe, reserved, unaware of his angular good looks. His mere presence in the newsroom brought the clattering typewriters of single women to an abrupt, hankering halt.

In the quaint parlance of the time, Howard was a "catch"—hard to get, socially well connected, a natural for the cultured social cosmos of Manhattan's movers and shakers. When he finally married a staggeringly beautiful socialite, my female friends and I writhed with envy.

And when, on a February afternoon, Howard ambled into a Manhattan restaurant for our interview, he looked as though he had stepped out of a time warp. Little about him had changed over the two and a half decades, save for the silver tufts that were making dignified inroads into his dark sideburns.

I expressed my surprise that he would agree to do this interview; he seemed to be the least likely candidate for a gut-spilling account of his emotional history and most intimate relationships. He raked his fingers through his hair and heaved a sigh.

Ten years ago I wouldn't have. But my father died this year, and I've been going through some changes. I've reached a point where it's not so important what other people think. I've never had any therapy, but I find myself feeling fragile, aware of my own mortality. I've been thinking about things I never thought about before.

He smiled apologetically and added, "Call it a midlife crisis."

Howard grew up in a Cleveland suburb, the second of two sons. I asked him to describe his parents.

I didn't know my father all that well. He had a separate life outside the family. I didn't know any of his friends either. I think he was very disappointed in himself. He was never successful. He was extremely well read. He should have been a teacher instead of a businessman.

The great secret in our family was that he was an alcoholic. It was his way of escaping his business failures. He was not there for me. Neither was my mother. She was the power in the family—rigid, had to have the last word. My father was afraid of her.

Howard's older brother was an introspective, studious boy who spent much of his time after school working in the science lab. But Howard was the star of the family—captain of the football team, president of the student body. "I was trying to get my parents' acceptance," he says. "The harder I tried, the more it was withheld."

"I like women," Howard said. "I could never do this interview with a man. It might be because I had this terrific grandmother whom I visited occasionally—she was very loving. I could tell her things I was afraid of, things that I wanted to learn, things I couldn't talk to my parents about. Unlike them she wasn't judgmental."

Curiously Helen, the woman Howard married, was the antithesis of his grandmother. "Helen was a challenge," he says. After six months of frantic wooing, he married his trophy wife—a woman who in ways was very like his mother: correct, controlling, reserved.

Within two years they had a daughter, Lauren, and were living the affluent life of a glamorous, influential urban family. I asked Howard what kind of father he was. He paused thoughtfully and then said,

> I was involved with Lauren, but not enough. I pretty much did just the Daddy things, like teaching her how to drive a car. I didn't encourage her as much as I should have. Her mother is the real power in the family—she was the one my daughter went to for help in homework and advice. When Lauren was little, sometimes I'd try to chat with her before she went to sleep, and Helen would say, "You've talked to her enough, she's tired." I did what I was told.

Howard explains that he was always haunted by the specter of his parents' loveless and acrimonious marriage, his father's drunken stupors, the slamming and locking of doors that separated the family into four camps. He learned very early in life never to ask questions, never to ask for help. And as his daughter grew, he was unable to encourage her to ask either.

> I was very slow to recognize that she was becoming a woman. I never discussed sex with her. But then, she didn't really talk to me about anything. When it came to dating, I may have given her some platitudes, but not much more than my father had given me—which was just about nothing. With Lauren I just did the minimum. Come to think of it, that's what my father did with me too.

Howard recalls for me the last time he saw his father. It was in the hospital, shortly before his father's death. A friend suggested that Howard tell his father how he felt about him—to express what he didn't get from him and what he did—to help him come to terms with their relationship while he still had the chance.

"Boy, I tried," he says. "A couple of times I started to say something. I wanted to say, 'I wish you spent more time with me. I wish you could have helped me. Why didn't you?' But I just couldn't. We just sat there."

Then he remembers that not long ago his daughter asked him a similar question: "She said, 'How come you never encouraged me more? How come you never talked to me?' I said, 'I tried.' It was pretty lame."

The recognition of the similarity between his behavior toward his father and his behavior toward his daughter stuns him into momentary silence. Finally he says,

> I don't know how much influence I've had on her, to tell you the truth. I think the only influence I've had anywhere is at work. People tell me that I made a difference in their lives that I have absolutely no recollection of. Recently a guy I haven't seen in years, who used to work for me, called me out of the blue and said, "I've gotten this big promotion, and I just want to thank you for giving me a break years ago." I was sky-high. I thought, Boy, this is what life is about: You give someone a break, you forget about it and think it doesn't mean anything. And what you've done is you've influenced somebody.
>
> It's ironic. I've spent most of my life not knowing what good I've done. But I've also not known what destruction I've caused in my own family either.

Howard shoots me a look of pained perplexity. The golden boy of the 1960s has reached the final trimester of his life with almost no idea as to what his life has been for. A random phone call from a grateful former employee seems to be the highwater mark of his fifty years. It is paltry recompense, he suddenly realizes to his horror, for having been a very good boy—in childhood, in marriage, in his career—who always did what he was told.

7

The Demanding Father

When I went to college, I talked about my father so much that every-one thought my mother was dead. I guess I made him sound like he's six foot nine and three hundred pounds, this huge all-encompassing man, because that's how it felt. In reality he's short and skinny, some-one you'd never notice in a crowd. I was scared witless of him. He has one of those tempers that when it goes off, it's better to be in Alaska. But a compliment from him, if you could get one, was better than gold.

—MELANIE, THIRTY

There's no mistaking this kind of father. You don't even have to *see* him to know what he's like; all you have to do is watch the reaction of his family when he gets home at the end of the day.

The kids sit up a little straighter, instantly turning from the television set to greet him; his wife trots to the front door, trying to catch the scent of his mood. If it is good, everyone heaves a small sigh of relief. And if it is foul, even the dog may hunker down deeper into the living room carpet.

This is the demanding father, the man who really *does* have all the answers, the man whose chair is the place of honor at the dinner table or in the living room, the man who makes the family rules: He leaves no doubt, imparts no ambiguity, about what he expects.

This is the parent to please. Bring home a report card with a B, and he wants to know why it isn't an A; arrive late for dinner, and his reprimand precludes making the same mistake twice; talk back to him, and he . . . well, it's better not to find out what he might do.

Such fathers cast a very long shadow over their children's lives. In some cases it is a benevolent shadow indeed, rather like that of a protective oak.

In other cases the shadow can be terrifying, for this father may be the sort who, if you ignite his anger, might even throw you across the room.

Demanding fathers come in two forms: the *authoritative* father and the *authoritarian,* or domineering father.

The Authoritative Father

Wendy, forty-five, recently suffered what is arguably the worst loss a parent can experience—her twenty-one-year-old son died of a rare form of cancer. All through his agonizing illness Wendy drew on memories of her father, who died when she was in college, for courage and fortitude. She says,

> Whenever I felt like falling apart, I would think of my dad. His strength was constant. When I was a kid, I was in an automobile accident and the doctors said I'd be in a wheelchair for life. My father said, "She *will walk again.*" He was so determined, so inspiring, that I did. At times I resented him, because we were both stubborn. But I adored him, and he adored me. All the qualities that have gotten me through the hard times I got from him. I always have a voice in my head that says, "You can do it. Press on."

This kind of father drags his children, sometimes kicking and screaming, into giving their personal best. For he has his eye not simply on the moment but on the future—he very much wants to prepare them for survival and happiness in the adult world, to see life as a series of challenging opportunities.

To that end he is willing to be the family heavy if necessary; he is seldom plagued by second thoughts and cannot be bamboozled. He doesn't expect always to be liked, but since he tempers his demands with affection, it's hard to *hate* him. For he is also able to express pride in his children's accomplishments, to share their joy when they meet or exceed either his expectations or their own, to allow them to be who they are—regardless of gender.

And while at times he may seem stern, he is fair: The daughter who loses a finals tennis match may, for that day, be relieved of her chores; the son whose girlfriend breaks up with him right before an exam will not be expected to pull a high mark.

The consensus among experts is that the children of authoritative fathers (or mothers) have the fewest behavioral problems and self-doubts. They know they can depend on him; they know exactly where they stand; and even if Dad is not exactly the Mickey Rooney of joviality, they can count on his love, supportiveness, and interest as well as his discipline, the blend of which gives them enormous security.

This rock-sure, loving authority has longlasting, beneficial effects on his daughters.

First, the daughter's cognitive abilities are enormously enhanced by a father who excites her curiosity, who stretches her limits by setting high—but not impossible—standards and who serves as mentor in her strivings outside the family. But he does not make the learning process easy. Rather than jumping in and solving his daughter's problems for her, he gently but firmly forces her to find solutions for herself and to profit from her mistakes.

Thus the daughter learns firsthand how to set priorities and goals in school and, later, on the job; how to defend her ideas; how to surmount obstacles—none of which is at the expense of her emotional side. Her father loves her whether or not she achieves, encouraging *both* her nurturing and mastering abilities, her empathy and her ambition. Just as he does his son's.

The second benefit to daughters of authoritative fathers is their robust sexuality. According to Dr. Seymour Fisher, those women who are the most consistently orgasmic—39 percent of his research sample—almost always had fathers who were authoritative, fathers who prize "morality, honesty, and strictness in adhering to rules."

The fathers in the Fisher study were not vague presences within the family; rather they were actively involved with their children. Their daughters had no anxieties about the solidity and *dependability* of the relationship—the keystone to their sexual responsiveness in their adult romantic attachments.

In all these ways the authoritative father—his inner security, his unflagging interest, his warmth and fair, gender-neutral expectations—inspires confidence, rather than slavish self-doubt, in his daughter.

The Domineering Father

The same cannot be said of the domineering father. Indeed, his authority is purchased at the *expense* of his children. It is reactive rather than inherent, contingent on the hoarding of power rather than the sharing of it. Instead of guiding his children, he *competes* with them. At the same time, to prevent their forming a united front, he divides and conquers, arbitrarily playing favorites and pitting them against one another.

The obeisance of his family is as necessary to his sense of self as is food for the body. And like physical hunger, his psychic hunger requires constant nourishment.

Yet his behavior is a study in paradoxes.

On the one hand he views his children's failure to meet his expectations as betrayals, since he wants them to reflect well upon him, to herald the fact that *he* is the wellspring of their accomplishments.

On the other hand he doesn't *really* want them to be *so* successful, *so* confident, that they pose a threat to his rank and command. Hence, the messages he gives can be very mixed, keeping his children hobbled and off balance.

Especially his daughters, as we shall see.

Domineering fathers come in guises of increasing harshness—from obdurate to cruel—which often overlap, including:

- The controller
- The tyrant
- The bully

The Controller

This kind of father sets rules from which there can be no deviation or debate, for he is the ultimate arbiter of absolute right and wrong. Rather than dominate physically, he wields his authority through intrusiveness and dogmatism, even on the most minor matters. Says a thirty-two-year-old woman,

> My father always has to get his two cents in. We could be talking about *rodents* and he'd say, "You don't know anything about it," or "You're too young to understand." Recently I

told him about a job interview I was going on. He said, "Don't wear the green suit. You won't be hired if you wear green." All these opinions and put-downs are because he can't deal with the fact that I have a brain, that I can think for myself, and that I can be independent.

The Power of the Purse. Any test of wills, however, instantly is weighted in the father's favor by his manipulation through money. Many of the daughters of controlling fathers told me that, in fact, money was the issue over which they fought most frequently. Financial largesse had very long strings—if anyone's dreams were going to be bankrolled, it was the *father's* for his daughter rather than her dreams for herself. As one woman said,

> My dad always made it clear that we kids couldn't survive without him and that as long as we followed the rules, he'd do anything for us, give us anything. He wanted me to go to Stanford and be a lawyer; I wanted to go to Oberlin and be a musician. So he refused to pay for my tuition.

Great Expectations. Some controlling fathers insist on their daughters' excellence in all things, chastising them for mediocre grades, or for not making the soccer team cut, or for not getting into an Ivy League college. These fathers encourage only the daughters' achievements, ignoring their emotional needs and snuffing out any possibility of intimacy and affectionate connection. Thus, as one researcher put it, a father may "be in favor of 'women's liberation,' except for [the daughter's] liberation to love him."

Low Expectations. Other controlling fathers become fixated on what they consider appropriate feminine behavior, promoting *only* the daughters' dependence, denigrating or even forbidding their attempts at mastery and achievement, including, for example, their ambition, or desire to travel, or wish to be self-supporting. These fathers want their daughters to cleave to traditional definitions of womanliness—to be demure, supplicating, unable to make decisions without Dad.

Keeping Tabs. Another way the father controls his daughter is by insisting on knowing every detail of her life, far beyond the reasonable realm of parental concern, and far more vigilantly than he does his son. In the process he instills in her the belief that she cannot survive alone. Says a twenty-seven-year-old woman who lives with her parents,

> My dad still treats me as though I were a kid. If I go out, he wants to know where I'm going, the names of my companions, how fast I plan to drive, the phone number of my destination. That may be part of the reason I'm afraid to move out and get my own place.

Obsession with Chastity. Such domination includes the controlling father's fixation—which can veer on prurience—on his daughter's virginity. One woman recalled that when she was a teenager, the minute she arrived home from a date, her father would give her the third degree:

> He'd say, "What did you do? What did he do? Did he hold you? Did he touch you? How did you feel about it?" I'd say, *"Daddy!"* His rationale was, "Don't you think I want to know when a man takes my baby into his arms?"

But for most of these fathers, the only interest they take in their daughters' sexuality is the conviction that they should have none—until they get married.

Frank, forty-two, is unapologetic about his double standard regarding the sexual behavior of his four teenage sons and daughters:

> I feel very strongly that girls should be married before they have sex. If I found out one of my daughters was sleeping with someone, I'd be pissed off beyond compare. On the other hand I encourage my sons to have some knowledge about sex, some experience. It's a completely unrealistic position of course, but that's the way it is in my house. You abide by the rules, or you don't live here.

Drawing such a hard moral line sometimes results in exactly that: The deflowered daughter is invited to decamp. For example Gloria, twenty-eight, no longer sees her father, not by her choice but by his. Five years ago she was living at home and dating a man with whom she wanted to go on a vacation. Gloria recalls,

My father said, "If you go away with this guy, don't ever speak to me again. You will no longer be my daughter." I went anyway, and he threw me out. He had this *thing* about premarital virginity—mine, of course, not my brother's. My boyfriend and I eventually did get married, but when I called my father to invite him to the wedding, he said "I'm not coming. As far as I'm concerned, you're dead." You've got to give him credit; at least he's consistent.

The Tyrant

This father rules his family by waging psychological warfare, cowing his daughters into servility. Such domination can include what Dr. James Garbarino calls "terrorizing," a form of emotional abuse that he defines as "threatening the child with extreme or vague but sinister punishment, intentionally stimulating intense fear, creating a climate of unpredictable threat, or setting unmeetable expectations and punishing the child for not meeting them."

The tyrant stops just short of physical abuse, at least with daughters, because, as one father put it, "You don't hit girls." With a logic all his own, he explained:

When my daughter was little, I spanked her. But when she started to become a young girl, I stopped. Up to the age of four or five, girls are more or less asexual. They're just little people. When they start to become girlish, you think, Well, this is not something you do to a girl. You do it with a child [sic], but not with a girl. I didn't touch her after that.

Nola, twenty-nine, told me that when she was growing up, she sometimes *wished* her father would hit her, the way he did her brother—anything to avoid his endless, harrowing lectures. She says,

My father was rough on my brother and really hurt him physically. But with me he used intimidation. I remember mostly being afraid of him. Anything could set him off: slouching, being clumsy. If I dropped something, he'd yell, *"What was that?"* I'd say, "Nothing." He'd scream, *"Don't tell me nothing!"* Then he'd go crazy.

He'd make me sit in a chair, haranguing me about being a good person—but what he was really doing was letting me know in no uncertain terms who had the power here. This could go on for hours; long after my bedtime I'd still be sitting there, sobbing. The more I cried, the angrier he'd get. Once I said to him, "Why don't you just smack me and get it over with?"

The Bully

Some fathers are simply sadistic, bent on degrading their daughters and breaking their spirits—and making them grovel.

When Jodie, thirty-two, was a child, the atmosphere in her house would go thick with fear the moment her father came home from work at night. She says,

> Here's an example. When I was around nine, my father said he would pay me five dollars if I could do a handstand for a full minute. I practiced and I practiced and I practiced, because I so wanted to please him and make him proud of me. Finally I was able to do a real handstand, and I showed him. He said, "Okay, here's the five dollars. But from now on you have to be able to do it *anytime I ask.* If you can't, you have to give the money back." Then he laughed.
>
> It just killed me.

Says Linda, forty-one, of her stepfather,

> One day when I was a kid, I wanted to ride my bicycle, which was in the garage. The only key to the garage was in my stepfather's pocket. I had arranged my life so that I never had to ask him for *anything,* but this time I had no choice. I said, "May I please have the key?" He said, "What?" And he made me repeat the question *seven times.* Then he slowly took the key out of his pocket. It was excruciating. He was trying to get me to say something fresh so that he'd have an excuse to whack me. Not that he needed one.

This is the bully, whose children not only are his prey but also are perceived as incipient anarchists. His is a siege mentality, panicking his family with his unpredictable hair-trigger temper, which can explode with the slightest whiff of mutiny, imaginary or real.

The bully has no scruples about striking children, let alone about "hitting girls." In fact it is the very ease with which his daughter can be intimidated that seems to enrage him even more. Tears don't stop the bully—the more a child weeps and cringes, the crueler he becomes.

And the younger the child, the better: Physical abuse is most common among children who are between infancy and four years of age.

Of course it is not fathers alone who beat their children. Parental violence is split about equally between mothers and fathers, with slightly more boys than girls being brutalized.

Nevertheless it is fathers, more than mothers, who are likely to pummel their spouses *as well as* their children. And it is fathers, more than mothers, who have the heft to *continue* wielding the physical upper hand when the children are beyond the single-digit years.

Irene, thirty-six, whose mother died when she was six, grew up with her alcoholic father, who assaulted her right up until she left home at eighteen. She says,

> Funny, he only hit me when he *wasn't* drinking. I used to *pray* he'd get drunk, because then he'd pass out, and I could get out of the house and not worry about my curfew. But when he was sober, he'd wait up for me, and if I was five minutes late, he'd beat the hell out of me. Anything could send him into a rage. I used to sit in the bathroom and cry, trying to figure out how I could commit suicide and make it look like my father murdered me. That way I could be dead and out of this life, and he could be miserable for the rest of his.

The Tyrannized Family

Curiously the domineering father at home is often the milquetoast at work, unable to assert himself in the outside world. The family may be the only place he feels he has *any* control. Hence a child who fights back can detonate his stored-up feelings of inadequacy. The child—unlike, say, the boss—is fair game, an easy target for his frustrations.

I interviewed one such father who periodically gets into power struggles with his belligerent eleven-year-old son, during which he sometimes beats the boy. Says the father,

> I'm the bad guy in the family, and it's really not my style. The truth is, I'm afraid of my son. If anything, I'm *too* liberal with him. I don't set enough limits. I'm a really a weak-livered pussycat. I feel like a schmuck, especially at my job. I should have been a vice president by now, and I think it's something about my wimpy style.

As we shall see, this sense of impotence stems from the domineering father's own childhood. He tends to have been rigidly disciplined, humiliated, or beaten by his own father, and repeats with his wife and children the behavior he learned early in life.

The Dominated Wife. Such men are often drawn to women who were similarly maltreated, women who may share their violent streak—toward the children, at least—and who behave toward their husbands as they once did toward their own fathers, desperately trying to placate them. Many of them relinquished promising careers and personal ambition when they were newly married, allowing their emotional and intellectual identities to be forfeited, eclipsed by their roles of oppressed wife and mother.

Such women tend to be "deselfed," as family therapists put it, trained to accept unacceptable behavior, compromising so often and giving up so much of themselves that little remains. It is as though they have been picked clean of their critical faculties.

As the ex-wife of a classic bully put it, "I was not much of a mother. When my husband was screaming at the kids, I'd either hope it would stop soon, or pretend it wasn't happening, or start to think that maybe he was doing the right thing. I simply had no judgment."

Consequently such women are unlikely to intervene on behalf of their children lest they themselves be berated or emotionally or physically battered and lest their marital status be endangered. By annexing their identities and control of their lives to their husbands, they slam the door on any possibility of individuality, of personal expression—and, often, of escape.

Therefore they set their children up for maltreatment, finding reasons to excuse, or explain, or deny the father's tyranny. More often they persuade themselves, as do domineering fathers themselves, that punitiveness is necessary to build character in children, "for their own good."

Family Secrets. It is this conditioning of children to believe that they deserve their maltreatment, and for wives to avert their critical gaze from paternal harshness, that ensures that such treatment remains shrouded in family secrecy.

In abusive families these "secrets" may include alcohol or drug addiction. An estimated 50 percent of child abuse involves a parent's drinking; between 30 and 40 percent involves drugs. Substance abuse does not *cause* child abuse, although it can dissolve inhibitions. However, it does nothing to *curb* it.

But whether or not alcohol or drugs figure in child maltreatment, the wives and children of malevolent fathers know what's at stake if they go public with their private pain: the family itself, without which they believe they cannot survive. At stake, too, is their tenuous sense of physical safety. If they "talk," there may be terrifying consequences in the father's reprisals.

And so, as addictions specialist Claudia Black puts it, children learn the rules: Don't talk. Don't trust. Don't feel.

And in families where the maltreatment involves only nonviolent intimidation, the rules are similar: Don't complain. Don't question. Don't be disloyal.

The Roots of Paternal Domination

The domineering father is a role for which men in this culture traditionally have been trained—and in fact after distant fathers, this is the most prevalent paternal style I encountered.

Given this country's macho values and forbidding, Puritan origins, patriarchal wrath is as American as apple pie. Indeed, when compared with other Western cultures, ours is unusually violent.

After child neglect, physical abuse is the most common form of child maltreatment, according to the National Committee for Prevention of Child Abuse: In 1989, of the 2.4 million reported cases of child abuse, over a quarter were for physical abuse. Violence toward children is on the rise, with lethal consequences; reported abuse-related deaths of children increased 38 percent between 1985 and 1989 alone.

Moreover, according to David C. Leven, an authority on domestic violence, while physical punishment of children is not con-

doned in Russia, Japan, or modern China, in the United States it
is a tradition that has resisted even presidential entreaties for
kindness and gentleness. Rigid discipline—as in "spare the rod,
spoil the child"—is considered a morally cleansing child rearing
necessity. Thirty states still permit corporal punishment in the
schools, whereas every European country except Britain prohibits
it.

Such culturally sanctioned violence simply reflects and under-
scores a conditioning that begins in the family.

The domineering father tends to replicate a rigidity and
hypermasculinity learned in his own childhood. The overwhelming
majority of domineering fathers I interviewed were systematically
taught, through unyielding or merciless paternal discipline, to fear
and "respect" their fathers. At the same time their fathers ridiculed or severely punished them for any trace of "sissyness."

Learning to Dominate Women. The father's behavior teaches his
son not just how to dominate, but *whom*—especially women. And
the behavior of mothers often amplifies that lesson.

While some of the mothers of the domineering men I interviewed were also hostile toward their sons, most were extremely
passive, doing nothing to circumvent their husbands' authority,
nothing to intercede on their victimized sons' behalf.

Many of these men felt utterly betrayed by their helpless mothers. A few even remarked that because of their mothers' inability
to protect them, the last thing they wanted in a wife, as one of
them put it, was "a wimp—I *hate* weak women."

Sometimes they hated their sisters. Not only were these men
treated harshly by their fathers, they often commented that their
sisters frequently were *not*. The men were lightning rods for their
fathers' wrath, while their sisters—because they were "girls"—
were spared.

Still, these men couldn't help noticing that the paternal double
standard gave boys one clear advantage: They had far more freedom than their sisters.

Perhaps the most indelible lesson of male domination of women
for these men came from observing their parents' marriages. Sons
carried with them the image of their fathers' sovereignty over their
mothers, and the mothers' subservient or obsequious behavior.
These marriages were the paradigm of heterosexual ardor: The
men learned to equate female "love" with compliance and masculine "love" with power.

Evocations. Some people believe that machismo is indicative of a hatred of women. But—as with distant fathers—many authorities argue that what's behind the domineering father's marital behavior is an essential *fear* of women. Says psychiatrist Ellen Berman,

> Part of that fear is that Mom is a man's first love object and the giver of all good and all bad. And part of it is the male mythos that says that in order to prove you're a real man, you have to have a woman who looks up to you and thinks you're terrific and doesn't have lots of complaints. An angry woman not only evokes all that old Oedipal stuff from childhood but really makes you feel like less of a man.

A man's daughter can evoke the same feelings. Long-forgotten memories of a helpless or vindictive mother's betrayal, or of favoritism toward a "weak" sister, or a father's mistreatment of his wife, can suddenly resurface when a man has a daughter: He looks at her and "sees" either his mother or his sister.

And very likely *he also sees himself.*

It is a psychological commonplace that parents punish in their children the thing they most dislike in themselves. Domineering fathers learned early on that any hint of "femininity"—as in vulnerability, sensitivity, and neediness—would be excoriated. They had to exorcise their capacity for empathy in order to get their fathers' acceptance—validation of the sons' "masculinity."

Thus the "weakness" a domineering father sees in his daughter is a painful reminder of the "weakness" that is lodged deep within himself, buried under layers of denial. He finds in his daughter's terrified, weeping eyes a loathsome reflection of himself as he once was—and, he fears, still may be.

Which is why her tears enrage him.

As Dr. Berman puts it, "The whole issue of being vulnerable is very scary for men. Intimacy feels like a step down, a loss of power." And since the intimidated daughter is so vulnerable, he "controls" *her* fear, rather than his own; her weakness becomes his strength.

Distortions. It is inevitable, then, that the domineering father will project onto his son and daughter distorted notions of masculinity and femininity, of strength and weakness.

For example, domineering fathers have definite ideas about what the "male" and "female" child ought to *look* like.

Dr. Joseph Pleck, an authority on sex roles, has remarked that many fathers of small-sized sons will try to bribe reluctant doctors into giving their sons growth hormones, in spite of the terrible side effects of those hormones. Thus the son—by virtue of his gender—is a physical extension of the father's sense of maleness and supremacy; the son is allowed to *look* the part, if not necessarily to act it—at least toward his father.

Conversely the daughter may be an extension of the father's disavowed emotional side. That is, she represents his own vulnerability and his concomitant need to *control* that vulnerability.

Thus he may want his daughter to be *diminished,* both psychologically and physically—little, lithe, pliable, emphatically unthreatening—a wish that is not lost on her, nor on the millions of women who believe that the only way to attract a man is to be wraithlike.

And if she does not fit the physical bill, he may once again call upon the medical community—this time to make his child *smaller.*

One twenty-three-year-old woman I interviewed, who is tall and generously built but by no means fat, said that throughout her life her father has needled her about her size.

> I've been waiting my whole life to get a compliment from him about how I look. When I was a teenager, I told him that I was mortified because I felt I was too big—my bones were *huge.* He said, "Let's find a doctor who can do something about it." That was not the answer I wanted to hear. I wanted him to say, "You're pretty just the way you are." If he caught me eating even a small bowl of ice cream, he'd say, "Don't eat that—you're a pig."

Fear of Sexuality. Paralleling the domineering father's opinions about acceptable feminine appearance may be his awareness of his daughter's sexuality and his unconscious guilt about his response to it.

It is not surprising that domineering fathers often become belligerent toward their daughters when they reach adolescence. As we saw in Chapter 1, a daughter's teens are a time when she is not only beginning to question parental authority but also when she is maturing into a woman, which can sexually arouse the father and sound his internal alarm about the incest taboo.

The domineering father is terrified by these feelings and re-routes his shame into rage directed at the daughter. He punishes her for his being stimulated, rather like shooting the bearer of bad news.

"My body was a source of great consternation for my father," said Nan, twenty-six.

> When I was around eleven, I was standing in my room in front of the mirror, kind of checking myself out, seeing what was developing, which was all so new. My father happened to walk by and yelled, "Don't do that!" At the dinner table if I fidgeted with my bra straps, he'd say, "Stop that!" It was definitely a message that you shouldn't have breasts.

And when at sixteen she began dating, her father became the keeper of the virginal gate, certain that every boy she went out with was a cad who had uncontrollable and devious sexual designs on her.

Dr. Majorie Leonard, in writing about such fathers, suggests that this kind of Victorian paternal hovering is, in fact, a defensive maneuver against their own imagined vileness. As she puts it, "By actively protecting their daughters from 'evil-minded males'—not themselves—they are able to deny their incestuous feelings, while projecting them onto others."

"Parentifying" Children. All of these controlling behaviors and distorted perceptions can be traced to the biggest distortion of all: Domineering fathers look to their children—especially their daughters—to give them the love they didn't get growing up.

According to Dr. Brandt F. Steele, abusive fathers are extraor-dinarily immature. Because of their emotional impoverishment, they are stuck in childhood and still have not separated psycholog-ically from their own parents. This lack of "individuation" robs them of empathy, even as it stokes their neediness and causes the reversal of roles between father and daughter.

As was noted in an earlier chapter, the daughter may be the father's last chance to be unconditionally adored by a female, his last chance to be seen as a hero, his last chance to get the unal-loyed love that he was denied in childhood. And when, under-standably, the daughter cannot fill the parental bill, cannot be the nurturing mother or father he never had, the father feels that it is *he* who has been wronged.

One woman told me that the worst beating her father ever gave her was when, at twenty, she told him that she was not happy living at home and wanted to move out. Says the woman, "That's the last thing I remember. He beat me unconscious. He felt I was abandoning him."

Such retribution for a father's childhood losses presupposes a certain narcissism—which, as was discussed earlier, is at the heart of much child maltreatment—wherein the emotional boundaries between father and daughter become blurred.

In the most brutal cases the childlike, grasping, parasitic, tantrum-throwing father suffers from what is called "malignant narcissism," a term coined by psychiatrist Otto Kernberg to describe a personality disorder characterized by paranoia, grandiosity, and an inability to feel another's pain. Such people, Dr. Kernberg told a reporter, "manipulate with no sense of how others feel inside. . . . [They] take pleasure in hurting others. They are extremely suspicious, seeing themselves as persecuted victims of a plot. They project their own cruelty onto their enemies."

Their "enemies," of course, include their insufficiently adoring or obedient children. But not, curiously, their *own* domineering fathers, whom they tend to idealize.

The Bad-Daddy Taboo. Because of the biblical commandment to honor one's parents, it is considered sinful to be angry with or hate them. The guilt induced by a culture that insists on the unequivocal authority and honoring of parents, regardless of their parents' dishonorable behavior, encourages children to take upon themselves the "badness" of the mothers and fathers who mistreat them. And when they are grown, the children may disgorge the badness, like an undigestible bit of food, onto their own children.

Thus domineering parents keep themselves and their parents right, and their children wrong. As Alice Miller tells us, "children who have grown up being assailed for qualities the parents hate in themselves can hardly wait to assign these qualities to someone else so they can once again regard themselves as good, 'moral,' noble and altrustic."

So powerful are their defenses, they are extremely hard to treat in therapy.

But the abusive father may be the most difficult, resistant patient a therapist sees—*if* a therapist *ever* sees such a father. Emotional denial is culturally ingrained in men, which nourishes the narcissism that allows them to blame their victims for the mal-treatment that they inflict.

For it is men, more often than women, who are discouraged from the kind of solitary introspection and soul-searching that might help them begin to take responsibility for their actions; to hold themselves accountable for attempting to wrest from their children the love they didn't get growing up.

And in training their sons also to vigorously avoid vulnerability —and their daughters *only* to be vulnerable—we see the fathers' abusiveness spiraling into the next generation.

Paternal Regrets. There are those courageous men who, with the mollification of middle age, *do* reflect back over their lives and *do* hold themselves culpable for their harshness.

Sidney, fifty, told me that when he was a young father, it seemed perfectly logical to him either to use or threaten to use a belt on his daughters, because that's what his alcoholic father did to him. He was terrified of his father, a man who "would actually rip kitchen cabinets off walls." His mother explained the father's be-havior by saying, "He's just working it out; it'll pass."

But something even he can't explain caused Sidney suddenly to *understand* his treatment of his children, to see the connection between his childhood and theirs: "I vividly remember the last time I hit them. I grabbed my belt, and all at once"—he snaps his fingers—"I saw my father's face. That memory stopped me. I re-membered my own terror. I'd never do it again."

Such remorse is something most domineering fathers are un-able to express. Apology is something they don't even consider. Certainly not with their children. It just isn't manly.

The Legacies of Paternal Domination

How a daughter weathers her father's domination depends in part on the severity of his behavior and in part on her own temper-ament and resilience. In general, though, most daughters of domi-neering fathers react in one of two ways: rebelling or capitulating.

Bad Girls. Temperamental "dissonance" between domineering fathers and daughters can be tumultuous if the daughter is in-nately assertive.

A number of women told me that they were "supposed to be

boys." In an effort to be more pleasing to their demanding fathers, a surprisingly large percentage of them became tomboys—an active revolt against "girlishness." Such behavior was as much reactive and compensatory as it may have been temperamental. It was one way to get Daddy's attention—perhaps the only attention they were getting at home, given their mothers' reticence and fears of contradicting their husbands.

Says Dr. Clarice Kestenbaum,

> One of my female patients, who has only brothers, was so unhappy not being a boy that she bound her breasts because she knew her father would turn off his affection the minute she wasn't like her brothers. As it happens, she could jump farther and run faster than her brothers when they were small. But when she developed fully into a woman, she went into serious depression because her father totally lost interest in her. He only wanted sons. She felt like an utter disappointment to him; he couldn't love her anymore, he was that blatant. That's abnormal parenting.

Tomboyishness is a coping mechanism that works even as it backfires. The tomboy is anything but compliant. Thus a coercive cycle of father-daughter friction can be established, a cycle that feeds upon itself.

As Dr. Michael Kerr has written, "Emotionally based conflict provides a type of solution to the relationship dilemma." Closeness and distance are simultaneously maintained in heated exchanges between the old guard and the new: Rage provides the distance and rage also provides the *contact.* Such relationships are perversely satisfying. As long as father and daughter are fighting, they can risk intimacy, however volatile.

And when the daughter is grown, so firmly is volatility embedded into her personality and her ways of relating to her father that she may remain tethered to him, and to all men, through rage.

Like a foreign correspondent looking for a war, the rebellious daughter may be drawn again and again to the "love" she knows—that of a frowning or critical or belligerent man. Or she may go in the opposite direction and look for a man *she* can dominate, and from whom she can exact retribution for her father's harshness. Or she may become sexually promiscuous, using her partners to prove she is as much a conqueror as her father was.

She may put all her energies into her career, neglecting her emotional needs. And because her feminine side was never encouraged, never a source of paternal delight, it can wither.

Good Girls. If the daughter is not naturally assertive, however, or if she has a rebellious older sister, she may deduce early in childhood that the way to avoid Daddy's wrath is to become the quintessential "girl." Thus it is her ability to be *masterful* that withers.

Such women comply with Daddy's wishes by tailoring their aspirations to fit his, since "ambition" results in the loss of his love and approval.

Marylou, thirty-nine, says that, of her brothers and sisters, she was spared most of her father's ire because "I was cute and bubbly and little. All I wanted to do when I was a kid was play with dolls; all I wanted to do when I grew up was to be a wife and have babies. I was no threat to my father."

Her older sister, however, was always in trouble with their father. Says Marylou,

> She was driven, a tomboy, always arguing with my father, standing up to him. I just closed off and did the opposite of whatever she did. I loved being cuddled and protected. It's very clear to me that that was a role I sought.

Supplication is rage turned outside in. Yet supplication can result in the dainty daughter's unconscious rage at the "weakness" of others. She may be drawn to tender men and then undermine that very tenderness, recapitulating her relationship with her father.

Says cute, bubbly Marylou, "The only thing my father cared about was achievement. The man I married is very successful, but guess what: The thing we always fight about is that I think he isn't ambitious *enough.* He spends time with our kids, which I think takes away from his career. I'm on his case about it all the time. Isn't that sick?"

And it is this male tenderness, however much a woman *says* she wants it in a man, that may in fact be something she fears—because "sensitivity" equates with weakness, and weakness equates with dependence. If her man is "weak," it means not only that he is not a "real man" but *also that she must be strong*—a characteristic for which her childhood may never have prepared her.

It is these anxious daughters of domineering fathers who are among the women who have the most difficulties in their sexual lives. Research shows that the more dependent and yielding the daughter, the more fearful she tends to be, which shows up in her sexual apprehensiveness.

The woman who is constantly off balance in her relationships with men, who cannot put her trust in the connection, is off balance in bed as well. Unable to believe in herself, fearful of disappointing others, feeling she has no control over her life, she will find it difficult to lose control the one place it is necessary: in orgasmic release.

Worst-Case Capitulations. In the most extreme cases of filial supplication, the daughter can become so addicted to male domination that she attaches herself to men who will batter her. Such women, in the complex convolutions of the mind, rely on brutal men to act out the rage they are unable to express.

Many battered women, however unconsciously, are silent partners in their abuse because they have been programmed for it. What is so deeply disturbing about this horrifying partnership is that these women delude themselves into believing they adore the men who batter them, or that they deserve their maltreatment and so are unable to break away from their husbands' brutal "love"— just as they were unable to break away from the "love" of their brutal fathers.

In all these ways the domineering father shapes his daughter's future romantic attachments, providing the paradigm of a love she can recognize and accept and to which she knows *exactly how to respond.* To get that love—unless she resolves her history—she must be powerful. Or yielding. *But not both.*

Thus the psychological legacies of daughters of domineering fathers, multiplied countless times across the generations, become *social* legacies as well. When little girls who have been menaced or beaten grow up, it is they, far more than their brothers, who tend to be victims of violence in their relationships.

A recent study by the U.S. Justice Department's Bureau of Justice Statistics found that 2.5 million women annually are raped, assaulted, or mugged. The violence done to them is *six* times more likely to be at the hands of someone they know or are related to than is violence to men. And when it comes to rape, the United States seems to be a leader: The rate is twenty times higher than in Japan, thirteen times higher than in Britain, and four times higher than in Germany.

But if women are in any way complicitous in how they are treated by men, it is not *only* because they have been socialized to believe in their powerlessness and not *only* that they have very real reasons to be afraid of men.

Rather, it is because the men in their lives—bigger, stronger, more forceful—have been trained to fear their own tenderness, to believe that the mark of real manhood is the inability to feel.

And men have the muscle and the power to make their beliefs stick.

Profile of a Domineering Father

When the slender, ascetic-looking man wearing sandals, jeans, and love beads slid into the seat opposite me in the booth of a New Jersey diner, I said, "I beg your pardon, I'm waiting for someone."

"Victoria, right? You said you'd be wearing red glasses. But the tape recorder was the tip-off," said the man, with a smile. "Earl?" I said, making sure that this was indeed the man who answered my ad, describing himself as a sixty-six-year-old ex-army drill sergeant, veteran of "Double-U Double-U Two," and retired construction worker.

"Love beads?"

"Yeah, well," he drawled, summoning a waiter to bring him a cup of herb tea, "I traded in my hard hat about ten years ago. People do change, you know."

He wanted to talk to me, he says, with a wry grin, because he's been on a decade-long process of self-discovery and was eager to "strike a blow for male sensitivity. I figured it would have more credibility coming from a rotten bastard like me. Until a few years ago my daughter, Chris, refused to see me at all. I don't blame her. I deserved it."

Earl grew up on Chicago's South Side, the son of a father who owned a construction firm and was seldom home, and an alcoholic mother. For much of his childhood Earl was on the streets, hanging out with gangs, and dabbling in minor theft. "I never did time," he says, wincing at the memory.

At eighteen he joined the army, he says,

to prove I was a man. I was a big, tough guy. I weighed one hundred eighty pounds, forty more than I weigh now. I was very powerful and physical, always getting into fights. Macho. I was sure I'd be dead by thirty.

He married at twenty-seven, right after the war, and his wife persuaded him to work for his father. "He was not a role model for me," Earl says. "I was convinced when I was a kid that I got switched in the hospital nursery. I was always emotional and passionate—he was a glacier. In all the years I worked for him, I don't think we exchanged more than a dozen sentences that didn't have to do with a job. Weeks would go by—*weeks*—when he wouldn't talk to me at all."

Things weren't much better for Earl at home. His wife began drinking, and Earl found himself spending more time at work. When he *was* home, he was, he says, "not a lot of fun."

I was angry most of the time. I was frustrated with my life. I treated Chris as though she were in boot camp. I was into blind obedience. Once in a while I slapped her; mostly I got in her face, scaring the hell out of her with my yelling.

In the meantime he began drinking heavily, and his marriage unraveled. "I wouldn't talk to my wife," he says. "I was fooling around. When my wife found out, she and Chris moved out, and she filed for divorce. Neither of them wanted to have anything to do with me. Nothing was their fault," he adds, matter-of-factly. "I made it happen."

When he hit fifty-five, Earl had what he calls "an Olympic-size midlife crisis," and turned his entire life upside down. Over the next five years he began reading books about spirituality and meditation and taking human-potential courses; he started exercising and became a vegetarian; he quit drinking and joined Alcoholics Anonymous; he left his father's firm and set up his own business.

And throughout he tried to make amends with his daughter, who refused to see him. Then one night she got into serious trouble. She called him from a police station, where she was being booked for drunken driving and pleaded with him to come get her.

"I realized that I had something to do with her problems," he says. "I knew I had to rebuild our relationship if I was ever going to be able to really help her, to make up for the early years."

At first Chris didn't believe that her father's efforts to talk to her, to see her and be there for her, were sincere.

> She didn't think I was legitimate. It's like she knew me as a macho guy for thirty years, and suddenly I've got religion, so to speak. I had a lot of trust building to do. I told her, "You can say anything you want to me. You can yell at me, curse me, tell me what I did wrong. Just let me have it. I'm here for you to let that out." She said, "Yeah, but. . . ." I said, "There's no 'but.' This is the real thing."

He fingers his necklace, ruminating on his rocky transition from streetfighter to soulmate. Finally he says,

> My other regret is that I didn't do all this when Chris was young. Like most men I did everything to avoid looking at the issue. I couldn't have talked to you twenty years ago—I'd be looking to grab you under the table. I didn't know you could be friends with a woman. They don't teach guys how to be fathers. They don't allow guys to have a soft side, to give up control. Even now it's hard for me. Sometimes I go into my head to try to figure out what the hell I'm feeling; it's still new territory. It must be something about the way guys are brought up.

With that he drains his cup, shakes my hand, and starts to leave. "I just want to say one last thing," he says. "I wish I could have straightened out my relationship with my father before he died. But he was never able to meet me halfway. He went to his grave thinking I'm an embarrassment and a fuck-up. What a shame."

8

▼▼▼▼▼▼▼

The Seductive Father

When I think about my father, he's just a big blank. I was never close to him, and he was never affectionate with me, never. But when I hit puberty, he suddenly seemed frightening, and I don't know why. This horrible feeling has remained with me to this day, that I'm afraid of him, that I don't want him near me, that he thinks of me sexually. He scares me and repulses me and I don't know why.

—ANNETTE, THIRTY-TWO

We hear about it, through the media, all the time:

• A nationally known child abuse expert and former FBI agent is sued by his two daughters for sexual abuse when they were children, and he loses. The daughters are awarded $1.2 million each by the court.

• A famous movie actress reveals in a magazine cover story that she was sexually abused by her stepfather during her childhood.

• A former Miss America announces in a speech that she was sexually abused by her millionaire businessman and philanthropist father from the ages of five to eighteen.

We are bombarded with information about it all the time, but we don't really *believe* it. Sexual abuse happens only to *those* people—you know, the psychos, the welfare recipients, the drunks, the dregs. Not to respectable people. Not to nice, law-abiding people. Not to people in the typical American family.

But that is exactly where sexual abuse is likely to occur: The white middle- or upper-middle-class two-parent family—the kind about which the neighbors say, "Such nice folks, so devoted to their kids, you never hear a bad word against them."

What we are talking about, of course, is incest—the parent-child "love" that most people dare not contemplate, a subject that is too terrible to comprehend.

Incest is the best-kept secret in America. After all, it's a crime that usually occurs when no one is looking, and most of its victims are people too little to defend themselves, too little, often, to know that what is happening should not be happening, or too scared to disclose it. And when they do tell someone, in most cases not much is done about it, as we shall see.

Not surprisingly incest is the least reported crime of all. Official reports require some form of substantiation—information that's difficult to obtain, since the only witnesses are usually the children themselves, whose testimony can easily be discredited, or who are easily pressured into retracting it.

Still, we do have an idea of its horrifying incidence. According to the American Humane Association, in 1989 there were approximately 384,000 official reports of sexual abuse of children, a twenty-fold increase since 1976. Eighty-two percent of the perpetrators were male—most often the biological father, but also stepfathers, uncles, grandfathers, and brothers—and their victims overwhelmingly female. (Unofficial reports, however, suggest that stepfathers are more likely to be abusive than biological fathers; that as many boys as girls are molested; and that a growing percentage of perpetrators are mothers.)

The true figures are probably considerably higher. Some authorities believe that for every case that *is* reported, another three to four *are not*—as members of the psychotherapeutic community well know from their rosters of female patients.

Says Dr. Marlin S. Potash,

A few years ago someone asked me, "What do you do to treat sexual-abuse victims?" and I said, "I don't treat them—that's really a specialty." But now I realize that in fact I do treat these victims. An absolutely staggering number of women I see have had some sort of sexually abusive experience. Based on my research and seventeen-year practice, I'm beginning to think that among all women, it's around 50 percent.

The consensus among experts is that as many as *fifteen million* American women were incestuously abused in childhood, half by fathers and stepfathers. As to the age of the child and duration of the abuse, it usually begins when the child is between the ages of seven and twelve and lasts for an average of four years.

But an incestuous experience, whether mild or brutal, need only happen once to leave its indelible mark.

Delicate Balance

Most fathers do not have to read the newspapers to know that incest exists and that it is the ultimate crime against a child. As we have seen in previous chapters, fathers are, if anything, hyperalert to the sexual overtones that lurk beneath the surface of their relationship with their daughters.

It is fathers, remember, who scrupulously try to keep their emotional and physical distance from their daughters. It is fathers who, even more than mothers, knock before entering a daughter's room. It is fathers who blush and look away when their daughters model their new bikinis and who change the subject when their daughters talk about their periods.

It's not easy being the father of a teenage girl whose sexuality is unfolding right before his eyes. How, he may wonder, do you monitor her womanliness and at the same time keep a lid on your own possible excitement? How much interest and demonstrativeness is too much? Too little? When does a father's compliment become a come-on? When does his affection become perversion? *Where do you draw the line?*

Jim, fifty-one, describes the pains he takes to ensure his sixteen-year-old daughter's ongoing trust in him, her faith that her daddy would never do anything to violate the incest taboo.

> I've read all those books about Oedipus, so I *know* what can happen. Long ago, when my daughter was three or four, I became conscious of when I was sexually stimulated by her. I was very, very careful not to let it show. I always respected her, always gave her her privacy, never pried into her personal life.

Stepfathers are even *more* acutely aware of the potential for sexual complications in their paternal role. They're not exactly *related* to the child, a fact that could, and sometimes does, undermine the moral prohibition against eroticism between them. But for many stepfathers the mere idea of behaving sexually with a stepdaughter can fill them with enormous guilt. As one stepfather told me,

> When my stepdaughter was little, sometimes she'd snuggle with me and I'd feel a degree of arousal and be terrified by it. I'd think, "Uh-oh," and quickly get her off my lap. There was such a taboo in my mind that I felt ashamed just *looking* at her and thinking, however fleetingly, "She's beautiful." When she became a teenager, occasionally I'd have dreams where we're alone in house and she climbs into bed with me; so powerful was the taboo that just before the moment of penetration, she'd turn into my wife. *Even in my dreams,* I wouldn't do anything.
>
> Oh, God, I can't believe I told you that.

Drawing the Line

In ideal circumstances the healthy, secure father does not pretend that he and his daughter are asexual creatures, devoid of sensual feelings. He acknowledges it in his head, but does not act on it. As psychoanalyst Alice Miller tells us, "Physical attraction and affection are always a part of love, and this has nothing to do with abuse."

Because the father is able to keep his generational distance, he can applaud his daughter's healthy development—complimenting her when she looks pretty, or talking easily with her about sex, or patiently advising her about what to expect of herself and of boys on dates—without violating the emotional boundaries of his role.

The loving, self-confident father reacts to his daughter's sexuality and puberty in a nurturing way, giving her appropriate guidance. Says Josh, forty-three,

> One night when my daughter was six, she started asking me questions about where babies come from. I answered every

question quietly, in loving terms, and the more I answered, the more she asked.

I felt very free discussing sex with her because she was asking not out of shame or embarrassment but simply because she wanted to know. Through the years I felt pride and happiness in her blossoming sexuality, in her developing so nicely, and in her looking forward to a great sexual and loving life with a man. I think she has a good feeling about her own sexuality. If I contributed to that, I'm delighted.

Another father was similarly helpful to his daughter in his ability to advise her about romance and sex. He recalls,

I wanted her to take her time getting involved sexually. But when she got to high school and fell in love with a really nice boy, she asked for birth control. I knew that meant she was no longer a virgin, so we had a long talk. I said, "Did you enjoy yourself?" She said, "Well, it hurt." I said, "It probably won't hurt the next time." I wanted her to know that I felt comfortable with the discussion and with the fact that she was no longer a little girl.

Crossing the Line

But the seductive father is not like these men. He is unable to maintain this delicate neutrality, this loving balance between his paternal distance and his daughter's need for his affection and attention.

At this point it's useful to define our terms: What exactly *is* incest?

According to Drs. J. Benward and Judith Densen-Gerber,

[Incest] refers to sexual contact with a person who would be considered an ineligible partner because of his blood and/or social ties (i.e., kin) to the subject and her family. . . . Sexual behavior recorded as . . . incest [ranges] from intercourse with consent; intercourse by force; attempted intercourse or seduction; molestation, primarily fondling of breasts and genitals, and exposure . . . all penetration, anal, oral, and vaginal, both passive and active.

In addition, writes Dr. Christine A. Courtois, "Incestuous abuse can include gestures, comments, and observation as well as actual body contact."

With these definitions in mind, incest can be divided into three general categories, representing intensifying levels of a father's sexual overtures and intimacy with a daughter:

- Excessive flirtation
- Creating an erotic atmosphere
- Seduction

Excessive Flirtation

A certain degree of responsiveness and flirtatious banter is normal and even desirable between fathers and daughters. Indeed many daughters take it as a wonderful compliment when, prior to going out to a party, their fathers admiringly say, "Don't break too many hearts." For a father *not* to notice how lovely his daughter looks in her prom dress, or for him to stifle the impulse to say "You look *gorgeous*" when she so clearly wants his approval about her appearance, denies his daughter one of the most important aspects of fatherhood.

But the line between flirtation and carnality gets murky when Daddy is *too* responsive to his daughter's appearance, when his admiration becomes *too* personal, when he is more complimentary toward her than toward his own wife. Such inappropriate behavior can bind a daughter to her father; responding to another man can feel to the daughter as though she's betraying their special relationship.

Says Shirley, thirty-five,

> My father flirts with everyone, and he always flirted with me. My mother told me he was fooling around with other women, but his affairs never bothered me—I always knew I was number one. I was much closer to him than she was. He responded and talked to me more than her. He was more affectionate to me.
>
> His flirtatiousness meant everything in terms of how I relate to men. I was so responsive to his flirting that I was

turned off to other men for years and years. He was number one for me too.

Even though Shirley's father never touched her in an erotic way, her sexual feelings were frozen in her loyalty to him. She and her husband—whom she ultimately divorced—seldom had intercourse, and when they did, she was unable to have an orgasm. She has always hated her body, she says, "because all it did was make trouble for me. After my divorce I thought, 'I will never be a sexual person, I will never like sex, I don't understand why people like sex.' I am still, in a real sense, my father's Virgin Queen."

Creating an Erotic Atmosphere

Some fathers set the tone of eroticism in the family by charging the atmosphere with libidinous electricity. Because of this loaded atmosphere—again, even if the father does not touch his daughter in an unhealthy way—the barriers to father-daughter sexuality begin to crumble.

One woman recalled the discomfort she felt when, at fourteen, she asked her father's opinion of a new outfit she had bought:

> I said, "Dad, how do you like it?" He slowly looked me up and down and replied, "Hmmm. I sure do like what's *in* it." It was the last time I asked for feedback about what I was wearing.

Most fathers—even those of sophistication and at least a nodding acquaintance with Freudian theory—are unaware of the effect on their daughters of such suggestiveness. One father told me that while vacationing with his family in Florida he committed a gaffe for which his teenage daughter roundly rebuked him:

> I saw this girl sunbathing topless, and I said, "Look! That girl doesn't have anything on top!" I saw another girl and I said, "Nice legs." My daughter said, "How could you say that? How could you *stare*?" What am I supposed to do, pretend I'm blind? She just doesn't want to accept me as a sexual human being. It bothers me.

Almost in the same breath this father added,

> My daughter's a cock teaser, there's no other word for it.
> She's a very sexy girl. She'll take off her jacket and throw out
> her breasts, trying to get a response from me. She accuses me
> of being sexual with her, and I am so careful to suppress
> whatever sexual feelings I have.

When daughters are little, their fathers' verbal eroticism precip-
itates a premature and disturbing awareness of their fathers' sexuality and their own.

And when the words are augmented by deeds, their awareness
deepens. One woman said that even at the age of six she felt
uncomfortable with her father's sexual provocativeness, which was
more than an accidental or sometime thing.

> He would always come out of the shower wearing a towel so
> loosely held that his genitals were exposed. Occasionally he
> would grab my mother's breast and look directly at me and
> laugh. Mind you, most of the time they were at each other's
> throat. It just confused the hell out of me.

All this suggestiveness and inappropriate behavior sexually
stimulates the daughter long before she is ready to deal with such
emotions, which in any case belong anywhere but with her father.
He eroticizes the relationship with this disastrous consequence:
She loses her innocence. And she may live with the specter of
what Daddy *might* do. Even if Daddy never touches her in a funny
way, she is constantly afraid that, unless she is very, very careful, it
could happen at any time.

Seduction

In the worst cases of paternal eroticism, her fears come true.

Sometimes seduction begins in little ways, so benign, so casual,
that they can't possibly be important: a father's chronically going
to the bathroom with the door open; a father who doesn't like it if
his daughter keeps her bedroom door closed; a father who wants
to keep his nine-year-old daughter company while she's bathing; a

father who still romps with his teenage daughter on Sunday mornings in bed.

Then the seduction escalates. The father suggests he and his daughter go skinny-dipping alone. The father insists that they shower together. The father crawls into his daughter's bed at night saying, "Your mother's not feeling well. I don't want to disturb her." The father puts his hand on his daughter's breast or genitals and says, "This is what you should never let any man do to you unless you're married."

Finally all traces of hesitation and ambiguity and self-control fall away, all boundaries and barriers dissolve, and the father masturbates or sodomizes or performs sexual intercourse with his daughter.

And then the father may say the words that declare to the daughter, as no other words can, that he knows what he is doing is very, very wrong and that she is a guilty party to it:

"Don't ever tell anyone. This is our special secret."

It is a warning that is redundant: The daughter *knows* that if she were to reveal the experience, she could be endangering her life, her family, and certainly her own fragile hold on the world—for her the family *is* her world.

What complicates incest abuse is that the daughter wants so very much to believe that her father loves her and will protect her. She will agree—having absolutely no choice—to any terms to avoid being abandoned by him. As Dr. Marianne Goodman puts it, "How can you really fight somebody if you want to be loved by them, and you know that their love is conditional on your agreeing with them or doing what they want?"

Nonviolent Incest. Most incest is not forced. The majority of incestuous fathers do not resort to violence, because it is unnecessary; a battered child may be too terrified or injured to cooperate. These fathers *woo* the daughter into believing that her cooperation is permissible and desirable by making her think that she is the only female in the whole world he loves. They exploit her sense of loyalty, her loneliness, her need for his affection.

Serena, forty-two, was adopted when she five, after having lived in a series of foster homes. But it wasn't until just before her puberty that her adoptive father, a physician, eroticized their relationship. And while he did not have intercourse with her, he might as well have. As Serena tells it,

I guess I fell in love with him, but unfortunately he encouraged it. When I was around eleven, I went on a diet. One day he said, "Let's weigh you." He told me to take off my nightgown, and I refused. He insisted that he was my father and I shouldn't be shy and he'd seen plenty of naked bodies before. So I did it, although I wasn't at all happy about it. I told my mother, and she got very angry with me. She said I flirted with him too much. After all I'd been through, I couldn't believe this was happening.

Curiously the following summer the mother went to a health spa for a week, leaving Serena and her father alone together. He had been extremely cold toward Serena in the months after she had revealed his behavior to her mother, and his silent treatment tormented her.

One night Serena was sobbing in her bed because he still refused to talk to her. He invited her into his room, apologized for his aloofness, and then, taking advantage of the opportunity and of her neediness, began exploring her genitals with his hand. "Don't ever let a boy go any farther than this," he said. Then he sent her back to her room.

It was the first and last time he touched her. Serena made herself so scarce—by staying after school with friends or by locking her bedroom door—that they were never alone together again. She never told her mother what happened. When she grew up and married, she never told her husband. Nor do her two grown daughters know. In fact, she says, the only person in the whole world who knows is her therapist.

Violent Incest. The daughter's silence is sealed by one fact alone: Daddy's power. It isn't unusual for a father to threaten violence—to the victim or to a sibling or to a pet or to himself—if she does not cooperate. *Actual* violence occurs in approximately 32 percent of the cases.

Since Daddy is big and strong and the daughter is small and utterly dependent upon him, she has *no* incentive to fight him. She is trapped by the reality of his domination and of her own vulnerability.

When Cheryl was three, her mother died. To bury his grief, her father began drinking heavily, an addiction that would unleash rages against Cheryl. For the next six years he first sexually molested and later repeatedly raped her. She recalls,

My father kept telling me that he wished it was me who died instead of my mother. He said that if I told anybody, he'd kill himself. For me sex meant death; love meant death. When my father got into my bed, I wanted to die. But telling him not to get into my bed meant that he might kill me, or he might abandon me. It got all mixed up in my head—he was all I had. Did I feel outrage? No. Outrage is an emotion you think you deserve to feel. All I felt was shame, and that my father would rather have me dead than have me tell anyone. So I didn't.

Silent Betrayals. The incestuously abused daughter knows to keep her mouth shut. Anyhow what's her word against an adult's—the biggest, strongest adult, her father?

Not much, because when a daughter *does* tell, most people, including her mother, *don't believe her,* not now, not ever.

The majority of authorities agree that the most common response is for the child to keep her awful secret. Tragically, write Drs. Brenda J. Vander Mey and Ronald L. Neff, "it is not the mother, another relative, a neighbor, or a teacher, but the victim herself who most frequently reports the abuse to the authorities."

Unless someone has the sensitivity to suspect that something is troubling her terribly, and the courage to do something about it, the child has no alternative but to bear her burden alone.

But these betrayals—especially if they began when the daughter was very young—set her up for *serial* abuses. When a daughter has been sexualized at such an early age, her neediness is so great that she becomes revictimized by people who are in a position of "trust"—such as teachers, clergy, baby-sitters, the fathers of children for whom *she* baby-sits—and who in any case have easy access to her. And later in life, as we shall see, she may continue to be prey to sexual predators, men just like Daddy.

And if her secret should leak out, teachers, relatives, friends, boyfriends, and, when she is older, lovers and spouses may say to her, "Well, how could you have let it go on so long? Why didn't you tell anyone? Are you sure you aren't imagining things? Are you trying to get some kind of revenge? *What did you do to provoke it?*"

As John Crewdson—citing studies in his book *By Silence Betrayed: Sexual Abuse of Children in America*—tells us, abused children almost never lie. And yet juries in abuse trials tend to identify with abusers rather than the abused—they usually believe the adult, seldom the child.

This skepticism will undoubtedly be fueled by recent studies indicating that extensively coached children can give inaccurate testimony in custody or child-abuse trials. Such skepticism may protect the innocent adult, but could also virtually guarantee that the child who *is* abused has no place to go with her story, will keep her own counsel, and will continue to be abused.

A Harvard Medical School and Massachusetts General Hospital study of incestuous divorced fathers found that even when there was considerable proof of abuse, the charges were disbelieved in court in 73 percent of the cases, and not one defendant was prosecuted. Moreover in nearly 60 percent of the cases the children were made to continue visiting their fathers.

The Disease of Denial. Freud himself made the appalling suggestion that his female patients' recitals of sexual abuse by their fathers were fantasies based on the women's attraction to their fathers, a theory long since debunked. Nevertheless people *still* deny the reality of sexual abuse of children.

Evidence of widespread social denial can be seen in the recent backlash against legislative and governmental efforts to spot sexual abuse and provide intervention services. Numerous parents seem to be more enraged by the possibility of being falsely accused than they are by sexual abuse itself. Yet denial is the very thing that keeps incest alive, that nurtures and breeds it like so much bacteria growing in test tubes in some dimly lit laboratory, far from public exposure.

And the laboratory—the breeding ground—is a child's family, in which she puts her total trust.

A Family Affair

Incest is not simply a clandestine sexual relationship between father and daughter; it is the result of a constellation of factors within the family, involving—directly or indirectly—all members of it.

The stage for incest is set in the parents' marriage. In most cases, as we shall see, the father was reared in a hostile or undemonstrative family and may himself have been sexually abused, and the mother has a similar history. Somehow male and female

victims of child abuse often manage to find each other in adulthood—and because of their own unresolved emotional turmoil,
they often triangulate a daughter into it.

The Mother's Role in Paternal Incest. Most wives of abusers were
severely maltreated, emotionally or physically, in childhood, and
have extremely low self-esteem. They tend to be passive and
wholly dependent on their husbands for psychological definition,
hence they willingly allow their husbands to set the family rules.

The wife of the incestuous father often has serious sexual problems and is either timid, or cold, or hostile toward her husband;
marital sex between them is minimal or nonexistent. But because
of her emotional fragility and lack of identity, maintaining the
marriage and her place within it mutes any awareness of her children's difficulties.

Such a woman is drawing on near-empty reserves of self-worth:
She has little talent for loving or nurturing, little skill for independent survival—and so she obeys her husband and denies the evidence of her own eyes and instincts. Unable to be either wife or
mother, and terrified of being abandoned, she is unconsciously
relieved to have a marital/sexual surrogate in her daughter.

It is inevitable, then, that the seductive father will turn to his
daughter to provide the love his wife cannot give him. And since
the daughter is so starved for love, her father's lavish attentions
may be her *only* experience of parental affection, however distorted.

Some studies suggest that most of these mothers do not collude
in their daughters' abuse, that in fact they often don't know about
it. Nevertheless sexually maltreated children, even if they don't
speak of their abuse, give off signs of it through mood change or
fear or some unusual behavior that the sensitive, alert mother
would pick up. Most mothers of abuse victims are immune to
these signs; in their emotional disconnection, they will do anything
to avoid the action that awareness of abuse would entail. And
even when they *do* know—if, say, they are given proof—they will
very likely accuse their daughters of lying.

Thus, as Dr. Irving Kaufman writes, the daughter is not a victim
of simply one dysfunctional parent but of *two:* "She is picked by
both parents to act out their conflicts."

As far as most daughters are concerned, however, the greater
violation, the more egregious betrayal, is the mother's, because

her denial or inaction or disbelief gives the husband an open invitation to continue his abusiveness.

As one survivor, whose father raped her throughout her childhood, put it,

> What damaged me even more than the incest was the fact that when I told my mother, she said I was making it up. Even when she caught him in my bed, she said, "You must have enticed him." She *knew* and she did nothing. The punishment I have had to live with ever since was that my own truth was denied. I will never forgive my mother for making me responsible for my father's brutality. To this day I have trouble wondering what I feel, questioning my own beliefs, because I wasn't believed at a time when my survival depended on supplying what my mother should have been supplying: sex for my father, protection and understanding for me.

Other Family Characteristics. Some incestuous fathers are pillars of the community, fervently religious and moralistically rigid, setting impossible standards for their children. Others are drug or alcohol abusers, beyond the fringe of society and the law.

Within the family itself there is little healthy physical demonstrativeness. Paternal love is expressed sexually rather than through tender or affectionate, nonerotic touch.

Members of these families tend to be isolated—not only from the wider community but also from one another. They usually have few close friends, and the children are not encouraged to form attachments outside the family or even within it. The abused daughter may be perceived by her siblings as their father's favorite, and they may hate her for it.

And the father will keep her on a very tight leash. He may ground her for months for the slightest infraction of the rules; he may not let her go anywhere without him; he may plead with her to stay home and keep him company.

Finally incest families are bound by secrets, the most important of which is the implicit or explicit injunction "Don't tell." It is the easiest of secrets for the daughter to keep. She has learned early, and well, that there is every reason not to tell what happened to her: No one will help. No one will believe her.

And there is noplace else for her to go.

The Roots of Paternal Seductiveness

What kind of man is capable of doing all that to a child? What workings of the mind allow him to touch sexually, or fondle, or penetrate his daughter's body? How is it *possible* for him to use his own daughter for his own sexual gratification?

While seductive fathers come in all guises, experts agree that they share one common characteristic: narcissism. Most of these men are not psychotic, not "wackos." Rather they are incapable of empathy.

It's not that the abuser is devoid of feeling; rather he can only feel for *himself*. So symbiotically attached is he to his child that in his narcissism he believes that that which gives *him* pleasure must also give *her* pleasure.

What drives the incestuous father to behave this way is a basic and unappeasable need to be admired.

The incest abuser has virtually no emotional boundaries. He is still a ravenous child, emotionally dependent on constant, instant gratification. He turns to others to provide validation of his worth, or power, or lovability. But his is an emotional void so wide and so deep that it can never be filled.

Some researchers believe that the incestuous father harbors a deep and abiding hatred and fear of women. In some cases this results in the father's domination of all members of the family—wife as well as children. In other cases the abuser is dominated by his wife; incest becomes a way of passive-aggressively getting back at her by projecting his hatred onto his daughter.

In virtually all cases, however, the incestuous father suffers from extraordinarily low self-esteem, which can be traced to his own childhood.

Some abusers were harshly disciplined, cruelly punished, or ignored by their parents. Others were emotionally smothered and given no limits. Still others were enmeshed in an incestuous relationship with either their mothers or their fathers.

But if there is one common thread to their childhood deprivations, according to Dr. Irving Kaufman, it is that they did not have enough maternal nurturing. Because the incest abuser was denied adequate nurturance early in life, he has not separated from his own parents. Consequently he has not grown up. He lacks a benevolent inner voice—an internal sense of security and confidence

—which would stabilize his life when it hits the rapids and which would regulate his impulses.

Thus he turns to his daughter to give him the nurturing he didn't get in childhood.

Still, the signal question looms: *why incest?* There are millions of people who grew up in emotionally deprived childhoods, people who do not act out their own childhood losses in this grotesque way.

Ultimately paternal incest is about *power*—namely masculine power over women, and the loveless intimacy for which men have traditionally been trained.

By any name, with or without gradual conditioning of a child, with or without a daughter's consent, incest is *rape*. And like rape, incest is never about the victim. It's always about the abuser, of whom the child is simply an extension, and about his need to control and dominate her.

Says Ronald Gaudia, deputy director of Westchester Jewish Community Services, who has established programs for the treatment of perpetrators, their spouses, and victims,

> There are two basic categories of incest offenders: one type has deep feelings of inadequacy. Choosing a child shows how ineffectual they feel. It's a way of getting some kind of recognition and attention. The second type is hostile and cruel.
>
> These men are not easy to work with. Most abusers deny what they've done. We've got guys here under court order, and they're still denying that they did anything. And when and if they finally get to where they can admit it, some of them get real depressed.

There are some incest offenders who do not wait to be turned in to the authorities to get help; instead they volunteer for treatment. Usually it's either because they are forced by their wives as the condition for not leaving them or because the fathers themselves are somehow able to take responsibility for their behavior.

A psychiatrist told me of a case that illustrates this latter category. The father had an obsessive love for his daughter, taking showers with her from the time she was two and excluding his wife from their special attachment. When the daughter reached adolescence, the father insisted on monitoring the daughter's every move, telling her that boys were forbidden to visit her at home, especially boys from ethnic minorities.

One afternoon, in an act of rebellion, the daughter brought home a Hispanic boy from her high school, just at the time the father was returning from work. He threw the boy out and locked the daughter in her room.

That night the father had a dream that galvanized him into seeking psychotherapy: He dreamed that he was having intercourse with his daughter. In treatment he recognized that his love for her was extremely unhealthy and that it was up to him to come to terms with his incestuous feelings, to apologize to her, and to allow her to have more freedom so that she could separate from him and become an independent, whole adult.

Unfortunately most abusers are not able courageously to take stock and do something about their behavior. Rather they deny it or they justify it. They say that their daughters "seduced" them, or they say they are only trying to give their daughters some firsthand "sex education."

Thus the incest abuser extorts from his victim a frail and fraudulent sense of power. Such a "solution" to his childhood deprivations is the mark of a bully who has lost every trace of humanity.

And his daughter, pressed into service as pawn, surrogate parent, and peer—unless she gets intensive help—is deprived of the ability ever to trust anyone again. Even herself.

The Legacies of Sexual Abuse

The damage done to the incestuously abused daughter is the destruction of her beliefs, the distortion of her gut instincts, the devastation of her mind, her body, and her identity. Says Dr. Goodman,

> The daughters of seductive or incestuous fathers, whether in manner or in actual fact, have the greatest problems and suffer the most. They have to put up emotional walls, because Daddy didn't. It creates enormous ambivalence in the daughter. It means that you can't trust anything—you can't trust good feelings, you can't trust bad feelings—because it's all terribly confused.

Coping in Childhood. What is the daughter who has been betrayed by the one man among men who was supposed to love and
protect her to do? How is she ever to feel that the world is a safe
place when her survival required that she yield to a father's violation of her body and perversion of her love?

With no place to go for help, how can she escape the agonizing
assault to her senses, her dignity, her appetites—all of which have
been so horribly exploited? How is she ever to feel at ease with the
natural, commingled inclinations of the body and of the heart—
the joy of normal heterosexual coupling—when love means shame
and degradation?

There's only one way to do all that: She must kill off a part of
herself. She must deny her experience.

A primary source of a daughter's denial is her own sense of
shame and complicity. For within the incestuous relationship exists
one component that is unique to this form of abuse: Unlike being
beaten, or ignored, or rejected, there is a degree of pleasure, however much it has been wrung from the child, however much it has
been corrupted by the abuser.

The victim does not merely identify with her aggressor; she also
loves him, and in some way may even love his touch, since that
may be the only attention she gets from *anyone.* The horror of her
"love" may send her reeling into denial, since she is unable to
sustain two strong emotions simultaneously: pleasure and disgust,
love and betrayal.

For this reason father-child incest is the most emotionally ravaging form of child abuse.

One way the sexually abused daughter manages to tolerate her
chaotic double life—at times the little girl, at times Daddy's lover
—is by "splitting" her father in her head: The "bad" Daddy is the
one who invades her body; the "good" Daddy is the one who takes
her to a picnic.

At the same time she "splits" herself: The "bad" girl likes his
affection, the "good" girl hates it. Little by little, however, good
and bad become so mixed up that they reverse. Little by little, that
which she "likes" she denies. She dissociates herself from her experience. She goes numb, training her body to feel nothing, her
mind to remember nothing.

And the badness becomes herself, not her father. Since she is
unable to fight him on any front, she simply takes on his culpabil-

ity; somehow, she feels, she asked for it, encouraged it, *deserved* it, making her a very, very bad girl indeed.

But that *also* is too intolerable an emotion to actually absorb. She must do everything in her power to banish the memories to a far-off precinct of the mind. The earlier the abuse began, the likelier she is to forget. By the time she is an adolescent or soon thereafter—when she finally begins to have a life of her own—it is as though *it never happened* or *is not happening.*

One way to exorcise it from her mind, as psychologists put it, is to "act it out." In adolescence she might become a reckless troublemaker; she might become sexually voracious; she might routinely get in trouble with the law.

Or she might become supergood: perfect in school, pristine in appearance, fastidious in the cleanliness and orderliness of her room, frantically searching for some semblance of control, some sense of virtuousness. She might become timid and nearly invisible; she might become a frantic caregiver; she might become a desperate achiever.

The mind furiously denies.

But the body betrays.

The body serves as judge and jury, doing penance both for her father's abuse and for her inability to prevent it. She might become an eternal patient in an unending series of illnesses. She might develop stomach problems, or become constipated or bulimic; she might have chronic bronchitis or frequent headaches or breathing difficulties. She might turn to drugs or alcohol to dull her pain, to mask the memories.

Or she might become anorexic, for here is another source for this insidious, predominantly female eating disorder. Her need to feel that she has dominion over some aspect of her life is extended to her regulation of the intake of food, with this goal: If she can eliminate all traces of her sexuality, all evidence of her femininity, she won't attract this kind of love, this kind of *feeling.* She starves herself into asexuality. It is a way to try to get Daddy *not* to love her.

Eventually her mind betrays her as well. She may become terrified of the dark, have repeated nightmares, be severely depressed or phobic or even suicidal. She may be hypervigilant, on a kind of twenty-four-hour watch; a sharp sound can send her jumping out of her skin.

Adult Legacies. This phenomenon of systematic denial produces what researchers call the delayed memory, the posttraumatic stress syndrome, the sleeper effect of sexual abuse. For it may only be years later, when it is safe—if it is ever safe—that she will dare to remember, dare to relive the experience in her mind. And, as we shall see in Chapter 16, remembering the abuse is the only way to free herself of its imprisonment.

But until then in adulthood the memories invade in short-circuited flashes, sparked without warning in guises too disconnected to be traced to their source.

The most banal occurrence inexplicably torments her. A shaft of light from an incandescent moon can seize her with panic (*it was always at night*); the smell of beer at a football game can fill her with nausea (*he was always drunk*); a song playing on a friend's car radio can plunge her into terror (*he played loud music to muffle her screams*); a toddler's outstretched arms can fill her with rage (*she was just that age when it began*).

Myriad dislocated associations, floating like malevolent spirits even in life's loveliest moments, can make her think she is losing her mind.

Reality becomes a series of inversions. The bizarre is the familiar; the familiar, the bizarre. Love and panic, affection and terror, intimacy and dread become so tangled that she may simply be unable tell the differences between them.

Worst of all, *real* love punishes her, because now it's an appetite that exhumes her horror.

And so the abuse gets played out in her love life—or lack of one. She may try to find a man she can dominate. She might look for a man who is indifferent to sex, rarely if ever touching her. Perhaps she'll turn to a woman, who will treat her gently, who will give her a sexualized tenderness that is more maternal than erotic. Or she may revictimize herself by finding a man who is similar to her father in his narcissism and/or brutality, recapitulating the "love" for which she was trained.

It all depends on her emotional resilience; on the length and severity of the abuse; on her ability to find other sources of solace and esteem; on her luck in the romantic draw; and on her capacity to form a trusting relationship with a therapist.

Some survivors *are* able to form loving attachments, with this caveat: They can relate well to men as long as they are not in bed. But once the sex act begins, they simply dissociate, sending their minds far, far away.

Getting her body to respond in a healthy, spontaneous way is the hardest thing an incest survivor can ever do. Because once memory emerges, even just a glimmering, it's not easy to treat it as merely an artifact of her history, not easy to keep it from flooding the reality of the moment.

Many survivors say that with the men they love they have to go through a series of orienting steps, mental maneuvers that will allow healthy love into their lives that they will not spurn, or destroy, or fear.

The survivor must constantly remind herself that *this* man is not her abuser, that *this* man loves her in or out of bed, that *this* man will not harm her.

As one survivor, a veteran of years of therapy, put it with a laugh, "You know, incest survivors deserve a sex life too!" She added,

> For a long time I didn't remember anything. But then the memories started coming back, and it was real difficult for me. I had to "leave" in order to have sex—I'd think about work. Sometimes I just couldn't do it.
>
> Thank God, my husband was wonderful. He read everything he could find and talked with other spouses of incest survivors. Now when I say I'm feeling invaded, he backs off. The way we've worked it out is he's given me total control. Sometimes we'll get started and I'll begin going away in my mind. Other times it's wonderful. But I call the shots.

Other survivors, those who haven't worked through their abuse, are not so lucky. As one, who was sexually abused by her father, uncle, and grandfather, put it,

> When my boyfriend performs oral sex on me, I am instantly three years old again. I look at him and I "see" my father. I try so hard to separate the memories from this man who loves me today, but it's automatic: My boyfriend's face becomes my father's. But since I love him, I don't want to disappoint him. So I shut off in my mind. I think of something else. I close down so that I can get through it.

So it is that, as a last resort, some victims are so exhausted, so frightened, and so discouraged, that they stop looking for love at all. They choose celibacy rather than revive the punishing emotions.

The toll of incest is lifelong and in some cases may cause the daughter to lose her own essential humanity. Perhaps the most damaging consequence of incest is that in the systematic repression of their own suffering, victims may—not always, but often—repeat the abuse with their own children, either by marrying another sexual abuser, or by denying their child's abuse at his hands, or by becoming sexually abusive themselves.

As Alice Miller tells us, such people "will unconsciously do the same to the child that was done to them, without having any idea of how much harm they are causing, since they themselves always had to distance themselves from their suffering."

Thus the harrowing phenomenon of incest reproduces itself in the next generation.

Profile of a Seductive Father

When I walked into the office of a San Francisco social services agency to meet with Larry, an "incest offender," as sexually abusive adults are called by therapists who specialize in their treatment, he and his therapist, Paul, were wrapping up a session. Paul and Larry had discussed this interview in advance and agreed that Larry would feel more comfortable and perhaps more open in discussing his experience if his therapist were present.

Larry is a youthful-looking forty-two-year-old landscape architect. Tall, fit, his blond hair cropped close, one might take him for a recently mustered-out military man. He greeted me with a firm handshake and a pleasant smile, but sat stiffly in his chair, his feet crossed at the ankles, his hands folded in his lap, a mixture of apprehension and resignation on his tanned face.

"I'll tell you anything you want to know," he said in a quiet voice shaded with the languid cadences of a southern accent. "The reason I decided to do this interview is because I want to reach those guys who want to get help for their problem, but don't know where to turn."

Larry grew up in Nashville, the youngest of three boys. He was, he says, a "surprise" to his parents, born when they were in their forties. His siblings were ten and twelve years older than he was. His father is a retired plumber, his mother a housewife.

"My dad was sort of the Jimmy Stewart type," says Larry, "tough but soft-spoken. He had this strap he used once in a while on my brothers. I caught some spankings, but not as many as my brothers did. They got beat plenty. But he never hit my mother. Funny—I had no trouble hitting my own wife and kids, even when they were little."

Larry describes his childhood as having been rather routine—except for the fact that the whole idea of sex and evil seemed to have been fused as far back as he can remember. A strict moral sense permeated his childhood; the family were Jehovah's Witnesses and went to prayer meetings or services several times a week.

"If you even *thought* of swearing or talking back to your father, you'd go flying through the door," Larry recalls. "My folks never taught me anything about sex. In my religion masturbating was a terrible sin; going to certain movies was a sin."

It wasn't his childhood that was bizarre, he says; it was an early sexual experience that left a lasting mark on his view of women and of eroticism. When he was five, he played genital show-and-tell with a neighboring boy, who told his father what they had done. The boy's parents came to Larry's house to angrily confront them with their son's "sick" complicity in this "evil game." Larry was forbidden ever to talk to his friend again.

And then, when he was eight, he saw a photograph of a naked woman on a gas-station wall and, he says,

> I got dizzy. It's like this demonic force was in the room. From that time on I never had a very healthy attitude about sexuality. I became a compulsive masturbater, and always with these pornographic thoughts, this sick fantasizing about all kinds of women.

The notions of good and evil governed Larry's adolescence and young adulthood. He was extremely religious; he was severely critical of men who were always "looking to get laid" and cheating on their wives.

And yet, he says, no sooner did he get engaged at twenty-three than he immediately cheated on his fiancée. He felt so guilty about each breach of his own ethical code that he would go to church and tell the minister of his moral transgressions, feel purified, and vow to mend his sexual ways, only to relapse later on.

I was trying to live according to a certain standard and at the same time I was capitulating all around. So I'd tell myself, well, at least I'm not a murderer. At least I go to church. Trying to make the good outweigh the bad somehow.

Larry and his wife tried to abide by the teachings of their church, to forswear birth control, to pray daily, to invite God into their hearts whenever they sinned.

In five years the couple had five children—two girls, Nan and Kara, and three boys. Nan was born blind; Kara—vivacious, energetic, "just like me in a lot of ways," says Larry, his voice thickening—was his favorite child.

And every time Kara sat on his lap, Larry would become sexually aroused. "She was just this cute, chunky little kid; and yet it would stimulate me. I didn't know that that was normal—I know it now. It's a matter of what you do with those feelings."

Larry's erotic response to his daughter terrified him. He thought it meant that he was losing a battle with the devil. He would pray to God to help him control his sensual feelings. He would vow to cleanse his mind of evil thoughts.

The year Kara turned eleven, Larry's life began to unravel. He was accused—falsely—of stealing a car from one of his clients. Until he was able to clear himself in court, proving that, indeed, someone else had stolen the car, his business plummeted. His wife, weary from so many pregnancies and unwilling to use birth control, had cooled to him sexually. His kids were beginning to show signs of normal rebellion, and he would beat them with a strap. His wife would have dinner late, and he would slap her. He recalls,

It was a time of real despair for me, of anger at God for all the financial troubles we were having, anger at my wife and kids, anger at myself for having lustful thoughts. All the normal boundaries of being a father just disappeared. One night I went into Kara's room—I just wanted some relief from all this frustration in my life. I only thought about me; I never thought about Kara. She was sound asleep, and I figured she'd never know what was going on.

Larry pulled the sheet back from his daughter's slumbering body, slowly removed her underpants, and began kissing her genitals. In a few minutes she stirred, pulled up her panties, and Larry quickly left the room. That night he plummeted into depression, anguished that he could do something so sinful, so selfish. His voice breaking, he recalls,

> With my other daughter, because she was handicapped, it was easier for me to see my fatherly role. But with this poor kid, Kara, I somehow thought of us as the same age, that she was really enjoying it, instead of thinking that she needed my protection. But I'd tell myself, well, at least I didn't penetrate her —it could be worse.

The enormity of his shame was such that he was unable to tell anyone about it. He vowed that it would never happen again, and three months went by. And then one night he again he went into Kara's room and molested her—and again he weighed what he did do against what he didn't: They were fully clothed, he reasoned. It could be worse.

Still, he was so horrified at his inability to "be a father" that he went to see his pastor, who listened sympathetically and invited Larry to join him in prayer. A year elapsed. Once more, when the pressures of his life became unmanageable, he went into Kara's room and held her until he climaxed.

Overwhelmed by the reality of his behavior, this time Larry sought professional help. He found the name of the social services agency where he, his children, and his wife have been undergoing treatment for five years. Larry sees his therapist privately and goes to an offenders' therapy group once a week; Kara and the other children and his wife see their own counselors in private treatment. He says,

> I should have gotten professional help from day one instead of thinking that prayer would take care of it. I'm still very religious, but faith alone can't help. You have to face what you've done. You have to look your daughter straight in the eye and say, "I did it. You didn't ask for this. I committed a horrible offense, and all I can do is beg your forgiveness." I didn't just hurt myself or her, I hurt everyone. I crossed a boundary. If anyone had told me when I was young that I'd ever molest my own daughter, he would have gotten a broken nose. But I had to admit what I did and go back over my life

to try to understand what made it possible for me to cross that boundary. I have to live with the daily awareness that my daughter will probably never trust me again.

I end the interview—which clearly has not been easy for Larry —with one last question: "Pretend that you could talk to every father in America who ever molested his daughter or even considered it, and didn't get help. What would you say?" He leans forward in his chair, takes a deep breath, and for the first time raises his voice above a whisper:

> The guy who does these things wants to stop. He wants to be cured of it. He wants to kill himself for what he's done. But he's got to be honest enough to say, "Yes, this appeals to me, there's something drawing me to it."
>
> Here's what I'd say to those guys: "Forget about what you have to go through; *you've got a child to save.* Maybe it isn't very 'manly' to get help, but you've got to bite the bullet and say, 'I'm the father. I violated a tremendous trust. I have to do what has to be done. I must get help.' "

9

vvvvvvv

The Absent Father

My parents divorced when I was five, and ever since the world has never been a safe place. Divorce teaches you that one morning everything can be fine and by nighttime the earth can fall apart. It teaches you to never count on anyone but yourself. It teaches you not to invest too much in anyone, because they could always leave.

—PAULA, THIRTY-NINE

It is a child's nightmare come true:

A father packs a suitcase and says, "I'm sorry, honey, your mom and I just can't live together anymore."

Or a father, without a word, walks out and never comes back.

Or a father dies.

And afterward nothing is ever the same. From that moment on, much of life becomes a matter of avoiding another good-bye.

Losing a father in childhood forever changes the shape of a daughter's identity—how she views the world and herself. Not only is her connection to the first and most important man in her life sharply curtailed or extinguished but all her perceptions, all her decisions, all her future relationships are filtered through that early, unimaginable, ineffable loss.

While there are many similarities among the women who grew up without fathers, there are also differences in the emotional impact of father absence on a daughter's life. Much depends on why Daddy left in the first place.

Absence by Divorce

Sandra, thirty, gazes into the distance, her thoughts far from the sidewalk café where we are sitting, and reconstructs for me the long-ago autumn morning when her parents split up.

> I remember it vividly, because it was my sixth birthday. I was looking out my bedroom window watching my parents, who were standing on the driveway, shouting at each other. Suddenly my father shoved my mother and jumped into his car. I ran outside, yanked the car door open, and screamed, "Don't go, don't go, don't go!" He said, "I have to," pulled the door shut, and drove away. No explanation. No good-bye. He just left. I felt as though the wind had been knocked out of me.

Sandra's experience is hardly unique, as we know from stark statistics that quantify the epidemic of father absence in the United States: Up to half of all children born in the 1970s and 1980s will, before they are grown, experience their parents' divorce and live in a single-parent home—almost always the mother's—for an average of five years.

Divorce is the closest thing to the death of a parent that a child can experience. Unlike death (except for suicide), however, it involves choice. And no matter how patiently parents explain to children that they are loved by both of them, no matter how ardently they try to reassure them that Daddy is not leaving them— only the marriage—on some level children can't help believing that Daddy chose to leave them too.

But they don't all feel that way forever. The long-term survival and emotional well-being of these children are colored by a number of variables.

Age of the Child. Most researchers agree that divorce is hardest on very young children, because the experience is so deeply embedded in their identities so early.

A three-year-old girl, for example, is at the stage of her psychological evolution when she is struggling with Oedipal issues— wanting to "marry" Daddy and have Mommy out of the picture. In the normal course of developmental events she would gradually come to understand that Daddy is spoken for. Eventually he would be dethroned, and she would turn to the outside world for a man of her own.

But if Daddy leaves during this crucial time, the sudden loss of his full-time availability can abruptly stall the resolution of the Oedipal triangle: Her idealization of her father can become frozen in time, like an insect trapped in amber.

In addition young children process the news of divorce with primitive thinking. Accustomed to having every need met in infancy, they assume that the world revolves around them. This "primary narcissism," as psychologists put it, is the means by which children begin to form a sense of their own separate identities.

Lacking the intellectual and emotional capacity to understand cause and effect, to fully grasp the reasons for their parents' divorce, young children marshal the limited, narcissistic reasoning they *do* have: They believe it is their fault when their parents split up.

Daddy might not have gone if, say, they'd been quieter when he napped, or hadn't knocked over that lamp, or hadn't etched his briefcase with crayons, which made him so very angry—angry enough to leave. And if children are powerful enough to make him go, maybe they're powerful enough to make him come back.

As we know, self-blame is one way children exert some sense of control over events. And the younger the child at the time of divorce, the more tenacious will be this guilt, this magical thinking, this urgency to try to get Mommy and Daddy together again.

For older children divorce has a lesser, but nevertheless lingering, effect. On the one hand they are well on the road to forming their identities and have a more rational comprehension of the marital situation, having witnessed, perhaps, years of parents' bitterness or sadness or even violence. They may even be thoroughly relieved to have the acrimonious atmosphere end at last.

On the other hand divorce can cause older children—especially teenagers—prematurely to detach altogether from their families, to look *solely* to peers and adult mentors for solace and support, relationships that can either be harmful or healing.

And should stepparents or new partners enter the scene, it is the teenager—who has usually found his or her rebellious voice— who seldom hesitates to express displeasure at the union and annoyance at having to form an unwelcome, artificial alliance with a stepmother or stepfather.

Gender of the Child. Another variable in the child's postdivorce psychological prognosis is his or her gender. Divorce affects boys and girls in quite different ways.

The overwhelming majority of children of divorce live with their mothers, and many authorities believe that boys suffer from these custodial arrangements more than girls. Boys living with single mothers have more behavioral problems in and out of school than girls and tend to be more aggressive than when they are in their fathers' custody, acting out their unhappiness soon after the family rupture. (Interestingly the same aggressiveness has been observed in girls living with single fathers.)

Since mothers and daughters identify strongly with one another and are likely to remain close—compared with mothers and sons —after the family upheaval, and since girls are trained to be un-complaining, it is as misleading as it is beguiling to assume, as many people do, that daughters who are in their mothers' custody are not terribly damaged by divorce. In fact some authorities believe that divorce is *more* harmful to girls because boys are raised to be less emotionally invested in relationships. Thus there is for daughters the "sleeper effect" of father absence, which doesn't show up until they embark on adolescent and adult heterosexual relationships.

According to Dr. E. Mavis Hetherington, daughters of divorce —especially if the loss occurred before the girl was five—become sexually active and marry earlier than daughters whose parents are still married or whose fathers died.

"I was fifteen when I started having sex," says Norma, twenty-nine, whose parents split up when she was four. "I found out *exactly* what the fuss was all about. I loved it. Even though I got a rather shabby reputation, I needed the comfort it gave me."

Most of the daughters of divorce I interviewed were similarly sexually precocious. But getting boys interested in them was the least of their troubles. The problem was getting and keeping their *fathers'* nonsexual attention. For gender also plays a role in the extent to which divorced fathers visit or financially support their children. Noncustodial fathers spend time or talk on the phone with their sons more often than daughters and, according to one study, are twice as likely to help sons as daughters with college tuitions.

When the daughter *does* see her father, each visit can be rather like a first date, during which she puts her best foot forward, only to have to reassert her winning ways the next time.

Says Lee, whose parents divorced when she was ten,

I saw my father, like clockwork, every Saturday. But it was always so awkward. He didn't know what to *do* with a girl. We'd go to restaurants or the zoo; sometimes he'd take me shopping. But it always felt, I don't know, *forced.* We didn't spend enough time together to just relax with each other. We'd always run out of things to say.

The Role of the Mother. The most important factor in a child's postdivorce adjustment is how the custodial mother weathers the emotional hurricane of marital undoing, and whether or not she can permit her children to love their father. For she must fill the aching void created by Daddy's retreat. And she can either help bend the child's life back into some semblance of normal, healthy shape or she can skew it further; she can encourage the continuity of her children's relationship with their father, or she can infect it with fierce possessiveness or accusations of their disloyalty.

It all depends on her own self-esteem and how she is able to handle the dizzying and daunting changes that are the aftermath of divorce. In all likelihood her income will plummet, even as her ex-husband's spendable dollars soar; friends and relatives may suddenly recoil from her emotional turmoil, as though it were contagious; she may have to get a job outside the home for the first time; she may be forced to move to smaller quarters; her children may have to start over in new schools and neighborhoods; they may have unreliable baby-sitters or become latchkey children, fending for themselves.

Other social supports may simply dissolve. For example Dr. Judith Wallerstein, in her fifteen-year study of the effects of divorce on families, discovered that of those families who belonged to churches or synagogues, clergy did not visit during the breakup of a marriage, whereas they might in other crises.

So busy are divorcees trying to endure, to salvage some portion of attractiveness and confidence, that they often regress emotionally, becoming in a sense their children's peers: frantically dating, desperately lonely, horribly insecure about the future. And their children may be denied the most routine parental attention. One researcher noted, significantly, that divorced mothers tend to read to their children less than do mothers in intact families.

The absence of a father may push the mother into a suffocating dependence on her children, especially her daughter. Not only is

the daughter the mother's gender partner and, often, sole confi-
dante, but she is also *entirely reliant upon her mother's goodwill.*

Now the daughter has Mommy all to herself, an isolated liaison
for which she never bargained and from which she may have great
difficulty extricating herself in the normal process of emotional
separation. With Daddy gone, she *dare not* become Mommy's rival, dare not see Mommy's flaws, because then Mommy might
leave too.

When the mother is the daughter's primary, if not only influence, the daughter, inevitably, may adopt her mother's attitudes
about men.

Lori, thirty-three, recalls that when her parents divorced, she
lived with her mother and grandmother, both of whom bore toward men an unbridled hostility they did nothing to conceal:

> They talked about men as if they were monsters and said that
> if I got anywhere *near* one, something terrible would happen
> to me. For a very long time I believed them: Men were "bad"
> and would "abuse" you. Of course that included my father.

According to Dr. Hetherington, daughters of divorce have more
conflict with their fathers, and perceive them as less competent,
than daughters of widows—in large measure due to the divorcees'
own anger toward their ex-husbands. At the same time, drawing
on their mothers' unhappy example, these daughters tend to view
men both as predators *and* as essential to their survival. As a
result, visitation with Dad can be a bittersweet blend of these
conflicting messages.

Since a daughter who loses one parent is terrified of losing the
other, it is not surprising that she often "splits" her feelings toward her divorced parents, seeing the custodial mother as "all
good" and the noncustodial father as "all bad." Such splitting may
be essential to maintaining her fragile sense of family, with longlasting consequences to the parent-child relationship and to the
daughter's later romantic attachments.

That many divorcees, in spite of their difficulties, are able to be
role models of strength and affection and fairness to their children
is an extraordinary feat. Because divorced fathers often don't
make single mothering any easier.

The Visiting Daddy. Many divorced fathers are also strong and
loving and just. They make herculean efforts to stay in touch with

their children—buying or renting homes near the marital abode, calling or visiting regularly, taking a tender and consistent interest. In some cases these fathers see *more* of their children than when they were living at home with their wives—which says something about the paucity of time fathers spend with their children in intact families.

In ways, being a visiting daddy is as hard on fathers as it is on daughters. As one man told me,

> Twice a week I would drive an hour and a half from the city to the suburbs and take my daughter out to dinner, and drive back again. During Christmas she'd come down to see me. I was living in a hotel room, and we'd put up this little tree. I had a deep emotional need to be with her. And I'd seen what happened to divorced friends of mine—their kids completely cut them off. I was never, ever, going to let that happen. Still, I was never with her as much as I would have liked. I missed all the day-to-day changes. It was a killer.

Visiting fathers who care deeply about their children often undergo feelings of crushing despair. Each visit is a reminder not so much of what they do have with their children as what they no longer have—or may never have had.

The gaps between fathers and their daughters can widen because of their different genders. These fathers wonder, What do you *do* with a girl, especially if she doesn't like sports? What if she needs sanitary napkins? What do girls like to talk about?

Many fathers don't know how to relate emotionally to daughters, and divorced fathers are no exception. Thus, visiting daddies may relate in other ways—through money and gifts and activity-filled, brief encounters. They have trouble just hanging out. Often they become far too indulgent, giving in to every whim, losing their critical ability to provide the kind of authority that gives the daughter some stability, some sense of structured continuity.

But at least these fathers try.

Devoted divorced fathers who insist on being part of their children's lives, and who do not use them as weapons in the dividing of marital spoils, appear to be a rarity: Fewer than one third of the fathers in Dr. Wallerstein's study were still closely and lovingly involved with their children five years after the divorce.

Because of their mothers' ambivalences as well as their fathers' behavior, visiting day for daughters can be more stressful than joyous. Many of these fathers bad-mouth the daughter's mother, or tailor the day according to the father's needs rather than the daughter's, or bring along a companion—often female—who is better at the idle chatter for which men often have little patience or aptitude. In these cases seeing Dad can do more harm than good.

Absence by Desertion

And then there are those fathers who simply drift away as the postdivorce years lengthen, seeing less and less of their children and eventually not seeing them at all.

It is a tragic and unavoidable reality that once a marriage ends, a great many fathers simply vanish. According to recently published findings of a nationwide study conducted by researchers at the University of Pennsylvania—which from 1976 to 1987 tracked over one thousand children of divorced parents from all socioeconomic levels—*nearly half of these children had not seen their fathers in the previous year.*

In most cases this paternal neglect is not due to the vindictiveness of ex-wives. In her study Dr. Wallerstein found that remarkably few divorcees actively try to prevent fathers from seeing their children. The specter of the vengeful ex-wife barricading the nursery door, as attorney Paula Roberts of the Center for Law and Social Policy in Washington told a reporter, is "usually a red herring, either to cover up lousy behavior by the abandoning parent, or as a bargaining chip to make the custodial parent accept less child support."

In my own interviews in only two cases did divorced mothers deliberately withhold their children from fathers. Both fathers said they had tried to see their daughters, to write to them, to maintain some kind of contact, only to encounter unlisted phone numbers or to have letters and gifts returned unopened.

But. In both cases there had, in fact, been occasional sightings of their daughters—a mutual friend found out where the daughter was, a relative had run into the mother—and the fathers *did not follow up* on these leads.

In the end it was indifference and inertia that kept these fathers from finding their daughters. And if a reunion was to be effected, it was almost always the daughters who did the legwork, broke through the silences.

Six of the women I interviewed were abandoned postdivorce by their fathers and did not see them again for from nine to thirty-five years. Only two of these fathers made the first move to reunite with their children.

Elaine, thirty-seven, whom we met in an earlier chapter, re-united with her father in adulthood. But in her case it was because she took the initiative to rekindle—or, rather, kindle—their con-nection.

Elaine had never known her father growing up. He abandoned his wife when Elaine was a month old, and she was always told that he had died. But something, some inexplicable hunch, made her believe that he was, in fact, still alive, still out there some-where.

When Elaine was twenty-six, her cousin violated the family se-cret, and she began a nine-year search for her father. She went to the Adoptees Liberty Movement Association, which helps adopted children find their biological parents; she scoured phone books whenever she took a business trip. Finally she wrote a letter to someone in the Social Security Department in Washington, who said he couldn't give out her father's address but would be glad to forward a letter from her to him.

"One day I was sitting in my office," Elaine says, "and the phone rang. I picked it up, and this voice said, 'I have a letter here addressed "Dear Frank." That's not what you should call your father.' My hands shook so hard, I nearly dropped the phone."

Two weeks later she was on a plane to Florida to meet her father for the first time. She recalls,

> I knew him the second I saw him—don't ask me why. We both burst into tears. We went into the airport bar, and each had a Scotch and chain-smoked cigarettes. He was very vulnerable, very tentative, very nervous—a far cry from what I had imag-ined him to be.
>
> All through the years, I had had these fantasies about him. I thought he might be Prince Rainier of Monaco, or at the very least a movie star. I imagined he'd find me and contritely lavish me with trust funds and expensive gifts, that he'd scoop me up and take me to his exotic estate and make up for

everything. Turns out he's just an average guy with huge insecurities.

All the women who met up with their fathers after long absences said that their reunions gave them a melancholy sense of completion. They were smart enough to know that, short of being held in solitary confinement by terrorists, a father who chooses not to see his daughter grow up rarely has a plausible reason for his absence and cannot in any way be excused.

So why did these women go to all that trouble? Because finding their fathers helped answer their aching questions, helped to put real, human, frail flesh on their fantasies.

Ultimately, however, the gains could not outweigh the losses, could not erase the decades of longing and rejection that had become so tightly woven into their essential identities. Too much time had gone by—too many taunts in school, too much precocious self-reliance and premature grit, too much financial insecurity, too much awareness of their mothers' struggles—to undo the unavoidable, agonizing *fact* that their fathers had apparently so very easily let them go. Only with therapy—and by spending real time with their fathers, getting to know what formed them—were they finally able to fill in the silences and release themselves from the past.

As for those abandoned daughters who *never* saw their fathers again, the loss they felt was an open wound, a lingering death. These daughters were not able to mourn because always there was the hope that their fathers might turn up. Every day was another reminder that they had been rejected, and as the days stretched into weeks, months, and then years, the feelings of rejection continued to pile up, obliterating, bit by agonizing bit, that very hope.

For these daughters the certainty of their fathers' deaths would have been preferable to the awful dangling reality that their fathers could walk out of their lives without a backward glance— that their fathers simply didn't care.

Until they resolved their incomplete histories, *all* the abandoned daughters felt uneasy, or frightened, around men. Gail, thirty-four, probably summed up best the cost of a father's abandonment:

> I grew up without any men in my house. All through college I
> had a twitch in my lip because when I was around men, I was

a wreck, I was so nervous. I never thought I would have a normal relationship with a man—it's because I never saw one. There was always this little voice in my head that said, "Watch out. This person is a man. And men don't stay."

Why Fathers Desert Their Daughters

Many divorced fathers would do almost anything to avoid being left out of their children's lives. How, then, to understand or even explain why a father would choose not to visit his child very often, or reject a child altogether?

In her longitudinal study Dr. Wallerstein gives us some clues. Infrequent visitation can be explained, in part, by obvious factors of logistical encumbrances—father and child may live hundreds of miles apart. Moreover for fathers to see their children *also* meant seeing, however briefly, their ex-wives, which revived the pain of the unhappy marriage. These visits revived feelings either of intense guilt—if the father had sought the divorce—or distress and abandonment—if his wife had initiated divorce proceedings. And for many fathers the pain was too much to bear.

The paramount explanation for the fathers' retreat, however, was their frail psychological underpinnings. Following their divorces many men became depressed, fearing their children would reject them. The fathers turned to their children for solace in a kind of role reversal, asking their children to be, in a sense, the agents of their fathers' recovery and healing, instead of the other way around.

These fathers didn't know how to be alone with their children. With the mother out of the family equation, fathers were denied her mediation. Having given over to her most of the parenting chores during the marriage, the fathers were lost without her ameliorating presence. Now Dad had to interact one-on-one with his children, with little experience to guide him.

Younger fathers seemed to fare worst. Men in the Wallerstein study who divorced in their twenties were "seriously derailed" ten years later. All had remarried, and 90 percent of those second marriages had failed. Their careers were anything but solid. And they didn't seem able to take care of themselves, let alone their children. Many moved often, unable to "nest," to set down roots that would have provided stability both for themselves and for their children.

Exacerbating all these difficulties was the paucity of close male friendships and supports in the men's lives—connections that might have helped ease their extreme loneliness and sense of isolation.

Hence, along with their own derailment was that of their attachments to their children and their paternal responsibilities—70 percent of these fathers paid irregular, or partial, or no child support.

Older divorced fathers in Dr. Wallerstein's study—those in their thirties and forties at the time of divorce—fared considerably better than their younger counterparts. They were well established in their careers, were able to take responsibility for the marital breakups, and in general had higher self-esteem. Ten years after the divorce most paid child support regularly, although in the same amount as originally decreed.

Age notwithstanding, my own research has led me to conclude that divorced fathers who abandon their children, either wholly or in part, share one primary characteristic: *They do not appear to have a paternal identity.* Rather, their sense of self is wrapped up almost entirely in their work and/or their masculinity.

In this culture being a nurturing, involved father has little social value. Without a mandate for men to prove themselves as *fathers,* rather than only as solitary achievers, men are often unable to comprehend the enormous psychic damage done to their children by their absence.

Abandoning fathers are first and foremost isolated, stoic *males.* The "feminine" attributes of forming mutually nurturing friendships, of compassionate, sensitive, active parenting, come somewhere far down the identity line, contingent on their attachments to their wives. And when their marriages end, their paternal identity ends with it.

Since so much of a man's self-worth is measured by his income, money can become equated with paternal love—and at the same time be a substitute for it. So when a divorced father remarries and has new responsibilities—a new spouse, new children, and a new mortgage—often there simply isn't enough "love" (read "money") to go around.

Without an *emotional* connection to his children from the previous marriage, it is very easy for a father to sever his financial connection. Through some trick of the mind he persuades himself that the unseen child doesn't have needs, doesn't have wants—doesn't really exist.

This lack of empathy, however, does not necessarily reflect his history. One of the surprises in my interviews of absent fathers was that of those who deserted their children, *all* grew up in intact families. What these men universally lacked, however, was a loving bond with their own fathers. In every case abandoning fathers were emotionally abandoned by their own fathers, or were treated by them with extreme harshness.

To repeat the question, how is it possible for a man to desert his children? If there is one unifying reason, it is this: Abandoning fathers are essentially immature, stuck in the primary narcissism of early childhood, unable to feel anyone's pain or joy but their own.

Maryanne, thirty-three, tells a story that illustrates this immaturity. Her alcoholic father, who had beaten her during most of her childhood, walked out on his family when she was eleven. Twenty years later he suddenly turned up—to borrow money from her. She says,

> I agreed to meet him for lunch, and he got plastered. It was clear that he had absolutely no interest in me. So I said I couldn't give him any money. After lunch I went back to my office. A few minutes later the receptionist called me into the lobby, and my father was sitting there in tears, rubbing his knee. "What's the matter?" I asked. He said, "I got into an automobile accident and I bumped my leg. My leg hurts." He wasn't seriously hurt. What struck me was that he was such a little child. I felt as though I ought to take care of him. It really upsets me that someday he might die alone. But I can't have a relationship with him. It would ruin my life.

Absence by Death

For a child the consummate abandonment is the death of a parent. Not only is the child categorically cut off from *any* relationship with the parent but the loss occurs at a time in her life when she is least able to absorb it.

Such a death is what sociologist Bernice Neugarten calls an "off-time" experience. Adults know that their parents must one day die, and those deaths are not unexpected. The child, however, has no such chronological inuring.

If she's very young, she's not even sure what death means. When, for example, Daddy's coffin is lowered into the ground, could it be that he's really alive and can't get out? How is it possible that he's never coming back? Maybe it's a mistake.

And maybe Mommy's next.

As we know, one of the most damaging consequences to daughters of father absence is that they have extraordinary difficulty separating from their mothers. And if ever a mother-daughter relationship is in danger of becoming overloaded, it is when Daddy dies.

Now there isn't even the *hope* of a father somehow taking up the parental slack, or pitching in when the bills mount up, or simply being there for the daughter when the mother is tired or out of sorts. Here again, the well-being of the mother is crucial to the child's emotional survival.

When Widows Love Too Much. Widowhood is a far easier social role than that of the divorcee. Studies show that widows have more family and social supports and feel less resentment about having to bring up children alone than divorcees.

Consequently their daughters have fewer problems with low self-esteem and less conflict with their mothers than do daughters of divorcees. Indeed, according to Dr. Hetherington, they are often closer than mothers and daughters in intact families.

Which is not to say they don't have problems. Mother and daughter can become *too* close. The mother turns to the daughter for the companionship she once had with her husband, and the daughter turns to her mother with the acute awareness that she is one parent away from being an orphan—to displease her mother in any way can seem life-threatening.

It is the very mutuality of this mother-daughter dependence that makes it so difficult for the widow's daughter to separate and grow up. With no father to help her ease away from her needy mother, the daughter finds herself pulled in three directions at once: eager to have her own life, loath to abandon her mother, and loyal to the memory of her father.

When Mourning Isn't Allowed. Some widows, unable to accept their own loss, have difficulty helping their children confront and accept theirs. Hearing a child's grief only redoubles feelings of helplessness and abandonment. Thus the child, temporarily at least, may be left in a kind of emotional netherworld, stranded with a loss she can neither comprehend nor mourn.

Elyce Wakerman, who conducted a study comparing the daughters of intact families, divorcees, and widows for her book *Father Loss,* found that three quarters of daughters whose fathers died in their childhoods were not encouraged to discuss their anguish.

Most of the women I interviewed whose fathers died in their childhoods corroborated Wakerman's findings. Daddy's death was often sanitized with euphemisms and well-meaning tall tales. Some daughters were told that Daddy went on a long trip; others, that he had gone to heaven; still others, that he was happy to be in some vague "better place"—but somehow not really, irrevocably, *dead.* Not really *gone.*

Says Eileen, fifty-four,

> One day when I was five, I was playing outside and my friends taunted me, saying, "Your father died, your father died." I said, "No, he didn't." I remember going into the house and being locked out of the living room. My mother and her sisters were behind this big door, screaming and crying, and I didn't know why. I felt utterly confused and alone because no one would tell me anything. Finally they came out and said that Daddy was away on business and wouldn't be back for a long, long time.

The child who cannot mourn her dead father also cannot separate from him, cannot give up the fantastic image of what her father was, or what she may have been told he was in the mother's glorious stories about him.

This "repressed mourning," as Wakerman puts it, means the child cannot say good-bye. And if she cannot, attachment to another man may fill her with intense ambivalence and guilt. As long as she clings to her father's perfect memory, she cannot give herself to a "perfect" romantic partner. For to love another wonderful man is to kill the glorified father in her head, to lose him entirely.

An inability to mourn carries with it another, more insidious message: *It's not okay to feel.* For if you are not allowed to express bad feelings, neither can you express good feelings. *All* feelings are to be avoided.

When Widows Blame Their Daughters. Widows can contribute to their daughters' unresolved pain in other ways. If the widow resented the father-daughter attachment, his death can unleash in her feelings of rivalry that may have been dammed up while the father was still alive. But without his tempering presence the mother has few constraints and can now convert her grief into unimpeded rage directed at the daughter.

Hannah, thirty-eight, worshiped her father but hated her mother, who was jealous of that affection. At seventeen Hannah wrecked her father's car. A year later he died of leukemia, which she recalls with harrowing self-reproach:

> It wasn't just that my father died, which was bad enough. I was forced to deal with my mother without his protection. My father was my best friend, and when I lost him, I lost everything. My mother made my life miserable. She told me that he wouldn't have died if I hadn't been such a hell-raiser.
>
> He never got mad at me for the rotten things I did. I put him through agony. In my head I know he would have died anyway. But in my heart I feel that I stuck a gun to his temple and pulled the trigger.

For some bereaved daughters what hurts most is this very sense of culpability. While the daughter of divorce may feel she caused Daddy to leave, the bereaved daughter may feel she caused her father to *die*. And without therapeutic intervention there is no earthly way she can rid herself of her punishing guilt. Indeed she may spend the rest of her life living under a self-imposed sentence of sadness and self-sabotage for it.

The Legacies of Father Absence

While there are differences in the causes of father absence, there are similarities in the emotional effects. Daughters who lose their fathers tend to share certain psychological legacies:

Fear of Intimacy. Consider the following two statements—the first, from a woman whose father died when she was nine:

> Over the years I've read a lot about how girls are affected by a father's death—that they choose unacceptable men because if those men leave, it's not going to really hurt you. And I've

certainly done that. I was in love with my father, and I've always picked men who are very different, men who treat me badly or who are emotionally unavailable. You can't get hurt if you're rejected by losers.

And this, from a woman whose parents divorced when she was eleven:

I think the reason I've always selected unacceptable men is because you know that if something happens, if they dump you or it falls apart, it's not going to really destroy you. You already know what it's like to have the worst happen. And you don't ever, ever want to feel that pain again.

According to Dr. Hetherington and others, it is daughters of divorce who tend to have the most troubled relationships. But *all* the women I interviewed who were denied an ongoing connection to their fathers seemed to have similarly rocky romantic attachments.

The theme among them was an inability to trust, to believe that a man won't go away. Indeed, counting on and loving a man was a leap of faith, because for them *a permanent relationship with a man was entirely theoretical.*

Most of these daughters tended to test the men in their lives—starting fights, finding flaws, expecting to be abandoned, or looking for excuses to walk out themselves. These women always knew where the emotional exits were.

Emotional Detachment. If all these daughters have learned anything, it is that the best way to deflect the pain of father absence is simply to close up emotionally.

While some daughters are flooded with feelings much of the time, and others are constantly on their emotional guard, they all share a profound emotional detachment—that is, they have trouble pinning down *exactly* what it is they feel or why, rather like being unable to pick out a single voice in a choir.

And when you disengage from feeling, in time you can't remember anything about your father. In time it's as if he didn't exist. Oh, you *remember* him—maybe how tall he was, maybe what he did for a living, maybe where he was born.

But you don't remember what he was *like.* You can't revive a picture of his face in your mind; you can't recall the feel of his embrace; you can't remember anything that would bring him back alive in your heart. Because if you can remember the pleasure, you will remember, too, the pain of losing him.

Fear of Dependence. Another pattern among these women is their anxiety about not being able to support themselves and of being financially dependent on a man. This is particularly true of women who are innately assertive, who are temperamental loners.

Ironically if these women are friends with anyone, it is usually men. It seems that the less masculine attention they got in childhood, the more they seem to *identify* with and imitate men—keeping their feelings hidden, preferring casual teasing and unemotional banter to the intimacies of female soul baring.

This phenomenon is a way of bringing Daddy back. Researchers have noted, for example, that when a husband dies, his widow often adopts his habits or mannerisms. Children often do the same thing—imitate the person who has departed.

Identification with men was especially noticeable among daughters who had conflicted relationships with their mothers. It was as though their only salvation was to be as much like their fathers as possible. Anything that smacked too much of "femininity" put them in perilous psychological proximity to their mothers.

Only in middle age could some of these women finally address that femininity—that is, their emotional side—and allow it to surface. Only then could they allow themselves to have emotional needs, permission that felt both like a gift and a curse.

As one forty-three-year-old woman, whose parents divorced in her teens and who recently married for the first time, put it,

> I adore my husband, and he adores me. But I'm deathly afraid that I'll forget how to be independent. Part of me just wants him to hug me and keep me safe from everything and pat me on the head and tell me it's going to be okay and to be his little girl. And part of me doesn't want to be *anybody's* little girl.

Fear of Independence. Other abandoned daughters go to the opposite extreme and are unable to be alone, ever. As adolescents they could not bear to be without a date on Saturday night; as adults they expended most of their energies looking for a man to marry. So desperate was this search that often any man who was the least bit convincing of his love and loyalty would do. These women jumped too quickly into love, were too frantic in their efforts to avoid loneliness and the horrible reminder of being left alone in the world.

These women were "relationship junkies"—an unkind term that aptly, if unflatteringly, describes women who cannot live without a man. Once a relationship reached the commitment stage, however, these women were on eternal alert, watching for any sign of diminishing ardor.

Inevitably they found it: The man who was a football fan loved sports more than he loved her; the man who needed time to himself was about to bolt; the man who encouraged her to find her own interests, to pursue her own dreams, was *really* telling her that he was about to pull out of the attachment.

And so these women, terrified of being reabandoned, redoubled their efforts to please, becoming, in the process, even more dependent—ignoring their instincts and neglecting their talents, unable to relinquish their desperate neediness.

Women who couldn't live without men also couldn't live without female friends—indeed, they are "friendship junkies" as well. They tended to overload their friendships, to identify *so* strongly with women that they turned to them for the kind of mothering they did not get in childhood. Not surprisingly their friends could not meet all their cloying expectations, resulting, often, in withdrawal—another abandonment.

Anxiety About Sex. As we have seen over and over, the woman whose father was either an intermittent presence or entirely absent often has difficulty in her sexual responsiveness.

As long as she reins in her feelings, her vulnerabilities, her trust —even if she is constantly looking for a man to define her—she can never *really* be crushed, the way she was in childhood. Holding back sexually is another way of protecting herself: If she doesn't allow this most private part of herself to be exposed, she can't be hurt. But the woman who "can't be hurt," who cannot risk loving, cannot be loved—and so cannot fully respond in bed.

Older Men. It is a cultural norm for women to be chronologically junior to their husbands. Most women marry men who are an average of five years older than they are. But a fatherless daughter who is romantically linked with a man *twice* her age is usually summed up as someone who "needs a father substitute."

In Elyce Wakerman's study she did not find this to be a strong pattern among her subjects (although she did find one group of women to whom it applied—women who had lost their fathers in adolescence). Rather the fatherless daughters in her sample were attracted to men who had ideal paternal characteristics—kindness, supportiveness, protectiveness—qualities that are in any case altogether desirable.

On the other hand, in Dr. Wallerstein's study there was a large group of young women who were attracted to older men. They, too, looked for fatherly qualities in their lovers. These women wanted the emotional and financial dependability of a seasoned partner, as well as—yes—his ability to "father" her by taking care of and nurturing her. Older partners were "good father and good mother rolled into one."

In my own interviews both phenomena seemed to prevail simultaneously: A substantial number of women—regardless of the age at which they lost their fathers—wanted a man who was both at least ten years older *and* who had these gentle paternal characteristics. In only two cases, however, was the partner old enough to be their father.

Rootlessness. Perhaps the most crushing legacy of father absence among the daughters I interviewed was this: *They weren't sure they belonged anywhere.*

Unless they were able to resolve their losses, they tended to retain a lifelong feeling that they simply had no emotional anchors. They believed they were untethered in an unfriendly universe.

This agonizing feeling of floating through life was exemplified by one woman, who, of all the women I met, suffered most from father loss: Between birth and the age of twenty-three she had had four different fathers.

Lorraine, forty-one, was adopted when she was an infant. Her adoptive parents divorced when she was five, and she never saw her father again. Her mother married and divorced two more times. Each of these men drifted out of her life.

Lorraine married at twenty-five and had a daughter. And although this marriage ended, having a child made her feel that at least as a mother she had one permanent attachment. Nevertheless she knows that soon she must let her seventeen-year-old daughter go, and she is struggling not to think of her as yet another person who will reject her.

Over lunch she explained the cost of too many fathers and too little consistent fathering. Hers was as concise and courageous a summing up of the legacies of father absence as I heard:

> My life is really a patchwork quilt. I loved all my fathers. I think of them as beautiful patches; it's just the stitches that are lousy.
>
> Catch me on a bad day and I won't be so sanguine. When you've had as many fathers and lived as many places as I have, you wonder if you're really here at all. And it shows in the men I choose. With so many male influences I don't know which to pick, so I pick them all, which, God knows, has given me a lousy romantic track record. It makes me feel very fragmented. My daughter is my only blood relative, the only thing that makes me know I'm not just some amorphous entity with no history, no father who ever really wanted me—and she won't be around forever. But catch me on a good day, which is most of the time now, and I will tell you that even with all those fathers I've had a hell of a life, and I wouldn't change a thing. I am just *determined* to be okay.

Profile of an Absent Father

If you met Alex at a party, the first thing you'd notice is his eyes. They look at you briefly from behind thick, horn-rimmed glasses and then dart away, scanning his surroundings as though he were a felon waiting to be caught.

A beefy man of fifty-four, his hair carefully combed in an unsuccessful attempt to conceal his baldness, his nervousness is palpable. He agreed to do this interview because, he says, "I wanted to take my 'medicine.' My daughter is twenty-five, and I haven't seen her since she was eight years old. I can't keep putting it off, and maybe talking to you will give me the kick in the pants I need."

The younger of two children, Alex grew up in Pittsburgh. His father was a bus driver and his mother a housewife. He has four strong memories of his childhood. First, he met his father for the first time when he was two. "Even though I was so young, I remember it vividly. He served in the army during World War Two, and he was wearing a uniform, having just been mustered out."

The second memory is when he was seven. His father and fellow union members were out on strike, and the family had to move to a tiny apartment. For a year his mother slept on the convertible couch in the living room with his older sister, and Alex and his father shared the only bed.

"My mother told me it was because she had ulcers, and my father's snoring kept her awake," Alex explains. "She also told me that she got the ulcers when she was pregnant with me. Nice."

The third memory was the postwar Joseph McCarthy years, when people's lives were being destroyed by the suggestion that they might be Communists. Alex recalls,

> My parents led a very circumscribed life and raised us to do the same. They told us that the FBI had a file on all of us and that once they got your fingerprints, they kept the file running, so you'd better never screw up. My parents always played it very, very safe: They said, "Don't make waves. Don't call attention to yourself. Stay out of trouble."

When Alex was growing up, he saw little of his father, who often pulled the night shift or went to sleep early. So Alex and his mother and sister spent a great deal of time together, going to movies or watching TV. Alex loved his mother, but was also frightened of her. It was she who meted out punishments, not by spanking but with terrifying reminders to be a good boy, because otherwise "the FBI might come and get you." Her threats were enough to keep him and his sister in line.

Alex's fourth childhood memory is that neither of his parents ever praised him for any of his achievements nor came to see him in the swim meets in which he competed—except once. He set a record for his school that day, and his father's only comment was, "Those other guys really fell apart, didn't they?"

Nevertheless Alex describes his childhood as having been happy.

At twenty-nine he married. His wife, whom he met at the Philadelphia insurance company for which he works, was very like his mother, he says with a laugh: "cool and judgmental and sexually repressed." Two years later they had a daughter, Karen. "I was ecstatic, and terrified," he says. "I adored Karen, but I couldn't relate, not until she showed some personality."

The marriage disintegrated within five years, and Alex moved out and began sending his wife child support. And then his wife announced that she and Karen were moving to Seattle.

Alex went to see his daughter twice and then stopped visiting. On his lawyer's advice he also stopped sending support checks. Says Alex ruefully,

> I was a schmuck for taking his advice. But I was so full of anger at my wife that I went along with it. I never tried to get in touch with Karen because I couldn't conceive of exchanging two words with her mother. I hate her fucking guts. I still can't even speak her name.
>
> For a long time I just pretended Karen didn't exist. When I'd allow myself to think about her, it would only bring up all the bad feelings. The bottom line is that I was able just not to feel. I put all my energies into my work.

Through the years Alex slowly rose up the ranks of the insurance company, eventually stalling out as claims manager. During that time he went into therapy, he says,

> to teach myself how to feel, to learn how not to be so scared all the time. I always felt guilty about surpassing my father. The reason I haven't made vice president is because I hold myself back. Twice a week I dream about my father, and he always looks like a zombie. I wish he'd go away. He hasn't released me yet.

But the biggest issue in Alex's therapy is that he's trying to work up the nerve to see his daughter, who returned to the East Coast five years ago to attend a college fifty miles away from where Alex lives.

The overriding emotion he has about Karen today, he says, is fear. He can't bring himself to go see her, even though she lives in Manhattan, an hour's train ride away. Several times he started writing letters to her, only to throw them away. Why doesn't he contact her?

Alex stares into space. Finally he says,

> That's the toughest question you've asked me. Have I not learned anything from my therapy? I pretty much squared away my feelings about my parents. But I haven't figured out my reluctance to see my own daughter. Karen's not *a* loose end—she's *the* loose end. I really want to know her. I have all

these fantasies about spending time with her—nothing earth shattering. Simple stuff. Chewing the fat. Hanging out together.

This is the only question he keeps evading. So one last time I ask, "Why don't you see Karen?" He locks eyes with me and for the first time doesn't let go:

Because I'm a chickenshit, that's why. I put it off and I put it off. The rational person in me says, "You're a fool." But the emotional person is just scared. I'm sorry I wasn't a father all through the process, all the way from infancy to young girlhood to adolescence. I deprived myself of a lot, I deprived my daughter of a lot. I take the full blame. What I recommend to fathers like me is this: *Do it.* Get in touch. *Get it over with.* The way I've resolved it is garbage. It's scarred both of us. I can't go to my grave with this one hanging.

It is a year later as I write this. Alex has still not seen his daughter, so afraid is he that she will tell him that it's too little too late.

PART THREE

Daughters: Patterns in Intimacy

10

Habits of the Heart

My father was the most important influence in my life. He made me believe that I could achieve anything if I worked hard enough. And he made me feel terribly attractive. Whenever I'd worry about ever getting a boyfriend, he'd laugh and say, "Are you kidding? I'll have to beat off the guys with a stick. You'll see." His whole approach was to make me feel good about myself, and most of the time he succeeded. I think if fathers do nothing else, that's a great thing.

—HARRIET, FORTY

When it comes to romantic love, some women have all the luck—and Julia, thirty-seven, is one of them. She has been happily married for a decade to a man who, she says, "is my best friend, biggest booster, the sexiest man alive." After all these years she and her husband still hold hands when they walk down the street; they horse around in the supermarket; they call each other several times a day from their respective offices, just to check in.

"He brings me flowers when I'm blue," she says. "We talk about everything. I trust him utterly. I have never, for one moment, been bored with him. If anything happened to him, I don't know what I'd do."

Then there are those women who are unlucky in love—and Peggy, thirty-three, Julia's sister, is one of *them*.

"It's the only thing about her that just stumps me," says Julia with an exasperated sigh.

> Somehow she finds one loser after another. Her first husband cheated on her and beat her up; then she lived with a guy who

was an alcoholic and lived off her. Now she's having an affair with a married man. My sister has a positive *genius* for finding the wrong men. Where does she *find* these guys?

Where indeed. Sometimes there's just no accounting for romantic taste—no sensible explanation for attractions that turn our brains into guacamole. Just ask Ingrid, forty, who recalls with a wistful smile the first time she fell madly in love:

> It was "mad," all right. I was in college. I saw this guy at a party, he looked at me, and I was done for. I'll never forget it. He came over to me, took my hand, and bells rang, the earth moved, rockets went off, every cliché in the book. I was convinced that if I didn't get him alone, I'd die. It was *crazy.* He could have been Jack the Ripper. Fortunately he wasn't. We had one night of spectacular lovemaking and soul baring. Alas, he was an exchange student and was going back to Europe the next day, so I never saw him again. I still think about him every now and then.

Why do some people suddenly, even recklessly, entrust all their dreams and vulnerabilities to a perfect stranger?

Why do others go from one lousy relationship to another, frequently changing partners who somehow are all the same—and all equally wrong for them?

And why do still others, against their better judgment, stay in attachments in which they put up with behavior that they'd never stand for in a stranger or friend?

Sometimes it's as if we're two entirely different people. One is the functioning adult who holds down a job, balances a checkbook, jogs daily. Then there's the *other person,* the one whose instincts, objectivity, and horse sense vanish the instant she or he falls in love, as though under a magic spell.

This almost-schizophrenic approach to ardor has puzzled poets since the beginning of time. "Love is blynd," Chaucer wryly observed in the fourteenth century, drawing on an adage that even then was shopworn. Shakespeare finished the thought: ". . . and lovers cannot see/The pretty follies that themselves commit."

But if love is blind—and the divorce statistics suggest that, at best, it has *serious* impairments of vision—it is not *deaf.* Because deep within each of us are voices from the past that crescendo when we are smitten, drowning out our otherwise rational selves.

In recent years students of human behavior have picked up where the poets left off, pondering the conundrum of this dual identity, taking the scientific measure of the intangible and inexplicable yearnings of the heart.

Dr. Phillip Shaver of the University of Denver is one of them. He conducted a study of 540 men and women between the ages of fifteen and eighty-two and found three distinct categories of romantic choice: Half his subjects felt secure in their partnerships; a quarter were "anxious clingers"; the remaining 25 percent would rather walk into a propeller than fall in love.

All these people had one thing in common: *Their attachments— or lack of them—were mirror images of how they related to their opposite-sex parent in early childhood.*

Dr. Shaver's findings were corroborated in a study by psychologist Carl Hindy. Insecure lovers, he told a reporter, "fail to develop stable expectations for love and affection in childhood, and grow up chronically anxious about what they fear will be a rejection from their partner."

The men in his study tended to have mothers who were not terribly loving or involved. The women, however, did have positive relationships with their mothers; it was their *fathers* who were emotionally distant or even hostile.

How romantic jitters were expressed, however, differed along gender lines. The men tended to be emotionally detached, whereas their female counterparts needed constant reassurance. These patterns were two sides of the same psychic coin: the dread of being unloved.

"People often instinctively repeat what they experienced in childhood, even if it was the worst thing in the world," says Dr. Marianne Goodman. But for women, she explains, the consequences are different:

> Women choose men like Dad because *it's what they know,* and if Dad was good, they're home free. But if Dad wasn't so good, if he wasn't emotionally present, they're in big trouble. Because, just as they did with their fathers, women tend to blame themselves when a relationship doesn't work out.

It is girls, more than boys, who are trained in childhood to make emotional connections and to form intimate attachments, as we saw in Part One. It is girls, more than boys, who are raised to believe that if an attachment falls apart, it is because they inherently lack the right romantic stuff.

Thus the role of the father in a woman's romantic choices is of incalculable importance, greater even than that of the mother. If a daughter was well fathered—that is, loved but given certain limits —her feeling of being valued as a *person* includes her confidence *as a lover.*

A well-fathered daughter will seek in her partnerships men who mirror the devoted father of childhood, avoiding partnerships that denigrate or compromise her. Having experienced the real thing when she was very young—and having been taught self-reliance— she settles for no less when she is an adult.

But if a woman did not have a loving, dependable father who could let her go when she was grown—*and if she has not examined the relationship*—she may remain emotionally tied to him. She runs the risk of being drawn again and again to men who reject her or who do not satisfy her emotionally or sexually. Alternatively she may recoil from love altogether. And always she will be haunted by the thought that she is essentially unlovable. Says sexuality authority and psychiatrist Avodah K. Offit,

> An appropriately warm and affectionate relationship with the father is the greatest basis for future warm and lasting relationships with men emotionally and sexually. I say this not by virtue of any statistic but by virtue of the absence of such relationships in most of the sexually unhappy women I've treated. I can't think of one who had a wondrous relationship with her father—except for those who did have such a relationship but lost it because of the early death of the father.

Duplicating the past in one's romantic choices—or in romantic or sexual aversion—is a dynamic the psychological community calls "the repetition compulsion." But women who love unwisely are not necessarily masochists. They do not repeat the past because they like the punishment; rather *they are trying to have one more shot at childhood, one more chance to rewrite their emotional histories.* Since that is an impossible task, they are frequently condemned to repeat it in their love lives—or lack of them.

In Part Four we will discuss what can be done about these self-defeating "habits of the heart," as journalist Daniel Goleman puts it, these no-win recapitulations of the past.

For now it's useful to explore how women feel about their fathers and how a daughter's family history is resurrected in her adult romantic and sexual behavior and choices.

Beginning with these questions:

Who is lucky in *paternal* love?

And—Catch-22—how is it that one daughter will seem to have a charmed relationship with her father *while her sibling may not,* as the sisters at the beginning of this chapter exemplified?

Family Systems: The Genesis of Romantic Patterns

As we know, the father-daughter relationship does not evolve in a vacuum. Rather, there are certain variables that can enhance or diminish it.

Birth Rank. Of all the perplexities of life, few are as confounding as the stunning range of attitudes and personalities to be found among children who share the same parents. Even the most well-meaning of mothers and fathers can reach the sobering conclusion that, try as they may, not all their children will feel equally loved and accepted.

For example, Adrienne, forty-two, is one of those rare people who are not tormented by ambivalence and self-doubt. A pediatrician with a large practice, she loves her work. She has been happily married for fifteen years to a man who fulfills her emotionally and sexually and who is an equal parent to their two well-adjusted children. She shakes off stress as though it were rain.

When I asked the secret of her serenity, confidence, and remarkable steadiness, her response was immediate:

> I had a terrific father. Don't get me wrong—my mother was also loving. But it's my dad who made me believe in myself. I remember my mom once telling me, "Don't act too smart—the boys won't like you." To which my father responded, "Hogwash—she'll get smarter boys."
>
> The two best lessons he ever gave me were these: "Don't ever be afraid to admit when you've made a mistake." The other lesson was "Don't hide from people; say what you feel.

Otherwise they'll have to guess—and they might guess wrong."

"So *that's* it," I said. "You and your siblings all had a wonderful daddy."

"Well," she slowly replied, "I certainly did. But if you asked my brothers and sisters, I'm not sure they'd agree. Even though we had the same father, we didn't experience him the same way. It's as though we all had different fathers."

Within the family one child's parental blessing can be another's curse. Some children seem to be like Adrienne—optimistic and self-assured—while their siblings are fearful or contorted by resentments.

Much of this unequal distribution of confidence has to do with birth rank. Indeed, in terms of how people behave, some researchers believe that birth order is as important as the luck of the parental draw.

If, for instance, you are a firstborn or only child, you are your parents' experiment—the first to feel their untried, undivided parental love or dismay.

Lacking older siblings, the oldest or only child identifies primarily with her parents, conforming to their ideals and demands, not the least reason being that she has no one with whom to share those demands. Since firstborns try to live up to the expectations of adults—teachers' as well as parents'—rather than of peers, they are likely to learn more and to bring home better report cards than younger siblings. Thus firstborns pave the way for younger siblings, setting the standards against which they are measured and measure themselves.

Middle children tend to be more gregarious and more dependent on the approval of peers than that of adults. For one thing they have the example of an older sibling—who has the credibility of generational sameness—to guide them in their decisions and to teach them the rules of the family road. An older sister who was grounded for a month for coming home late from a date, for instance, is a lesson not lost on her younger sister or brother.

At the same time younger children are buffered by birth order from their parents' sole concentration. Hence they are treated with more indulgence and are called upon less to take on responsibilities.

As a result middle and younger children identify with both parents *and* siblings. Because they are more loosely attached to their mothers and fathers—indeed, often feel like outsiders—they frequently have an easier time separating from them and a better sense of their own individuality. Consequently they are more able to take risks. A study of revolutionary scientific thinkers, such as Charles Darwin and Nicholas Copernicus, for example, found that most of them were middle children.

But it isn't just the daughter's birth rank that determines how well she and her father relate to one another; one also needs to consider the *father's own sibling experience.* And here, as Dr. Walter Toman, an authority on birth order, tells us, the child's *gender* must be factored into the sibling equation.

Let's say a father has two daughters and a son, the first- and thirdborns being girls. Let us also say that the father himself was the firstborn of several boys and has no sisters. Who among his children will get the nod of his special love?

At first it may be the firstborn girl; Daddy will identify most with her because *they share the same birth rank.* But once the boy is born, *he* may outrank his older sister; since the father has no experience with sisters, he feels more at ease with boys.

As for the third child, she may trail behind the other two in Daddy's devotion. This less well-loved, perhaps envious, daughter probably has no idea that her father's perceived favoritism toward her older brother and sister may have more to do with the fact that the father was one of several boys than with any flaw in the daughter herself.

What has all this to do with a daughter's later love life? Only this: *Sibling connections, or lack of them, become the foundation for her way of dealing with conflict in peer relationships.*

Just as children tend to repeat in their adult relationships their experience of their parents, so, too, do they often replicate their sibling ties. Even when they are explosive, these connections are what children *know*—a critical piece in their interpersonal training.

As one researcher put it, "siblings are often the first partners in life, the first 'marriages' where primary intimacy can be learned." Hence birth order, and whether or not one has siblings, affects not only our relationships with our parents, but it may also be at the root of many of our conflicts with our romantic partners.

According to Dr. Toman, "rank conflicts" occur when two

firstborns marry each other. Neither wants to give up their leadership position.

"Sex conflicts" erupt between partners who had no opposite-sex
siblings. They have trouble reading each other's signals. For a
woman who had no brothers, men are unquestionably "other,"
especially if her father was emotionally distant or if her parents
divorced. Such a woman, says Dr. Frank Pittman,

> will base her idea of a relationship on fantasies—Scarlett
> O'Hara and Rhett Butler, or Spencer Tracy and Katharine
> Hepburn. She'll have a distorted sense of the difference be-
> tween men and women. When you're in a situation where
> everyone is the same gender, that's when someone of the
> opposite sex becomes strange and foreign.

Peer conflicts occur in couples where both partners are only
children. The day-to-day give and take of sharing a life with someone of one's own generation is completely alien to them. As one
woman put it,

> I've always wondered what it feels like to have siblings, and I
> was musing about this one day with a friend who has three
> brothers, sort of fantasizing about how wonderful it would be
> to have a big brother I could lean on. My friend laughed and
> said, "Well, you could have had a big brother who beat you up
> or locked you in a closet." It never occurred to me.

Consequently only children are likely to look for a "parent"
rather than a "peer" in their romantic partnerships. If two only
children should become romantically linked, says Dr. Toman, they
have the poorest marital prognosis of any blend of birth ranks:
Neither is particularly eager to *be* the parent figure for the other,
nor to give up being the center of a "parent"/partner's life.

Among the couples least likely to experience rank and sex conflicts, says Dr. Toman, are these: First, a man who is the oldest
brother of sisters paired up with a woman who is the youngest
sister of brothers—the man is used to the senior position, and the
woman is used to being outranked by males. Another compatible
combination is an only child and a partner who has an opposite-
sex sibling.

While all this sounds terribly complicated, it is important in terms of how couples learn to tease out what are profound differences between them from what may simply be evidence of their disparate family histories.

For example, Amy, twenty-nine, is an only child who is married to a man who has four brothers and sisters. Initially the couple's vastly different childhoods created great strain between them. Says Amy,

> At first it was very hard for me to adjust to being part of my husband's family. He and I used to fight a lot because he thought I didn't like my in-laws. But then he realized that I just wasn't used to so large a family. When they all got together at Christmas, their sheer numbers and the noise level overwhelmed me. Now when we visit his family, he's learned to say, "Amy's taking a nap." He knows I need to take a book and hide somewhere. I need down time.

But birth rank is only one piece of what a woman brings to her relationships in and out of the family. Another is the role she may have had to adopt in her family of origin.

Roles. Children unwittingly are asked by their parents to play certain parts and often are not treated equally, in large measure because of the parents' unresolved childhood histories.

Take, for example, the scapegoat—a role that is *assigned* by a parent. Let's say a father had a younger sister who was favored and who in addition outdistanced him in school and elsewhere. He may unconsciously see in his daughter the despised sister. Thus he may "punish" his daughter for his sister's transgressions by denigrating the daughter's achievements. Another daughter, who does not resemble the privileged sister, might not stoke the fires of these ancient, subconscious vendettas.

How will the scapegoated daughter respond? She and her father will be emotionally bound together in conflicts or sullen silences.

What of the favored daughter? She may have earned her privileged status by default, perhaps because she evokes her father's happy memories of his adoring mother or sister. And while being Daddy's favorite may do wonders for her self-esteem, it may be a prize for which she may dearly pay in terms of her sister's jealousy.

The degree to which a parent has become a mature, "individuated" adult who has separated from his or her own parents is what Dr. Michael Kerr, an authority on family-systems theory, calls the "level of differentiation." Differentiated parents are able to treat their children equally—that is, tolerate individual tempos and personalities and allow their children to try out their beliefs within the safe arena of the family.

But parents who are undifferentiated see their children's opposing viewpoints as betrayals, if not sabotage. They project onto their children hidden emotional agendas and resentments from the past. These parents play favorites as a hedge against their own repressed feelings of unworthiness and insecurity, ensuring their children's emotional and psychological dependence on them rather than teaching them to depend on themselves.

Favoritism can also be caused by what psychologists call "splitting": Children often play out the unresolved "good" and "bad" feelings their parents have of themselves. The preferred child may be a reflection of the parents' good feelings about themselves; the black sheep may represent the parents' disavowed, unpleasant side.

The result, of course, is sibling rivalry, which often is a reflection of splitting. For instance a parent who dislikes one child may unconsciously allow him or her to be punished, sometimes brutally, by another—the punishing child may be expressing hostility that the parent feels but is unable to express. Thus the parent is inserting a lifelong wedge between them.

One has only to observe a family function, say, a wedding or Christmas dinner or Passover seder, to see the consequences of paternal favoritism and splitting—how firmly entrenched are our family roles, how obdurate our sibling grudges. The minute we gather together with our families of origin, all the old resentments and sarcasms, all the alliances and private jokes surface, as though the clock had stopped in childhood.

Moreover one has only to watch aging siblings scrap over the worthless pots and pans and scuffed furniture of a deceased parent's estate—like toddlers over toys—to see how desperate is the need to wrest some last, pathetic, tangible measure of their parent's devotion.

In all these ways siblings inherit their parents' unresolved rancor. Culpability for their rivalry needs to be placed where it belongs—at the feet of the parent who unevenly doles out his or her love. As Dr. Stephen P. Bank tells us, that rivalry is "part of a fabric which was woven *for* the siblings, not just *by* the siblings."

Of such stuff are family triangles made.

Triangling. As we know from family-systems theory, children are often drafted by their parents to play certain roles for another reason: to reduce marital tension. As long as the kids are wrangling, parents do not have to examine their own marital conflicts. Rather they farm them out, concentrating, say, on a "problem" child or vying for the loyalty of a "favored" child.

Indeed it is a daughter's perceived mandate to divide her loyalty that is one of the most common sources of father-daughter animosity. She may feel duty-bound to side with her mother when her parents argue and to view her father as the villain in the marital piece. And in loyally disliking her father, she may *barely notice* that all the while her mother is constantly trying to placate her father. Thus the daughter is exploited by her mother in this triangular way.

But sometimes marital discord gets played out between *mother* and daughter, with father doing the exploiting. Let us say that a daughter is extremely close to her doting father and perceives her mother as a domineering nag. In this case the daughter sympathizes with the beleaguered father and constantly quarrels with the mother; father mollifies mother, confides in the daughter, and the daughter takes the rap.

In both cases the unhappy marriage remains intact, and the daughter is left with its punishing aftermath—estrangement from one of her parents.

When daughters are asked to play these roles—adversary or ally—they stabilize the family by sacrificing their own needs and identities. They have no choice but to distort themselves in order to become that which *will* please their parents, on whom they are utterly dependent.

A daughter who is the unwitting repository of her parents' unresolved childhoods and marital unhappiness has, in a sense, two masters. In her efforts to please them both she must be one person to her mother, another to her father.

The result is that she has within her two voices—two false selves—each of which "answers" to her parents. And when she is grown, these voices, rather than her own, may resonate in all her attachments.

She may behave one way toward women, another toward men.

And in her romantic pairings she either may react to her partner exactly as she did toward her father, or exactly as her *mother*

did. Or she may alternate, first one way, then another, depending
on the circumstances and her stress level.

These warring voices sometimes resemble a telephone party
line; sorting them out will be the focus of chapters 16 and 17.

Temperament. Finally we come to the child herself—the inherent qualities she brings to the father-daughter bond.

It isn't easy trying to figure out how much of our behavior is
innate and how much was shaped by the roles we were forced to
adopt in childhood. For if a parent clearly dislikes *who* a child
uniquely is, it will have everything to do with *how* she is.

Indeed sometimes it takes the assistance of a therapist to sort
out this gridlock of emotional alliances—to help us recognize the
person we had to be in order to survive in the family and to find
our true self, the person we were at birth, before we had to make
so many bargains.

A child's temperament is an extremely important wild card in
how children *perceive* parental favoritism. The way we process information may be influenced by our genetic makeup.

According to recent research there are three core temperamental qualities that change little over one's life; anxiety level, friendli-
ness, and "eagerness for novel experiences." Other qualities, such
as morale and feelings of satisfaction or isolation, are often *reactive,* varying according to external events and the people involved.
As Dr. Paul T. Costa, Jr., who has conducted studies on personality, explained to a reporter, "What does change is one's role in
life, and the situations that influence your temporary behavior one
way or another."

Yet there are those children who, amazingly, seem to be impervious to harmful parental influences—who, because of a certain
constitutional sturdiness, salvage their sanity and humanity and
identities *despite* parents who are psychotic, brutal, and/or chemi-
cally addicted. These "resilient," "transcendent," "indomitable,"
or "invulnerable" children, as they are variously called, are astonishingly healthy in the face of family disarray.

What spells the difference between a child who is bruised or
even destroyed by such chaos and the child who thrives in the
midst of it? Is this luck? Researchers think not—except for the
"luck" of being innately cheerful and sociable in the first place.
Some researchers believe that because invulnerable children often
are blessed with winning ways, they elicit from their parents whatever love they have to give.

According to authorities on invulnerability, these children tend to share certain characteristics:

First, in infancy they had one person—an aunt or grandparent or even a parent, before troubles blotted out the ability to love and nurture her or his children—who gave them an early acquaintance with tenderness and devotion.

Second, resilient children are extraordinarily creative. They seem to invent themselves; through their own imaginativeness or artistic self-expression, they cushion themselves from their tumultuous surroundings in a kind of psychological damage control.

A third trait these children have in common is that they know where to go for help. They are not afraid to turn to others for a reassuring hug, or for advice, or simply for peaceful, friendly respite.

Finally hardships imbue resilient children with a psychic hardiness. They see their deprivations as a series of challenges to be overcome, which spur them to take on even greater challenges.

This hardiness was observed in a study of four hundred famous twentieth-century men and women, over 75 percent of whom experienced grinding poverty, parental rejection and divorce, or physical handicaps in childhood. Resilient children, according to Dr. E. James Anthony, are simply "good copers," whose greatest quality is their extraordinary capacity for self-repair. In short, when handed life's lemons, they make lemonade.

None of which recommends a childhood of gothic horrors as a character-building parental tool. For these survivors pay a huge price for their childhoods: Their very temperamental capacity for distancing themselves from adversity may *also* sabotage their capacity for intimacy. They may have enormous difficulty forming romantic attachments in adulthood and pull back when anyone gets too close.

Sad to say, resilient children are extremely rare. Most children, when faced with unrelieved parental cruelty or unfair treatment, are unable to hang on to their true selves—*especially daughters, who by virtue of gender alone are conditioned to be defined, and to define themselves, in terms of their attachments.*

Thus a good temperamental fit between father and daughter is a *crucial* variable in their relationship, because the daughter who feels accepted and loved by her father does not have to develop a false self for him. When there is a good fit, the daughter has an enormous psychological advantage.

Says Monique, forty,

> I was always an oddball. In the 1950s girls were just supposed to be stupid and submissive and quiet and decorative, and I was none of those things. I was interested in science and sports, which was totally beyond the social pale. Luckily my father was exactly the same way. We did all kinds of things together, including rewiring the house. It didn't seem to bother him in the slightest that this was "boy stuff." We just had a perfect personality match-up.

Childhood is the time when daughters learn both how to *be* in a family and how to *be* in an intimate relationship with a man. Daughters are shaped by the first man in their lives. Yet Daddy is not the same person to all his daughters. Sisters who share the same father will get different versions of him, depending on their temperaments and the roles they are asked to play.

That role-playing will be the template for how daughters behave in their romantic attachments when they grow up.

Coming of Age

There is no more terrifying or exhilarating event in a young woman's life than the day she moves out of her parents' house into her own, crossing the threshold of her adult life. This is the moment when she will discover how well she has been prepared for the world of adult work and love. And if her father was affectionate and dependable, escorting her through the seasons of her life with encouragement and stability and flexibility, she will be able to chart her course well in both areas.

But if she was not well fathered—if she was too indulged or neglected or mistreated—while she may navigate well in her job, when it comes to healthy romantic love, she will be on uncharted territory. She will bring to her adult life *two* identities—the woman who functions in the public world and the child within who surfaces in private matters of the heart.

The otherwise achieving, competent woman may be eclipsed by the girl when she falls in love. Unconscious memories of Dad will beckon her back to her childlike expectations and fears and hopes

—even her passions—as the studies mentioned at the beginning of this chapter illustrate.

Yet there is something vaguely disquieting about the notion that the dictates of the heart can be so scientifically computed, so tidily pigeonholed in psychological terms, as though one's difficult childhood were a romantic death sentence. Many people yearn for the perfect partner to make it all better, to banish the wretchedness of loneliness and lovelessness.

The hungry heart wants to believe in miracles, just as we did when we were children. And so we wonder: Is there no place for love songs? For dreams? For wishing on stars?

These are the questions I posed to Dr. Nina Evans, a psychiatrist. I wanted to know if she could explain the phenomenon of "love at first sight"—specifically, to explain what's happening on an enchanted evening when two strangers lock eyes across a crowded room, and, without exchanging a word, feel a powerful electricity between them. In such situations how can one point a Freudian finger at early childhood as the agent of desire?

Dr. Evans replied,

> People have experiences in childhood that are triggers in later life—experiences that determine what's good and what's bad, what's pleasurable and what's not. We don't react to strangers in a vacuum. We bring something to the party. We respond to the *familiar*. We're attracted by someone's body posture, speed of speech, voice tone, gestures, and facial expressions, components of attraction that were conditioned by the past. So if a woman sees someone across a crowded room who has characteristics that are very similar to her father's when she was a child, it's likely to elicit a fairly strong emotional response.

To illustrate the point, Dr. Evans described the case of a woman who told her, "Everything I've had to learn as an adult I've done well at. But what I apparently learned as a child was how to pick men, and I always manage to find the ones who are rotten to me. This can't be chance alone; it doesn't happen to any of my friends in the same social situation."

In her therapy the woman began to find the commonalities in the men to whom she was attracted. Says Dr. Evans,

All these men had a specific set of qualities: They made a lot of eye contact and stood very close to her; they were flattering and confiding; they swept her off her feet and then disappeared. She was responding to a very early, conditioned set of triggers.

So. Do daughters "marry" their fathers, as Freud believed? Researchers have delved into this oft-repeated maxim and have come up with a variety of conclusions:

Sociologist A. Aron, for example, did a study comparing the characteristics of people's parents with those of their partners and found that most men and women tend to select partners who are similar to their mothers. This finding may be due to the fact that our first lessons in love are learned from our mothers, reinforced by their greater involvement—relative to fathers—in our lives.

But family therapist Augustus Y. Napier, in his own practice and research, found that this tendency was truer for men than for women.

So I put the question of the father factor in female attraction to Dr. E. Mavis Hetherington because of her pioneering, exhaustive studies about the role fathers have in the shaping of daughters' attitudes toward men. She replied,

The old psychoanalytic theory that women keep seeking to reenact their relationship with their fathers in their relationships with men holds true only for girls from one-parent families. They had little or no contact with their fathers and have a very unrealistic image of men. Whereas girls from intact families work through their relationships with their fathers as they go through adolescence and adulthood. Even if Dad was a "no-good son of a bitch," at least he was real. And you can deal with reality much more than you can deal with abstraction.

Which returns us to the major premise of this book—that fathers have as great an impact, if not greater, on their daughters' romantic choices *by their emotional absence* as by their presence.

Some of the women in my own research sample were indeed drawn to men like their mothers. Some were drawn to men like their fathers. And some were attracted to a combination of the two. *It all depended on whether or not Daddy was around and how he behaved when he was around, when they were growing up.*

This, then, is what fantasies, and dreams, are for: to give us, in myth, what some of our fathers could not give us in fact.

Seasons of Love

For a large percentage of the women I interviewed, their relationships with men changed as they aged. For some these changes occurred within one ongoing relationship—that is, both the women and their partners evolved along similar lines simultaneously, and the relationships deepened over time.

Other women found that as they matured and evolved, their choices of men improved dramatically. These women simply weren't the same people at thirty-five or forty-five that they had been at twenty-one. Consequently many of them changed partners at different times in their growth, each partnership healthier than the last.

An important variable in these patterns was the sequence in which the women resolved their feelings about their parents. Most —not all—of the women took far longer sorting out their relationships with their fathers than their relationships with their mothers. After all, in general, mothers are not abstractions in their daughters' lives; hence dealing with Mom is a relatively easier task, which doesn't mean it is *easy.*

By the age of thirty-five or so, however, most women have either examined or resolved many of their conflicts with their mothers. This is not true of their relationships with their distant or remote or abusive or divorced fathers.

Part of the reason for this delayed resolution has to do with the difficulty many daughters have in understanding what is often essentially only hypothetical: the healthy, loving, mature male-female relationship. For many of these women, men are a mystery because *fathers* are a mystery, and the women's romantic relationships are frequently driven more by fantasy than by reality.

Patterns in Intimacy

The process of demystifying men begins with recognizing the unhappy patterns in our romantic choices—our reasons for choosing the partners we do or our reasons for choosing *not* to have a partner. Specifically we need to examine what keeps us from achieving healthy intimacy or from feeling good about ourselves without it.

The issue to be explored is not harmonious singleness, or harmonious living with someone, or harmonious marriage. Rather, it is to find out why we may be unhappy in each of these three areas and how that unhappiness may be a reflection of our unresolved relationships with our fathers, our unfinished filial business.

Failure to separate emotionally from Daddy—or failure to have attached to him in the first place—lingers in women who *repeat* their unhappy romantic patterns: being repelled by intimacy, or getting involved with partners who are married, or who are unresponsive, or chronically unfaithful, or cruel, or who disappear.

The unresolved father-daughter relationship lingers, too, in women's *sexual* patterns: inability to achieve orgasm; revulsion toward sex; nymphomania; inhibited sexual desire; aversion to all sex, including masturbation.

Such repeated behavior becomes a vicious, and pernicious, cycle, reinforcing a woman's insecurity. It is a *reaction* to an earlier emotional wound, rather than a healthy choice. As Dr. Offit has written,

> The way a parent handles emotional attachment and separation will affect what turns a person on or off in later life. Supreme sexual exaltation through loving marital dependence can hardly be a consequence of having been subtly or overtly frightened, neglected, punished, berated, ignored, or otherwise abused.

The unresolved father-daughter relationship is reflected in the following areas of romantic choice:

Staying Single. One way to avoid addressing our feelings about our fathers, to say nothing of our ambivalences about men, obviously, is to gallop away from any romantic commitment. Such avoidance can take many forms: celibacy, platonic friendships with men, working so hard that one doesn't have time for love.

Another way to stay aloof from intimacy is to cling to romantic idealism—to hold out for the "perfect" man.

Many of the women I interviewed who are still single in their thirties and forties are following the mandates of the baby-boom generation, trying to establish their careers and bankrolling their ability to live without a man. Culturally, at least, they don't need to be defined by a romantic attachment. And in fact it's extremely healthy for them to take as long a hiatus from matrimonial commitment as they need to allow the girl within them to grow up.

Emotionally, however, many of these women feel uneasy about their solitary lives and express a longing for a romantic commitment—it's just that, as they often put it, "There aren't any good men out there." But, as we shall see, many of these women, in holding out for the "right" man, may simply not be ready for *any* man.

Instead they cling to the fantasy of the perfect lover and partner, the unblemished hero who will have all the answers and provide all the protection that their fathers may not have provided—or, alternatively, fathers who *did* provide it but could not let their daughters go.

Living Together. Some women split the connubial difference by living with a man without the arguable benefits of matrimony. Numerous studies have pointed to the fact that whether or not a couple lives together prior to marriage has little bearing on how a marriage will fare. As we know, cohabitation is quite common: Nearly half of people in their early thirties have at one time lived with a member of the opposite sex. But such informal living arrangements don't seem to guarantee that the relationship will be strengthened by marriage.

Withal, many women prefer to stay in the twilight zone of uncommitted commitment. That way they can keep their psychic bags packed. They can be dependent *and* independent, rather than *interdependent* in the best romantic and psychological sense.

Marriage. Healthy intimacy and interdependence can be avoided in marriage as well. For many women *something happens* when wedding vows are exchanged. Now the couple is a legal, social, and psychological *family*—to which all the old dependencies, ambivalences, and survival mechanisms of the *original* family are transferred.

When a woman becomes a wife, often it is as though someone threw a switch: Suddenly—and unconsciously—the spouse becomes the father of childhood, and *she becomes the child she was,* the false self of old. Sometimes marriage feels vaguely incestuous.

As long as a woman feels conflicted about Daddy and about men, and as long as she's playing an outdated role, she cannot be *real* to a spouse, nor can she perceive him as real. When our false selves are in the new family—and in the marital bed—it's difficult to figure out *what* we feel, especially if those feelings are tangled in the past.

In all these ways women often operate on romantic automatic pilot, continuing in adulthood to feel and behave toward men as they once felt and behaved toward their fathers. And unless they have the courage to examine how those early attachments are being played out in their romantic lives, they may live in fantasy or anger, or a combination of both.

Both romantic idealism and perpetual rage keep us childlike: As long as *this* man—*any* man—doesn't measure up, I don't have to trust. As long as he is so flawed, I can keep my defenses up. As long as he is less than I want, I don't have to examine either why I allow myself to stay in an unrewarding relationship *or why I cannot ever let my guard down with anyone.*

In recognizing self-destructive patterns there are psychological riches—clues as to why we compulsively repeat the past—that enable us to begin changing the present and the future. If we are to change these patterns, we must first recognize where they first take shape: in childhood.

It is in our romantic patterns today that we can begin to unlock the secrets of the past. Because of her early conditioning a woman may fall into one of the following categories:

• *The favored daughter*—who looks for men who either cannot measure up to her glorified father or who *do* measure up, giving her the same special, indulgent treatment her father once did and requiring little in return

• *The good daughter*—who, in her desperation to find and keep a partner, gives more than she receives, because she believes she cannot survive without a man

• *The competitive daughter*—who feels most alive when matching wits with her partner or who only knows one way to relate to men—through hostility—or who may use her demanding career as a way of avoiding the whole issue of intimacy

- *The fearful daughter*—who is terrified of men and becomes either dominated or brutalized by her partner, or is frightened away from the romantic field altogether
- *The maverick daughter*—who is a free spirit, able either to be at ease with her unusual, even eccentric self, or else is derailed in childhood and angrily punches her way through self-destructive adulthood

Sometimes these categories overlap—that is, some women behave one way with one man, another way with a different partner. Some women try on different behavioral styles—perhaps a Good Daughter early in life, a Competitor later on—as they get closer to healthier identities and healthier reasons to remain unattached or to become attached.

These categories include qualities that are both endearing and endangering. The point in reading about them is to figure out which is which, to discover which corroborate our good experience of our fathers and which the bad, which reflect our true selves and which the false.

By examining the habits of her heart a woman can begin tracing them back to their source: the lessons of love she learned from her father and whether or not they enabled her to separate from him and find her own romantic and sexual identity.

The purpose of the next five chapters is to help the reader find herself so she can begin to understand how her relationship with her father colored her romantic choices. By courageously examining those choices, she can begin to free herself from the destructive ones.

11

The Favored Daughter

My father and I have always had a very special bond; it's like I'm almost part of him. I can remember thinking when I was a little girl, "I'm even closer to Daddy than Mommy is because he and I are related by blood." I identified so strongly with him that when he got reading glasses, I pretended I was nearsighted so that I could get glasses too. We're just kindred souls. When he dies, I don't know what I'll do. I worry about it a lot.

—MAGGIE, THIRTY-SIX

Some women seem to walk through life as though on a nobleman's cloak. They carry themselves with a certain enviable presence—a sense that nothing bad will ever happen to them, a confidence born of knowing exactly where they stand in the world.

More than anything they exude an air of *entitlement*—the expectation that life will go smoothly for them, that they deserve to be treated well, and that they will always get exactly what they want.

It is an expectation that is bred in the bone: For these are the daughters who are the clear favorites of their fathers—women who grew up fiercely protected, lavishly praised, the paths before them plucked clean of any impediments. From their earliest years these daughters are aware that they, more than their siblings, are chosen children and can do no wrong.

The daughter who is adored by her father may see a side of him that her brothers don't, experiencing his particular tenderness and safekeeping. With a girl a father can let down his guard and express his nurturing, feminine side, free of the mandate to produce a "real man," relieved not to have to adhere to a certain emotional austerity.

And to be *preferred* by her father over her sisters gives the favored daughter the feeling that she is somehow charmed—that she is the queen of the prom, while they are merely members of her court.

Heady stuff. Being singled out for Daddy's special love can make a daughter feel terrific about herself. After all, no one *hates* winning a popularity contest. But paradoxically it can simultaneously have the opposite effect.

This is not to suggest that fathers should disguise the love they feel for their daughters. What is being discussed here is favoritism that can, whether you're a girl or a boy, exact a high cost within the family: If you're a clear winner, then someone else is a clear loser, which does nothing to promote domestic tranquillity, as we saw in the last chapter. And if you win the favoritism of the *opposite-sex parent,* that victory has important implications for your future heterosexual attachments.

The daughter who "wins" her father in some ways also loses — for paternal favoritism toward daughters is quite different from maternal favoritism toward sons. As Freud observed, "A man who has been the indisputable favorite of his mother keeps for life the feeling of a conqueror, that confidence of success that often induces real success."

But to be a daughter who is anointed by her father's partiality can be another matter altogether, for this is a gift that can at the same time be a debt.

To rework Freud, a woman who has been the indisputable favorite of her father keeps for life the feeling of being a privileged character, a privilege that is often the quid pro quo for her dependence upon him.

The difference in the effects of parental favoritism toward opposite-sex children can be traced, in part, to how boys and girls are raised—the former to be independent, the latter to be defined by relationships. Girls aren't supposed to be conquerors—boys are. Hence the privilege that favored daughters enjoy frequently feels as though it is at someone else's expense.

It all has to do with what psychologists call the "locus of control," or "ownership," and how it often differs for men and for women. In general, men are encouraged in the family and in the culture to claim their own success—to stand out in a crowd, to take total credit for their achievements. Whereas women are trained to *share* their glory—to be self-effacing and say such things as "I couldn't have done it without help." This inability to own their achievements—because it is so isolating from attachments—is the heart of women's classic fear of success. Consequently, when good things happen to favored sons, they usually feel they deserve it; when good things happen to favored daughters, they frequently feel they got lucky.

As a result being Daddy's darling girl can be a mixed blessing. To begin with, it sets a dangerous precedent.

Ginny, thirty-eight, vividly remembers the exact moment she became aware that her father's exalted opinion of her was not shared by the rest of the world. She says,

> The first time I went to a party, no one but my date asked me to dance. I can't tell you what a shock it was not to be the belle of the ball. I was devastated to discover that not everyone thought I was as great as my dad said I was. It took me a long, long time to get over the expectation that everybody would automatically love me.

Unlike other categories of daughters—women who try to wrest from their attachments the love they didn't get from their fathers growing up—favored daughters are constantly trying to recapture in their public and/or private lives their special status.

There are only two problems: First, in order to get an adult version of Daddy's love, *favored daughters often have to remain girlish,* because that's how they got to be Daddy's favorite in the first place. And if it worked once, it *ought* to work again. Second, these daughters are frequently uneasy about winning Daddy's favor. Since girls aren't conditioned for the isolation of being the best—especially if it causes someone else to be unhappy—they often feel that they will be punished for it.

The Making of a Favored Daughter

When a daughter is accustomed to having love come her way through no effort of her own, she is unlikely to be prepared for the realities of life. The jewel in Daddy's crown is trained for royal treatment, not for disappointment. She is groomed for receiving affection, not necessarily for giving it.

This is the essence of narcissism—the absolute certainty that approval and adoration are one's due.

But there is in the narcissist a countermelody of doubt; maybe I don't *really deserve it.* Since the advantages the favored daughter enjoys may be more a matter of fortune than merit, of parental largesse than personal grit, she may have the unsettling awareness that her special status in life requires that she put on an act. There is a small voice within her that says, "Keep dancing, keep smiling, keep performing, because the minute you stop, Daddy will take all his love away."

These twin messages—*I'm entitled* and *I'm a fraud*—fuse in the favored daughter.

Part of her special treatment has to do with the luck of the sibling mix. The majority of favored daughters I interviewed are firstborn children with younger brothers. Being first up in the junior rank of the family—and being either the only girl or having a younger sister who trails a distant third behind the brother—allows them to corner the market of paternal devotion.

A girl is no threat to a father's authority; nor does she challenge a brother's traditional gender role, because a father's expectations of him are different, as was discussed in Chapter 1. Thus the favored daughter tends to have both seniority and no serious competition for her place of honor.

Appealing to Daddy is easy for little girls. They sense early on the particular power they have over their adoring fathers, employing a weapon unique to their gender: flirtation. The swiftest path to Daddy's heart is to wriggle, to giggle, to flatter, to cajole—*to be all girl* so that Daddy will love and protect them and also let them have their way. When Daddy says no, they stroke his face or flash a beguiling smile, and in no time Daddy finds himself saying yes, even if it contradicts his wife's wishes.

Such ploys do not come from nowhere. Unlike little boys, most little girls are not encouraged by their fathers to debate a point, to stand up to pressure, to openly compete. Moreover, as we know, it is fathers more than mothers who flirt with opposite-sex children. Favored daughters are often molded by their fathers into lovely ornaments, their very identities predicated on a certain delicacy, like fine china, requiring special handling. And what daughters glean from this royal treatment is the value of manipulation.

Pretty as a Picture. If these daughters are sometimes vain and self-serving, grasping and cloying, the fault is not entirely theirs. Favored daughters tend to be physically attractive, an important ingredient in their fathers' attentiveness—and, for that matter, the world's. Pretty little girls get special treatment from *everyone.* Studies show that beautiful children tend to have more attention heaped upon them than plain children—including by teachers, who often excuse the naughtiness of the comely.

Female beauty has always been not just a bonus but a *value.* Consider this bit of advice from a popular turn-of-the-century beauty manual:

> As the girl ripens into the woman, every experience in life teaches her that her share of its successes and pleasures will be in proportion to her own ability to win favor, to please, and that *the first and most potent influence is physical beauty.* [Emphasis added.]

While such words may rankle in feminist quarters today, the profitability of such films as *Pretty Woman* and of diet and beauty books targeted for women remains enormous, de facto evidence of the cultural clout of female pulchritude, especially of the *youthful* variety.

With fathers how a daughter looks still counts, and daughters know it. As long as they're Daddy's manicured pet, they'll never have to worry their pretty little head about a thing.

It is an unspoken social contract between father and daughter, this mutual admiration society, and daughters are well aware of the bylaws: Idealize Daddy and you'll get your heart's desire. Argue with Daddy and you'll feel his temper or, at the very least, the withdrawal of his favoritism.

Not surprisingly researchers have found that girls whose parents are indulgent and loving to the point of suffocation tend to be more dependent than children whose parents are strict. The daughter who was not given any frustration to tolerate—whose every deed was punctuated with the words "You're so *cute*"—learns to live by her winsome wits, and to get by on a smile.

But there's more to the egotism of the favored daughter than simply her artfulness; another strand of her psychological wiring has to do with the addictiveness of unconditional love.

Highs and Lows. Happiness researchers—psychologists who study who is happy, who isn't, and why—have turned up some interesting findings. Ed Diener and his colleagues at the University of Illinois, for example, have discovered that there's a big difference between happiness and elation; the variables are *frequency* and *intensity*.

Ecstasy is an exhilarating emotion, all the more thrilling because of its rarity. If, for instance, you find a fifty-dollar bill lying on the street, you are likely to jump for joy because not only wasn't it expected but also it's not something that happens very often; it doesn't really change your life or how you feel about yourself.

Were you to find a fifty-dollar bill every day of your life, however, in time the windfall would begin to lose its zing. Soon you would *expect* to find it. It is the "habituation" of intense good feelings that makes their opposite so painful, like the sudden withdrawal of drugs.

Children who are accustomed to being treated well internalize that treatment and have a permanent sense of well-being. But children whose every need is instantly gratified and who are constantly praised to the skies do not have the same sense of well-being; rather they may feel despair or rage when that gratification is withheld, or when everyone doesn't glorify them in the same way.

Many favored daughters are unaccustomed to being criticized. Rather *they're used to being seen as perfect*—every drawing in school worthy of the Prix de Rome, every composition a candidate for the Nobel prize, every pose worthy of a *Vogue* cover. These daughters are programmed for continual encomiums and automatic acceptance, and when they don't get it, they're stunned.

People who are used to constant attention and flattery become inured to the merely pleasant and become "peak seekers." They expect the highs, and when their unrealistic goals or expectations are not met, they are not simply disappointed, they are devastated.

Thus "happiness" alone does not guarantee mental health and well-being. A tempering dose of disappointment—an occasional taste of frustration and learning that you do recover from it—goes a long way toward producing long-term contentment. Indeed the ability to ride out the bad times without feeling doomed is essential to survival. When happiness is not taken for granted, and when one is acquainted with its opposite, it is more easily savored and has more lasting effects.

Hence the father who extorts from the favored daughter this

unspoken promise—"Stay true to me, be my loyal *little* girl, and I'll give you the world"—is setting her up for failure.

Daddy's Little Girl

The operative word, of course, is *little.* For as long as a daughter is petite and pink and pretty, she can be her father's toy, the object of his unabashed affection. But as soon as she begins to grow up into womanhood, her privileged status is on the line.

Says Dr. Marianne Goodman,

> If you're Daddy's little girl, it means you cannot be Daddy's grown-up girl, because that makes you too much like his mistress. That means you have to keep yourself small. Your development could make you attractive to Daddy in a threatening way.

If, in addition to becoming womanly, the daughter should begin to assert herself, she threatens Daddy's authority as well. As long as she's not a sexual creature with a mind of her own, however, it's quite easy for her father to accept her and love her to bits.

Consequently the favored daughter may find a variety of ways to *stunt* her development.

One way the favored daughter keeps herself small is by making Daddy her hero, the only man who *really* understands her, the only man whose opinion really counts. She idealizes her father long after he—and she—should have been dethroned. Such hero worship stands in the way of her forming healthy heterosexual attachments later on. Says psychologist Louise J. Kaplan,

> A certain amount of idealization is normal in childhood. Children feel less if they think their parents are less. During adolescence there's a huge challenge of this idealization—and the more a daughter is attached to her father in an infantile way, the more difficult it's going to be for her to establish relationships in her own generation.

Another way for a favored daughter to remain unthreatening is to attach herself to a man who, like Daddy, will keep her dependent. The favored daughter may marry a man whom Daddy takes into his business; or she may join forces with a man who passes paternal muster—agreeable and passive, but no real challenge to the father's sway over his daughter or to their special bond.

A third way to remain Daddy's little girl is to be his psychological bride, to adhere to a kind of emotional, sometimes actual, chastity—failing to find sexual fulfillment in her romantic attachments and channeling all her erotic energies into her career.

In all these ways the favored daughter—unless she examines the high cost of her privileged position and resolves her relationship with her father—may encounter difficulties in her romantic attachments when she is grown. Until that resolution takes place, she may find herself falling into one of two roles: the Princess or the Heroine.

The Princess

Everyone knows that no woman has it all—except, or so it appears, for women like Alexandra.

The tall, lithe, graceful brunette greets me at the door of her San Francisco house and extends a slim, welcoming hand. "How nice to meet you," she graciously says in a voice so seductively hushed that I must lean closer to hear her clearly. Gazing at her, I am reminded of Audrey Hepburn in *Breakfast at Tiffany's,* and suddenly I feel too big, too loud by half.

Alexandra, forty, ushers me into the living room of her Victorian mansion, regally perched atop Russian Hill. The symbolism of having the city and the Bay—if not the world—at her feet is not lost on me. But, I quickly discover, it is not at all how she sees herself.

Alexandra pours tea from the silver service on the table before us, sinks into a down-filled couch, and describes the dark side of her gilded existence:

> I was the apple of my father's eye, and I'm living a life he orchestrated. My husband, the son of my father's best friend, is successful. He buys me anything I want; we travel all over the world. And it's not enough. We fight all the time. He can't understand why I'm not happy. Every time I try to tell him that I wish he'd pay more attention to me, he just walks out of the room, because he's heard it so often. Just last night he

screamed, "I'm not your father!" I try not to think about it too much. If I don't raise an issue with him, life is wonderful.

Women like Alexandra seem to their envious acquaintances to be shallow, self-centered, and parasitic, as indeed some of them are. With so little asked of them growing up—except of course to be decorative and never to complain—and no real survival skills, it's not surprising that many of them are hungry for constant attention, and at the same time afraid to examine why.

Many of these daughters consciously set out to find someone just like Daddy. They tend to be drawn to powerful, ambitious men whose success reflects well on them and who will protect them and keep them in the pampered style to which their fathers accustomed them.

Often, however, those expectations are sown not just by Daddy but by Mommy as well. As the joke goes, "A princess has always had at least two in help—her mother and her father."

Many of the princesses I interviewed enjoy their fathers' permissiveness with little interference from Mom. That's because there's something in it for *both* parents. In babying the daughter and discouraging her self-sufficiency, they ensure her permanent allegiance to and dependence on them.

In these cases the mother may underscore that dependence by giving the daughter tips on the care and feeding of a man: "Don't try to 'wear the pants'; always let a man win at tennis; agree with everything a man says, and then do what you want; make him feel that he's in charge, but we"—*wink, wink*—"know better."

As one woman told me,

> I was my father's favorite child because I was naturally cheerful and cute. I was also extremely bright, but I quickly learned to keep my scholastic record a secret. That's because a woman who's accomplished is not my dad's idea of what a woman should be. He thinks a woman should be beautiful and loving and live her life in service to a man. My mother believed the same things. She always said, "Don't act too smart, or the boys won't like you. You just have to cotton up to them; they always like a pretty face and a smile." My father never disagreed with that. I got the picture. In my marriage I play an ingratiating role. I know where my bread is buttered.

Such daughters have little incentive to separate from either parent, to be independent strivers. Rather they are trained to follow in their mothers' footsteps, to marry someone just like Dad and behave just like Mom.

And so they often take the marital route to "independence." Most of the princesses I interviewed married in their early twenties, moving from their fathers' house to the marital abode, in the guise of separation—but *emotionally* they lived on with their fathers.

Having sacrificed their independence and their adult identities to maintain the uninterrupted flow of their parents' indulgence, *these daughters want something in return.* They expect the men in their lives to treat them as privileged characters, just as their parents did.

Thus some princesses run the risk of getting involved with men who are as narcissistic as they are. These women read their partners' seductiveness—and, in some cases, pathological charm—as adoration. Because of their self-involvement, these women are able to tolerate their partners' infidelities for a time because they cannot imagine losing the romantic sweepstakes.

One woman, an only child, told me that she remained for fifteen years in a marriage to such a man—also an only child. After each of his extramarital indiscretions he would be profuse in his apologies, abject in his guilt. Each time she would forgive him. Eventually she reached the point where she was able to see how skewed her perceptions were. She says,

> I went into therapy to figure out why I stayed with this guy so long. I realized that my father, whom I adored, had never scolded me, never punished me. He thought I was perfect; so did my mother. What I discovered about myself was that I simply assumed I would be able to tame my husband because I was so wonderful. I bought all his promises of reform because he was so overwhelming in his contrition. He once told me that every time I spoke, he "felt immortal." His lovemaking was incredible, especially when we were making up. So it became easy to ignore the fact that at dinner parties his hand would wander up another woman's skirt.

When the princess's partner cannot or does not meet the expectation for which her parents trained her—that she will be utterly adored no matter *what* she does, that she is too precious ever to be rebuked—these daughters feel, at best, confused and, at worst, betrayed. No one ever told them that the rules get changed in the outside world.

Winning Daddy, Losing Mommy. Sometimes, however, being Daddy's princess is a Pyrrhic victory—for being Daddy's favorite often means that you *aren't Mommy's.* Many favored daughters are consorts to their fathers, stand-ins for their mothers because the parents' marriage is troubled. The mother perceives the daughter as her rival and retreats from the daughter. Daddy, taking advantage of the situation, becomes the daughter's best pal and rousing champion.

The princess's estrangement from her mother can result in the compromising of the daughter's female identity. Some adoring fathers disparage their wives and draw their beloved daughters into a mutual trashing of Mom. Such sharing by father and daughter of malevolent confidences is at once seductive and shattering, because the daughter's bridge to Mommy—and to all women—may be burned. In denigrating Mom she is in a real sense denigrating herself.

In these cases the princess is stranded in an intimacy with her father that, even without overt sexuality, is nevertheless too close for comfort. How will she manage? She may have little choice but to identify *solely* with Daddy.

In her studies of the children of divorce, which compared these children with those from intact homes, Dr. E. Mavis Hetherington found a subgroup she called "opportunistic-competent," who seemed to function extremely well—they were popular, did well in school, and were energetic and curious. But the girls, more than the boys, tended to share a characteristic not found in other children from divorced families: They were manipulative and egocentric and tended to play parents off against each other to get what they wanted.

Some girls from intact homes where there was a great deal of conflict also had these characteristics. They were more reactive to that conflict than were boys and usually had one parent to whom they were unusually close and one parent by whom they felt rejected. These children tended to seek out adults in power, such as teachers and parents, and to ingratiate themselves to those people, but their friendships with peers were short-lived.

Because princesses tend to identify with their fathers, some do very well in their careers. Since they tend to be more comfortable with men than with women, they often surround themselves with men at work or at play, finding male mentors.

It is not men these daughters fear, it is *women*. Says Dr. James Meltzer,

> There are some fathers who imply to their daughters, "You're different; you're more like me than you are like your mother." They are critical of their wives, which is very upsetting to the daughters. It heats up the triangle; the mother is angry and envious because the daughter is getting all Daddy's love and attention. So what the girl learns is, "You'd better be careful, not of men, but of women's envy. Align yourself with strong men, but watch out for women, because they'll stab you in the back."

Evelyn, forty-one, a lawyer, has always gotten along well with men. It's women, she says, who rattle her.

> My father only wanted girls, because he was never an athletic kid. He'd talk to me about his business; he'd ask me for my opinion about things. So I don't have any problems with men. I know how to talk to them. I am very good at working the good-old-boy network at the office. I pump men up with flattery and I get promoted. Where I have problems is with women. I let them bully me. I fall apart if a female friend is mad at me. I think it's because there's always been this tension between my mother and me.

Interestingly the man Evelyn married is not a bit like her father. Rather he's like her *mother:* unemotional, self-centered, subtly sabotaging. After Evelyn's most recent promotion her husband's sardonic reaction was, "Great. That'll jack us up to a higher tax bracket."

No one is more surprised than Evelyn that she didn't marry someone like Dad. She is unaware that by marrying her mother's psychological twin she is giving her mother one more chance to win the Oedipal war. It is Evelyn's way of punishing herself for having won it the first time, when she was a little girl—a phenomenon that is extremely common among favored daughters.

The Princess in Bed. Since these daughters tend to be narcissistic, they subconsciously believe that experiencing, rather than giving, sexual pleasure is their due. Seducing accomplished men is second nature to such women; they simply sexualize the flattery they've used right along with their fathers.

One thirty-five-year-old woman recalls with chagrin her outrageously flirtatious behavior when she was in her twenties:

> I was a real catch and conducted myself accordingly. I had three dates a day every weekend. I felt like a hooker. But then, when I really got into it, I liked it. I was extremely sought after and had innumerable affairs with very rich men. But I was never straight with them. I'm a very good listener, an excellent complimenter, and I always played the little coquette, the "aren't you big, wonderful, strong, terrific" bit. It was the easiest thing in the world.

Dr. Seymour Fisher in his studies of women and sexuality found that narcissistic women—those who invest a great deal in their looks and in being the center of attention—have a higher intercourse (if not orgasm) rate than other women. For them sex is "attention."

And while masturbation is one form of their great self-love, it is also wanting in one respect: As Dr. Avodah Offit tells us, the narcissist may find masturbation "something of an embarrassment, a social and sexual failure." Better to have an audience; better yet to have someone else do the "work" of helping them build up to sexual release.

These women have no trouble *receiving* pleasure; where they fall short is *giving* it. Thus they require a partner who will continue to adore them physically.

But some immensely self-involved daughters are not content with one partner. Their love is too important not to spread around. These women assiduously avoid committed relationships, preferring to use their sexuality in a series of liaisons.

Frequently they use their sexuality as a form of power. This is true of some narcissistic incest survivors; the "favoritism" they experienced with their fathers was sexual.

While most incestuously abused daughters retreat into fear or rage, the narcissist feels a distorted sense of omnipotence. According to incest authority Christine A. Courtois, these daughters were often "parentified" in childhood—that is, asked by their mothers or fathers to provide the love the parents didn't get from their own parents. Consequently the narcissistic incest victim may be aware of having an insidious sense of importance. In childhood she may have acted out her sexual "power" through repeated sex play; in adulthood she may use it in compulsive, serial sexual partnerships.

The narcissistic woman most frequently bedded by a lover does not, however, necessarily feel that she is the best loved. Such women often discover that the attentions of their lovers or husbands just don't measure up to Daddy's. Says Dr. Robert U. Akeret, "Daddy's princess has all these expectations that the man in her life is going to be very similar to her father in an all-embracing way. She's very likely to be disappointed."

The Heroine

Other favored daughters are not so much vain and seductive as they are self-sacrificial. So symbiotically attached are they to their fathers that devoting their lives to Daddy and to his ideals is the high moral purpose of their lives.

Kathleen, thirty-four, is such a daughter. When she was little, she used to sleep with her father—"like spoons"—in his twin bed in her parents' bedroom. "It was because I always had nightmares and was frightened at night," she says. "My mother put a stop to it when I was four"—a habit that most mothers would never have allowed to take hold in the first place.

At eighteen Kathleen went away to an Ivy League college on a full academic scholarship but dropped out after her freshman year and returned home. "I couldn't bear to be away from my father," she says matter-of-factly.

Kathleen works as a secretary in a local elementary school. "Success doesn't interest me," she declares. Five years ago she married a man who, she says, "is very much like my father—gorgeous, loving, supportive." But, she adds,

> Unlike my father he's also passive. He gives up easily. When he's working around the house, trying to repair an appliance, for example, he'll say, "I can't do it," and I'll have to fix it.

If not for his passivity, he would never have agreed to Kathleen's marital terms. "I was very up-front with him. I told him before we got married what my priority was: I could never live very far from my father. My dad isn't going to live forever, and I don't want to have any regrets. My husband agreed. But sometimes my refusal to live anywhere else causes strain between us."

She adds with a laugh, "Being my father's favorite is wonderful, but there are definite drawbacks!"

Punishing Happiness. For some heroines what suffers is not simply their romantic attachments; they also undermine their talents and discount their abilities.

Fear of success is a by-product of their devotion to their fathers. They dare not outdistance their dads. Of course that's not what these daughters consciously think. They believe that becoming an independent, achieving woman will make them less available for their fathers, an absence that would be so profoundly hurtful that it's simply not worth it. They say things such as "He's so unhappy when he doesn't see me," or "I would die rather than let him down." It's as though their autonomy would literally kill their fathers.

Other heroines do not undermine their masterful sides. Rather they undermine their ability to connect emotionally with anyone outside the family, using their careers to keep romance at bay.

This tendency is also unconscious. In fact to hear them tell it, they're *desperate* to get married. I interviewed a number of favored daughters who cannot fathom the reality that at thirty or thirty-five or forty they are still single. Many of them date a great deal, but somehow they never really *commit,* erecting barriers to real intimacy. If a man gets too close, they bail out of the relationship or in some way sabotage it.

Staying unattached can for an indefinite time keep Daddy enshrined in idealization and all other men at an emotional distance. As novelist Mary Gordon wrote of her father, who died when she was a child, "I lived at the center of the heart of a passionate man. He loved me simply, utterly. . . . *Certainly, I knew he was bringing me up to be no man's wife.*" (Emphasis added.)

The independence of heroines does not go unpunished. In many ways they do penance for leaving Daddy. Phobias are not uncommon in these daughters. Such anxieties are a desperate attempt to push far down into the subconscious their adult identities and appetites. Writes Dr. Michael Kerr,

The most fundamental way to think about [acute anxiety] is that the less a person has grown away . . . from his family, the more anxiety he has about being on his own and assuming responsibility for himself. Some people deal with this by never leaving home; others leave and "pretend" to have grown up. The degree of pretend is betrayed by the amount of anxiety associated with trying to be a responsible adult.

Naomi, thirty-three, an architect, suffers from panic attacks, usually when she's about to take a business trip. These attacks puzzle her because, she says, she had such an idyllic childhood.

When she was growing up, her loving father set the tone of her extraordinarily close family. So happily married are her parents that, she believes, if something were to happen to her mother, her father could not go on—"I'd have to be watched," he once told Naomi. It's one of the reasons she feels particularly protective of him.

Another reason she is close to her parents, she says, is because she is their only daughter. "That's what daughters do," she says. "They stay more in touch." She is certainly expected to do so. At twenty-five she wanted to move out, but her mother asked her to wait a year.

My brother had just gone off to college, and she said that it was too much to lose both of us at once. My father didn't disagree. By his silence I knew he wanted me to stay as much as she did. Looking back, I shouldn't have acceded to their wishes. It took me three more years to work up the courage to get my own place.

What confounds and saddens her most about her life is the fact that she's still single. She says,

I'm *dying* to get married. I was sure I'd have a husband and two kids by now. I just don't understand it. I thought only unloved daughters of neurotic parents have trouble finding the right guy. I had a *perfect* family, a real *Leave It to Beaver* childhood. How come I'm almost thirty-four and I haven't even come close to finding a partner?

For one reason, like many favored daughters, Naomi is impatient in love. She wants to cut to the romantic chase, where boy pursues girl, conquers her, and slips an engagement ring onto her finger. When she meets a man to whom she is attracted, she spends more time looking for signs of commitment than on evaluating *her* feelings for him.

It's as though she needs a declaration of love before she'll get involved in the friendship part of courtship, the gradual building of trust and discovering of mutual interests and intriguing differences, the negotiating of wants and needs.

But even when a man *does* commit, it's not enough. There's always something wrong with him. As Naomi ruefully admits, "If a guy isn't a challenge, I just turn off."

A favored daughter's chronic inability to find the "right" man allows her to sidestep the whole issue of separating from her father. Says Naomi,

> I adore my dad as a father, but I wouldn't want to marry someone like him. I want someone more exciting. I think the reason I haven't found someone is because I'm not looking for somebody "nice" and "stable" and "kind" like my father.

It is quite an admission, evidence that she dare not *choose* someone like Daddy because she dare not leave her father. Emotionally she is still a little girl who feels that to commit herself to a man with those qualities—a man like Daddy—would be the ultimate disloyalty, the ultimate infidelity. The ultimate separation.

The Heroine in Bed. Consequently many heroines are psychological—if not actual—virgins, repressing their sexual appetites or finding partners who make few sexual demands on them, or recoiling from intimate attachments altogether.

Says Nell, thirty-seven, an editor,

> I think my being sexually inhibited had to do with being loyal to my father, who absolutely adored me. I was his best friend. In some way sexuality smacked of incest. In retrospect that's what the meaning of sex was for me—forbidden. So you certainly dare not let yourself go. It wasn't a moral question; it was a question of frigidity. I married a man who had absolutely no interest in sex. And I poured all my energies into my work.

The Cost of Being a Favored Daughter

It's not easy giving up Daddy's unsullied adoration and the belief in his magical perfection. If the favored daughter is loath to peer beneath the shiny surface of her special relationship with her father, one can hardly blame her. She fears that she will find the wizard behind the curtain, and the illusion, the protection, the devotion, will vanish. Should that happen, she will be abandoned to a self-reliance and emotional maturity for which she is totally unprepared.

To keep the magic going, she may transfer to her romantic liaisons—or lack of them—the unfinished business of her childhood: *her inability to separate from her father.*

She may be haunted by the belief that she is not loved by her partner as much as Daddy loved her. She may dare not love another man for fear that her father will stop loving her. She may be bedeviled by feelings of her inherent phoniness, the sense that her true self somehow got lost in childhood, and that she must keep on dancing for Daddy. She may be devastated at the ebbing of her youth, horrified to discover in middle age that investing only in her ornamental qualities has left her an emotional pauper.

Worst of all, *she may never grow up*—and her father will remain the hero of her heart.

Profile of a Favored Daughter

I knew Barbara only slightly in college. I'd stare at her in class, watching the boys stumble over their own feet in their attempts to impress her, and I'd wish that I could be her: a blond goddess of physical perfection, a golden girl who seemed to glide through life with every advantage, skewing the law of averages for the rest of us.

But Barbara wasn't a student for very long. After her freshman year she dropped out of school to marry a man she met over summer vacation.

Recently we ran into each other at a department store, discovering that we lived a mile apart, and we renewed our acquaintanceship. I could see that little about her had changed. Still a golden girl; still gorgeous and privileged; married to an investment banker who is respected by his colleagues; two kids with whom she and her husband travel to the south of France each summer; an estate serviced by a butler, a maid, and a gardener.

And as I got to know her better, little by little my glorified image of her and her life began to take on darker hues, dappled by reality.

The second-born of five children, Barbara grew up in an affluent suburb of Dallas. Her older brother was a brilliant, outspoken achiever, who constantly argued with their father, the vice chairman of an oil company. But Barbara, who was the quintessence of femininity, was her father's delight. She says,

> My dad was big and warm and kind, and he never placed any demands on me. He was much more accepting of me than my siblings or even my mother. He was always there to pick up the pieces for me. My sisters and brothers see him quite differently; they felt shortchanged by him. He was a taskmaster to them, but not with me. I was the least smart of my siblings, and he just didn't have any expectations of me. Grades weren't important. It was important to have a good time, and I did. I was just a happy-go-lucky kid, and my dad thought I was adorable.

I'm struck by the contrasts of Barbara's life and personality. On the one hand she's extremely well read, she's an astute judge of people, she's a concerned and involved mother.

At the same time she paints herself as an airhead, a brainless southern belle who's not terribly good at anything. And when she talks about her marriage, her feelings of unhappiness and inadequacy are particularly raw:

> By marrying so young I took the easy way out. I guess the most rebellious thing I ever did was to marry someone whose background was so different from mine. Jeff came from a poor family and worked his way through college and was still in business school when we met. Marrying him was an impulse. I jump into things before I think. It was stupid, because I got pregnant immediately, and Jeff and I were just two moronic kids who hadn't grown up yet. We didn't have a chance to form a relationship first.

After Jeff's graduation the couple moved into a house in Dallas that Barbara's father bought for them. Living in her father's shadow was, she thinks, probably the worst thing the couple could have done—because Barbara spent as much time in her father's house as her own. "I was still such a kid that I looked to my father for approval and direction. He helped us a lot." And all the time she kept comparing Jeff to her father, who died five years ago. She continues, weeping,

> The problem is, Jeff gives more to our kids than he gives to me. For a long time that was okay, because I was getting it from my father. But once he died, I turned to Jeff and found we didn't have much together. And when I started asking for more of a connection, he wasn't ready for it. I always let him be in charge before. I let him baby me, so we didn't have a very mature relationship. I think he always thought of me as another of his kids, because that's how I acted. Now I want a husband. I guess I switched the rules on him. Our worst arguments are because he won't tell me how he feels about me.

One reason he won't, she admits, is that she keeps her guard up with him. The way they communicate is through anger. She picks fights and gets hysterical, he becomes a glacier.

> I scream and carry on, and he just stands there saying nothing. If I push hard enough, eventually he explodes. He'll kick a chair or something. He says I drive him to it. I know I do.

Barbara has a very clear picture of what's wrong in their marriage: Her expectations of her husband are those of a child. She looks to her husband to define her; she has a hard time finding ways to feel good about herself. She has never had a job because, she says, she's qualified for nothing. She hasn't the patience, she says, to get a college degree.

She tried therapy for a while, but abruptly stopped going after about six months. It's a subject that makes her squirm, because, she says, "I *know* I need it. But I guess I'm not ready. Because if I really look, I'm afraid of what I'll see. I'm afraid it'll mean the end of my marriage. At forty-five I'm not exactly cut out for anything else."

Barbara pulls out a handkerchief and wipes her eyes, aware that

she has painted herself into an emotional corner and cannot summon the courage to find a path out of it. And then, suddenly, she
brightens. "I'll tell you my dream if you promise you won't laugh,"
she says with a broad smile.

> Now that my kids are grown, I want a little house in the
> country with a white picket fence and no servants. I want to
> do my own cooking, my own cleaning, my own laundry,
> maybe a little gardening. I want to make my own preserves.
> Me, in the kitchen, making preserves—imagine. Life would
> be heaven, and I could put up with anything. Because then I'd
> have Jeff all to myself.

12

▼▼▼▼▼▼▼

The Good Daughter

Someday I'd like to have a relationship with someone I don't have to be totally focused on pleasing. Every time I go out on a date, I keep thinking, "Do I look okay? Did I say the right thing? Am I funny enough? Smart enough?" I'd like to be with a man for companionship, not out of some neurotic need. But for that to happen, I have to put to rest this thing with my father. Because that's what I always did with him: I was always trying to please him.

—MARCI, TWENTY-NINE

"Be a good girl."

Nearly every woman has heard these words at some point in her life, and she knows exactly what they mean: Be conciliatory. Be agreeable. Be attentive, uncomplaining, giving, kind, ladylike. Above all, *be forgiving.*

In exchange your parents will protect, house, feed, clothe, and shelter you from the big bad world. You might even be treated to a toy, or a trinket, or, if you're *really* good, maybe a new dress.

If there's one thing women know very, very well, it's how to be very, very good. Indeed, being sensitive to the feelings of others is one of the things that women do best—within reason of course. Softheartedness does not necessarily mean softheadedness. Even the most generous of women know the difference between collegiality and exploitation and are discriminating in their emotional investments. They have a psychic quota of loving-kindness.

But some women are relentlessly, even recklessly giving; they are *desperate* to please. These are the daughters who are *supergood.*

The trouble is, they don't know how much goodness is enough. They cannot bear to have anyone mad at them, even someone they don't much admire. It isn't simply that these women want to be liked. Rather, being in anyone's bad graces, however briefly, feels as though they have no purpose in life.

Particularly in their intimate attachments. For these are the women who cannot live without a man, who in fact will do just about anything to get and keep a romantic partner. For them the worst fate is to have no one to love.

The world is full of good daughters. You see them everywhere:

In gyms, trying to be even more appealing
In corporations, allowing others to take credit for their work
In bed, faking orgasms with their partners
In doctors' offices, being treated for depression or eating disorders

It is to these women—the women who are never so happy as when they are helping someone—that this chapter is addressed.

The Making of a Good Girl

All children start out being "good." It is the way they gain acceptance from their parents, the people upon whom their very lives depend. And when their goodness is greeted with parental love and support and limit setting—coupled with the freedom to form their own opinions and beliefs—these children learn how to become solid, compassionate citizens of the world.

But some children feel they must solve everyone's problems in order to be loved. This eagerness to please comes from a variety of sources.

One of them is temperament. Certain children are unusually sensitive and perceptive, instantly able to pick up the scent of people's moods and draw on their own empathy to solidify their place in the family.

Goodness is also related to birth rank. In general, second-borns and middle children are people pleasers. An older sibling has already staked out the achievement path; a younger sibling, if any, has cornered the market on immaturity and irresponsibility. Hence middle children choose the role that is open to them: They are the family diplomats and appeasers, adept at mediating different points of view. It is cheerfulness and compromise at which they excel.

Especially in the world beyond home. According to authorities on birth order, the paramount characteristic of virtually all secondborn or middle children is that they tend to go outside the family for the attention they do not, or cannot, get within it. Because they often feel like outsiders, these children settle for less and have lower expectations in their relationships than firstborns. They are extraordinarily loyal and are likelier to abide an unfulfilling attachment longer than their siblings.

A third source of a child's goodness is the degree to which his or her parents use reward, punishment, and praise as childrearing tools. As psychiatrist Rudolf Dreikers pointed out in *Children: The Challenge,* many parents, in response to a child's doing something well, will gush, "What a *good girl [boy]* you are!" rather than say, "It's wonderful that you can do that all by yourself."

The well-meaning parent confuses the *doer* with the *deed;* it is the virtue of the doer, rather than the mastery involved in accomplishing a deed, that is underscored. Thus, failing to be rewarded with praise can make the child feel that she or he has failed.

Of all the variables of goodness, however, *the single most important predictor is the child's gender.* This is especially true in traditional families, where a degree of fight and mischief in boys is expected—and, it could be argued, required: A son's naughtiness and challenging of authority proves that he isn't a mama's boy, isn't a sissy.

Girls in traditional families, however, are not easily forgiven their spunk. One never hears the expression "Girls will be girls" applied to misbehaving daughters. To prove they aren't boys, aren't "mannish," these daughters must be demure and not call attention to themselves; they must conform. They must be "good."

The family and cultural catechism by which girls learn how to be good begins early. In childhood they receive a litany of the virtues of self-sacrifice: They are told over and over again to share, to give up or give away, and to grin and bear their disappointments. They are roundly rebuked for being "bad"—too loud or opinionated or "pushy."

For many of these girls, giving becomes a conditioned response to anyone's needs. So thorough and automatic is their generosity toward others that they forget how to ask for themselves. Asking is selfish. Asking is aggressive. Asking is what boys do.

And so good girls put their own needs last, behind those of the people they love or who control their lives: Mommy. Daddy. Teachers. Employers. Friends. Lovers. Spouses. Even their children.

"I learned early in life to tell people what they wanted to hear, things that I didn't even believe," says Sybil, thirty-eight. "I learned to be an actress. Even today there are times when I don't know who I am—the actress or the real me."

"It was just understood in my family," says Gayle, fifty-five. "I was to be the caretaker; my brother was to be the achiever. So he was sent to college, and I was sent to charm school."

"When somebody needs me badly enough," says Joanne, forty, "I think it's love."

If there's one problem good daughters share, it is this: They dress up their needs and pass them off as *other* people's needs, which they must then satisfy. If, for instance, they feel lonely, they find a friend who is even *lonelier* and pour their energies into making that person feel accepted. With such children the false-self personality—the one they invent to placate a hostile or indifferent world and to be loved by their parents—is angelic.

And when they feel neglected or unappreciated, they work even harder to please. It is a subconscious, socially acceptable means by which girls are able, circuitously, to feel good about themselves, to avoid being stranded in the world, and to have a sense of control.

Good daughters feel valued primarily in their attachments rather than their achievements. Love is women's work—indeed it is their mission—which is why so many of them are found in the helping professions, such as teaching or nursing or counseling. What these daughters want more than anything is someone to depend on them so that they can feel a sense of purpose. The good daughter has a powerful incentive to be as virtuous as possible: Her need to please comes from altruistic strength, the feeling that she is not simply needed but *indispensable* to the well-being of others.

However, such "strength" is frequently a mask for emotional deprivation.

The Overly Helpful Daughter. The daughter who instantly chirps "I'll do it!" when a parent asks for volunteers; the daughter who puts herself in the middle of her parents' scuffles, trying to placate them both; the daughter who listens patiently to Mommy's or Daddy's marital woes; the daughter who can't concentrate in school because she is worried about a parent's business problems —this is the child who is dying to please.

Her parents' "weakness" becomes her source of strength. So does everyone else's. The good daughter is everyone's best friend, spending hours on the phone advising her chums about their boyfriends or family troubles, lending money or clothes that somehow never get returned.

These daughters are "overfunctioners," turning their neediness inside out. It's perfectly acceptable to sense the needs of others and to offer assistance. It's perfectly awful to sense your own needs and not have them met.

Says Cathy, nineteen,

> The other night I said to my boyfriend, "I wish I had the money to go to medical school and become a doctor. There's so much cruelty in the world, and I feel I ought to do something." He said, "Why do you always feel it's your responsibility to fix everything?" I said, "Because that's how I grew up. I had to take care of my family. I had to take care of everyone."

Children of alcoholics often adopt this helpful role—they are called "enablers"—as do the children of depressed or abusive parents. Maltreated children tend to believe they deserve their maltreatment, and one way to ameliorate that treatment is to alleviate the parent's stress, or anxiety, or sources of irritation—whatever it is that makes Mommy or Daddy behave so badly.

Children of divorce are also prone to such behavior. They often become "parentified," especially daughters. Almost all of the "caring-competent" children of divorce in Dr. E. Mavis Hetherington's studies were girls. A key ingredient in the sensitivity and relative emotional sturdiness of these daughters was that they were called upon at an early age to care for others—either their siblings, or their alcoholic or depressed or lonely mothers, or a frail grandparent. (It was different for the sons in the custody of single mothers. The difficulty of having no father or father figure counteracted the esteem-building qualities of being responsible for others.)

Such parentification of children of divorce, according to Dr.

Judith Wallerstein, is not *true role reversal*, nor is it always psychologically beneficial. She writes,

> Rather, these new roles . . . are complex and unfamiliar. . . . Children who end up playing these roles are often those who naturally feel a great deal of empathy. They pity the adults around them and are frightened about losing their parents. Feeling vulnerable, they tend to yield to the parent's wishes and threats. Their sensitivity becomes their undoing, as they assume multiple roles to support the parent's neurotic needs.

"Parental" children, however, can also be found in intact families that are not characterized by chemical dependence, psychosis, or physical or sexual abuse. While the dynamics are subtler, it is still the girl who is likeliest to adopt this helpful role.

Especially if her father is domineering and controlling. Such fathers tend to be married to women who are submissive, and their daughters learn that the way to please Daddy—hence all men—is to be like Mommy.

That doesn't necessarily mean that the daughters *like* Mommy. Often they feel ambivalent about their mothers; that's because their mothers need them so very much. These daughters frequently feel altogether *too* necessary to their mothers, who are punishing if filial solace is not forthcoming. These mother-daughter relationships can become stifling, even hostile.

To avoid being swallowed up by her mother, it becomes *crucial* for the good daughter to please her father, to make sure he doesn't leave, because she needs him to help her separate from her mother. So she may imbue him with magical qualities: He *would*, if he *could*, defend her or spend more time with her—it's just that he's working so hard. Thus she may become a one-woman rescue team: She will make Daddy's home life as peaceful as possible.

To increase the odds that Daddy will stay, the good daughter becomes the family savior, stepping into the hornet's nest of her parents' arguments.

Says Eva, thirty-six,

> My mother was always needling my father, just to get some attention from him. He'd go crazy and they'd have violent

arguments. I'd jump in the middle and say, "Please don't fight." I'd be shaking. I was like the parent in the family, advising my mother and my father. I didn't want that role, but they gave it to me when I was a little kid.

The overly helpful daughter strikes this bargain to compensate for the loss of paternal stability and warmth and intervention. She becomes the family caretaker. *She* will keep the family together.

There's a hitch, however: Because her emotional boundaries are so porous, she is unable to set limits on how much responsibility she is willing to take on and frequently becomes overburdened. Worse, she is unable to extricate herself from her parents' emotional entanglements.

For all these reasons and in all these ways, good girls are not trained to be self-sufficient, to be independent, to give their own needs the same priority as they give everyone else's. Rather they are trained to be someone's helper, someone's healer, someone's nurturer, someone's partner. *Someone's wife.*

The Tyranny of Femininity. Good daughters must not simply be giving; they must also be "superfeminine"—that is, irresistibly, relentlessly, girlishly attractive to the opposite sex. And in childhood the most important man to attract of course is Daddy.

Since it is fathers, more than mothers (see Chapter 1) who tend to be the arbiters of gender-appropriate behavior, girls learn early on that the way to get their fathers' approval is to be compliant and adoring. Yet good daughters never feel that they are *pleasing enough* for their fathers.

Daughters who are considered to be extremely feminine generally come from families in which the fathers have exaggerated ideas of masculinity and femininity. The most "feminine" daughters tend to have fathers who take a dim view of aggressiveness.

As a result—according to research on gender behavior—while boys affirm their masculinity in terms of being accepted by other boys, girls test their femininity not in terms of how acceptable they are to other girls but in terms of *how males react to them.*

These findings were corroborated by the good daughters in my sample. Many of them had fathers who held rigid beliefs about how girls should behave. Says Mimi, forty-nine, "My father was extremely puritanical. In his house the man was king, and my mother and I were expected to follow his orders. If I bought nail polish, he'd throw it away. If I wore lipstick, he'd make me take it off. He didn't want me to grow up."

Such rigidity precludes real paternal warmth and serves only to make the daughter try even harder to be good, as though it were her particular task to balance the emotional weight within the family: The less Daddy gives, the more the good daughter is inspired to give.

Consequently if there is a common denominator among good daughters, *it is that most of them suffered from "father hunger."* The greatest loss of their childhoods was that they did not experience a healthy, affectionate, reliable, and supportive relationship with their fathers.

And because they harbored the belief that their fathers' cool or harsh treatment of them was due to some terrible flaw within themselves, these were the daughters who became the neediest of having a man in their lives.

Thus the good girl, beginning in adolescence, may turn to the outside world to find her hero—a man who will rescue her from all her family obligations and paternal losses.

Boy Crazy. The degree to which a daughter is "boy crazy" is in direct proportion to the amount of time her father spent with her in childhood. As psychologist Henry Biller writes, "Father-deprived girls are more likely to become . . . completely obsessed with boys—as they desperately seek affection from a male father figure."

If she did not have a loving and involved father, the good daughter will not simply turn to friends or mother surrogates for solace, although she may well do that. Of far greater urgency is to find a *father* substitute. Discouraged by her parents from becoming autonomous, she doesn't know how to stand on her own. Hence, she takes the most logical route out of the family: She mounts a frantic search for a boyfriend, from whom she will borrow a sense of autonomy. She transfers all her needs to a man who can be *both* parents to her—both protective and nurturing.

This urge to merge is indicative of the good daughter's fragile sense of self. Writes Dr. Michael Kerr,

> If a person grows up under strong pressure to adjust to the anxiety, emotional reactivity, and subjectivity of others, [her] life becomes strongly governed by emotional, feeling, and subjective processes. . . . As [emotional] boundaries dis-

solve, *there is increased pressure on people to think, feel, and act in ways that will enhance one another's emotional well-being.*

It is understandable, then, that boyfriends become the father-hungry daughter's salvation. She craves physical affection and strength, both of which combine in a lover. And the way to get and keep a man is to please him in all ways—especially sexually.

The Good Daughter in Love

Some good daughters are drawn to passive men; others are attracted to controlling men. Either way these daughters often fall in love and/or marry in haste, rather than gamble on the possibility that a better opportunity will come along, as though *this* were their last chance for love. As one woman put it,

> I didn't find my husband to be particularly attractive. But he was the right religion, he was intelligent, and I felt, How am I ever going to find anyone like this again? I was trying to get my strength from him. He wanted to marry me, and I said yes, and it's as simple as that.

Good Daughter, Passive Partner. Of course it isn't as simple as that. Women who were called upon to be the family saviors respond reflexively to men who "need" them.

Such women often become involved with passive men. They continue to give too much in their attachments and marriages, just as they did in childhood, and to receive too little in return. "Strong" men don't "need" them. Consequently their partners often bear a startling resemblance to their needy mothers. At work here is the conditioned response spoken of earlier, the result of having been so extraordinarily invested in the emotional lives of their parents.

Inevitably the good daughter's anxieties increase the more she gives, because her own needs aren't being met. Thus just as there is an urge for closeness, so is there often a simultaneous urge to flee. For even as she gives away so much of herself, she also reserves a tiny place for herself—an oasis of skepticism and doubt and fantasy.

Several of the good daughters I interviewed commented that

there is an invisible wall they construct around themselves that their partners, no matter how loving or passive or gentle, are unable to break through.

Says Laura, twenty-seven,

> It's hard to be vulnerable to a man, because it was dangerous to be that way as a kid. My father was just never there for me. So my guard is always up. My husband would never cheat on me. *I'm* the one who thinks about having an affair. I have all these fantasies about other guys, even though I'd never act on them. It's like a kind of insurance. I think, "Well, I could always get another man." I can't give my all to someone, and my husband senses that. The other day he said, "I can feel that you don't totally open up and that you're not with me entirely." I said, "I just have this fear in the back of my head that someday you're going to do something to hurt me, or let me down, because you're a man." I don't want ever to be a victim, like my mother was. So I don't allow myself to be loved. I can't give him a break.

Good Daughter, Dominating Partner. Other good daughters are drawn to domineering partners, men who do the controlling and who make the decisions. (Women who link up with brutal men will be discussed in Chapter 14.) These women seek relationships in which they can lay down the burden of premature responsibility and be taken care of. In these cases their partners are often carbon copies of their fathers.

Jocelyn, forty, is the second-born of three girls. "I was the wonderful daughter," she says, "the goody-goody. My sisters had a harder time with my parents and got into more trouble, because I was always held up as the 'nice' one."

Jocelyn didn't spend much time with her father when she was growing up. He owned a small electrical appliance store and worked six days a week. Says Jocelyn,

> He wasn't a big communicator. I don't remember his ever saying, "I love you." Recently I called him up, and at the end of the conversation I said, "I love you." He said, "Thank you." I said, "What do you mean, 'thank you'? Say 'I love you.'" He mumbled something; he couldn't get it out. The best he could do was "Me too."

When she was twenty-two, she married a lawyer, a union that produced four children. She makes no bones about the fact that she "spoils" her husband. If he says he'd like a cup of coffee, she jumps up to make a fresh pot. If he's hungry, she'll stop what she's doing to fix him something to eat. Of their marriage she says,

> I don't feel taken advantage of by him. I really like doing all that stuff. Maybe it's because I see a different side of him from what other people see. He's certainly not shy. When he has something to say, he says it. He has a temper, and some-times it just blows. With most people he comes on strong, but not with me. But then, I don't give him a really hard time. Of the two of us he's the stronger. The biggest problem we've had is with our kids. Sometimes I'm too protective, and I'm not sure that's good, because it takes authority away from him. There is a point where the father's the father, and what he says goes. I guess I'm old-fashioned that way. I tend to give in and I don't know what's the right thing to do. He always knows. He's the strong father figure I didn't get growing up.

For Jocelyn, having an outspoken, protective husband makes her feel secure. The bargain they have struck—that he be the head of the family and she, as she puts it, its "heart"—seems to suit the couple's respective temperaments.

But for other good daughters, giving over so much authority to their partners can have painful consequences. Such daughters use their dependence as an emotional hedge against abandonment. They martyr themselves for the sake of their marriages and their children. They "cover" for the husband's neglect of his wife and children. They will pay any price for peace.

Says Dr. Marianne Goodman,

> Some women feel that the man is more mobile than a woman, that a wife can't leave the home, can't leave the kids. She's stuck. So she needs the man to take care of her. Therefore she has to protect him and accommodate him.

Not that this long-suffering behavior is a conscious attempt to manipulate. These women truly believe that being second marital banana is in the best interests of family harmony. Some of them, however, admit that their "weakness" can in fact be manipulative.

They know the degree to which they allow their neediness to control others.

Marilyn, forty-six, is such a woman. She has been married for twenty years to Jim, a man she describes as a "real catch. He had his own insurance business and could have had his pick of any of the women he knew. I couldn't believe it when he asked me to marry him. I'm not exactly a beauty queen."

Marilyn, whose mother died when she was eleven, grew up in the shadow of her beautiful older sister and her aloof, intellectual, and exacting father. Because Jim didn't finish college, her father disapproved of the match. For the first several years of her marriage she felt torn between her father and her husband, desperately attempting to keep them both happy, trying to make them believe that each was the center of her life.

The strain of trying to please the two most important men in her life eventually took its toll. She developed colitis, an illness that would flare up whenever she felt stress. During her frequent medical emergencies, her two daughters were called upon to run errands or make dinner, or to be quiet so that Mommy could rest. Says Marilyn,

> I cannot deal with my own anger or anyone else's. All my life I've been an apologizer. I dominate by being weak. I think at times I've manipulated my kids by being ill. It's the only time I give myself permission to express my needs. I have far less trouble expressing annoyance at my kids than at Jim. In many ways he's just like my father. He tends to lecture and gets mad if I interrupt him. He likes to control the money, the kids, me. When he's mad at me, I just retreat and don't tell him how I feel. Or I say "I'm sorry," just to break the ice.

Elena, fifty-three, also married a domineering man. But in her case being long-suffering has literally bankrupted her.

She lives in an immaculate, slightly shabby house in an affluent suburb. Her son is a graduate of an Ivy League college and pulls a high income in his profession. Elena never had her child's advantages, nor did she really want them. All she ever wanted was to be a wife and mother.

When she was nineteen, she married Theo, a man who, she says, is exactly like her father: demanding, uncommunicative, vain. She says,

My father always made all the decisions in our house, and that's what Theo did. I've always been the person who jumped—first to my dad and then to my husband. I felt that if I ever did something to make Theo leave, my father would blame me. He was always on my husband's side. So if Theo was being mean or irritable, I'd tell myself that he was working hard, that I'm not perfect, either, that I shouldn't be too judgmental, shouldn't be selfish. I accepted everything, because that's what I did with my father.

Five years ago Elena discovered her husband was having an affair with a much younger woman. It wasn't the first time he had been unfaithful to her. Elena knew about Theo's occasional dalliances over the years, but never thought he'd actually *leave* her.

After all, she'd put him through medical school; she'd helped the family budget by baking bread and growing vegetables in the summer and canning them "to save a few pennies." She kept the house spotless and inviting, and her body trim, for her husband.

"I was superwoman with the family," she says. "Everything ran like clockwork. I did everything I was supposed to do." But Theo never seemed to be happy, not even when his medical practice erased their money worries. So Elena would blame herself for his unhappiness, for his wandering eye, and work even harder to be a better homemaker, a more adroit lover, a more proficient gourmet. And when he was cranky with her son, she'd cover for him.

I'd say, "You know, your daddy really loves you. He's doing the best he can, even though he hurts your feelings and isn't home very much. We have to back him up; we can't be selfish."

And in fact her hard work seemed to pay off. Her husband once told her, "If you're a good girl, I won't divorce you."

He left anyhow.

Today Elena is trying to make sense of what went wrong in her marriage and in her life. Since she has no real fight in her, she did not put up an argument when her husband insisted on a minimal financial settlement. By day she works in a nursery school as a teacher's aide, trying to maintain her dignity and stay off welfare. At night she lies awake, wondering if she'll end up as a bag lady.

Without a husband, and without a child for whom to care, she seems rudderless. Trying to put a brave face on her troubles, she says,

> Looking back, I realize I let Theo completely control my life. I'd try to talk to him about the things that bothered me, and all he'd say was "Not now." So I'd say, "Anytime you're ready." Sometimes he'd be so apologetic; he'd make all these promises about turning over a new leaf, that he'd go see a marriage counselor with me, that he'd spend more time at home. Later he'd deny he'd ever said those things. He had me convinced that I'd made it all up.
>
> My fantasies made me not see the reality. I gave and gave and gave until the well was empty, and it wasn't ever enough. Not for my father, and not for my husband.
>
> But maybe I'm being too critical. I can't really blame them —they're both good men. They did the best they could.

The Good Daughter in Bed

Sexual intimacy for the good daughter can be joyous—a wondrous blend of profound love and physical passion, of tenderness and touch—the expression of her deepest feelings of commitment and caring. Or sex can leave the good daughter with a feeling of incompletion and longing. It all depends on how much of her childhood she brings with her into the bedroom.

One of the most painful consequences of being a good daughter is that along with her emotional needs her sexual needs are often unmet.

The Sexually Passive Daughter. For "helpless" women their sexual difficulties are partly due to their very inability to ask only for themselves or to give their own pleasure an equal priority: They hope their partners will figure out what they need.

One of Dr. Seymour Fisher's findings in his studies of female sexuality was that those women who were best able to concentrate on their own bodily sensations and needs—that is, to concentrate only on themselves—were able to achieve orgasm relatively easily.

Many good daughters, however, do not give their sexual needs a high priority. Rather it is their *partners'* needs that are paramount. These women concentrate more on satisfying their partners and making them feel that they are good lovers than on being satisfied.

Says Dr. Avodah K. Offit, author of *The Sexual Self,*

A major theme among the women I treat is their difficulty in asking men to do this or that, to touch them in a certain way. Women are very tender with the male ego. They're afraid of offending their partner's pride because men like to think they know how to perform.

As many researchers have noted, part of this sexual altruism has to do with a daughter's moral training in childhood. For some good daughters the whole issue of sex is "messy," both physically and morally. In their minds sex is tainted with shame. In childhood they were discouraged from masturbating or punished for doing so; they were also taught that premarital sex is sinful.

For these daughters marital obligation and procreation and religion may make sex justifiable, but that doesn't mean that such sanctions make sex immediately pleasurable. When a woman has been told all her life that sex is wrong or evil, that passion and desire are the work of the devil, it's hard suddenly to feel good about it once she is married.

Thus some women experience extreme ambivalence about the pleasure they feel when being touched and sexually aroused. Theirs is a kind of libidinous stage fright, ashamed of or embarrassed by the passion that floods their bodies and eclipses their "moral" reserve and self-control. After all, a sexual partner is a *witness* to the good girl's "wickedness."

Consequently she may prefer to have sex when the lights are out, or when she's had a drink first, or only when she doesn't have her period, or only when her children are asleep or, better yet, when they're staying over at a friend's house.

For other good daughters sexual intercourse is not so much a moral crossroads as it is just one more area where it is more blessed to give than to receive. For these women sex is subject to a kind of misguided etiquette. In their eagerness to please they often *pretend* to be sexually satisfied. The biggest sexual gift they can give their partners is the orgasm they fake.

Says Dr. Offit,

Many men have an investment in women's orgasms. It's as if their masculinity is afflicted if women don't have orgasms. Men have more of a division between affection and sex.

Whereas most women are less concerned about sexual function than wanting their partners to be affectionate and caring
—they pretend to have orgasms so their partners will feel that
they have performed well.

According to numerous psychologists, this need to be pleasing
at the expense of her own sexual pleasure is a consequence of a
woman's inability to please her father.

Says Dr. Marlin S. Potash,

A remarkably common theme among my female patients is
that they can't relax in bed. Many of them say, "Sex isn't
about *me*. It's about my husband or lover." They're terrified
that they're not attractive enough, or that they're too passive
or too aggressive for their partners. They say, "If I'm myself,
the guy's going to leave. I can't really enjoy myself." Translation: I have to be vigilant. I must make myself over to keep
him, to keep "Daddy," to get "Daddy" to come home. Sex is
about pleasing the father figure; it's about the terror that
you're not going to be able to please him, and then you'll be
alone and not taken care of.

No wonder these women don't have orgasms. Their dads
just weren't there for them. They were cared for by their
fathers from afar. So the women come to tolerate being taken
care of from afar in bed too. You have sex, but it's not for
you. You fake orgasms so you won't be abandoned.

An integral component in the good daughter's confusion about
sexual pleasure, then, may be her underlying fear that all good
things will end, especially love. Women who infrequently or never
experience orgasms have little confidence that their intimate attachments will endure. Unlike consistently orgasmic women, they
have vivid memories of paternal loss—fathers who were seldom
home, or who appeared to be unconcerned about them, or fathers
who divorced or abandoned them, or fathers who died. Or fathers
who sexually abused them.

For such daughters separation anxiety—the fear of the loss of a
loved one—makes the buildup of sexual tension particularly
threatening.

But even if she cannot or does not achieve orgasm, or reaches it
only occasionally, sex for the good daughter is, in most cases, nev-

ertheless highly valued and extremely meaningful. It gives her a feeling of being wanted and of being cherished; indeed the best part of sex is the tenderness.

Hence the sexually passive daughter may make this compromise in her head: She may love the cuddling, the being held, the affectionate components of sexual intercourse—and at the same time hold herself back in a self-protective way from true orgasm. She may give her body, not her unqualified trust.

The Sexually Eager Daughter. For other good daughters sex is more than reassuring; it is one of the few ways that they allow themselves to be assertive. Indeed for some of them sex *is* love, a conditioned response to a man's attentions. Their erotic appetite is often a consequence of their acute father deprivation.

I found a number of women—whose fathers had either died or were divorced or emotionally absent—who used sex as a kind of magical release from reality. At some point in their adolescence or early adulthood, they compulsively began seeking sexual partners, rather than girlfriends, to assuage their neediness.

Says Margaret, fifty-one, whose father died when she was four, "It wasn't until I was in my late thirties that I had close female friends. The great hunger was to find a man. I had countless affairs."

Such yearning for physical closeness makes perfect sense to the woman who didn't get enough of it from her parents in early childhood. It can be argued that making love is the closest thing to the intimacy that an infant feels at its mother's breast. Intercourse is all but literal physical union—two naked bodies bound together, skin to skin, mouth to mouth, genitals to genitals. In the heat of passion it's possible, for a few exquisite moments, to feel "lost in love," not knowing where your body and identity end and your lover's begin. At such moments nothing matters but the partner in whose arms you are held. For this kind of good daughter, sexual abandon is a great escape, a kind of libidinized balm.

One woman, whose father was a salesman and frequently on the road and whose mother was an alcoholic, recalls the first time she played "doctor" with a boy:

> I was seven, and the boy from next door, who was around nine, wanted to pretend that I was sick and that he was going to take care of me. What better game for someone like me, who didn't have anything like a normal family. He said he had

to "examine" me and told me to pull down my panties. I knew it was sort of naughty, but I loved the attention. He was so persuasive and nice, I did it for him. Which figured in all my attachments later on. If a man was nice to me, I would immediately go to bed with him.

Like sexually passive daughters, many of these women also feel ambivalent about their passionate attachments and a bit sheepish about their hearty sexual appetites. Some guiltily confessed that they had frequently masturbated ever since they were children to relieve their stress or unhappiness. Others worried that they might be "oversexed." They lamented that they wanted sex more than their partners or spouses and that the imbalance in their sexual appetites was the cause of frequent arguments.

An example of both phenomena is Natalie, thirty-one, a speech therapist who has been married for five years to a man she describes as "sweet, but not much of a go-getter." She says,

He always plays it so safe. One time on vacation we were swimming in a lake, and I wanted to have sex then and there. He said, "Are you crazy? People will see us!" I giggled and said, "Only if they're underwater." He got furious. So now I'm trying to tone myself down. But the truth is I want to make love with him all the time.

For some sexually eager daughters, their desire to please can become self-destructive. Just as they have difficulty knowing how much goodness is enough, so, too, do they have difficulty drawing the sexual line.

When Ellen, twenty-five, was growing up, her father was always a remote presence and her mother was unusually belligerent toward her. In high school Ellen was an honors student and extremely popular, but she did not have any boyfriends. Except one: Carl, her math teacher.

Carl was everyone's favorite teacher. He was kind, empathetic, and willing to listen to his students' problems. Ellen could talk to him in a way she had never been able to talk to her parents. Often, after school, she'd go see him just to ventilate. The more she got to know and trust him, the more she revealed about herself.

She told him about how hard she always tried to be perfect. She told him about how she would pull her hair out in clumps, or dig her fingernails into her skin, because she was so desperately un-happy at home. She told him about experimenting with drugs. Says Ellen,

> Carl was incredibly supportive and understanding. Then one day he said, "Why don't we meet later?" I knew exactly what he wanted. He was the first man I ever had sex with. I believed he loved me—I still believe that. He was risking his entire career for me. He was the only man I'd ever known who totally accepted me for myself. The affair ended when I graduated.

Carl was the last "older" man with whom she became involved. Once she got to college, she was attracted to almost any male student who paid attention to her. And as time went on, her need for male attention became increasingly frantic and harmful.

"I was never coy," she says. "I was just immediately sexually available. Every guy I went out with I fell in love with. I thought I was in love with all of them. I allowed myself to be used, because I wanted to be loved."

Whenever she went to a party, she'd drink heavily. One night she was so drunk that she lay down on a couch and a boy lay down on top of her. "The next thing I knew, he was inside me. Lo and behold, I got pregnant," she says.

Ellen got an illegal abortion, which traumatized her—the abortionist used no anesthesia. Nevertheless she did not obtain birth control and continued to be sexually active. A year later she again got pregnant, this time by a student whom she had been dating for several weeks. The boy offered to marry her, and because she couldn't face another abortion, she agreed; the marriage lasted eighteen months.

Today Ellen is the divorced mother of a five-year-old daughter —"my love child," she says, smiling wanly—and she works as an art director in an Atlanta advertising agency. She's in therapy trying to contain the damage of having had a father she could never talk to; to find out why she is drawn to men who exploit her sexually; and to discover why her neediness eclipses her good sense.

"I have to watch myself constantly," she says. "I still want to give men whatever they want. It's a tough habit to break."

The Price of "Nice"

Whether they are married or single, and whether their partners are passive or controlling, it's only a matter of time before good daughters begin to resent giving more than they receive.

For within the good girl may be a very angry girl, the one who could seldom get her father's attention, the one whose relationship with her mother was too close for comfort, the one who wasn't ever allowed to express her own opinions and who always had to smile bravely and move uncomplainingly to other people's rhythms.

Not that these childhood losses and compromises are always conscious. In fact, to keep her awareness and hostility below the flash point, the good daughter may find other ways to vent them. It all depends on how bleak her treatment was in childhood, how frenetic her need to please, how fragile her sense of self. And of course rage isn't ladylike. Rage isn't something good girls are supposed to feel.

In some cases the good daughter's anger takes the form of a kind of tyranny of her goodness—she needs someone weaker than she is. She may seek out relationships that corroborate her virtuous strength. And should a friend, or partner, or child become strong, *she will try to make them weak* by pointing out their flaws or their mistakes and "heal" them with her love.

In other cases she needs someone stronger than she is to act out her anger for her. It is not uncommon to see couples where one partner is altogether charming and kind and forgiving, while the other is nagging or opinionated or sour, and to think, "What does she [he] see in him [her]?" Just this: The "good" partner gets the "bad" partner to be the villain and remains the innocent bystander.

In still other cases the good daughter may suddenly feel exploited and then explode out of all proportion to the reality of a given situation—say, at a friend who is late for a lunch date, or a child who accidentally upends a glass of milk. A lifetime of rage can be detonated by something relatively inconsequential. It's safer to vent one's anger at a friend or a child than on one's partner, upon whom one's identity or support depends.

Safer still is to turn one's anger inward, to punish the "bad girl" within. One form of self-directed rage is an eating disorder—anorexia or bulimia—in which the good daughter punishes herself for her appetites and needs. (More serious self-destructiveness will be discussed in Chapter 14.)

As we shall see in Part Four, when good daughters are able to take stock of their emotional histories, they can eventually take responsibility for their own contribution to their emotional impoverishment. They can assess the cost of their niceness and the pain of being so eager to please. They can gain a sense of control over their own happiness and choices and sexuality.

But until they do, they may persist in the belief that love and goodness will automatically be rewarded. They may continue to be stunned every time they are exploited. They may be repeatedly dismayed when their generosity is unappreciated and puzzled that no matter how much they give, it is never enough.

Profile of a Good Daughter

I liked Candy, twenty-four, on sight. The beaming face that appeared at my house on a dreary winter afternoon was almost a literal breath of spring. Stamping the snow from her feet, she apologized for being late. "The roads are murder," she said, removing her colorful ski jacket and knitted hat and shaking loose her short auburn curls. I assured her that five minutes does not constitute true tardiness.

Candy's demeanor matched the voice that had called a week earlier in response to my ad—energetic and enthusiastic. "This is the first time I've ever been interviewed," she said, blushing, as I turned on my tape recorder. "Forgive me if I sound a little nervous."

Candy is a good girl. A very, *very* good girl. She is, she says, constantly at her family's and her friends' "beckoning call." In fact ever since she was a little girl, she was the one in the family who always tried to cheer everyone up.

Candy is a second-born—she has an older brother. She grew up in a small town in Tennessee with her father, who owns a farming-implement company, and her mother, a housewife.

When she was a child, she and her father were close. He would tell Candy his problems, about how his father died when he was young and how lucky Candy was to have a father. "My dad loved me but hated my brother," she says. "That's because my mom always sided with my brother. I hate to say it, but my father was really abusive to him. I think he felt there was competition there. Daddy didn't feel that way with me, though."

Their relationship changed abruptly when Candy was fourteen. She and her family went to see a production of *Fiddler on the Roof,* and when they got home, her father said it was time for her to go to bed. She replied, "I don't want to. I want to stay up with you guys." She recalls,

> All of a sudden this man who never laid a glove on me slapped me across the face so hard, my nose bled. He was all pumped up by the play, especially the part about the daughter disobeying the father. I was disobeying him. I was hysterically crying. Later he apologized; he said he wanted me to respect him more. It's funny, because I was always respectful toward him. He didn't really mean to hit me. He's a good man, but he's like a time bomb. He keeps everything inside.

After that night Candy's relationship with her father changed. He stopped confiding in her and began showing more attention to her brother. Candy insists that it doesn't bother her.

"I was always the peacemaker in the family," she says. "I was so critical of myself. If anyone was mad at me, I'd say, 'What did I do?' I'd try to get my dad to ease up on my brother; I'd try to get my mom to be nicer to dad. I'm always trying to get everyone to talk to everyone. I'm always in the middle."

Compounding her problems with her father was the fact that his business began to fail, hit hard by a drought. "I felt so bad for him that I made myself the scapegoat," she says. "I took the blame for all his problems, thinking that if I were a better person, his business would get better. I was trying to be the problem solver."

Because she couldn't really talk to her father, she found herself getting involved with men who would take advantage of her. Recently she began therapy to examine how the need to be the family cheerleader has spilled over into her romantic choices. She explains,

> I always go to men who have problems. I'm always getting involved with these guys who can't give. I'm always giving of myself sexually and in other ways, and I'm tired of being

shortchanged. I'm tired of men telling me I'm a tease and that I have to prove I'm not by going to bed with them. Men always misconstrue my being nice; they think I'm coming on to them.

What propelled her into therapy was her most recent relationship. A man she had known in high school began pursuing her because, he told her, he "needed a friend." He was unable to get a well-paying job, and, he said, Candy was so comforting, so easy to talk to. One day he called at the office where she works and said, "I really need to see you. Can you come over?" Candy left the office and drove to his house. Weeping, she recalls,

When I got there, he was like a little boy who needed a mommy. I sacrificed myself sexually to try to comfort him. But afterward he suddenly got very cold. He made me feel very guilty and ashamed that I slept with him, and I didn't think I did anything wrong. After that night he stopped calling. I'm so angry with myself for letting it happen again.

I ached for this endearing young woman, so eager to say the right thing, so anxious to create a good impression, so desperate to be loved. She wants nothing so much as to make other people happy—to get married and take care of a family. And she is astonished to discover how far she is from her goal and how easily she confuses being needed with being loved.

A week after our interview she called me up to thank me for "listening to all my troubles." Then she added,

I just wanted to tell you one more thing—it came up in my therapy session today. I was thinking about all the men in my life and I realized I had never had an orgasm. I brought it up with my therapist because I thought there was something wrong with me. The therapist said that I've always put up a shield because I don't trust men and that when I'm mentally ready to let a man get close to me, instead of me always trying to solve their problems, I'll be able to have a loving sexual relationship.

For now, she said, she's stopped going out with men. She wants to learn to be by herself. "I need to learn how to have a different kind of relationship. My therapist says love doesn't always have to be sexual, that you can truly be friends with a man. Oh, God, I hope she's right."

13

▼▼▼▼▼▼▼

The Competitive Daughter

My father was the type who couldn't express love—only approval or disapproval. Once I got a B on a report card, and he said, "What's this?" I said, "Why don't you say anything about all the A's?" He said, "I expect that. I expect you to be perfect." The good news is that he trained me to be extremely capable, so I am very successful—I can take care of myself. The downside is that I'm a driven workaholic. I can't make a mistake, and I'm always walking on eggs. One false move, and it's all undone. I feel as if I'm only as good as my last accomplishment.

—JUDY, FORTY-THREE

One of my oldest friends is Pamela, who, as I am fond of reminding her, is the only perfect person I know. She's an internationally known author and lecturer and has a devoted husband who is not the least threatened by her renown and staggering income. She is a brilliant thinker, a consummately charming hostess, and unfailingly generous friend. Worst of all, she effortlessly maintains a perfect size-eight figure.

But if there's one thing about her I envy, it's her unshakable self-confidence and equanimity in the face of pressures that would land most people in a sanitarium. This is a woman who churns out books, keynote addresses, and television appearances, all on five hours of sleep a night, and never loses her cool or her stamina. I have never seen her stage a tantrum or fold from self-doubt.

"Let's not get carried away here," she tells me, hosing down my admiration of her.

There are no free lunches. I handle stress well, it's true. But there's been some fallout from my success. For one thing I have two younger sisters who have always felt they can't measure up; it's not easy having a big sister like me. And there have been times when I haven't been as available to my husband and kids as they would like. I just spread myself too thin. And I *hate* to lose.

Try as she may, Pamela is unable to paint a black lining in her silver cloud. The fact is, she knows *exactly* who she is and cannot be toppled from her self-assurance, both as a world beater and as a woman. She does not brood about past mistakes or circumstances that are beyond her control; she simply forges unambivalently ahead.

The same cannot be said for my friend April. She's the head of her own company, a cosmetics firm she founded twenty-five years ago. Thrice divorced, she is the first to admit that her career path is littered with emotional losses. She is eternally looking over her shoulder to see if anyone's gaining on her; she has few friends; she never takes vacations; she is feared by her employees, who are intimidated by her brusqueness; she cannot seem to sustain an intimate partnership, much as she would like one.

"I don't suffer fools gladly," she says, expelling a rueful sigh. "I have zero patience with stupidity or inefficiency. I don't ask more of others than of myself—but then, I never relax. I don't have an identity apart from my work. Even when I had emergency surgery, I was on the phone talking to clients until they wheeled me into the operating room."

Both these women are competitive daughters, for whom an ordinary life of human scale is unthinkable. Such daughters recoil from the strictures of stereotypical womanhood. Not for them the confines of hearth and home, although many do in fact marry and have children. Rather they need a larger canvas on which to define themselves.

Their emotional and intellectual wanderlust must find its expression beyond family and sexist constraint. They have charted life courses that have propelled them into the world of accomplishment, of influence, of wealth. And if there have been sacrifices along the way, well, the same can be said for their male counterparts.

But of course it's not the same. For men success and masculinity are synonymous. For women success and femininity are frequently uneasy companions, often at war with each other.

The Competitive Edge. There's something about women at the top that especially captures our curiosity and interest. One looks for the chink in the scented armor, the weakness in the impenetrable facade. Three decades into the feminist movement, such women are still subject to a certain cultural derision: They "made it," their critics sniff, because they do not know how to be real women.

Some people can't wait to see a powerful woman tumble. Senator Pat Schroeder weeps after a primary defeat, and the traditionalist nods in righteous recognition: See? She's a "woman" after all. Leona Helmsley is indicted for not paying her taxes, and stories of her ferocious temper and tongue-lashings are trotted out. See? That's what happens when women try to wield power in the broad arena usually vouchsafed only for men.

There are those unusual women—my friend Pamela is one of them—who are able to live lives of stunning accomplishment without feeling their gender identity is compromised and without becoming arrogant. For them, work and love, strength and tenderness, are not mutually exclusive. They are able to blend both aspects of their characters, unencumbered by internal conflict and turmoil.

But many more competitive daughters, like April, are torn apart by their ambition. Somewhere along the line these women got the idea that they had to *choose* between their work lives and their emotional lives. There is little room or time for love. They funnel all their energies into their masterful sides, while their empathetic, nurturing sides are neglected or, in some cases, wholly ignored. A narrowly focused drive is essential to their self-definition.

Competitive daughters—whether imperturbable or conflicted— are not average women; they do not want average lives. And they never have.

The Making of a Competitive Daughter

Female achievement is spawned in a variety of ways—through innate ability, or birth order, or by virtue of the lucky break where hard work and opportunity meet. But of all the variables of female success, *the most significant is the competitive daughter's relationship with her father.*

Let's examine these variables one at a time.

Temperament. Sustained achievement almost never occurs without the inner determination that characterizes competitive daughters virtually from birth. Most of the ambitious women I interviewed knew from earliest childhood that they were destined to lead special lives—if not exactly marked for greatness, at least *not* marked for the mundane female stereotype.

Many of these women have a particular talent for living—all possess a boundless zest. As children they walked and talked early, they seldom napped, they asked a million questions, they could not be idle. They were blessed with energy, intelligence, curiosity, and above all tenacity.

Such children are nothing if not persistent. They view their setbacks as one less hurdle to vault, believing that the law of averages will eventually turn in their favor. Indeed they are ignited into action, rather than discouraged, by challenges.

What sets them apart from other children, however, is not simply their lustiness. Rather it is that they are remarkably free of fearfulness. Much of their temperament may be their luck in the genetic draw.

According to Harvard psychologist Jerome Kagan, who has investigated the biological components of temperament, of those children who are fearless in infancy—roughly 30 percent of all children—90 percent are *still* gutsy at the age of seven. These youngsters, Dr. Kagan speculates, may have central nervous systems that simply preclude skittishness; they just aren't as physiologically predisposed to stress as other people.

Of course one competitive child's beguiling boldness can be another's obnoxiousness. Dr. David Kiersey and Marilyn Bates, researchers of temperament, cite two personality types who are most likely to succeed.

One is the "Dionysian" sort—the impulsive, tireless worker who loves change and who thrives in a crisis. Such people do not gnaw on the probabilities of failure—or, for that matter, of success. Instead they simply lunge, often unprepared, for a goal, a task, a novel experience. They are extraordinarily sanguine; people love their company and are charged by their enthusiasm. But few people know them well, since they are not given to emotional nuance and grow restless when they feel confined.

The other type most likely to achieve is the "Promethean" temperament. These people crave competence and knowledge. In their constant quest for self-improvement and expertise, they are inordinately hard on themselves. Self-doubt goads these people in their pursuit of personal excellence. Prometheans are absolutely certain of their own opinions because they've studied all the possibilities. Hence they often give the impression of insufferable arrogance.

Birth Order. Where the achiever places in the sibling roster has a great deal to do with her need to win. Firstborns and only children, as we know, are expected to do well—to reflect favorably on their parents, to be, in a sense, family ambassadors.

But a substantial minority of secondborns and middle children *also* make good in their careers, albeit for different reasons. These achievers tend to have distant or even hostile relationships with their same-sex parents and reach out and wrest from the world the attention or approval they do not get at home.

Whatever their birth order, achieving children are the object of sibling jealousy. Virtually all of the achieving women I interviewed had a sibling who resented her for unwittingly setting what seemed to be an impossible standard of success.

The Father Factor. Which brings us to the father-daughter relationship. Research indicates, not surprisingly, that women who succeed identify more with their fathers than with their mothers, more with traditional male values than female ones.

Nowhere is this more apparent than among tomboys—girls who act like boys. Many competitive daughters were in childhood anything but hothouse flowers; a substantial number of them were more comfortable playing with boys than girls, with wearing jeans than pinafores.

The desire to be the opposite sex, or at least to have its *advantages,* is over two times more common in girls than boys—especially between the ages of four and eleven—and most tomboys eventually outgrow it. Still, tomboys are not necessarily born that way. There's evidence that circumstances force them to conclude that it's better to be male than female.

According to Dr. Ken Zucker of the Child and Family Studies Centre at Toronto's Clarke Institute of Psychiatry, tomboyism is primarily learned behavior. For example, some girls wish they were boys because their mothers resent being female and pass on that gender disdain to their daughters. Other girls become tomboys because they want to be more pleasing to their fathers. Still other girls are treated like boys by parents who wished for a son and got a daughter instead.

Thus, depending on their family histories, competitive daughters tend to fall into one of three categories:

- *The protégée*—whose father was a loving mentor, encouraging all her abilities, and whose mother was supportive and warm.
- *The ersatz "son"*—who is the "boy" her parents never had, or the "boy" who makes it easier for Daddy to relate to her, or the understudy for an older brother who died.
- *The substitute "husband"*—who, because her parents divorced or her father died, was raised solely by her mother and who became the "man" of the family.

The Protégée

Daphne, thirty-four, an only child, is the youngest president in the history of a major book publishing company. Her father always believed she would be an enormous success. When she was growing up in London, he'd tell everyone that she was going to become the first female prime minister of England. "Make that 'first *Jewish* prime minister,' " she jokingly edits.

> I am a clone of my father. The difference is he's 1941, and I'm 1991. He wanted me to be the best I could be, and as far as he was concerned, nothing would prevent it. He felt I could be a pioneer—a female who was also enormously successful.
>
> He adored me. He wanted me to tell him what I felt and thought. We always fought, because we're both volatile. If I argued with him, he'd say, "I forbid you to speak to me that way!" and I knew in my heart of hearts that's *exactly* how he wanted me to speak to him—to stand my ground, just like him. He always dominated my mother, but he never dominated me, and she had the good sense not to stand in the way of our relationship. He demanded and he commanded, but he never shut my mouth. He just gave me my head. I'm called hard. I'm not hard. My father wasn't either. We're just *stubborn;* we don't give up.

Fathers like Daphne's look upon their gifted daughters with enormous pride, grooming them for greatness, coaching them through their adolescence and young adulthood and pulling every possible string to help them advance quickly in their careers. But such fathers also appreciate their talented daughters' "feminine" qualities—their efforts to look attractive, their sensitivity and understanding.

For these fathers femininity and female success are not mutually exclusive. Moreover they are not rattled when their daughters reach puberty. Such loving but exacting fathers are able to reframe their tender feelings for their budding adolescent daughters, replacing the physical intimacy of childhood with mentorship—even debate, which they encourage.

Protégées are allowed to argue, to defend their opinions with their fathers—a quality, says one group of researchers, that has an enormous impact on the daughters' ability to hold an opposing point of view without feeling that they will be rejected. "Conflict," the researchers write, ". . . may reveal depth in parent-child relationships and in the context of warm involvement may have positive rather than negative implications."

Another study of female achievers showed that their fathers were "brilliant . . . personally secure, vital, and achievement-oriented." These fathers prized their daughters' femininity—which may have been a factor in their not viewing their daughters as competitors—at the same time having high expectations of them. Of equal importance, the marriages of these supportive fathers were harmonious. As a result their daughters felt cherished by their fathers *and* by their mothers, both of whom prepared them for autonomy.

Similarly the protégées in my sample were hybrids of both their parents' values, incorporating into their core identities the "masculine" and the "feminine." But they also profited from the two sides of their fathers' evolving paternity: the tender, playful daddies who romped with them and scratched their backs and read them bedtime stories in childhood, and the fathers who tailored that intimacy as the daughters moved into womanhood. The weight of Daddy's love was the same—only its contours changed, in tandem with the changing contours of the daughters themselves.

As Dina, thirty-six, puts it,

My mother provided nurturing for me, but my father was really my role model; he was so much more exciting. He never said to me, "Girls don't do that." He taught me how to build furniture. So today I can enjoy being a "girl"—shopping and nesting and all that. But I also can't sit still. I always have to be doing something productive.

The importance to the emotional futures of daughters of this paternal permission to compete and disagree cannot be overstated. Daughters whose loving fathers prize both their achievements and their sensitivity do not regard assertiveness as antithetical to femininity. Such paternal acceptance and affection are as integral to the daughters' sexuality as they are to their professional success, as we shall see.

The Ersatz Son

Some competitive daughters start out as their fathers' favorites, only to be abruptly demoted later on. This withdrawal of paternal favoritism occurs for a number of reasons: The daughter's emerging ambitiousness may cut against the grain of her traditional father's gender expectations; or the daughter is upstaged by a younger brother, to whom Dad shifts his allegiance and interest.

The most common cause of paternal distancing, however, is the daughter's puberty, when she is obviously no longer a child. Even girls who were encouraged by their fathers to do boyish things, such as help fix a car or play football, suddenly stopped being Daddy's favorite when they developed breasts. From then on their fathers pushed them toward matrimony and traditional femininity.

The Untouchables. One reason for this sudden switch in paternal favoritism, this attempt to marry off gifted daughters, is that it may be a subconscious way for the father to send his daughter safely into someone else's arms—a deflection of incestuous attraction. But it could also be that the rebelling competitive daughter threatens to upset the power balance in the family headed by a man who insists that all power reside in himself.

Still, these daughters know nothing of their fathers' psychological confusion or insecurity or sexual jitters. They get their fathers' message—if not its meaning—and rework it to fit their own temperaments, unlike, say, their more timid or combative sisters.

Competitive daughters compute Daddy's distance as a mandate to be as achieving as possible, hoping to attract their fathers' admiration, if not affection.

It is this sudden paternal retreat and its psychological impact of which competitive daughters speak with particular sadness.

Adele, forty-one, is the president of a shipping company. Her father was a wealthy businessman, her mother a submissive housewife who lived contentedly in her powerful husband's shadow. Casting a nostalgic eye at a silver-framed photograph of her father, Adele says,

> For a long time I was my father's darling. We were a perfect match. He loved my spirit. But as soon as I hit my teens, suddenly I became chattel, just like my mother. The only time my father would talk to me was when we played poker—we'd play for hours. He taught me all the tricks. My business acumen is a direct result of those card games. I much preferred his company to my mother's. But I didn't want him to control me the way he controlled her. I determined very early that I had to become economically independent. For me marriage was out of the question; marriage meant being like my mother. I wanted to be in charge, like my father.

Other competitive daughters, however, *never* were their fathers' favorites; indeed, their fathers made it clear that by virtue of gender alone they were disappointments.

When Frieda was growing up, her father made no secret of his bias for sons: "Too bad you're not a boy" was the litany of her youth. She says,

> He treated me like a little doll when I was small. But when I became an adolescent, our relationship became stormy. We fought about everything—school, money, what I was wearing. He was very, very critical.
>
> I figured the way to please him was to be *like* him. So I became a terrific athlete. I could run faster, bat a ball farther, climb a tree higher than any boy on the block. In a way I *was* my father—the flower of his seed. That drive affected my life tremendously, the idea that you must succeed and do well. But it also made me wonder if I would ever be attractive to

men. I hated being a girl. It took me a long time to feel like a woman.

Outclassed   Mothers   and   Siblings. Occasionally,   however, Daddy's retreat is fomented by a domineering mother who is envious of her firstborn daughter's gifts and of her affinity with her father. This maternal jealousy often erupts with the birth of a second girl.

Here mother and younger daughter form an alliance against father and firstborn, splitting the family in two and creating in the favored daughter enormous ambivalence about Daddy's love.

"I'm the son my parents never had," says Greta, forty-two, a network news correspondent. "I had all the attributes of a firstborn boy: I was a very quick, did everything well, won awards all through school. I'm just naturally compulsive. So my father poured all his hopes into me. It made my mother wild with jealousy."

Greta's success also caused enormous friction with her younger sister, Tina, who quickly became her mother's clone. Tina had trouble in school. Her grades were mediocre, she was shy, she was neither athletic nor terribly attractive, unlike her older sister. Says Greta,

> I was the star and she was not, and she resented it bitterly. So my mother began to make me feel ashamed of my successes, saying they were the cause of all my sister's problems. If I won something, I was scared to bring it home because of the reaction it would produce. My father was secretly pleased about my achievements, but he dared not say so—at least not in front of my mother and sister.

Winning the sibling race didn't make such achievers feel like big shots. Rather winning was bittersweet. The rush of success was accompanied by an undertow of regret. There were no clear victories. Each kudo was paid for in a sibling's defeat and, all too frequently, a mother's reminder of it.

This is an example of the unresolved Oedpial triangle. The daughter is unable to integrate both father and mother into her identity. Rather she must choose: Either be like Dad or be like Mom. Of such things is lifelong sibling enmity made.

The   competitive   daughter   who   wins   Daddy,   however clandestinely, and loses Mommy and one or more siblings, has little difficulty accomplishing. Where she runs into trouble is *attaching.*

When winning a father's love equates with the loss of her mother—her female role model—or a sibling—her generational peer—all her future relationships may be imperiled. She may be stranded in the impersonal working world of men with few female friends, quarantined by ambition from true intimacy and warmth.

The Second String. Other sonlike achievers are secondborns whose older brothers died and to whom their fathers transferred their hopes and expectations. These daughters felt honored by their fathers' favoritism, however much it may have been by default. For these women the compulsion to succeed was a way of assuaging their fathers' grief—in a sense, picking up the banner of the fallen male sibling and finishing his course.

Leah, thirty-five, whose brother died four years before she was born, always felt loved and appreciated by both her parents. If she suffered at all in childhood, it was because her father, a commercial airline pilot, was away so much. "I missed him desperately," she says. "But when he was home, he was so wonderful. He'd read to me, or take me on walks, or he'd come into my room just to talk. Still, the time we had was spent in minutes, rather than hours."

Leah's mother was a gentle, elegant woman who worked part-time in the local public library. And while Leah adored her, it was her father upon whom she patterned herself. Sometimes he'd take her to the airport and let her sit in the pilot's seat of a jetliner. "It was thrilling," she says.

> I decided I wanted to do what he did. I became a pilot too. I'm absolutely driven—it's my nature. I felt if I took my mother's career path, I'd be lost, but if I took my father's route, I'd find myself.
>
> Still, I could never really make up for my brother. I could aspire to my father's profession, but I could not be a fantasy person.

As Leah talks about her father, it is with obvious love. But there is one subject that she touches upon only glancingly, as though eager to enter it quickly into the record and then to sprint past it: The day she took her first solo flight, her parents accompanied her to the airfield. When she landed, her father was nowhere in sight. Later he was found in a hangar, chatting with a maintenance worker.

Why, I asked her, did he leave? She wistfully replies, "I don't know. Maybe he was feeling competitive. Maybe he was thinking, 'This is what my son would have done.' To this day I don't know why he left."

"Did you ever ask him?"

"No. I guess I didn't want to hear the answer."

She mulls over the question a moment longer. Suddenly she pulls up another memory: "When my younger sister was born, my father disappeared then, too, because, he said, he was so disappointed that it wasn't a boy."

Leah winces at the thought that no matter how rosily she recalls her father's attentiveness, and regardless of how hard she tried to be a good "son," she could never be the child of her father's heart. She was, after all, only a girl.

Motherless Achievers. Other circumstances can cause an achieving daughter to become an ersatz son, to wit, when her mother dies. In this case identifying with Daddy is not simply the easiest way to get his attention; it's also a survival mechanism—a way to guarantee that he won't "leave" too.

Carlotta's mother died when Carlotta was twelve. Her father, a professor, was, she says, a "dominator"—immensely dashing, talkative, opinionated, erudite. His career and trips to conferences made the few hours he *was* home a tiny but critical window of filial opportunity. Says Carlotta, forty-eight,

> My mother was the feeling person; my father was the brain person—it was almost a caricature of sex roles. I was never really fathered. My father only spoke to me if I spoke to him. So after my mother died, I reframed his unavailability as a plus: I saw it as giving me "space" so that I'd be autonomous and have my own life. The truth is, he just wasn't ever really thinking of me.
>
> You see, I couldn't be both motherless and the child of an unloving father. I couldn't let myself see that there was this hollow shell where I thought my father was. The only way that he could be a father to me was to give me self-respect as an intellectual.

So I apprenticed myself to him; I was his intellectual heir. I wanted to *be* my father when I grew up.

The "Substitute Husband"

A number of competitive daughters became successful not simply because of their inherent grit but because they had grit thrust upon them. These are the daughters who lost their fathers due to death or divorce and who felt that, almost overnight, they were promoted from child to grown-up—particularly if they did not have older brothers.

When Celeste, forty-three, the owner of a midtown Manhattan restaurant, was nine and her brother two, their father was killed in an automobile accident. From that day on she felt she had to take care of her mother—a loving but unassertive woman who relied on Celeste to support her emotionally and later financially.

There is about Celeste an air of quiet assurance; nothing seems to rattle her. Given her early loss, she is unusually free of anxieties. She says,

> I idolized my father, and we have a lot of the same qualities. I have his solid core. I have his physical strength. I'm a brave person—I don't get flustered. Maybe it's because I've been through the worst—I lost my father, and it made me stronger.
>
> After his death I became the decision maker in the family and my mother's protector. And when I grew up, the last thing in the world I wanted was to be financially dependent. The thought of not having my own money scared the hell out of me because my mother was so needy, and because men were not to be counted upon—they might die. It was much safer to rely only on myself.

Other competitive daughters were brought up by divorcees who were not only angry at their ex-husbands but resentful if their daughters continued to see or be loyal to their fathers. Unlike most children of widows, these daughters had no choice but to split their allegiances—and their identities.

Maria, thirty-seven, is executive vice president of a large advertising agency. She recalls that when she was nine, she sat huddled next to her weeping mother as her father angrily packed a suitcase and stormed out of the house, never to return. Says Maria,

> There was no question whose side I was on. My father was a shit. Once he left, he seldom sent child-support checks. My mother was the fragile, victim type, so I was always the one who wasn't fainting, wasn't sick, wasn't falling apart. I had to take on the masculine role; I was the man of the house. So I didn't complain, I didn't give anyone any problems. I just brought home the bacon and was very, very responsible and independent. In high school I was a straight-A student and class president. I worked thirty hours a week to help support the family because my mother's income wasn't enough.
>
> But I also became very hard, very brittle. The emptiness of not having a father became a kind of "I'll show *you*" thing: Achievement helped fill in a lot of emptiness.

These daughters are forced to grow up in a hurry. Indeed, the younger they are at the time of their parents' divorce or fathers' death, the sooner they become miniadults, testing their mettle outside the family. Fatherless girls tend to get higher grades in school than daughters from intact homes. And while they are piling up achievements, they spin dreams that will carry them as far from economic and emotional want as possible. They are determined never to need anyone ever again.

Addiction to work helps to forestall feelings of worthlessness and abandonment. What drives these daughters is the unconscious wish to be too busy to feel. One way to numb the pain of life without father is not only to *become* him but also to have so many projects and activities that there is no respite, no empty hours, into which an awareness of their painful emotional losses might tumble.

Behind this workaholism is sometimes a smoldering narcissism and grandiosity. No matter how much power, income, and press coverage these daughters acquire in adulthood, a sense of satisfaction eludes them. No success is sufficient to dissolve their feelings of fraudulence. Never sated by their plaudits, never feeling they deserve their success, they are eternally playing catch-up.

In all these ways fatherless daughters keep their fathers—*and their idolization of or disappointment in them*—alive, frozen in the daughters' grim determination to remain resolutely autonomous, to be always in control.

None of which augurs well for their intimate attachments.

The Competitive Daughter in Love

Those women who are inherently loners and whose work ethic is not a defense against pain and self-doubt are generally protégées, who are content to lead lives of solitary achievement. Should love come their way, their partnerships are equal parts affection, friendship, and autonomy.

Writes Dr. Henry B. Biller,

> Women who can comfortably pursue their occupational interests and develop their intellectual competence as well as be successful wives and mothers are more likely to have come from homes in which both parents were positively involved with their children.

Most of the competitive daughters in my sample, however, at one time or another had serious difficulties in their love lives: Work and love represent a psychological split.

For some, career has always dominated their emotional agendas. Love, if it is ever to happen, is relegated to the sometime, the amorphous, distant horizon. They neglect their emotional and intimacy needs, pushing them out of sight.

Then there are those achievers—generally from abusive childhoods—who in youth were *desperate* for love to the exclusion of everything else. Only when they began to acquire a measure of self-confidence were they able to tap into their innate talents, their suppressed ambition, and become fierce competitors.

Here, too, love sometimes presented problems: Once they found their professional voices, many were afraid that love would send them reeling back to the neediness they worked so hard to overcome.

Thus the romantic patterns of competitive daughters vary widely.

Flying Solo. One of the components of achievement is a thick skin—an immunity, whether feigned or authentic, to vulnerability, and a need to be in control. Being invulnerable means keeping one's emotions in check. Falling in love means sharing or even *losing* control.

Some achievers can't risk it. They are *terrified* of love—it feels as though they are careening through space. The only relationships they can abide are those with male colleagues, men who are kept at bay by professional camaraderie and one-upmanship.

For such women, heterosexual love and female friendship are to be avoided. Says Betty, fifty,

> I never had any real girlfriends until about ten years ago. For the first time I became interested in forming female friend-ships, because I no longer saw women as bitchy and manipu-lative. I never trusted women before; I only confided in men —and only in the office. I realize now how much I missed.

For women who cannot get close to a female friend, having a balanced, intimate relationship with a man is next to impossible.

One fifty-five-year-old competitor said that she *tried* throughout her twenties and thirties to marry. Indeed she got engaged to one man after another, because she knew that's what her parents ex-pected of her. "But," she says with a laugh, "my body kept rebel-ling. Either I couldn't sleep, or I couldn't *stop* sleeping, or I got shingles. My body told me what my prefeminist mind couldn't: 'Marriage is not for you.' I was able to put it off until I was forty-one—a neat trick for my generation."

As for younger competitive daughters, the postfeminist climate that has brought women into the executive suites of corporate America allows them to avoid matrimony. These women can af-ford to be choosy—and many of them unapologetically choose to remain unattached and invulnerable.

Says Lila, twenty-eight, a journalist,

> Marriage fences you in. You can't go anywhere or do anything without consulting or reporting to somebody. With my work schedule—being shipped around the globe on various assign-ments—a social or family life just isn't in the cards. Maybe I'll change my mind someday, but right now the last thing I want is to be a wife.

Of such single-minded daughters, Dr. Marianne Goodman says,

I have a number of female patients who, even in their forties, have never married. In almost every case the daughter has consciously refused to identify with her mother and has gone to the opposite extreme of what her mother was. And the best way to do that is never to become a wife, never to become a mother, because they're so afraid of becoming like their mothers. These women perceive that there are only two options: be like Mom and hate it or be alone. Clearly there is another healthy choice—to have a relationship with a man that is different from the "remembered" one between mother and father. Often these women have made their parents caricatures. In therapy they are helped to see their parents as real people and to see more accurately the relationship as it existed rather than the black-and-white situation they imagine it was.

There are those unattached competitive daughters who hate *all* men. For example several of Dr. Goodman's female patients had abusive fathers and grew up witnessing paternal belligerence and forming protective alliances with their mothers. Says Dr. Goodman, "It was guerrilla warfare—we women against men."

Then there are the daughters of incestuous fathers—women who, through ambition, made certain that they would never have to rely on a man for anything and vowed to become as strong as men. Since love and shame and even physical pain are indistinguishable to them, the safer course is to feel as little as possible—to channel all their emotions into their careers and to become social isolates.

Other determinedly single competitors are the daughters of fathers who either died or were emotionally or physically absent. These daughters compensate for the loss of father by restoring him through their own ambition—what Elyce Wakerman calls the "restitution" theory. In idealizing their fathers, they cannot betray him by loving any other man; they are instead married to their work.

Combining Forces. At least half the achieving women I interviewed did not marry until they were in their thirties, forties, and fifties. And when they did, most chose men who were gentle and loving.

More so than other women, competitive daughters are singularly adept at finding nurturing partners. Some are able to relinquish their need to control and allow themselves to be taken care of and at the same time to express their own tenderness and vulnerability. There is no crushing ambivalence, no fear that to love and be loved means that their strong identities will evaporate.

That's precisely the case with Celia, forty-three, head of a public relations firm. By the time she met Hank—whom she eventually married—two years ago, she was weary of being so stoically independent, so careful not to exude a whiff of neediness. She says,

> He was the first man who wasn't threatened by, or who didn't make fun of, my success. With Hank, it was "Wow! You'll be able to support me!" He's my good daddy, lover, and best friend all wrapped up in one package. He lets me be the star, but there's nothing wimpish about him. In certain areas I'm the dominant one, but I'm very careful not to abuse it.

But other competitive daughters, who are also drawn to loving men, cannot sustain their romantic attachments because they don't know when to *stop* competing. These are daughters who have achieved partial separation from their parents; they have come of age economically and professionally but haven't finished their emotional evolution to true separateness. Many had fathers who were, as Dr. Biller puts it, "aloof, perfectionistic, and self-disciplined" and who did not provide for their daughters enough emotional support for them to develop solid self-confidence, the kind that is unafraid of expressing emotions.

So conditioned are such daughters to equate masculine tenderness with weakness and servility, they perceive gentle men as chumps. These women *must* dominate others—just as their fathers dominated them. Thus they become involved only with passive or easily intimidated men, in whom they quickly lose interest. Says Becky, twenty-eight,

> My ex-boyfriend was an adoring type. He thought I was wonderful in every possible way. So I picked on him constantly. I had no respect for him because he worshiped me. He was like a puppy. I got rid of him in a hurry. Come to think of it, I've dumped a lot of men like that.

Still other competitive daughters don't lose interest in their low-key partners, because a weak man satisfies their need to control.

The easiest way for such daughters to deny their own vulnerability is to make sure their partners stay weak. The tragedy of this bargain, of course, is that they find themselves right back where they started in childhood: deprived of the love and advocacy of a caring, confident man.

One forty-five-year-old woman, a wealthy fashion designer who recognized the destructiveness of her marital behavior, divorced her passive husband and went into therapy to come to terms with her need to always have the romantic upper hand. Today she is ready to express her own vulnerability in a much healthier way. She says,

> I never tried to find a man to take care of me. Because I was raised to be so independent and mistrustful of men, I never looked for a kindly father figure in my lovers. Right now I wouldn't mind one! I'd like to be nurtured for a change.
>
> That feeling was a long time in coming.

When a competitive daughter is ready for healthy love to come into her life, it has remarkable consequences, not just emotionally but professionally as well.

In a landmark study of achieving women by Drs. Margaret Hennig and Anne Jardim, there were interesting differences between those women who found love and those who did not.

The women in one of the researchers' samples—none of whom had brothers—were the firstborn and undisputed favorites of their fathers. By their mid- to late thirties these women had reached the higher rungs of middle management, and their fathers were aging rapidly or dying.

It was at this point in their lives that, for some of them, femininity became a priority for the first time. Having established solid careers, they were able to address their long-neglected emotional needs. Many changed their hair and clothing styles, no longer feeling they had to appear defiantly asexual. They eased back on their work commitments and began dating. These women were able to take a chance on love and female friendship.

Interestingly, expanding their identities in these ways had an extraordinarily beneficial effect on their careers: They rose to vice president and president in their companies. In giving themselves permission to form intimate attachments in their personal lives, they were able to relate better to their colleagues.

The Competitive Daughter in Bed

For those achieving women who do not polarize love and work and who are not conflicted by what they consider "masculine" and "feminine" behavior, sex within a loving relationship can be joyous.

For other competitive daughters, however, sex is yet another contest—and often a weapon. Because competitors want to do everything well, being *the best in bed* is almost as important to some of them as being the best out of it. The ability to achieve orgasm, then, is part of their mastery; indeed, so sexually expert are they that they can be libidinously intimidating—"impotizing," as Dr. Avodah Offit puts it, their partners in their eagerness to outdistance them erotically, as though sex were a marathon.

Still other achievers have trouble shifting gears from the boardroom to the bedroom; confident though they may be at work, some of them lack confidence sexually. In a way they feel like neophytes—plagued by the thought that they don't know what to do in bed, that they are sexually unappealing, that they don't know how to attract a man.

Says Rita, thirty-one, a venture capitalist,

> Sometimes I look at myself in the mirror and I wonder, "What could a man possibly like about this body?" I have never, ever believed I'm sexually attractive. I've always believed that I was chosen by men for my abilities, not because of my sexuality, even though I'm bursting with desire to express love in a sensual way. Maybe it's because I've had no real practice with men loving me for myself. Certainly my father gave me no warmth, no touching, no model—only expectations for success.

It is the competitive daughters who are fatherless or whose fathers are remote who frequently have the most difficulty with sexual vulnerability. Says Elizabeth, a physician whose parents divorced when she was twelve,

> My father was incredibly controlling and cold. His idea of a hug was to place his fingertips on your shoulder and briefly press down. I was the oldest living virgin when I had sex for the first time—I was twenty-six. It wasn't until eight years

later, when I married my husband, that I finally had an orgasm. He's a perfect match for me—he's laid back about everything. Sexually he's wonderfully relaxed and bawdy. There's only one problem: I've always relied on myself, so I've never been able to ask for anything. It's hard for me to ask in bed. Sometimes I'll just move my husband's hand if I'm having trouble reaching climax. But I can't seem to say, "Would you touch me here? Would you go down on me?" It's all I can do even to tell you.

The Cost of Being a Competitive Daughter

Many achieving women—such as Pamela, mentioned at the beginning of this chapter—had parents who encouraged both their competitive and their feeling sides. These women successfully combine work and love, achievement and emotionality, the ability to take care of and be taken care of. Life is not wasted on such women. Their energy and enthusiasm allow them to taste and savor all the good things in life.

For many other competitive daughters, however, prize winning comes at a high psychic price—they pay dearly for accomplishment.

Some pay through loneliness. These are the women who are unable to form intimate attachments, who are so much a part of the good-old-boy network that, emotionally, they are in a sense good old boys themselves. Anything "feminine" is to be denigrated, including female friendship.

Such isolation precludes the capacity for mutually loving, freely sexual romantic attachments. The resolve never to need or to want results in the inability to receive love. Risking all for the tangible success, risking nothing for the uncertainties of love and sexual abandon, many competitive daughters spend their entire lives trying to measure up, alone.

And for some of them the price of their perfectionism is painfully apparent when they *do* form romantic partnerships: The self-control of such women can become self-denial.

These are the women who cannot take any form of criticism. To admit they cannot do everything well means that they can do *nothing* well and that they are essentially unlovable. Said one woman,

It's only recently that my husband can say something mildly critical and I don't put up my dukes, translating his comment as an indictment of my entire worth. I tried all those years to please my father through achievement. I had no ground rules about what was lovable. So I've always felt that my husband didn't want me because I was lovable but because I was useful to him in some way.

The other day he said, "Why do you get so upset if I tell you, say, the coffee is a little bitter? Don't you understand that it's a superficial thing and has nothing to do with my love for you?"

I screwed up my courage and said, "I guess I don't. What makes someone lovable?" He gave me this elegant answer: "I love you for your humanness."

I burst into tears. No one ever said that to me before.

Some achievers find, over time, that the weight of their responsibilities and the denial of their emotional and spiritual needs become overwhelming. They simply burn out, having breakdowns, or developing ulcers, or suffering heart attacks. Driven to be as powerful as men, they may acquire "masculine" power and plaudits, but they also acquire the health risks of driving male ambition.

Many competitive daughters in their thirties or forties are able to assess their losses, to stop attempting to be their own fathers, and to allow their neglected nurturing and feeling sides to blossom. Shifting emotional gears is not always easy for these women; the competitive daughter has the most trouble summoning the nerve merely to be human and to admit she needs help.

Those who do admit that need are, in a way, far ahead of other women. Having taken responsibility for their own lives, having achieved economic security, these women can *afford* to be generous to themselves. The very determination they applied to their careers they now apply to finding a way to get beyond needing to be defined solely by their credentials. They allow themselves to be angry at the fathers who suffocated their femininity. These women stick to and profit from therapy, just as they profited from their professional tenacity. Relieved to finally stop trying so hard, they transform themselves.

When the courageous competitive daughter is ready to relinquish her agonizing, rigid, angry, lonely control, she has a chance, for the first time, to feel whole.

Profile of an Achieving Daughter

When I arrive at the Chicago condominium forty stories above
Lake Michigan, I am greeted by a housekeeper who says, "Kimberly will be right with you. She's on the phone."

A few minutes later Kimberly rushes into the living room, apol-
ogizing for keeping me waiting. "I gotta get out of this business,"
says the forty-six-year-old financial planner. "The market is in the
dumper. But I *love* it. Every day is another crisis."

Sitting cross-legged on a couch, Kimberly says we only have
ninety minutes for our interview. Her bridegroom of six months is
flying home from a business trip, and she's to pick him up at the
airport. "I'm *crazy* about the man," she says.

Kimberly grew up in a small midwestern town, where her father
owned a grocery shop. Father and daughter always had a special
relationship, she says. It was her mother who was her nemesis.

> I wasn't afraid of her. I defied her, because my father adored
> me. She was hell-bent on making me into a prig. She was
> always giving me Toni home permanents and putting me in
> frilly dresses. He didn't want me to be a boy. He just accepted
> me for who I was and thought I was adorable. I was very
> bright and very independent, and very, *very* stubborn; I still
> am. I was a tomboy; I always trusted boys more than girls. For
> a long time I said, "I can't be friends with girls because
> they're terrible." Maybe it's because when Daddy wasn't
> home, my mother would hit me. She absolutely loathed me. I
> used to tell her that someday I'd get even with her.

As much as Kimberly worshiped her father, she knew she had to
grow up fast and get out of the house and the town in which, she
says, she felt suffocated. Suddenly, when she was eighteen, her
father died. Six months later she was on a plane to Chicago.

She didn't have a plan, she says. All she knew was that she was
never, ever going to get married. Her financial career happened
almost by accident. She got a job assisting a high-level investment
banker, and because she was a quick study, she was rapidly given
more and more responsibility.

> I was terrified someone would find out I didn't know what I
> was doing. But to mask that, I just pretended I knew every-

thing. My love life just went down the tubes. I never picked out appropriate men. My business was my survival; it became my identity. It actually was who I was. Weekends were an agony. I didn't have any friends because I was so hostile.

When Kimberly was forty-three, her mother, whom she saw only on rare occasions through the years, died. Suddenly a series of awarenesses galvanized Kimberly: She was no longer young; she was, except professionally, utterly alone; she had nothing to show for her hard work but money.

Around that time Ernie, fifty-two, who was recently divorced, came into her life—as a client. She was sitting in her office discussing his investments, and he casually mentioned that he was taking his daughter, whom he adores, to dinner.

Suddenly Kimberly burst into tears. "I had never done anything like that before," she says. "It was an absolute no-no to be open with a client. But suddenly I found myself talking about my father and how much I envied Ernie's daughter."

That night Kimberly broke another rule: She joined Ernie and his daughter for dinner. In the next two months she saw Ernie every night—and she fell desperately in love for the first time.

He told me, "I love you exactly as you are. Everything that you've done in your life is part of who you are now." But all this scares me. Ernie is as wonderful as my father was, and I don't want to confuse who the two are. I want to love Ernie for being Ernie, not for being a substitute for my father.

What I'm most scared of is that I'll forget how to take care of myself if I let Ernie take care of me. He's the first man I ever felt safe with. I don't want to run away from this. The funny thing is, there's a huge part of me that *loves* having Ernie nurture me. But I also worry all the time that something will happen to him—that he'll die and leave me, like my father did.

Before I leave, Kimberly takes me into her bedroom to show me a picture of her father. Suddenly she starts to weep. Pulling out a tissue, she says,

Does everyone you interview cry when they talk about their fathers? I can't talk about him without crying. I wonder if he was as good as I think he was. I never had as much of him as I wanted—so I'll probably never know.

14

▼▼▼▼▼▼▼

The Fearful Daughter

No one ever told me not to express my feelings as a kid. I just knew from day one not to. I'm like my dad that way. I never had an identity, not really, and because I don't, what I do is meaningless. I never realize the consequences of my actions, whether it's not paying my bills, or binge eating, or getting involved with rotten men. I'm never aware of the reality until it's literally hitting me over the head, like when the IRS closed my bank account. It's like I don't exist. I feel as if I could disappear from the earth, and no one would ever notice.

—CORRIE, THIRTY-TWO

When I was in my twenties, I went to an election-night party, where I met Claudia and Eric, a couple I had seen occasionally at other functions but didn't really know. Eric, a big and burly stockbroker, held forth at angry length about the candidates, while his wife, a plump and altogether amiable but rather nervous housewife, politely listened.

Midway through the evening Eric—braced by several drinks—tossed a racial slur into the conversation. Claudia blurted out, "Oh, I'm sure you don't mean that." Suddenly Eric's cheeks flushed a furious red, and he shouted, "Shut your fat mouth! No one asked your opinion." There was a sharp intake of breath as the group fell into embarrassed silence.

Claudia studied the cocktail napkin in her hand. I turned to her and whispered, "Good for you."

Her head jerked up, she fixed me with an even gaze, and said, "I don't need rescuing."

Claudia's reaction puzzled me, not because I expected her gratitude—clearly I should have aimed my comments directly at Eric—but because she appeared to take no offense at her husband's cruelty. Indeed she seemed almost to be defending it.

Since that night over twenty years ago I have met hundreds of variations of Claudia—women who are dominated by the men in their lives, women who appear to have no point of view, women who rely on others to orchestrate their thoughts and behavior. The opinion of the last forceful person to whom they spoke becomes their own—until the next opinion maker comes along. Such women have little sense of self apart from people's reactions to them. Often they don't even know *what* they feel.

Should someone be angry with them, these women are not merely upset—as, for example, is the good daughter, who throws herself into a flurry of chirpy reform. Rather these women *freeze*. It's as though their lives stop, and the next step might plunge them into an emotional abyss, a fate almost literally worse than death. To be berated is the emotional equivalent of an execution.

This is the fearful daughter, a woman who is terrified of criticism, terrified of confrontations, terrified of being caught in a mistake.

More than anything she is terrified of her own passions, especially anger. That's because she feels *everything:* All emotions seem to have equal weight, to be equally crushing. Because she is so reactive, so sensitive, she cocoons herself in anonymity.

To avoid attracting attention, she subordinates and protects herself in one of two ways—either in a relationship with someone who is controlling or even overpowering or by totally isolating herself from all attachments.

In the former category she sends her emotions off to some safer place—a lover or spouse, perhaps, who orchestrates her every move and is her mouthpiece; a parent, maybe, who still makes all her decisions; an employer, from whom she wants nothing so much as perpetual second billing.

In the latter category she cannot sustain any close relationship, social or professional. She prefers to live alone and frequently is self-employed. Respite from feeling—from *people*—is achieved in her voluntary solitary confinement. By withdrawing from life, nothing can ever touch her, not good feelings, not bad feelings. Alone she doesn't stir anyone's scrutiny or ire or curiosity. Alone she doesn't risk the heat of intimacy, or the pain of abandonment, or the humiliation of failure.

But the fearful daughter doesn't start out with all these self-effacing defenses. Once, long ago, she was just a sweet, shy kid, not so very different from a lot of people.

The Making of a Fearful Daughter

Being reserved is a characteristic of many deep thinkers, people who see life not as black or white but, rather, fascinating in its varying hues, its subtleties, its ambiguities. Such people, to rework Henry James, wish to "strike as many notes, deep, full and rapid, as [they] can." Indeed, the external reticence of such people often belies an active inner life, a rich imagination and profound intelligence.

For the fearful daughter, however, superficial impassivity may mask inner storms that threaten to capsize her. Her cautiousness is, in fact, the end result of a constellation of cultural, genetic, and psychological factors—as much imposed as inherent.

Temperament. Shyness and timidity are among the traits that have been the subject of study for most of recorded time. Over two thousand years ago in ancient Greece, Hippocrates speculated that certain people are "phlegmatic"—sluggish and unexcitable, biologically predisposed to take the low, slow emotional road. Today such behavior is called "introversion" by the psychological community.

There's a lot to be said for introverts. Without them, the collections in libraries and art museums would be slim indeed. In their book *Please Understand Me,* David Keirsey and Marilyn Bates, authorities on temperament, describe introverts as "territorial" and "intuitive" rather than "sociable" and "practical." That is, they are depleted, rather than animated, by groups; it is the solitary life of the mind, the adventure of introspection, that excites them. Because they tend to be extremely creative, their preference for privacy can result in extraordinary productiveness. Many writers, artists and musicians spring from this introverted pool.

Introversion shows up early in life. Timid youngsters—roughly 15 percent of all children—are not necessarily *fearful.* Rather they are "slow to warm up," overwhelmed by new places and faces, and need to be introduced slowly to them.

When such children are fortunate enough to have parents who are sensitive to their emotional prudence and who value their imaginativeness and lack of impulsiveness, these children eventually feel at ease with their understated personality. Timid children often outgrow their cautiousness; many a salesperson or television correspondent was once a shy child who, with love and encouragement, finally found her or his voice.

But many adults—including teachers—misread shy children, thinking them stupid. Ours is a fast-paced culture that looks upon shyness with a degree of disapproval, if not downright suspicion. Because introverts are ponderers, they are often written off as "nerds," which drives them deeper into themselves. Dr. Philip G. Zimbardo of Stanford University believes that most shyness is *learned behavior*—either a reaction to being denigrated or an imitation of a role model who is also shy.

For example, the seesaw of closeness and distance in relationships, according to Dr. Avodah Offit, is first negotiated within the parent-child connection. In the normal course of developmental events children experience the three-tiered components of interpersonal attachment: In infancy they learn touch *bonding,* followed by *attachment*—the recognition of parent figures—and then *separation* in the form of parental limit setting. Most healthy relationships contain components of all three experiences. Family therapists call this dynamic "self-in-relationship."

But if an introverted child did not get enough healthy parental touch and attachment, the child may be so starved for human connection that separation becomes anathema, a kind of death.

When parents of introverts perceive them as "losers" or "wimps" and withdraw their love and attention, these children, in time, may not experience their temperamental and intellectual depth as assets. Rather such children may view them as afflictions that invite—indeed deserve—ridicule.

Introverted children are easily intimidated and often are made to feel guilty by parents who are punitive or domineering or cold. Such parents may take advantage of their shy progeny, who are easy targets for emotional, physical, and sexual abuse.

In such circumstances a shy child's innate reserve can turn to fear and shame.

Without family nurturing and understanding, then, what starts out as shyness in childhood can become fear in adulthood—fear of too much distance and, paradoxically, fear of too much closeness, as we shall see.

Birth Order. Sibling rank also plays a role in a person's essential cautiousness. Many fearful adults grew up in families in which they were youngest children. In a Yale/Harvard study of shyness, for instance, two thirds of the subjects had older siblings who bullied or denigrated them.

Lastborn children tend to be composites of other people's opinions and directives—not just mothers and fathers but senior siblings as well, who boss them around and make fun of them. This is particularly true of "change of life" babies, who are accidentally or deliberately conceived long after the baby-making years of most people are over. These children are raised in households where *everyone* is a parent or parent figure. Either they are overprotected and coddled or they are teased and treated cruelly—perhaps, as is often the case, a bit of both. The most timid of such children often become invisible in the family, by default or by design—lost in the emotional shuffle.

Gender. Fearfulness comes with the territory of being female. In fact in examining the core components of stereotypical femininity, researchers in one study concluded that key ingredients are "fearfulness" and "inhibition"—hardly a surprising finding. It is an undebatable fact of life that girls and women are picked on and mistreated physically with far greater frequency than are boys and men.

Tragically this is especially true within the family. The most obvious example of gender-based mistreatment is incest abuse by fathers of daughters. Virtually all incest victims are frightened enough of their powerful fathers to keep quiet about such treatment, or to pretend it isn't happening. Even when daughters tell someone—their mothers or another relative—little is done about it.

Most incestuously abused daughters drive their memories underground, only to have them emerge in childhood and adulthood as physical symptoms, or snatches of memory, or simply a creepy feeling that steals over their bodies. Daughters who are abused in early childhood are most likely to forget the abuse.

As for physical abuse, here, too, we see the gender components of fearfulness. Teenage girls are much more likely to be brutalized than are boys, simply because they are not strong enough to overpower a father who is bent on beating them. The consequence of paternal violence, whether experienced directly or merely witnessed, paves the way for a fearful daughter's future revictimization.

In Dr. Judith Wallerstein's study of the children of divorce, for example, of those who grew up witnessing violence in their families, half later became involved in abusive attachments. Of the girls, three quarters were victims of their boyfriends' violence; of the boys in violent relationships, *all were abusers.*

Domineering Fathers. For most of the fearful daughters in my sample, it was their fathers who ruled the family. The daughters were clones of their submissive mothers, following their intimidated examples.

These fathers tended to be dictatorial, cowing their wives and children into obedience—especially fearful daughters, who throughout adolescence and adulthood remained abject rather than rebellious.

Mindy, forty-three, an only child, recalls that when she was growing up, any display of feelings on her part would send her father into a rage. She recalls,

> Recently I figured out why I always cry whenever I start talking about feelings. My father was an absolute tyrant who yelled constantly. His scariest yelling was when I showed emotion. One time when I was six, a bird flew into my bedroom, and I ran screaming hysterically into the living room. My father bellowed, "What's the matter with you! It's just a bird, for Christ's sake. Stop crying this instant!" To this day I still feel shameful and worthless and undeserving whenever I have a strong feeling.

Fearful daughters of domineering fathers are helpless prey, easily victimized through physical and sexual abuse, and the most likely to suffer from anorexia nervosa; Mindy suffered from all three.

Overwhelming Mothers. Sometimes, however, it is the mother who exacerbates the shy daughter's fearfulness.

A substantial number of fearful daughters in my sample had domineering mothers, who were critical or opinionated or ruled through martyrdom. These relationships were extremely complex, symbiotic, and ambivalent—*exacerbated by their fathers' psychological or physical absence.* These fathers played small but telling roles in their daughters' lives. Some were merely passive; others were involved only to administer periodic punishment. Some were di-

vorced, appearing sporadically; others were absent because of desertion or death.

The domineering mothers of fearful daughters were able to
march into the void left by uninvolved fathers. These mothers
tended to infantilize rather than parentify their shy daughters. At
the same time the daughters were so defeated by their mothers'
outspokenness or narcissism—and so neglected by their fathers—
that they were unable to express their own feelings, especially
their rage, to anyone. Rather they survived in the family by allowing their mothers to steamroller them emotionally.

Ella, thirty-nine, was a change-of-life baby whose emotionally
constricted father deferred on all domestic matters to her critical
and vain mother. Says Ella,

> I always did exactly what my parents wanted. Whenever they
> were angry, I would grovel. Even in my twenties I actually
> convinced myself that they were always right. I'd think, "How
> could I be such a rotten, ungrateful, inconsiderate person?"
> But the bigger influence was my mother, because my father
> gave her center stage. She died when I was twenty-five. I'm
> certain that had she lived, I never would have married, be-
> cause anyone I picked, she would have said wasn't good
> enough. I couldn't do anything without her approval.

For such daughters it becomes a matter of psychic life and death
not to outdo the mother. Thus, fearful daughters avoid competition,
not only with mother but in their careers as well.

Cultural Causes. So widespread is fearfulness in women that it
must be seen as more than merely a symptom of psychological and
family dysfunction. One need only examine the alarming statistics
regarding depression, battering, date rape, sexual abuse, and eating disorders—*whose victims are overwhelmingly female*—to see
that female fearfulness is a symptom of cultural dysfunction as
well.

Psychologists have long observed that far more women than
men suffer from depression. An estimated seven million American
women—one woman in four, as opposed to one in eight men—are
or will be clinically depressed. Most of them go untreated or are
misdiagnosed.

Some social scientists have theorized that female depression is a
consequence of women's greater ease—compared to men—with

talking about their unhappy feelings. As Dr. Donna Moreau, clinical director of the Children's Anxiety and Depression Clinic at Columbia Presbyterian Hospital in New York, told a reporter, "Boys just don't have the same kind of social network as girls. If they feel depressed, they can't talk about it. They end up withdrawing."

Recently, however, female depression has been linked to social rather than simply psychological causes. A 1988 study of college women from intact homes found that depressed adolescent girls frequently have fathers who are psychologically unavailable to them—a characteristic of a great many American fathers.

In 1990 a report by the Task Force on Women and Depression published by the American Psychological Association went even farther. It stated that female depression is more a consequence of women's acquaintance with sexual and physical abuse, poverty, and single parenthood—conditions more common to women than to men and indicative of the power differential between them— than almost any other factor.

One of the most significant findings of the report is that *37 percent of depressed women had been significantly sexually or physically abused by the time they reached the age of twenty-one.*

As we have learned, sexual abuse by fathers of daughters—in which the threat of violence is always implied—is reaching epidemic proportions, and may be even higher than the APA report just described indicates. Such abuse is reflected in statistics regarding psychopathology. As many as 40 percent of sexually abused children demonstrate pathological symptoms immediately; in adulthood 20 percent continue to suffer from serious psychopathology. These statistics are probably woefully deflated, given the denial by the victim's family, the culture, and, of course, the daughter herself.

As for mental cruelty that passes as "discipline" for children's "own good"—a common childrearing practice—noted psychologist Alice Miller has this to say:

> If there is absolutely no possibility of reacting appropriately to hurt, humiliation, and coercion, then these experiences cannot be integrated into the personality; the feelings they evoke are repressed, and the need to articulate them remains unsatisfied, without any hope of being fulfilled. It is this lack of hope of ever being able to express repressed traumata by

means of relevant feelings that most often causes severe psychological problems.

The abused fearful daughter's inability to express her anger—and her consequent depression—is inevitable in a culture that considers displays of temper and assertiveness to be unfeminine. Like the good daughter, she displays her rage in socially acceptable, albeit self-defeating ways. But the list of self-destructive behaviors is far longer for the fearful daughter—behaviors that may never be diagnosed as depression but that are symptoms of it, including:

- Slovenly appearance and extreme weight gain or loss
- Flinching when touched, even accidentally
- Inexplicable exhaustion
- Phobias
- Drug or alcohol addiction
- Hypervigilance and anxiety
- Suicidal thoughts and wishes
- Stomach ailments, including constipation and ulcers
- Sexual dysfunction

More than anything, these are symptoms of rage—turned inward.

To summarize the formation of the fearful daughter, she tends to have some or all of the following characteristics: She's shy or introverted; she's an only, lastborn, or change-of-life child; she has a symbiotic attachment to her mother and feels distant from and/or frightened of her father; she is unable to express her anger in a healthy way; she may have been physically or sexually abused; she is raised in a culture in which women are dominated by men.

For all these reasons the fearful daughter has no trouble being an instant supplicant in her attachments. She has been conditioned to roll over and expose her emotional underbelly.

Indeed supplication is her primary defense. Where other daughters defend against vulnerability through self-centeredness, or self-righteousness, or competitiveness, or unbridled fury, the fearful daughter *embraces* her vulnerability in a misguided attempt to avoid even greater harm.

The fearful daughter brings to her adulthood a catalog of perplexing anxieties and ailments. Nowhere are they more pronounced than in her intimate attachments—or lack of them. For it is in the affairs of the heart that her attachment to her father—whether painfully close or distant—is recapitulated.

The Fearful Daughter in Love

Among the many anomalies of how daughters express their fearfulness is the fact that they often function well in certain areas of their lives. For example, they may have good friends and are able to hold down a job. *But they fall apart when they fall in love.* Suddenly they become unaccountably anxious and insecure, even terrified.

Fearful daughters manage their romantic jitters in a variety of ways. Let's examine them one at a time.

One Is Enough. Many fearful daughters fall under the psychological umbrella of what Dr. Offit calls the "schizoid" personality, a term she uses to describe people who are unable to form close bonds with others. Schizoids manage rejection by becoming emotionally disengaged, a self-protective coping mechanism. For them emotional intensity in a relationship subconsciously reminds them of the neglect or abusiveness of their parents.

Of the unattached fearful daughters in my sample, many are repelled by marriage because of the searing memories they have of their parents' unhappy marriages.

In some cases these daughters had mothers who were critical and nagging and self-centered, and fathers who were alternately mute or explosive. Dorie, thirty-nine, an only child who grew up with such parents, has never married. When I asked her why, her answer was instantaneous:

> I remember saying as a little kid, "I will never get married." To me marriage was so awful, because my parents fought all the time. I figured that if I ever had kids, I'd destroy them because the chaos in my family made me unfit for motherhood. I decided I wanted no part of marriage and children—and so far I haven't found a reason to change my mind.

Being single, however, does not mean that Dorie's life is empty or uneventful. She's a fairly successful free-lance book designer; the walls of her airy apartment are covered with her paintings. She has a wide circle of friends. She's even trying to combat some of

her many phobias. Recently she decided to try to overcome her
fear of heights and took an Outward Bound mountain-climbing
trip.

And being unattached doesn't mean that she wouldn't like to
have a significant other in her life. The trouble is that with men
she becomes another person. This otherwise capable woman turns
into a clingy child the minute she meets someone to whom she is
attracted. She explains,

> My friends aren't sick; only the men I go out with are sick.
> I've always felt incomplete without a man. But the men I go
> for are always unavailable. Either they're married, or just
> broke up with someone, or are unable to commit. One way or
> another they're all like my father—they're rejecting or cold.
> For a while I even went out with a guy who beat me up. He'd
> just gotten out of jail for a narcotics conviction. Since then
> I've not been seeing anyone. I'm getting to the point where I
> think I'm just not cut out for romance. And since my life is
> pretty busy, I don't really feel the need for it. I'm really better
> off by myself.

Mothers also play a role in the fearful daughters' decision to
remain single. For the daughters of narcissistic, denigrating mothers, fear of "achieving" in Mom's domain—marriage and children
—is intolerable. Rather than go up against such mothers, these
daughters recoil from so "competitive" a move as matrimony.

For other fearful daughters their singleness is a reflection of
their excessive need to remain loyal to the mothers who took the
daughters' part against difficult or negligent fathers. Such daughters are often symbiotically attached to and dependent upon their
mothers, united with them in their mutual hatred of their fathers.
Some of these daughters never leave home.

This is especially true of the daughters of seductive fathers
whose advances were forestalled by their protective mothers.
These daughters often remain bound to their mothers; in most
cases they never marry and remain frightened of any attachment
to men.

Still other fearful daughters remain single because their relationships with their fathers rendered *all* men predators. It's not
simply that they can't find a good, gentle man. Rather it's the
conscious or subconscious assumption that to be male is to be

potentially abusive. The better course, then, is simply to withdraw entirely from the romantic field.

"It's the easiest thing in the world," said one woman. "Just gain fifty pounds and keep it on; that way men won't be attracted. That's what I did."

Fearful Marriages. Other fearful daughters do not recoil from attachment. Rather they rush into it, often replicating their childhoods in unhappy partnerships. It's what they know. These daughters grew up with unhappiness; they are conditioned for despair.

Here again, where once they may have been competent—at work, at least—they may fall apart when they fall in love and/or marry.

In his book *Success and Fear of Success in Women,* Dr. David Krueger describes a study of phobic women whose anxieties did not erupt until *after* they were married. These women all came from families in which emotional thriftiness was highly prized. In essence they were not allowed to be children, to be free spirits, to be rambunctious. Rather they were miniadults whose primary goal was to avoid their parents' criticism.

For these women marriage was an opportunity to become the children they never were. Indeed wedlock gave them a sense of security that was absent in childhood. Many of these women were drawn to men who were echoes of their oppressive fathers; others were attracted to men who resembled their narcissistic mothers.

To avoid upstaging their husbands, these women again became dutiful supplicants, just as they were in childhood. They either quit their jobs or sabotaged their careers. Indeed the closer they got to reaching their goals, the more nervous they became.

Many of the fearful daughters in my sample similarly escaped into marriage so as to be spared the anxieties of solitary achievement.

It's what Ariel, fifty-three, the only child of an extremely dependent mother and controlling, distant father, calls "a deal." Says Ariel,

> Not marrying was simply not an alternative for women of my generation. But I didn't marry just any man; I deliberately married a strong man who would take care of me, because I was never taught to take care of myself. He's the daddy person; he's on the hook to support me. And in exchange for that enormous responsibility, he gets to have a lot of control. He

likes to be in charge—he's very like my father that way. Sometimes I stand up to him, but usually I'm ambivalent; it just wipes me out.

It's clear to me that I have given up certain things in exchange for being taken care of. I haven't pursued a career with the tenacity I might have. I'm more amenable than is probably good for me. It's a deal. Is it a bad deal for me? I don't know. I'm having my cake and eating it—and choking on it.

Such "deals" can put some fearful daughters in physical peril. These are the daughters whose husbands are brutal, either physically or through bullying and intimidation.

Eve, thirty-four, is the youngest of three children of an alcoholic father; her mother, who adored her, was too frightened to prevent the beatings her father meted out to his wife and children whenever he was drunk.

At nineteen, Eve married Norman, ten years her senior—"to get away from my father," she says.

Norman once said that he married me because he wanted to have someone *he* could push around for a change—his father had beaten him when he was a kid too. Right after we got married, Norman managed to get fired from his job. I was working full-time and he'd be watching television when I got home, and complain that the house was dirty. He had a bad temper, and he'd hit me if things weren't just so.

I always felt I had to be perfect for someone to love me, so I'd wear my ass out trying to be perfect. I'd clean like crazy. I'd overlook it when he went out with other women or didn't come home at night. He told me, "When you bug me too much, I don't want to have anything to do with you. When you're nice to me and don't complain, that's when I really love you." So I never complained. I felt, "This is how you keep a man; you don't complain."

Six years later her husband left her for another woman. Since then Eve's taste in men hasn't gotten any better. She says,

I have no interest in men who are regular, who are nice. If I don't have to wait by the phone, I'm not interested in the guy.

It's like if I don't have to work for it, it can't be good. When I think of all the men I've dumped because they were kind to me, I could kick myself. I figured they were wimps, they weren't manly enough. Any real man isn't nice to a woman. That's what I grew up with, and that's the only thing I feel comfortable with. Weird, isn't it?

Psychologist Marlin S. Potash has treated a number of women like Eve in her practice. She says,

These women tend to go from one horrible affair or marriage to another. They replay their experience over and over again. Most of them don't even know they're replaying it. They don't really remember their abuse in childhood. They just push it down and it pops up as a phobia, or it boils just beneath the surface. And because they can't recall it, there's all this tightening up. In therapy they can replay the abuse in a safe way. They can learn to trust the therapist enough to be brave, to begin remembering.

Not surprisingly the braver these women become, the more they recall, and the stronger they get. As their self-esteem grows, their romantic choices—including, often, the relationships they are currently in—improve dramatically.

But without the courage to utilize their temperamental sensitivity and examine their ambivalences, they may cling to the "security" of a partnership and paradoxically at the same time wall off a part of themselves within it.

With little to give and so great a need to receive, such daughters are unable truly to attach in a deep, meaningful way. They may be dominated or subservient in their attachments, and at the same time not really *be there* as whole adults, as we shall see in a moment.

Lesbianism. Some of the fearful daughters I interviewed were too terrified of men to imagine having a committed heterosexual relationship. Instead they formed loving, sexual attachments with women. Most of these women had fathers who were bullies—they abused their daughters emotionally, physically, and/or sexually—and mothers who were too insecure or frightened to leave their husbands.

For some of these daughters a lesbian relationship provided

them with a solace and tenderness they craved—but, they said, homosexuality was not their core sexual identity. Rather their female intimate attachments were substitutes for the love and nurturing they didn't get from their own mothers.

Such a woman is Lonnie, forty-three, whose father was a tyrant and whose browbeaten mother died when she was fifteen. Lonnie married at twenty-three, but her husband was killed two years later in an automobile accident. For several years she lived alone. Then, when she was thirty, she met Diana, a lesbian. Says Lonnie,

> After my husband died, I just caved in. I couldn't go home, because I hated my father. I was so devastated that I think I was looking for a mother figure to comfort me, and Diana filled the bill. I worried about being attracted to her, because I thought it meant I was sick. But I was so terrified of being taken advantage of sexually. I just couldn't face the dating scene. And I had never really mourned for my mother. With Diana I could just cry and cry in her arms. She was wonderful to me. But after a while the sex part was embarrassing to me, so I ended the affair. I'll tell you something, though—I miss the hugging and the closeness. I've never had that with a man.

Other frightened daughters who formed committed lesbian attachments are not at all ambivalent about their sexual orientation. Most of these women had been sexually abused by their fathers—but, they said, their romantic choices had nothing to do with their childhoods.

While incest can severely confuse a woman about her gender identity, it does not *create* lesbianism per se. According to incest authorities, sexual abuse can underscore the inherent lesbianism of a woman and make the acceptance of her sexual orientation easier to acknowledge. In other cases lesbianism is part of the recovery process of sexually abused heterosexual women; the trauma of the incest experience may "block" a woman's heterosexual orientation, temporarily or permanently.

In all these ways fearful daughters try to reduce their anxieties through their romantic choices, whether in isolation or in a relationship. Unless they resolve their feelings about their fathers, a part of them may always be imprisoned, the part where trust and safety and security were never experienced, never nourished in

childhood, the part that cannot truly believe that
harm them emotionally or physically.

For the woman who is too terrified to expre
one of the most effective ways to protect herself is to
dysfunctional.

The Fearful Daughter in Bed

Fearful daughters often have extraordinary difficulties in their
sexual lives, depending on the kind and degree of emotional deprivation or physical damage they experienced in childhood. So conflicted are their identities that love and loss, arousal and apprehension, may be hopelessly tangled. The only thing they know for
sure is that sex is a mixed bag; what they don't know is *why*.

A certain cautiousness or detachment often characterizes the
sexual behavior of those fearful daughters who did not get enough
healthy bonding in childhood. For instance they may, in their emotional starvation and dependency, covet the structure of an ongoing relationship but withdraw when it becomes *too* close—that is,
sexual—because they are terrified of rejection or exploitation.

Sexual dysfunction takes a variety of forms. In some cases fearful women can manage sexual closeness, including orgasm, but
only in relationships that are not too *emotionally* close; in order to
keep their psychological distance, these women choose men who
are controlling.

In other cases fearful daughters may become extremely
aroused, and then suddenly something clicks off, like a short cir-
cuit, and desire dissolves. Or the sex they have may be routine and
impersonal, performed more out of obligation than passion—and
as seldom as is maritally manageable. They'll find myriad reasons
not to have sex with their partners: They're just not in the mood,
or they've got a lot on their minds; or they invent a headache or a
reason for their partners to be angry, killing the sexual moment.

Some fearful women feel vaginal pain during intercourse that is
nonmedical in origin; others are tormented by death fantasies.
Still others make themselves emotionally leave the scene during
sex and think of something else—otherwise they'd bolt. This is
especially true of victims of physical and sexual abuse, who may
spend their entire adulthoods suppressing memories of that abuse
and being unaccountably terrified in the arms of a lover or spouse.

In these cases the woman may be there in body, but just barely. Says Dr. Offit,

> Among women who had cruel fathers or who were incestuously abused—physically hurt during the process—I often do find an absence of feeling. These women may not experience anything physically—there's an absence of attraction, of desire, of interest. When a woman has been seriously damaged that way, she may simply not understand what sex is all about. Often there's a lack of comprehension. But sex, union—and, in its deepest connotation, love—is so integral to human survival that women who have been abused or abandoned or maltreated may be capable of dissociating sex from affection, from caring, from bonding. They may perceive it as a separate function.

Then there are those women who are simply averse to all sexual contact. Even an embrace can cause them to feel panic, because they think of it as a prelude to eroticism. Says an incest survivor,

> There's a part of me that will never heal. Sometimes sex is okay; it depends on how vulnerable I feel. Being aroused is the toughest piece in the world for me; it's a punishment cycle. When I'm aroused, I instantly start getting bad feelings, not wanting to be touched. My husband understands all this. We were in our relationship a long, long time before I could allow touch of any kind. When we're in bed, I try to stay in the moment, but I can't control the flashbacks. If I'm having a flashback, I start to shut down, and he's the only person in the whole world who can help me ease out of it. He puts zero pressure on me. The worst scar, though, is that I have so much trouble receiving love. To memorize love and know that it's not ever going to leave, blows the doors off your defenses. The way I grew up, if you didn't protect yourself, you might die.

As these examples illustrate, dealing with sexual dysfunction is extraordinarily complex. For one thing unlike, say, an eating disorder, never liking or having sex won't *kill* you. But the emotions it evokes can be killing.

For some frightened daughters passion may be terrifying because it is not a gentle emotion, nor is intercourse generally a gentle form of closeness. Thus sex may be too close for psychological or physical comfort. These women may be willing to sacrifice *all* touch, however tender, in order to avoid the terror that it evokes. Unconsciously controlling their bodies through rigidity or by holding back the storms of passion may be the only control some fearful daughters can manage. Keeping desire below the boiling point may be the only way they can hang on to a portion of their being. By not losing themselves sexually, they do not lose themselves emotionally.

Other fearful daughters, however, are drawn to "violent" passions and brutal partners, because they cannot separate sex from being treated cruelly. They generally had fathers who were physical or verbal bullies; the paternal closeness and "love" the women grew up with was violent. For these women love can become dangerously distorted.

The Price of Fearfulness

If domineering, abusive men repress their own "feminine weakness," fearful daughters repress their own "masculine strength."

One of the costs of fearfulness, as we have seen, is the loss of healthy sexual desire and emotional fulfillment. Not ever to be touched in a loving way—whether it is a hug from a friend or sensual touch by a partner—can have a devastating effect on one's psychological well-being.

Another price of fearfulness is the cost to a woman's physical health and well-being: The fearful daughter is the personality type most likely to be trapped within a physically abusive relationship—or to be revictimized in serial encounters with men.

"It wasn't just my father who molested me," says Torie, thirty-nine.

> I must have this sign on me that says, "Please touch." When I was seven, the man who tuned our piano helped wipe up a soda I had spilled by putting his handkerchief on my crotch. On the subway when I was nine, a man finger-fucked me through my coat. It's like I was asking for it, but I wasn't—I hated it, but I was too scared to react. Even now men seem to think they can put their hands on me—it doesn't happen to

any of my friends. I must be doing something to invite it. I can't stand thinking about it.

Finally, as we have seen, the fearful daughter is the woman most likely to suffer from chronic physical or mental illness—the price of her self-inflicted anger, her unexpressed rage. As Alice Miller puts it, "neuroses are a result of repression, not of events themselves."

The longer the fearful daughter puts off examining her anxieties and emotional conflicts and confusion, the greater the toll they may take—because sometimes even the fear is more than she can bear. The most severely damaged of these daughters simply shut down psychologically.

Fearful daughters are the least able to erect healthy emotional boundaries because they are the least emotionally separated from their parents. Consequently in extreme cases some of them can, indeed, become psychotic.

According to Dr. Michael Kerr, schizophrenia does not occur within a vacuum. Rather it can be conceptualized as a reciprocal process—a *response* that is learned early in life by those children who may be biologically or genetically wired for it. He writes, "Chronic psychosis and depression can be thought of not just as diseases but as *symptoms* of having given up too much self to the relationship system."

When the fearful daughter can examine her anxieties and trace them back to their childhood source, she can begin to uncover her own repressed strength.

In some cases fearful daughters are fortunate enough, resilient enough, and healthy enough to find partners who will nurture them, helping them heal from their childhood losses. The men they choose often come from loving families, or have resolved their own difficulties, and appreciate the sensitivity and sweetness of the fearful woman without taking advantage of those qualities. These happy partnerships often come late in life. Several of the fearful daughters I interviewed overcame their anxieties by degrees in therapy, going through many relationships or failed marriages before they were able to find and sustain a healthy one.

Fearful daughters who have been maltreated by their fathers can and do recover, although the process is far from easy. When you love your abuser—your father—forgetting the abuse may seem like the only way to hang on to the love. But remembering is essential to healing; the costs of denial are so devastating that the experience must be unblocked for the lingering evidence of that abuse to ebb.

And although the fearful daughter may be the most vulnerable and even damaged of women, she may also be the most *treatable*. Because she often is sensitive, and creative, and intelligent, and able to tolerate ambiguity, she can draw on those very abilities to get beyond her early history, and learn to live a life not of fear but of healthy appetite and even adventure. She can learn how to strike all the notes in her rich emotional repertoire, as we shall see in Part Four.

Profile of a Fearful Daughter

I am sitting in the newsroom of a large metropolitan daily newspaper waiting for Yvonne, forty-seven, a syndicated columnist. She rushes up to me, introduces herself, and apologizes for keeping me waiting. "I'd say it's one of those days," she says, her broad smile deepening the laugh lines in her cheeks, "but all my days are like this. I was just meeting with one of my sources, a young woman who's about to sue her father for raping her. It's going to be some story."

Yvonne was to be one of my "experts" for this book because of her prizewinning articles on domestic violence. But soon into our conversation, we determine that of greater help would be her own story. She agreed to tell me the most intimate details of her childhood, providing I didn't attribute them.

To anyone who doesn't know her history, this vivacious, brilliant, and witty woman would appear to be the antithesis of the frightened daughter. As we talk, it quickly becomes apparent that the woman I see today has carefully pieced together a persona from the debris of her shattered childhood.

Yvonne grew up in a small New Hampshire village, where her father was a high school football coach and her mother a housewife. When Yvonne was three, her mother died, and her father began drinking heavily. Although he was a member of a fundamentalist church, his religious convictions did not prevent his incestuous abuse of Yvonne. Until he remarried four years later, he battered her physically and repeatedly raped her. She recalls,

> I was blamed for everything by my father. I was told I couldn't be trusted, so I never got to go on school outings. For years and years I tried to get his approval and my stepmother's too. But she was addicted to tranquilizers, so I couldn't go to her for anything. I certainly couldn't tell her what was happening to me.

By the time she was in high school, Yvonne managed to erase all memories of her father's treatment of her in childhood. She began gaining weight, and by the time she graduated, she had ballooned to over 170 pounds. At eighteen she moved out of the house, got a job working in a local newspaper as a receptionist, and began drinking—but only at parties. She wasn't, she told herself, a real drunk like her father, only a social drunk.

The editor of the paper took a protective interest in her. He began giving her small assignments, and each story got better than the one before.

But the drinking increased. She met an extraordinarily kind man who was also a newspaper reporter, whom she married during one of her "dry" spells; soon the couple had a daughter, Deborah. Yvonne was in no way prepared for motherhood; her daughter's screams from colic would sink her into depression.

Yvonne was fired from her job. Her husband threatened to leave her if she didn't get help. She signed herself into a rehab hospital and was able to overcome her addictions with the ongoing encouragement of her therapist and a support group.

Meanwhile she began free-lancing—she knew the pressures of working in an office were more than she could take. Little by little her work began to attract national attention, and a newspaper syndicate signed her on for a personal-opinion column.

Her marriage seemed to be solid—well, in every area but sex, which she was frequently too tired to manage. Her daughter, with whom she had formed an extremely close and loving relationship, was doing well in school. Relatively well. Because as she got close to puberty, her grades began to drop, as did her weight. Yvonne figured her daughter was going through teenage rebellion; she ignored the weight loss.

Then one weekend when Yvonne was around thirty, she was out of town on an assignment, and her husband called her to say that Deborah had swallowed a bottle of aspirin. That night she flew home. At eight o'clock the next morning she was in her therapist's office even as, next door, Deborah was starting her own therapy. Says Yvonne,

> Watching my daughter fall apart made me realize that I had a huge piece of unfinished business to take care of. I had never really confronted my father, nor examined how our relationship had damaged me. I was trying to give my daughter the perfect life, but I hadn't really taken care of the child inside me—the child I was, who hadn't grown up.

Over the next two years Yvonne began stripping away the layers of denial that were somehow being horribly played out in her daughter. It was as if Deborah were the living proof of Yvonne's own repression.

And gradually the memories started to emerge in her body—especially at night, when her husband wanted to make love. For the first time, whenever he reached for her, she'd flinch. Where once oral sex was a part of their sex life, now it made her gag. And then one morning, when they were in the middle of intercourse, all the memories came crashing into her awareness.

She pushed her husband away and began screaming.

Tears slide down Yvonne's cheeks, choking off her narrative. After a few moments she collects herself and says,

> I told my husband everything I was feeling; that when he entered me, I felt like I was three years old again and that he was my father. I remembered the time my father put his penis in my mouth. I remembered telling my mother, who told me I had just had a bad dream. I remembered telling my grandmother, who held me but never did anything about it. My husband put his arms around me, and we wept together.

Since that day twelve years ago Yvonne has devoted her entire career to the prevention of child abuse. Her articles always produce an avalanche of mail. Yvonne answers every letter herself, because, she says, "There's no way I can ignore them; my articles open wounds. These people are reaching out, and I always steer them to experts who can help them. No one helped me when I needed it most. I'm no saint. I just want to do what I can to stop this shit."

And in the meantime her daughter, now twenty-five, is in her final year of medical school; she wants to become a psychiatrist. As for her marriage, Yvonne says,

> It was dumb luck that I married that man. I can't imagine why he stuck with me through all those years when I just couldn't open up, when he'd want to talk to me or hold me and I just wasn't there. I still have trouble in the sex department, but I no longer feel as though I'm going to die. That's because if I start to feel frightened, my husband just backs off. He says I make up for it in other ways. He's unbelievable.

As she walks me to the elevator, she says, "I wouldn't wish my childhood on anyone. What I've tried to do is to use the memories of it to find a sense of purpose in my life and in my work. If there is a silver lining to all this, that's it."

With a wave of her hand she turns and runs back to her office.

15

The Maverick Daughter

You know that story about the Ugly Duckling? I always felt very different from everyone in the family—like I was the wrong kind of egg stuck in this nest and I didn't belong there. I didn't get along with either my mother or my father. Maybe it's because I was such an oddball—very rebellious. I remember thinking at the age of five that I had to get out of there. I knew I was going to do it someday. There was no question. Ever. Ever.

—HEATHER, THIRTY-ONE

When I was in the fourth grade, the kids on my Manhattan block were divided into three camps: those who picked on people; those who were the pickees; and those who were mewling cringers, praying they wouldn't be noticed.

I was no dummy—I was one of the mewlers. I knew *exactly* what I had to do to avoid being ganged up on: be nice to Loretta, the thuglette who was the ringleader of the unsavory girls in the neighborhood. I carried her books; I stooped into a humble parenthesis; I eagerly offered her my Good Humors, the prewar, prepubescent, epicurean equivalent of protection money.

Loretta fascinated me. Even at ten she seemed invincible—at her happiest, it appeared, when beating the hell out of a boy. You could have hit her with a hammer and she wouldn't have blinked, let alone shed a tear. Meanest kid I ever met. Caustic. Cutting. Cruel.

I wanted to be just like her.

Soon after I began conducting interviews for this book, I met her alter ego, a novelist whose name, Tammy, stands in hilarious contradiction to her personality; even she sees the humor of it. "My first sexual experience," she deadpans, "was getting a crew cut when I was nine."

At forty-three one can still see in Tammy's electric-blue eyes flickers of the fire that burned within her when she was a little kid, being hauled daily into the principal's office for blackening someone's eye. It is a fire that has been banked by years of therapy; ten years ago she started examining her history of burned bridges and hotheaded outbursts, the scorched earth of her shattered relationships.

Soon after she began psychoanalysis, she attended a weekend retreat with her psychiatrist and therapy group. She recalls,

> I announced to the group, "I can beat up any man in the room." And I did beat up one of them. I was certain that I was strong enough when I was angry to kill anyone. I was capable of such rage, you cannot imagine. I would get out of cabs in the middle of the street and throw rocks at them. Hard as I appear, though, inside I still feel like a scared little kid. I have an absolute *horror* of hurting the feelings of anyone I love. Bottom line, no matter how crazy I've been in my life, I'm not a bad person.

This is the maverick daughter—well, one version of her.

According to Webster's dictionary, a maverick is "an individual who refuses to conform to his group." She comes in a variety of forms, all of them blatant.

Sometimes she's simply an eccentric who lives an unconventional life and doesn't care—or much notice—who knows it. Sometimes she's an artist or dancer or writer whose work creates storms of morally or aesthetically outraged protest. Sometimes she's an academic terrorist, lobbing philosophical grenades on college campuses and in political treatises. Sometimes she's a daredevil, driving the fastest cars, skiing the steepest mountains, pushing her physical limits as far as possible.

And sometimes she's like a runaway train. She may be dangerously promiscuous; she may pick fights in barrooms; she may scream at cops; she may find herself in court—or in jail.

The maverick daughter is always unusual, the triangular peg that does not fit into the square hole. When her incandescent energy is channeled into productive pursuits, she can be heroic—

blazing trails and redefining femininity, even the way we look at the world. History is filled with such female upstarts: Joan of Arc, Elizabeth I, Elizabeth Cady Stanton, Amelia Earhart, Isadora Duncan, Simone de Beauvoir.

But being a tough woman is, culturally, an oxymoron. The maverick is not simply "different"—frequently she is called "difficult," the elegant translation of saltier adjectives by which she is described behind her back—nutcase, ball breaker, bitch, among them.

As off-putting as mavericks can sometimes be, however, one can't help admiring certain of their characteristics, not the least of which is courage and, often, an exalted code of ethics. Their indignation is nothing if not righteous.

Dr. Augustus Y. Napier calls such people "rule breakers." Of them, he writes,

> Beneath the surface . . . there is a strong, gutsy kid. . . . I have a special fondness for the rule breaker. She takes a stand against the forces of conformity and coercion. . . . These kids . . . stand up, they speak out; they declare themselves.

The female maverick's problem is not so much that she is different; her trouble is that she isn't easily *accepted*, a condition she often brings on herself, with considerable help from the culture. Most mavericks tend to be anything but meek. They have *definite* ideas and are not a bit reticent about expressing them. Not for them the fate of their paler, more fragile sisters, who go belly-up at the first hint of trouble. Yet paradoxically the maverick wants nothing so much as to *belong.* However, she wants to do it without being brought to heel. If the maverick is to be singled out for a showdown, she'll take no prisoners.

What is so confounding about the maverick is that what you *see* is not necessarily what you get. Of all daughters the maverick may in fact be the most vulnerable and intuitive of the lot. Who but a hypersensitive soul would notice an eyebrow lifted slightly in contempt, the condescending lilt in a laugh? Put another way, if one is sluggish or thick-skinned or altogether indifferent, one is surely more immune to social slights and emotional subtleties.

Within the maverick is a duet of voices—the tough and the

tender, the masculine and the feminine, the prizefighter and, often, the terrified child.

The Making of a Maverick Daughter

How mavericks cope with their uniqueness depends almost entirely on the "group" into which they are born—that is, how they were treated in childhood.

Some maverick daughters come by their unconventional ways honestly. They view the world through a different lens and are entirely at home with their atypical selves. They generally come from families wherein being different was the norm—in England they are called eccentrics or, perhaps, "dotty."

If these mavericks have trouble finding their niche, it is only *outside* the family; within it, they are allowed to follow their own unusual rhythms. And in most cases they were their fathers' protégées, a liaison of which their mothers approved, or at least did not intrude upon.

Such a maverick is Mattie.

As I pulled into the driveway of her unprepossessing Vermont frame house, nothing about the neatly clipped hedge and carefully tended garden prepared me for the forty-year-old woman who, with her husband and daughter, lives inside it.

The living room resembled the setting for a Stephen King novel, and I had one of those split-second journalistic moments of panic: Is this interview, I wondered, *really* necessary? The wall above the fireplace was smudged with menacing soot; the floors were covered with piles of yellowing newspapers, magazines, and books. An antique radio sat on a dusty table, its vacuum tubes spilling out like so many glass bones. Occupying one corner of the room was a five-foot cage in which a boa constrictor was coiled in sleepy repose, digesting something or other.

But then I entered the kitchen and saw on the table a plate piled high with still-warm brownies and chocolate-chip cookies, a vase filled with wildflowers, and two place settings with delicate teacups and Victorian silverware. The sweet-smelling cinnamon coffee and homemade goodies persuaded me to stay.

A good thing too. Because of all the women I met while researching this book, Mattie was by far the most brilliant, inventive, amusing—and original.

Mattie is a witch.

"I've come out of the broom closet," she laughs. "But not to everyone. This is a tranquil New England town, filled with stalwart, God-fearing patriots. My husband is a member of the local chamber of commerce; my daughter is a Brownie. Can you imagine . . . ?"

Mattie, a writer of computer software programs, is the only child of a retired engineer and his wife, a Sunday schoolteacher. Growing up, Mattie was always extremely close to both her parents, but especially her father, whose hobbies were restoring old cars and radios. Of her childhood she says,

> I didn't have too many girlfriends because I was interested in things that girls weren't supposed to be capable of understanding—science, astronomy, electronics, machinery, cars. I did those activities with my dad. One of my very early memories was watching him repack a wheel bearing, scooping grease and bearing components into a wheel hub of a 'forty-nine Cadillac. Working on cars was more fun than playing with dolls.

I asked her if she ever had the sense that her father had wished for a son. She replied, "No. I think my dad was very advanced for his time. He never thought in terms of 'boy stuff' and 'girl stuff.' He would have treated any child this way. He wanted me to know how things work so that I could fix them myself."

Which is not to say that her father saw her as sexually neuter. When she reached puberty, he didn't suddenly stop hugging her but, she adds, he wasn't "overly sexual either." He found another way to acknowledge that she was indeed female.

> For my sixteenth birthday he bought me a lacy nightgown and peignoir set. It was the perfect gift, permission to be a woman instead of a child. My mom helped him pick it out.

But interest in things sexual and romantic came late to her. She wasn't terribly keen on dating. Most of the boys she knew in college were intellectual comrades.

> I was so unfeminine. I'd be sitting in a bar having a riveting conversation about oscilloscopes or the Palomar Observatory

with a male friend—who meanwhile had his arm draped around the cheerleader of the moment. I could never fathom why smart boys wanted to date dumb broads. I certainly didn't want to be someone who was decorative but stupid.

Mattie majored in astronomy and later got a master's degree in electronics. At twenty-two she began to find her virginity tiresome, so one night in the backseat of a car she got involved in "some frantic slap-and-tickle with my chem-lab partner. I thought, 'You don't usually do this sort of thing—but what the hell. It's fun.' "

Her college years were extremely difficult in one respect. Certain members of the faculty tried to pressure her into switching her major to elementary education, to meet a "nice boy, get married, and have kids." It was a huge contrast to what she had always heard from her father: "Be yourself." She adds, "The basic attitude he gave me was to make up my own mind and find out things for myself."

Mattie credits her father for supporting her maverick ways, for accepting her brilliance, curiosity, and experimentation and even encouraging them. Fortunately she married a man who could be a clone of her beloved father, giving her similar permission to be herself.

Of her being a witch—which, she says, is really a hobby, devoted mostly to healing—her parents' reaction is this:

> My dad is amused by it and a little bit proud. My mother said, "Well, at least you believe in something. But no biting heads off chickens in the graveyard at midnight."

I have gone on at some length with this particular case study because it stands out in stark contrast to many of the mavericks I interviewed—and not just because of Mattie's unusual hobby.

As Mattie's example illustrates, the maverick who is accepted by her family does not have to resort to outrageously antisocial behavior in order be loved in the family. She can find her niche and lead a life of stability and productivity.

Such family acceptance of being a female "weirdo" is remarkably rare. For most maverick daughters, defying the social order is evidence not simply of their intrepidness but also of being singled out for ridicule in childhood. Like cornered animals, they lash out at the people who punish their nonconformity—especially their parents.

Different Drummers. Temperament, of course, has everything to do with the maverick's fate in the family. Some children are simply out of sync with the rest of their kin. The maverick's innate boldness and quirky curiosity are likely to set her apart from the start.

Of all temperamental categories, the maverick's is the most difficult to pin down, because so often they give out confusing signals. In some ways they resemble the competitive daughter—many are tomboys for instance. But the maverick is not necessarily desperate to win. Rather she is desperate to be allowed to approach life in her own way.

Perhaps the best explanation for the maverick's temperament is that she is probably what Dr. David Keirsey and Marilyn Bates call "Apollonian." This personality is in a constant and often circuitous quest for self, in restless pursuit of identity and individuality. The researchers write,

> [The Apollonian wants] to be what he is meant to be and to have an identity which is uniquely his. His endless search most often causes him guilt, believing that his real self is somehow less than it ought to be. And so he wanders, sometimes spiritually, sometimes psychologically, sometimes physically, seeking to satisfy his hunger for unity and uniqueness.

Not to be allowed to be unique can sometimes derail the maverick daughter. Her confused parents may see the volatile pain in the neck, not the visionary. Thus many mavericks, feeling like strangers in the family, become extremely argumentative or abrasive.

A primary reason they feel like outsiders has to do with the sibling gender mix of the family into which they are born.

Brotherly Love. One of the startling findings in my research is that over 80 percent of the maverick daughters in my sample had brothers. No other group had so lopsided a sibling history.

Those mavericks who were firstborns and whose brothers were younger began life with their parents' undivided attention—in most instances their fathers took a particular interest in them. These daughters were their fathers' potential protégées, but with the arrival of the secondborn—*a boy*—their fathers changed their paternal tunes. These mavericks found themselves being rejected by their fathers, and their brothers captured the bulk of Daddy's time.

As for those maverick daughters—the majority—who had older brothers, the heirs apparent had already cornered the market on paternal favoritism by virtue of birth rank *and* gender. Mavericks were born into the breach, constantly trying to measure up to, or be the tag-along of, their big brothers.

Family Feuds. Another characteristic of many maverick daughters is that their parents' marriages—those that haven't been terminated by divorce—tended to be anything but serene.

"Problem children" often have the bad luck to be born at the worst possible time of their parents' lives—during the breakup of a marriage or a parent's serious illness or unemployment. Or they are the "wrong" sex. Such children are often unwanted kids, symbolizing one more area of stress, rather than joy. The unhappy result is that in childhood many mavericks did not have a reliable ally in either parent.

Even if Daddy loved the maverick, he was too remote, or too busy trying to earn a living, or too preoccupied with his sons to be of much use to her. More likely he was so outraged by her unconventional or "unfeminine" behavior that he was as tough on her as he was on his sons. In the worst cases he would try to force her to be a "real" woman through incest—several of the mavericks I interviewed were survivors of sexual abuse.

That left Mommy, who was not in such great shape herself. Most mavericks had conflicted relationships with their mothers, ranging from strained—a matter of a temperamental misfit—to downright hostile. The majority of mothers were either belittling or cruel to these daughters. Life with Mom was a constant battle of wills.

The remaining mothers were women who were simply too docile or too intimidated by their bewildering daughters to be relied upon for any kind of consistency or limit setting. As one researcher pointed out, rebellious children are often desperate to "provoke establishment of rules."

To be fair, aggressive children are a handful. If Mom's marriage gives her no solace, an insult added to that matrimonial injury is a daughter who is both assertive and "odd." The maverick is unable to be her mother's sympathetic, conventionally feminine soulmate.

Mom's only real family ally is likely to be the sainted son, who is her unambivalent love object—the only male in the house who utterly adores her. Or she may take a shine to *another* daughter who is more to her temperamental and social liking and with whom the mother can be a "girl."

Thus the maverick—fired in the caldron of disapproval—may find herself an outcast within the family—ambivalently loved or ignored by her father, the object of her mother's disappointment or fear or even scorn, and outclassed by her brothers.

Says Liz, twenty-eight,

> I was the only girl. I had two older brothers. I can remember sitting at the dinner table trying to talk. I even have tapes of it. You can hear me saying, "Mommy, Mommy," or "Daddy, Daddy," in this little voice. My parents would be talking to my brothers, and when I tried to get them to talk to me, they'd look at me with this blank expression for a second and then turn back to the boys.

How, then, is the maverick to get attention within the family? Certainly not by conforming to sexist convention—by being, for example, self-effacing or unctuous or coy. Such behavior would only push her farther into the family shadows, farther from her unusual self.

Far better to be *brazen*—to be as smart as, vocal as, tough as her brother. But her parents *already* have a boy, thank you. And if they have unwavering expectations of how boys and girls ought to behave—and have a sample of each gender right under their noses— it is all but inevitable for the maverick daughter to be at best neglected and at worst punished for her unusual interests or unruly behavior.

The maverick has all but literally to fight for her life in such a family. So she might as well do the very thing that will *guarantee* their attention: be chronically in trouble. She may eternally be in hot water with teachers, employers, friends; she may abuse drugs; she may be an inveterate runaway. She has nothing to lose by being so mutinous—indeed she has everything to gain. Her family *needs* someone to blame for their difficulties; unbeknownst to all of them she is actually doing them a favor.

The Scapegoat. Whatever the reason, the family troublemaker is invaluable to the family. For one thing she is the lightning rod for everyone's hostilities. Without her they might have to suffer their conflicts in silence, or get help and solve their own problems.

Instead they turn on her—or, to be more precise, they turn *to* her—to vent their frustrations. After all, the kid deserves it: If only she'd behave, abide by the family rules, be a good little girl, she could spare herself their wrath.

Another value of the scapegoat is that she acts out everyone's anger for them. The more devilish the maverick, the more angelic everyone else appears to be. To keep her in her restless, rambunctious place, they react in a number of ways. One is to *worry*. And the more trouble she gets into, the more they worry, which only makes her *more* troublesome.

As Dr. Michael Kerr tells us, such parents think of the troublemaker as the cause of their woes rather than "a reflection of their own anxiety-determined functioning." Thus parent-maverick interaction can be mutually reinforcing. Writes Dr. Kerr,

> It is easier to "help" the "sick one" than to look at one's own emotional problems. The emotional functioning of the parents is the major determinant of whether anxiety escalates in a nuclear family.

Scapegoats also serve to keep their parents' marriage together. As we saw in earlier chapters, when parents can agree about a child, at least they have one thing going for them—in this case their mutual rage at or fear of her.

The final psychological bonus is to siblings: While the maverick is taking parental lashes, they get off scot-free. Many a troublemaking daughter has, in fact, been innocent of a family offense— say, denting a fender. But because of her rebellious personality, it's easy for parents simply to *assume* that she is culpable. Even if her parents later take back their accusations, the damage has been done: The scapegoat has her role underscored by their automatic assignment of blame—and her siblings have little incentive to cover for her.

When her parents are abusive, what starts as simple reinforcement of the troublemaker's behavior becomes almost a mandate to the maverick daughter. Where some parents occasionally ponder whether or not their anger at the scapegoated child is an overreaction, the abusive parent has no such second thoughts. With mavericks these parents have little difficulty justifying their cruelty.

One of the components of child maltreatment is the parents'

perception of a child. According to Dr. James Garbarino, psychologically abusive parents view one or more children as "different and exceptional, even as the one who elicits the maltreatment." And, heaven knows, the maverick is exceptional.

For all these reasons mavericks feel compelled to choose fight over flight or supplication. They're not about to wimp out, because to do so would be to lose their importance in the family and to jettison their identity. They're not about to drop the one defense mechanism that, in the case of abused daughters especially, may have saved their sanity or even their very lives.

But being the scapegoat is not simply a glaring symptom of family dysfunction. An overriding explanation for the maverick's behavior is that she identifies so strongly with the people who attempt to oppress her.

Identifying with the Aggressor. Hostility can be seen as the flip side of fear; that is, as long as one is angry, one can erect sturdy barriers to feelings of helplessness. And the surest way to avoid feeling helpless is to identify not with the weakest parent, as timid daughters do, but with the parent who is in power: *Daddy.*

Many maverick daughters are in fact caricatures of masculinity.

Theresa, thirty-three, grew up with her violent, alcoholic father and overprotective mother. When Theresa was fifteen, her mother died after a brief illness. To make sure she wasn't overwhelmed by her father, and by men in general, Theresa became as macho as she could be—not an easy task, given that she was five feet tall. She recalls,

> I was a clingy kid—my mother wouldn't let me out of her sight. But almost immediately after she died, I became tough. I consciously decided that I would never cry again. I became a bad girl, hanging out with bikers, always wearing jeans and leather jackets. I started drinking Johnnie Walker Black on the rocks with a twist. I'd go by myself to bars and order five shots in a row and never get drunk, just so that people would notice me—this tiny girl who could drink anyone under the table. I was trying to shape myself into my father. I wanted to be able to hold my own with men—to think like a man, to be as strong as a man. Because I was *terrified* of them.

Other mavericks identify with their fathers not simply out of fear but out of longing, even if their fathers are cruel or addicted.

One woman said the reason she started drinking at twelve was so that she'd "know what Daddy felt like when he was drunk. I wanted to find out what made him tick. In a strange way it was a way to get closer to him."

Many of these mavericks are the daughters of divorce whose father hunger is so acute that they, too, try to *become* their fathers, filling in the void of their absence by identifying with them. As Dr. Judith S. Wallerstein writes,

> It is a tragic irony when divorce allows a mother to escape an abusive husband, while her children are trapped by their identification with him . . . reinforced by their fears of becoming like the victim mother. In fact, the more capricious and rejecting the father, the more intense is the children's admiration and the more powerful are their efforts to be like Dad.

Sexual Rebellions

Of course there's a limit to how "masculine" a maverick can be. It's not necessarily that these daughters want to *be* men; mostly they just don't want to feel scared.

Thus when they emerge into adolescence and adulthood, they discover one more way to express both their freewheeling individuality and their anger: sex. Most of the mavericks in my sample were sexually promiscuous beginning in their early teens.

But their sexual aggressiveness was a double bind, in part because of their anatomy. For misogynous men, sexual aggressiveness toward women is an example of the abuse of their greater physical power. Rape is nothing if not anger turned against—indeed, thrust inside—the weakest opponent.

Women are incapable of committing rape with their genitals; a woman can have intercourse only by being *entered*. Nevertheless they can be sexually vengeful by becoming sexually indiscriminate.

Promiscuity does provide a kind of satisfaction for some mavericks. What more effective way to say "Fuck you" to her father than to "fuck" almost anyone else? What better way to assert independence and originality than defiantly to *not* be a father's virginal child, his chaste property? What more ego-deflating method of punishing Dad than to be a tarted-up, predatory, female opposite number?

As one woman put it,

> My father always rejected me because I wasn't a boy, even though he already had two sons. Ever since I was small, I wanted to be a boy. I used to stand in front of the toilet and pretend I was a boy. It wasn't that I was attracted to women— it was that I didn't feel accepted as a woman by my father. But when I became a teenager, suddenly I was noticed by men. I became very promiscuous. I wore tight, low-cut dresses. I wanted to bring out the beast in everyone else without having it brought out in me. I even pretended I *didn't* have orgasms when I *did*. I had a very high sex drive, but orgasms made me feel ugly and low. They made me feel too vulnerable.

Other mavericks are promiscuous because they are desperate to assuage their father hunger. Said a thirty-year-old woman,

> My dad was simply never there for me, even when he was home. So when I hit my teens, I started picking up men who were much older than me. It wasn't even the sexual part that I wanted. It was that I wanted to be accepted by an older man because I didn't have that with my dad. Until I got married, every relationship I had was with older men. I didn't have orgasms with them. I just wanted them to hold me and make me feel okay about myself. Some of them did.

In the most extreme cases mavericks can become so alienated from affectionate human connection that they are sexually self-degrading. Studies of prostitutes indicate that a large percentage were sexually abused in childhood. This kind of maverick suffers from what one researcher calls "the disorder of hope." By selling sex, she reframes her father's hideous exploitation of her love for him. She gets men to "pay" for her father's egregious violation of her trust.

The whole issue of sexual love can be grotesquely distorted for some mavericks, for whom the only good sex is dangerous, even perverse sex. They engage in sadomasochistic sex, allowing themselves, for example, to be whipped. Such women, according to Dr.

Avodah K. Offit, may be acting out behavior they learned in child-hood. Their parents, she writes,

> may . . . produce someone who cannot enjoy sex unless hu-miliated in much the same way that their parents gave atten-tion. Another possible result is the creation of an equally aggressive mimic, who mistakes giving punishment for giving love and can only have sex if there is some subjugation to it.

The Maverick Daughter in Love

As these examples illustrate, mavericks are often veterans of serial sexual relationships, if not of mutually enriching love. The Catch-22 of such sexual acting out, however, is that it only serves to deepen the maverick's psychological dependence on her father. By living libidinously in angry reaction, she shores up her emo-tional attachment to him. Sexually she reinforces it in the most intimate way possible, using the men she "loves" and leaves or is left by as stand-ins for the father who rejected her.

Because of their early, stormy, or distant relationships with their fathers, the problem for many mavericks is not in finding the right man; the problem is in *wanting* to find him. With so little acquain-tance with gentle masculine love and approval, they are not condi-tioned for tenderness and trust and belonging—they are condi-tioned for *survival.* They want to be the ones who reject, not the ones who are rejected. Thus they may recapitulate the disap-proval, abandonment, or abuse—whether physical or emotional—of their fathers in their romantic attachments.

Some mavericks *deliberately* choose men who are emotionally unavailable, rather than risk another rejection. Enjoying sex only in the absence of emotion is a common theme among these women. As long as a man is not really worthy of her respect, she can have fun in bed.

Other mavericks become involved with men who are passive, from whom they attempt to provoke a strong response. Here again, the maverick replicates her relationship with her father, continuing to play her troublemaking role. Says Martha, twenty-eight,

I guess I just rub men the wrong way. I bring out all my boyfriend's worst qualities. We have this little game we play. I'll start a fight, and he'll try to ignore me, so I'll bug him more. Then he'll get mad and threaten to hit me, and I shut up. When I realize he's *not* going to hit me, I hit the roof. I'll show him I'm not scared and get furious at him for trying to make me feel bad. My mother used to do the same thing to my father: He'd get red in the face, and she'd say, "Go ahead, *hit* me," and sometimes he would.

Some mavericks never marry. For one thing, they frequently are unschooled in the ways of the heterosexual heart and do not know how to be themselves with men. For them men are simply aliens.

Then there are mavericks who remain single because they are simply too scarred by their abusive fathers ever to risk any kind of closeness to a man. This is particularly true of those daughters who survived their fathers' brutal or incestuous behavior by becoming angry enough to make their escape.

In these cases their anger worked for them. They used their rage to pull them out of the hurricane of childhood into something resembling a normal life—establishing careers, forming cautious friendships. But in matters of the heart the flames of rage at their fathers burn brightly on. Says Brenda, thirty-two, a television producer,

No man ever asked me to marry him. I was never in one place long enough. And I think I scare men to death. I am hyper-alert around them. I can trust certain men now, but boy, do they have to work for it. They really have to slave—they have to bleed. My sense of security doesn't come easily.

Some of these incest survivors are lesbians, a life-style, culturally at least, that is out of the mainstream. For these mavericks, homosexual relationships may be the only way they can feel love without the risk of physical menace, the only love that doesn't require constant defense. But even here the maverick may still have trouble with trust, if not with sex: The fire exits are always within view.

In matters of the romantic heart, then, the maverick is likely to bring about the very thing she most dreaded in childhood: rejection.

Many of the mavericks I interviewed were able to recognize the toll of their romantic choices. After galloping through years of angry attachments, furious emotional advances and retreats, they finally became too emotionally exhausted to continue to ignore their demons and sought help. Often these women were ultimately able to form loving attachments.

However, until the maverick is able to examine her rage, she may find herself becoming abandoned over and over again, emotionally or literally. In choosing lovers whom she can bully or who are unloving, eventually she may push so hard that they leave her. Because she lives life on a dare, always looking for or provoking the flaw that will give her permission to erupt—to bring her metaphorical father back—she may drive her partners away.

The Cost of Being a Maverick Daughter

With each unhappy romantic encounter the maverick gathers proof that all men are crummy—either too weak or too strong. She transfers her feelings about her father to all men because she dare not acknowledge the depth of her own loss. To really feel the pain of it would be to see how raw are her wounds. The irony of course is that only by truly grieving for the child she once was and mourning the father who could not accept her can she finally relinquish the very rage that keeps him in charge.

The cost of the maverick's coping mechanisms is not confined to her love life. Unless she is like Mattie, the "witch" described early in this chapter, and has the good fortune to have parents who accept her being an oddball, the maverick may be a loose cannon in other areas of her life as well.

She may, for instance, become estranged from her family of origin. Since many mavericks felt like such outsiders from their earliest days, they may cut off from their parents or from their entire families.

Divorcing one's parents—and it is almost always the maverick who exercises this option—is the final familial act of a rejected child. Those who do so usually have tried every other alternative to avoid such an unsatisfying solution to their seemingly hopeless family ties. But cutting off does not mean getting rid of anxieties about oneself, one's attachments, one's choices. It merely reduces one area of anxiety and overloads the others.

Their work lives for instance. Some mavericks do fine in their careers—as long as they're in charge. Better yet if they own the store. Sometimes the maverick is too volatile to engender loyalty in her employees. Moreover her fear of criticism and anticipation of attack keep her at a managerial distance.

Consequently those mavericks with the best career track records tend to be those who are self-employed, who will drive themselves as hard as some of their fathers once drove them, only this time on their *own* terms. Money *matters* to these mavericks. It is their ticket away from insecurity, from abandonment, from conformity. More than anything it is their psychic insurance against ever feeling helpless or dependent again—providing they don't burn out.

Other mavericks, no matter how achieving, continue to feel like outsiders. Some are resilient children—and they are nothing if not mavericks—who survived horrifyingly abusive childhoods; in adulthood there is a kind of hollowness that haunts them.

Still others have employment records that are rap sheets of incompletion and failure. One thirty-nine-year-old maverick said that she's had seventy-five jobs over the last twenty years. It's not that she is incapable of working hard, she says; it's just that people try to make her something she's not.

> I'm the type of person who, if you encourage me and if you trust me to do things my own way, will go to the end of the world for you. I'll work twenty-four hours a day for peanuts. But if you tell me there's only one way to do things and that I'm hopeless, that's what I'll be. My father used to think the way to get us kids to work hard was to say, "You'll never be able to do that." So now if I work for a boss who is a dictator, I'll just quit. I don't care how interesting the job is or how much it pays.

Another area that exacts a price in the maverick's life is that of friendship. Like competitive daughters, mavericks frequently have few female friendships. Unlike competitive daughters, they tend not to have male friendships either.

Those friends mavericks *do* have are likely to be gay men. These men are able to provide the strength and comradeship of a man without the complications of sex and domination. They are *"female"* enough for mavericks to be at ease with discussing their deepest feelings. And, like the maverick herself, gays are cultural mavericks.

"I don't have to keep my guard up with homosexuals," one maverick told me. "I can be honest with them. I don't have to play games. I can look beautiful and not get hit on. Gay men let you be yourself."

The final cost to mavericks is that they may self-destruct psychologically. Feeling like the eternal ugly duckling, never finding a nest in which they can contentedly be their unusual selves, those who don't end up destroying themselves through overwork or drug addiction or dangerous pursuits may simply decide to take their own lives quickly and dramatically.

Yet the maverick is also the daughter who may be the likeliest to seek help—of the offbeat sort. Most mavericks have one more string in their unusual bows: Because they're not afraid to be different, the social stigma of needing help may be the very thing that attracts them to therapy, both traditional and the more exotic, such as human potential and New Age movements.

Today's mavericks have an enormous advantage over their female forebears, who were burned at the stake or stoned in the public square for their penchant for choosing *only* the road less traveled. These women, once they find ways to stop derailing, are the very people who blossom—burst, really—into their true selves. And once they do, they can indeed become the kinds of visionaries who change the world, even if it's only the world of their vivid, lusty, courageous private lives, loves, work and causes. These originals pave the way for the mavericks to come—both male and female.

Profile of a Maverick Daughter

Looking into the unlined, cherubic face of Dulcy and watching her contentedly nurse her newborn twins, it's hard to imagine that this thirty-three-year-old, serene mother and housewife once lived a life that would easily provide the plots of several Dickens novels.

There was early childhood in Detroit, when for three years she watched her mother die by inches of cancer. These were the years when Dulcy was silenced by family secrets—Mommy's sickness, Daddy's alcoholism—and by the loneliness of no one to talk to.

There were the grade-school years, when Dulcy's father was

alternately violent or seductive, either beating Dulcy or threatening to get some "relief" in her bed.

There were the high school years, when Dulcy lost track of time, dropping acid with the other "oddballs" after school or consoling herself at night with vodka in the arms of some man she'd met at a disco whose name she would forget by morning.

There was her early adulthood, when she escaped her father and careened into a hasty and hideous marriage that nearly cost her her life because she was so brutally beaten.

There were her late twenties in Chicago, when she finally discovered Alcoholics Anonymous and began putting together the shards of her life; getting her college degree and working full-time as a waitress, so poor that she had no furniture or telephone; starting a career as a paralegal and moving on to a commodities exchange where she started making "serious money."

And now there is Dulcy the happily remarried, full-time mother, living in a velvet, manicured Illinois suburb, proudly pointing out the filigreed wallpaper she herself has hung in her spotless kitchen.

"I'm a maniac for order," she says with a wry grin, swinging wide the pantry drawer to show me her alphabetically arranged canned goods. "Gee, I wonder why."

She puts her babies into their bassinets, sits down with a cup of herb tea, and tells me about her "normal" life.

Normal is a word she uses with particular care and even reverence. She says it slowly, as though blowing a bubble of iridescent, changing, magical hues. Because normal today is not what it was when she was growing up.

> I remember as a kid thinking God had made a mistake. I was supposed to be a boy. I didn't feel like I was a real person. I always felt I wasn't normal, that there was something intrinsically different about me, a wall between me and the rest of the world. It wasn't until I joined AA that I found out my childhood *was* normal—for alcoholic families.

To understand how Dulcy got from the normalcy of family craziness to the normalcy of a conventional, structured, predictable life —from wishing she were a tough boy to gratitude that she is a woman whose body can grow and suckle babies—is to understand the determination and spirit that propels some mavericks out of nightmares into realized dreams.

The one tiny, cherished piece of Dulcy's childhood was that she knew her mother loved her and wanted her to have everything—to read, to learn, to grab life and shake the good things into her own hands. She would think of her mother from time to time as she picked her way through the emotional maze of her life.

She'd look for people to emulate: the executive down the hall who told her where to shop for tasteful clothes; the therapist who told her she could learn how to be the good kind of normal; the second husband who taught her that not all men get their kicks from punching women.

For years every step forward seemed to be followed by two in retreat to her old self. She'd crack from trying so hard to be a real person. She'd fall off the wagon, or she'd binge on food; she'd pick a fight with her husband, or she'd jump into her car and race through the night to nowhere.

But eventually the side trips into the "other" normal got briefer, and the good normalcy became more routine.

Easing out of what you learned in childhood sounds so simple. All you have to do is make up your mind and *do it,* right? But it's hard letting go of the perilous familiar and trusting the safe unknown.

Even today Dulcy sometimes looks at her husband, a physician, and wonders: "Maybe tomorrow he'll slug me, out of the blue. Maybe tomorrow he'll decide I'm ugly, I'm no good, I'm a terrible mother." But those thoughts are rarer and rarer, as the old Dulcy is shed for the new. She says,

> Listen, it's not always wonderful. My husband I both have tempers. But you have to understand that for so much of my life there was no safety net. The one thing I am absolutely certain of is that my husband is my safety net. It was only when I met him that I started to feel feminine, that I could have orgasms, that I could wear frilly things and not feel I had to be a tough guy to survive.
>
> Motherhood transformed me. I was not able to make a friend until recently. Now I sit with the women at parties and talk about developmental psychology and Pampers.
>
> Jesus, I sound like a jerk.

She pauses, not happy with her remarks, because they don't really explain what she means—they make her sound as if she traded in her brains for provincialism. To buy thinking time, she gets up to pour us each another cup of tea. Then she says,

> What I'm trying to say is that I'm reliving my childhood now. I never had a real family. Having a loving man lets you be a *family. That's* what I mean by normal. I want to be the mommy I never had and give my kids the daddy I never had. I am vicariously living through my children. Someday I'll get back to my career. But not now. Not now. I need this too much.

Dulcy walks me to the door, and together we stroll out into the sunshine. She waves to a neighbor driving by, then stoops to pick some flowers out of her garden for me to take home. As I climb into my car, she rests her hand on the door and adds one last thought:

> There's a part of me that will always miss the wild days a bit. But it's because of them that I know how good my life is today. There's also a part of me that will never totally trust any man. And since I don't expect my husband always to be there for me, every day I treasure the fact that he *is.* I'm happier than I ever imagined it was possible to be. And I'm trying like hell not to screw it up.

PART FOUR

The Demystification of Men

16

Rediscovering Our Fathers

I think it's possible to understand your father. But first you have to work through your feelings to reach some kind of resolution. That's what I'm trying to do—because I feel like a prisoner of my relationship with him where men are concerned. You know what's really crazy? I love my father—but I hate him too. It's very confusing, and very sad. I'm just never relaxed with men, and I'm tired of it. I don't want to live the rest of my life this way.

—PEG, THIRTY-TWO

When I started researching this book, I believed that daughters could comprehend both their fathers and mothers and their feelings about them in exactly the same way. I was both right on target and wildly off the mark.

With mothers, daughters at least have gender and—notwithstanding feminist changes in the culture—social roles in common. A daughter's connection to and understanding of her mother may sometimes be wobbly, even ruptured, but theoretically at least it's a relatively direct route, paved by their profound similarities.

But fathers are another matter. As we saw in Chapter 1, fathers and adult daughters contemplate each other over a chasm that in some ways forever separates them from *total* empathy.

After all, they don't share anatomical engineering. They don't share family and cultural training for "appropriate" behavior. They don't share many of the gender-specific skirmishes encountered in the outside world—girls being "catty," boys being "bullies," women being "hit on," men trying to "score," fathers being judged by their incomes, mothers by their ability to nurture. Fathers and daughters each have different—albeit almost entirely arbitrary—proving grounds and yardsticks for self-worth.

So the route to father-daughter understanding is something of a leap of the imagination. Most fathers are simply mysterious figures to their daughters. That's why Mom is often called in for assistance, interpretation, translation—counsel that even at best is so much guesswork because Mom, not being male, may not understand men any better than her daughter does. All Mom has going for her is her own experience—a brother, perhaps, an uncle, maybe, a lover or husband or several of each, and her own father, whom she may not know all that well either.

Nevertheless fathers and daughters have more essential similarities than either—even the most estranged—may realize:

They both have or had parents whose conditions for acceptance, approval, and love they tried hard to meet.

They are both pressured by sexist stereotypes and assumptions about how they ought to think, feel, and act.

They both know what it is to taste joy or loneliness, success or failure.

They both have defense mechanisms against emotional vulnerability.

They both want to be loved unconditionally by the other.

It is with those differences and similarities in mind that we begin the complex process of sorting out how daughters can come to terms with their fathers, how they can rediscover their fathers—or perhaps discover them for the first time—and reframe their relationship.

One of the surprises of my research was the stunning number of women who don't even *know* that they don't really know their fathers. For the majority of adult daughters these are the givens of fatherhood: Dad always at work, Dad behind the newspaper or in front of the TV, Dad enforcing the rules, Dad roughhousing with brothers, Dad teasing at the worst possible moments, Dad repairing a broken doll or helping with a science project, Dad eyeballing a daughter's date or tracking her virginity.

Most daughters never question Dad's role, his emotional unavailability, his different way of parenting. That's how fathers are, they think, that's what fathers do; it's always been like that and always will be like that and it's no big deal. After all, daughters still have Mom, or at least a girlfriend to pick up the slack.

When daughters telephone home and Dad automatically says, "I'll put your mother on," they may find his comment mildly amusing and altogether predictable—"Oh, that's Dad"—but they may not really consider that they can have a great deal more of him— or that they *ought* to have had a great deal more of him right along.

They especially don't know how very integral he is to their identities, how *great* a role he has always played—if only in absentia— in their feelings about themselves and about men.

The problem is that daughters don't *expect* their fathers to be there for them the way their mothers are.

They don't *expect* their fathers to weep and express their deepest feelings and self-doubts.

They don't *expect* their fathers to take a serious interest in their emotions or thoughts.

They don't *expect* their fathers to really talk to and understand them, to really be a friend.

But most daughters do expect all that from their lovers and partners.

Daughters find out in a hurry—at least subconsciously—what they didn't get from Daddy when they fall in love: all those unmet, undreamed-of, or denied expectations of fathers surface when the man of the moment, or the husband of thirty years, is late, or fails to notice a new dress or celebrate her job promotion, or is testy, or ignores her feelings and needs.

Now they feel Daddy's influence, but may not recognize it for what it is. All they know is they're often inordinately cautious or angry or weepy or anxious with men, frequently out of all proportion to the situation or current event. Their unrecognized or unresolved feelings about the father of childhood—their reactions to his silences or his thunder—come tumbling out in intimate partnerships.

These feelings can be oddly familiar. A distant mental bell rings, but where is it coming from? A twinge of recognition registers, but of what? To find explanations, daughters pick up the phone and make a lunch date with a girlfriend. Or pay Mom a visit. Or drop in on a sister.

Daughters don't go to the source of their confusion about men. They don't talk to *Dad himself,* because they don't know he's what makes the bell ring, he's why they feel these odd twinges with men. And even if they *do* know, they don't want to rock the paternal boat. Why mess with the past? He'd never open up. He wouldn't know how to begin to talk about this stuff. He'd be too embarrassed or annoyed or gruff. Or just too busy.

Anyhow, that's Dad.

He'll never change.

What's done is done.

You know how men are.

Knowing What You Missed

In reading the last six chapters, you may be counting your blessings that you had the good daddy you had. Those attentive, loving, actively involved, nonsexist fathers who today are in their fifties, sixties, and seventies had almost no social support for their compassion and sensitivity and eagerness to be equal parents to their daughters and sons. They had almost no applause for their need to put their families first. Given the recent interest in the "new, nurturant father," the good daddies of previous generations are sociological miracles.

Thus it's much more likely that you are among the daughters who never had a daddy like that. You may have been hobbled by your father's double standard for boys and girls. You may have been a disappointment to him because you weren't a son. You may have been ignored, or ridiculed, or abused by your father. You may not even have lived with him—he may in fact have deserted you or died.

Reading about good fathers, then, you are beginning to get an *idea* of how much you missed—as if it hasn't already crossed your mind—although you may not be entirely sure what to do about it. You may even believe that your relationship with your father is utterly hopeless and that all you care about is damage control, simply trying to get on with your life.

It's possible, though, that you fall somewhere in the middle: You're so certain that your father was a paternal paragon that it simply flummoxes you that your love life or your marriage is slightly-—or very—unsatisfying.

Some women have read this book hoping to find tips on forcing the men in their lives to change. These women are convinced that their less-than-fulfilling attachments are entirely the fault of lovers or partners who could be "fixed" if only they'd get some therapy—a beguiling thought, since there's usually some truth in it. Other women believe that if *they* change, say, by taking off some weight or learning the latest surefire sexual technique, they will turn their men into panting love slaves.

What many women don't realize is that even if they could select the perfect mate from some cosmic central casting, they'd probably keep repeating their underwhelming romantic patterns. Somehow the past continuously asserts itself in ways that have nothing to do with their partners.

Explanations for these repetitions of emotional history are not to be found in their partnerships, although there are clues. Explanations are to be found in an examination of their relationships with their fathers.

Perhaps you identified with one particular kind of daughter in the last section. Depending on your temperament and history, you might be gathering glimmerings that what is missing in your life today is de facto evidence of what was missing in your childhood connection to your father. For these are among the painful legacies of fathers to their daughters that, if unresolved, are carried over into the daughters' romantic choices:

Favored daughters did not get enough objectivity and limit setting.

Good daughters were not encouraged to value their capacities for assertive strength.

Competitive daughters learned that they were better off concealing their "feminine" vulnerabilities.

Fearful daughters were conditioned to equate love with loss or harm.

Maverick daughters were taught that to be different was to be unacceptable.

Thus you may recognize that in trying so hard to please your father, or in trying so hard to punish him or prove him wrong, something in your identity got lost.

Long before a woman can make reasoned, healthy romantic choices and alterations in her romantic patterns, she has to resolve her relationship with her father—the first man in her life—and how she feels about him. Whether or not her father was altogether "good enough" or distant or thoroughly monstrous, the idea is to be able to leave behind the old model of heterosexual love and friendship she learned from Daddy and to construct her own adult model.

Until a woman can do that, her choices of and relationships with men may be overly defensive—stalwartly insisting that all men are unreachable, hopelessly insensitive jerks—or overly dependent—giving her autonomy over to the men in her life. Either way, imprisoned by her automatic reactiveness to her father, she lacks real control over those choices.

One purpose of this chapter, then, is to help daughters to find out what they missed with their fathers so that they can better understand their relationships with men outside the family, whether at work or in love.

The larger goal here, however, is not simply or even necessarily to help women find nice guys or to improve their partnerships (see Chapter 18), or to learn how to compete with men in their careers, or to change the social order that is so damaging to women *and to men* (see Chapter 19)—although these are among the benefits of resolving the father-daughter relationship.

Rather the goal of this chapter is to understand the *father within,* to single out from the chorus of voices from the past *his voice* and to recognize his influence in the shaping of his daughter's identity and sexuality.

The key is to really get to know the actual father—whether or not he is alive or even around—to pull him out of the shadows, apart from Mom, away from the newspaper, and really *see* him.

Resolving the father-daughter relationship is a three-part journey of discovery:

* *Remembering*—finding out what you got and didn't get from your father in childhood.
* *Healing*—working through your feelings of anger or sadness, and mourning the child who didn't get enough fathering or the right kind of fathering.
* *Reconnecting*—viewing your father through the prism of your own maturity and finding out what shaped him, with or without his cooperation, so that you can understand why he behaved as he did and separate your wounds from his.

Let's examine these parts one at a time.

Remembering

In order to unravel confusing feelings about your father, you need to examine the past—to dig up memories of the father of your youth. But the journey back into childhood is not without risk.

The Hazards of Discovery. Many women feel that to acknowledge their fathers' parental failures, to see Dad's flaws, is to violate a sacred canon: family loyalty.

"Honor thy father," the Bible commands. Set aside for the moment that your father may not have honored you. The first hazard of seeing the real man with all his imperfections is that it forces you to separate from him emotionally and give up the rosy notion that he can fix anything, do anything, is an all-powerful hero.

Another hazard of recollection is that it lays siege to the fortress of your defenses. Exhuming the past can be threatening because it shakes apart your foundation, the persona you so carefully constructed to get or keep Daddy's love.

The very survival mechanisms that helped you to get along with your father, or to attract or to avoid his attention—the false self you created *just for him*—are the ones that you may still employ in your intimate attachments, but they may no longer work: The false self was tailored for *that* father and may not fit *this* lover or spouse. And in any case the choices of the false self are unreliable, because they are not the choices of a mature adult.

Says psychologist James Meltzer,

> If a woman grew up thinking that men are what makes the system work and that men have the power, then to question that is to be subversive to the social structure and even her own emotional structure as well. It can scare the hell out of her. If she felt that the way to survive was to align herself with a powerful man, and suddenly you ask her to *stop* seeing men as all-powerful, she's really up a creek.

To take another example, some daughters survive childhood by thinking of their fathers as unredeemable brutes, which gave these daughters permission to summon the gall angrily to reject Dad and stomp into adulthood. To suggest to such a woman that some men are indeed vulnerable and loving—that there are good guys out there—is not only to undermine her fiery and perhaps lifesaving defenses, it is also to whet an appetite for love that she may have struggled long and hard to banish.

Challenging a daughter to see her father in a new way—asking her to give up her total worship or total vilification of him—presents her with a terrible dilemma: If she tampers with the very cornerstone of her survival—the false self—what's left? The child within who is afraid of being abandoned by Daddy.

Hence some women are afraid to look back. They find ingenious ways to deny their own experience, to keep Daddy enthroned on idealization or entombed in amnesia or rage.

Denial and Blame. There are countless ways to avoid examining your relationship with your father. One is to mythologize him—to persist in seeing him as perfect, to protect oneself from seeing his dark side.

Then there are phobias, which are nothing if not catch basins of unresolved, uncomfortable feelings. And let us not forget all those other awareness killers—sleep, food, alcohol, drugs.

Blame is another way to sidestep working through our feelings about Dad. Blaming Mom or Stepmom is an extremely common theme among many of the women I interviewed. Indeed the very ease with which narcissistic or hypercritical or hypersensitive mothers can be blamed is exactly what deflects our attention from *another,* if not *the other,* source of our anxieties about ourselves and about men—Daddy.

Says Vivica, forty-two,

> I was afraid to let go of the fantasy that my father was perfect, that he was the protector, because then I'd really have come to terms with my mother, who was never there for me. It took me a long time to realize that he was a very self-indulgent man who always paid more attention to what he wanted than to what any of his children needed from him emotionally. I had to believe he was Santa Claus—otherwise I'd have no one.

Blame can be used in other ways. Holding a sibling or even yourself entirely responsible for the frayed father-daughter tie is a useful defense against seeing Dad as he really is. So is blaming Dad himself—it's easier to cut off from him than to examine your relationship to him and hence your own emotional conflicts.

But let's be clear about our terms: Fathers are *accountable* for their treatment of their children. Accountability helps put the past where it belongs and opens up the future. However, accountability can sometimes be a dressed-up version of blame.

To blame your father for everything that goes wrong in your adult life is to refuse to hold *yourself* accountable for what you do about those early paternal disappointments or injuries. Blame gives us license to fail. Blame keeps Daddy at the helm and very close by.

In denial and blame we remain emotionally bound to our fathers through our obeisance or belligerence. We do not see them with adult perceptions but, rather, as frightened or angry child to giant, all-powerful parent. We simply trade one pain for another. Or we trade one *hope* for another: Maybe Daddy will finally notice us, or maybe this new man or this new job will make up for Daddy's unavailability.

By ignoring the past you virtually guarantee its perpetuation. Says Dr. Marianne Goodman,

> This is what growing up is about: recognizing who your parents were, appreciating what they could give, acknowledging what they couldn't give, feeling the disappointment, and moving on.

Unless you can get beyond your defenses and see your father's *humanness,* you may not be able to accept your own. You may not allow yourself the chance to develop that part of you that got left behind.

By bringing *all* aspects of your father, rather than selected memories, into your adult consciousness—cushioned by your chronology and adult seasoning—it's possible to fill in the blanks of his silences, or his absences, or his negligence, even his misguided good intentions. It's even possible to still forever the terror of his abusiveness.

Recognizing your father's errors is not to dishonor him. Rather, ignoring them and failing to believe the evidence of your own eyes and ears and sensibilities is to dishonor yourself. If you can't see the fallible, real man, neither can you see yourself, or the people you love—friends, lovers, children—as fallible and real; they can only be *all* good or *all* bad.

Getting at the Memories. The point of emotional journeys back to the father of childhood is to *defuse* the past and its hold on us.

The first step is to start at the end: to decide what you dislike about the patterns of your relationships with men today, whether comradely or professional or intimate, and to find out what causes you pain—that is, to pay attention to those moments when you react strongly in specific ways to men.

Do you, for example, unquestioningly follow to the letter the advice of any male lawyer or accountant or physician? Do you feel that a lover is about to bolt if he says he needs some time alone? If your male boss calls you into his office, are you certain that you're about to be reprimanded or fired? Are you convinced that any man who pays affectionate attention to you is entitled to your body?

Alternatively, are you stunned when you cannot attract any man at a party? Do you assume that you are the one who will get a job promotion just because you feel special or privileged? Do you use sex for favors or assume that sex will be rewarded in some way?

Or are you unable to walk away from a wholly inconsequential fight with a man? Do you routinely find yourself engaging in arguments with strong or domineering men in a kind of verbal arm wrestling? Do you resolutely refuse ever to ask the counsel of any man? Are you unable to resist dominating or manipulating "weak" men? Of the sensitive men you know, is there a part of you that denigrates them simply because they *are* sensitive?

Then there is the matter of sex: Do you have serious and ongoing problems in bed?

These responses and difficulties—examples of unresolved emotions rather than rational thought—are often symptoms of unfinished father-daughter business. Hence they provide useful springboards into the past.

The second step backward, so to speak, is to start uncovering memories of your father.

Below is a list of questions—drawn from my interviews with therapists—to bring the father of childhood out of the shadows of selective memory:

• What are your earliest memories of your father? What are your strongest memories of him? What is the happiest memory and what is the unhappiest memory?

- Which parent did you run to when you fell and hurt yourself or when you had a problem, and what happened?

- What was your father's attitude about your crying or expressing anger? Did he overreact, threatening, for example, to punch you or someone else out? Did your pain result in his being *more* pained, requiring you to comfort him? Was he indifferent?

- When you asked him questions—or when you asked him certain kinds of questions—did he usually or always say, "Go ask your mother"?

- How and when did your father praise or reward you, or punish you, and for what?

- What kinds of presents did you make for him when you were a child, and what was his reaction to them? Was he pleased, or annoyed, or perfunctory?

- Did you ever spend time alone with your father, or was your mother always or frequently in tow? Did he, for example, ever take you to lunch or an outing apart from the rest of the family? How often?

- Did you believe that your father favored your brother or, perhaps, a sister over you? Were you his favorite?

- What were your father's dreams for you? Did he say, "What's the point of sending you to college? You're just going to get married"?

- Did your father encourage you to be independent, and if so, how? Did he say or imply, "Girls can do just about anything boys can do"?

- Did your father encourage you to be dependent? Did he, for instance, say, "No real lady ever calls up a man," or "The reason your brother can go camping and you can't is because he's a boy"?

- How was money handled in your family? Did Dad pay all the bills and put Mom on a strict allowance, saying, "Women don't know the first thing about finances"? Did he make frequent references to the provisions of his will, letting you know that good behavior—as he defined it—would ultimately be financially rewarded? Did he make all the "big" decisions in the family, such as where to live, what to buy, where to go on vacation?

- What was your parents' marriage like? Did Dad denigrate or humiliate Mom? Did he say to her, "Don't worry your pretty head about a thing—I'll take care of it"?

- Did you ever get the feeling that in loving one parent, you were being disloyal to the other? Did your father encourage you to collude with him and "gang up" on Mom? Did you ever feel you had to choose up sides? Why, when, and for what?

• How did your father behave with his own father? His mother?

• Are there *no* happy memories of your father? Are there *no* unhappy memories?

As you answer these questions, you will find patterns not only in your father's behavior but in your own as well. You will begin to put together a portrait of your false self and why and how it took shape—what you had to do or be to please your father, or at least to stay out of his way.

After posing these general questions it's important to ask yourself sexual ones in order to discover your father's attitude about eroticism in general and about your sexuality in particular. Such questions also help you to find out whether or not your father was seductive or incestuous because, as we know, these painful memories are often repressed:

• Did your father change his behavior toward you when you reached puberty? What was he like before, and then after? How did he react when you first got your period? Did he even know you got it?

• What was his reaction to your dating? Which boyfriends did he like, and which did he forbid you ever to see, and why?

• What did your father tell you about sex? Was the subject verboten? Did he take too great an interest in your love life, pressing you for intimate details about what you and a date or boyfriend did alone together?

• Did your father make sexual cracks and judgments about women—as in "Get a load of those jugs" or "Rape victims all ask for it"?

• Did your father walk around the house without his clothes on? Did he always shower or urinate with the bathroom door open?

• Did you ever get a creepy feeling when alone with your father? Were you ever afraid to be in his company without a third person present?

• Did your father insist—other than in early childhood—that you never lock your bedroom or the bathroom door?

- Did he ever stare at or fondle you in a way that made you feel uncomfortable?
- Did he ever touch your nipples or genitals other than in the most obviously accidental way?
- Did he ever say, "Don't tell your mother we were alone together—this is our special secret"?
- Did he ever threaten to harm you, or a sibling, or a pet, or himself, if you didn't do something? (This is a question for those women who can't remember sexual abuse but *can* remember being threatened or intimidated.)
- Did your brother ever abuse you sexually? (Sometimes a woman can remember fraternal incest, but totally blocks out paternal incest.)
- If your father abused you sexually, what did you do? Did you keep it secret? If your father was found out, what happened? How did each parent react?

When the answers to any or all of these questions are elusive, family albums can yield important information. In looking at photographs you can notice certain patterns: Either Dad was never in the picture, or he never stood close to anyone, or he stood close only to your brother or to Mom. Maybe he gained a lot of weight or abruptly lost weight, a symptom of stress or illness; maybe he always had a bottle of beer in his hand; maybe he never smiled.

The idea behind all these questions and investigations is to begin shrinking our fathers to human scale and to tease out that which was good as well as that which was bad. Even the woman with the happiest of childhoods is able to remember the *one* time her father lost it—slapping her, for instance, because she came home late from a date. And even the most brutally abused woman can remember the *one* talk she had with her father when he told her a little bit about his business or about his childhood, the *one* time he bought her a toy or was fun to be with or went to bat for her.

As you collect information and impressions about your childhood, certain emotions may emerge. For women whose childhood losses were relatively minor and not terribly damaging, simple remembering may indeed be enough to end their confusion about Dad and about men. Thus the answers you have gathered may be sufficient to clear up any doubts about your father or yourself.

But for other women, recollection may be a Pandora's box of

pain or terror. Such women need to do something with the over-whelming feelings that are evoked. Resurrecting them is not for the faint-hearted or ill prepared and may require outside help and support. Having unearthed the anguish, it must now be dealt with in a constructive way.

Healing

There are many resources for binding up the wounds of child-hood loss—books, spirituality, psychotherapy, and self-help groups among them. Many women, depending on their histories and the complexity of their difficulties, choose one, or even all, of these paths to healthy adulthood.

Here we will concentrate on two approaches that may be neces-sary if the others fail to produce real healing: therapy and support groups.

Therapy. One of the purposes of therapy is to provide an atmo-sphere of trust in which you can safely relive your childhood and play out the sorrow or rage *without being judged.* Therapeutic in-tervention can help to free you from a sense that you are impris-oned by the past and that you have no alternatives or grounds for realistic hope.

One of the tasks of therapy is to help you mourn your childhood —to grieve for the child who was improperly or inadequately fa-thered—so that you can separate emotionally from your father. This is not self-pity; rather it is saying to yourself, with a therapist as good parental stand-in, "You didn't deserve the childhood treatment you got, you didn't ask for it, you are not responsible for it, and you were entitled to something better."

Learning to express anger is also a critical piece of therapy, especially if you were never allowed—or never allowed yourself— to feel rage at your father but, rather, volunteered for tearful self-blame for his neglect or mistreatment. Constructive anger can be emboldening, permitting you to take back the power you may have had to sacrifice in childhood in order to be accepted and to sur-vive.

For example, a woman who idealizes her father and is afraid of sullying his sacred image may have to develop healthy anger at the ways he may have infantilized her or made her too dependent on him. Such women need to form a more mature, realistic love—to separate real feelings from fantasy, their strengths from their fears, so that they can learn to stand on their own.

Says Courtncy, thirty-six,

> I remember some negative things about my father, and I hate them. It hurts to remember them, because if I see his warts, I can't feel special the way I did with him when I was a child.

Getting rid of unconstructive anger is another therapeutic task. Women who were abused by their fathers in childhood, for instance, often and understandably excoriate them, keeping them on an eternal pyre of rage or vengeance. These women have to develop compassion, if not necessarily love, for their fathers, in order to get beyond their own volatile reactiveness. They need to find some path to an understanding of what shaped even the most egregious of fathers.

Says June, forty-one,

> It's only recently that I've been able to see my father as other than a son of a bitch. He was just a glaring example of a screwed-up childhood. He was always a very angry man, and he took it out on me. But I think he was acting out of what he was deprived of and just passing it down, and not out to "get" me, even though it felt like that at the time.

Acceptance is the final piece of therapy—knowing that nothing you could have done in childhood could change your father and that nothing you can do today will change him. All you can change is your *reaction* to him. Acceptance means you stop trying to win your father's approval or to wrest an apology from him. Acceptance means looking forward instead of being sucked back into the past.

Perhaps the best way to describe how therapy works with a compassionate, well-qualified professional is to take a worst-case scenario: incest, the most ravaging and most father-daughter-specific form of child abuse.

Many incest victims can't mourn the past or feel the anger because they are totally unable to remember their childhoods. To remember is to relive the guilt, the terror, the revulsion, the shame —and even the pleasure. Many, if not most, incest victims dare not remember because dissociating from the experience allowed them to survive it. In some cases, if the abuse occurred only in infancy, they *cannot* consciously remember because they had no language with which to incorporate it.

Either way they block memories of the abuse, which lives on in their fears of men, their fears of sex. It lives on in their somatic responses and in their unfathomable, symbol-filled nightmares and their inexplicable panic attacks.

The hardest aspect of incest to absorb, let alone make sense of, is the incongruity of two simultaneous truths: the pain and the pleasure, the betrayal and the affection. That is why the over-whelming majority of incest victims *must* have sympathetic professional help to recollect and to heal their incest wounds. The memories are too searing, too confounding, too punishing to handle alone.

Healing through therapy is a reciprocal process that rests on the *one* emotion the incest victim most fears: trust. Therefore, when she can somehow come to trust a therapist, trust that her memories won't be used against her, and trust that love won't kill her, it is a triumph of hope over experience.

For many incest victims there comes a moment in adulthood when memory literally begins to serve, which will inspire them to seek help. This phenomenon of sudden awareness—whether making vague connections or experiencing total, vivid recall—of long-ago sexual abuse is called "delayed discovery," which occurs years, even decades, after the incest itself.

Sometimes memories return when the victim has an ongoing sexual relationship with a loving man. Or when she gives birth to a daughter. Or when an older daughter gets a certain look in her eye.

Sometimes it happens when the victim is at work. One woman, an attorney, was in court cross-examining a man accused of sexually abusing his three-year-old daughter. Suddenly recollections of her own father's sexual abuse erupted into her awareness, causing her to scream at the judge, "These men just get away with it!"

Sometimes the victim remembers the abuse in the middle of therapy that she started, she thinks, because her marriage isn't working or she wants to improve her career—and the real reason she sought professional help is beginning to boil in her subconscious.

A therapist recalled for me treating a woman—let's call the patient Louisa—for years before the incest memories crept out.

Once, seemingly out of the blue and almost as a non sequitur, Louisa asked the therapist, "Is it possible that somebody could have been abused and not remember it?"

In subsequent sessions, Louisa fought a desperate duel with her protective amnesia, which up to then had stifled both her lingering sense of deep and abiding shame for having enjoyed her father's caresses *and* her equally harrowing awareness of his betrayal.

Gradually Louisa bravely began to recover shards of recollection. And then one day she had a breakthrough session with her therapist. She was talking about her father's molestation of her and began to weep. "I liked the abuse," she sobbed, "so it must have been okay."

Her therapist replied,

> No, no. You liked it *and* you didn't like it. Your *body* liked it; *your mind hated it.* Right now, if I took a needle and shot you up with heroin, your body would like it. It wouldn't mean you chose it, it wouldn't mean it was good for you. But you'd like it.

That session produced a quantum leap of psychological growth for Louisa, because it helped her finally to integrate her experience and to end her need to keep pushing it out of sight.

These, then, are among the tasks of therapy—slogging through denial, blame, mourning, anger, distrust, acceptance—and they do not work overnight. Therapy is a long, often wrenching, often exhilarating process—not a quick fix. It takes years to erect defenses, whether of supplication or rage, against one's father. So it takes time to dismantle them and to replace them with self-esteem and sturdy emotional boundaries.

By constantly covering the same material in what seems like an endless litany, new memories are added and old fears eliminated. In time, where once a woman was fearful or defensive, now—having taken the power of her strengths and sensitivities into her own hands—she can, in a profound sense, be reborn.

Self-Help Groups. For some women, therapy may not be enough, or even the appropriate path, for them to repair their childhood wounds. This is especially true of women recovering from substance abuse, whose resurrected fears might send them reeling back to their addictions. Self-help groups can provide another route to healing.

An enormous part of their appeal is the feeling of community they offer. Moreover, many groups, particularly twelve-step programs based on the Alcoholics Anonymous model, unite around a single issue. These groups pick up where therapy leaves off. What self-help groups can provide that traditional therapy often cannot is *identification:* Simply hearing about someone else's experience can help you remember your own. Seeing someone recover from similar childhood wounds can inspire your own healing.

Says a member of Co-Dependents Anonymous,

> It wasn't until I joined CoDA that I was able to make sense of my lousy relationships and my suicidal feelings. My mom died when I was three, but I remembered nothing of my childhood. One night I was at a CoDA meeting and I heard a woman talk about the messages she got from her past. All of a sudden I started hearing all these death messages from *my* past—things like my father saying, "I wish it had been you instead of your mother." I finally got it: No *wonder* I thought I didn't deserve to live.

For many women self-help and support groups of all kinds can lead to full recovery, often in tandem with traditional therapy. Ultimately it doesn't matter which route you take to the resolution of conflicts—as long as you remember, and heal.

Reconnecting with Your Father

Having resurrected the memories of childhood and mourned your paternal losses, it is now possible to take the final step to father-daughter resolution, the acid test of healing: reconnecting with your father, if only the father of memory.

Mommy alone can't make the father-daughter connection all better. A friend or lover or spouse can't make it all better. And in some ways even therapy or self-help are not enough to get beyond all your childhood reactions to Dad and your conditioned responses to men.

The last piece of father-daughter resolution is to know your father and/or find out all about him. Discovering the unique challenges and conflicts of his life can help you finally understand, if not necessarily forgive, why he treated you as he did in childhood.

Occasionally, learning more about him can result in admiration of him. He might, in his advanced years, be inspired to discuss your early years, his role in your pain, and become a friend.

Even if he can't, at least you will be able to test your growth and the sturdiness of your emotional boundaries. When you can be with your father—or with the memories of him—without losing your boundaries, you will no longer be in danger of repeating the past in your intimate connections. You will discover at last that your father—like most men—is not so mysterious after all.

17

▼▼▼▼▼▼

Reframing the Father-
Daughter Relationship

*I really had four relationships with my father: The first was when I was
a little girl and he just adored me. Then there were my teens, when he
was always working, and when he was around, all we did was fight.
Then after I got married, we were sort of polite strangers. But the last
relationship was when he was old and sick—that was quite different.
He was so vulnerable that you couldn't do anything but love him. I
really got his tenderness and who he was; his courage and his character came through. We came full circle. I felt such a completion.*

—SYLVIA, FIFTY-ONE

When Amanda, an only child, was twenty-five, her mother died
after a long and agonizing struggle with cancer. Amanda and her
difficult mother had always had a volatile relationship, uname-
liorated by her mother's illness or Amanda's ministrations to her.
Her mother's death and their lack of emotional closure left a void
in Amanda's life, throwing her into a sinking spiral of angry, confused grief.

Amanda had no one to turn to. She had not seen her father
since she was five, when he abandoned her and her mother; her
grandparents all were dead. Her paucity of female friends and her
nonexistent love life made her acutely aware of how alone she was
in the world.

Yet when an acquaintance suggested that she try to find her
father and attempt a reconciliation, Amanda snapped, "Not for a
million bucks!"

"My life was a mess," she recalls. She was riddled with self-doubt. She had an unchallenging job and no particular goals or ambition. She had no interests or social life beyond the nightly television lineup.

As time went on, and as Amanda's empty existence became a black hole of depression, the idea of seeing her father again began to gnaw at her. She wanted to connect with him—yet she didn't. She desperately needed a daddy, but she hated her father for dropping out of her life.

Jolted by her mother's death and terrified of a future that seemed so bleak, Amanda went into therapy to try to begin constructing a future of meaning and purpose.

Six months later her therapist suggested she contact her father, and this time she took the advice. She called a distant cousin who knew where her father was and got his phone number in Michigan. That night she collected her courage and dialed the number.

"Daddy?" she said to the man who answered the phone. "This is Amanda." She recalls,

> The first words out of his mouth were "Did you know that your mother had brothers and sisters who were killed in a car crash before you were born?" Imagine! His very first words, even before I had a chance to tell him Mom had died. I had always been told by her that he was this evil man. And here he was telling me something I never knew, to help me understand her.

A week later Amanda boarded a plane for Michigan. When her father picked her up at the airport, she recognized him instantly: "I have his face," she says with a wry grin. For five days father and daughter engaged in a painful conversational marathon, punctuated by tears and rages on both sides. Says Amanda,

> I felt like a time bomb was going off inside me. We got into some pretty heavy rows. I said, "How could you just disappear?" But it was hard for him too. I was pulling the rug back from my life and exposing all the garbage underneath. Every time he tried to change the subject, I dragged him back.
>
> Eventually everything came out: He showed me letters he had sent me that had been returned unopened. He said the reason he left was because my mother's mother had always put herself between my parents. Grandma and Mom con-

stantly accused him of having affairs. He said, "Finally I did have an affair because I was so sick of being falsely accused of it." That stuck in my head. It was like he was really human; they had always made him seem so inhuman.

I tell you this story not because it had a Hollywood ending—the visit was the only time Amanda's father set aside his own bluster and vanity long enough to open up and "be human." Rather I relate this story because it had a very happy aftermath: Thanks to Amanda's reconnection with her father, she was able to accept him and to find answers to all the dangling questions about her childhood. She says,

> Seeing him again helped to get rid of all my expectations that he'd somehow give me everything I never got from him in childhood. I wanted him to be there for me and really communicate—to be a real father. What I found out is he just isn't capable of it. He's not a bad man—he just can't do it.

Now, nine years later, at thirty-four Amanda has achieved a separate peace. In completing her emotional self-portrait, she has come to terms with her childhood. She has a sense that her history can no longer harm her—because she doesn't live there anymore.

The Goals of Reconnection

As we saw in Chapter 1, the challenges adult daughters face with their parents tend to be characterized by two general themes: Most daughters need to detach from their mothers, because the relationship is so very intense. But with fathers, the psychological mandate is different. Most daughters need to *attach* emotionally to them, because the relationship is usually so distant. For you cannot truly separate from your father if you didn't spend much time with him or were never very close to begin with.

Thus, for the majority of daughters it is important to try to reconnect with their fathers in adulthood: to get to know their fathers once and for all—in ways they didn't in childhood, or adolescence, or even young adulthood—and to reframe their relationship beyond blame and outmoded dreams.

Perhaps the most significant incentive for reconnecting with your father is that it may be your last opportunity before he dies to clear up some mysteries and misconceptions about your childhood, to correct or fill in the blanks of faulty memory, to ferret out the lore of your youth.

For your father—unless he abandoned you or he died—is the *other* eyewitness to your history. Parents are the primary emotional and factual archivists of our infancy, early childhood, and adolescence. More than anyone, they have tracked not only our first steps but in many cases every step of the way between birth and adulthood. Even fathers who spent much of their time at the office or buried in a book have more information about us — mothers excepted—than almost anyone else; and in most cases Mom has usually been filling Dad in right along.

Forgiveness Versus Understanding. Once again, a definition of terms is in order. Most adult daughters would love to have a good relationship with their fathers or improve the one they do have. But reconnecting doesn't necessarily mean wiping the slate clean, doesn't necessarily lead to forgiveness and reconciliation.

All children automatically forgive their parents in childhood because their survival depends on seeing their parents as perfect. But once they are grown, children are, to one degree or another, able to survive on their own, and forgiveness takes on a greater ambiguity and complexity.

Moreover forgiveness is a loaded concept; it implies that one should be able to turn the other cheek and discount one's own feelings. Indeed failure to "forgive" one's parents can lead to a certain judgmentalism on the parts of others that does nothing to help a child claim her own experience. Says Dr. Potash,

> One of the mistakes friends, relatives, and even therapists sometimes make is to say, "Make friends with your daddy or mommy, forgive them." If your father was cold or negligent or abusive, you *are* allowed to say of him, "He was a terrible parent."
>
> The important thing is to get beyond such childhood experiences and not be permanently paralyzed by them—to concentrate on your own growth rather than thinking you asked for your father's treatment and that you are a bad person if you don't forgive him. More useful is to say to yourself, "Well, that's what I had back then, but I can have something better now. I'm no longer a helpless child."

Forgiveness does not of itself result in a daughter's maturity and equanimity. And in some cases it may not even be appropriate: Some fathers are so unrepentantly cruel, malignantly narcissistic, addicted, or brutally psychotic that reconciliation—let alone forgiveness—isn't even an option. It's difficult to imagine, for example, that a daughter who was tortured or raped by her father—and whose father has never taken responsibility for his behavior—could ever feel a scintilla of forgiveness for such actions.

This is where the distinction can be made between forgiveness and understanding. When a daughter can *understand* what caused a father to behave as he did, it helps to defuse his power over her. When she can feel tenderness for the boy within her father—the frightened child who in all likelihood himself was humiliated or beaten and sexually abused—she can begin to make sense of how the adult man came to be, *which has nothing whatever to do with her.*

To understand your father does not mean that you must love him. It doesn't mean you must forgive him, although in time you might. It means that you can and must let go of your anger or fear in order to avoid derailing—or being attracted to someone like him.

As for reconnecting with an abusive father, in some cases—although certainly not all—it is possible, as we shall see later in this chapter, to arrange circumstances of personal safety for a daughter to test her boundaries with him face-to-face. But even if that isn't possible or realistic, it's still necessary to learn what forces in a father's own generational and family history caused him to self-destruct, so that she can leave her childhood behind.

A New Beginning. The errors of most fathers are those of omission rather than commission. If fathers were, say, overprotective, or had whimsical dreams for their daughters that seem purely nineteenth century, generally it is because they are citizens of their own generation. In attempting to do their paternal best, they were drawing on memories of their own childhoods and the mores of their own parents.

Thus, for the majority of adult daughters, reconnection with their fathers is a comparatively easy process. Indeed the odds of improving and reframing your relationship with your father are extremely good.

For one thing your father is no longer a kid. Many daughters see their fathers' vulnerabilities for the first time when those fathers have completed the career-building years or withdrawn from the breadwinning battlefields into retirement or illness or old age.

The seasons of a father's life are an important component of his emotional availability. As we know from the work of Daniel Levinson and other researchers, it is in the final trimester of life that many men become aware of and long to take care of their own unfinished emotional business: to love and be loved in ways they were too busy—or too culturally indoctrinated—to attempt in their younger years.

Ironically many fathers are even more eager to make amends with their grown children than are the children themselves. Says family therapist Ellen Berman, M.D.,

> I have found over and over again that fathers are far more willing to talk than their kids, who are still dealing with the internalized parent in their heads. By the time a woman is an adult, her father is heading down the road toward fifty-five or sixty and he's actually willing to communicate, if you approach him right. Most men, even if they didn't talk while the daughter was growing up, tend to mellow as they get older. They want to reconnect with their children and feel that they're leaving some kind of legacy.

So the time may be ripe for you to get to know your father—and he you—perhaps for the first time, and almost certainly in a way you never did before.

You yourself have some advantages in this effort. To begin with, you may have a clear head start by virtue of your gender. If any grown child can get through to Daddy, it's usually his daughter— the child he is most likely to have shown a particular tenderness when he was a young father, unencumbered by the mandate to be an unemotional, "masculine" role model. Your father may still see in you—if only in his sentimental memories of your childhood— the one female who ever came close to perceiving him as he wanted to perceive himself: an adored hero.

Another advantage you may have is the weathering of your emotional storms in therapy or support groups or by reading self-help books. If that's the case, you have a leg up in the maturity department. There is scant payoff for you to continue to be either the dutiful, obedient, flattering, placating little girl or the trouble-making, attention-seeking, provocative one.

For all these reasons, reconnecting with your father in adult-hood can be a unique opportunity to see him through the prism of your seasoning and his. Now it is possible to accept him at last as he is, not as you wished he could have been or fantasized that he actually was.

Reality Check. "Sure, sure," you may be thinking, "it all sounds so simple. I just have to call Pop on the phone and he'll dissolve into a puddle of contrition. Fat chance."

But the idea isn't to corner him and shout *"Gotcha!"* or to manufacture trouble where it doesn't exist. The idea is to *demystify* him.

Let's imagine that you are a once-intimidated little girl who now wants to reconnect with your father, the opinionated autocrat. The very *thought* of sitting down and attempting a heart-to-heart at this late date may seem daunting. As strong as you may have become in other areas of your life, this one gives you hives.

Perhaps you are still trying to protect him—and yourself—from your disappointment in him. Many daughters told me they'd often wanted to sort out certain issues with their fathers and get to know them better, but hadn't because they didn't "want Dad to feel bad." As one woman put it,

> I'm afraid to rehash the past because it might jeopardize what we do have. I'd love to let my hair down with him, but he's so sensitive that I don't want him to hate himself or feel guilty.

On the other hand perhaps you *can't wait* to rush home and tell your old man off because your feelings about him are still raw. Of this impulse, says Dr. Berman,

> It's tempting for some people to confront the parent with their most fearful or angry complaint. The problem with that is that the parent doesn't know where this is coming from, and will get very defensive.

These reactions are evidence that you are still *reacting* rather than *interacting* and that your emotional boundaries are shaky. The challenge is to go back into the relationship not with a laun-dry list of demands or as a last-ditch effort to win his approval. Rather it is to see your outlines, separate from his.

Agenda for Reconnection. These, then, are the goals of father-daughter reconnection:

• Uncovering your father's history—finding out the forces that shaped him, his decisions and choices.

• Defining yourself in *relation* to him—holding on to your own identity, regardless of the pressures or temptations to slip back into childhood roles.

• Settling old scores—telling your father in a reasoned way what he means to you, what he gave you and what you feel he didn't; or, if it isn't possible to do so in person, ending the grudges and vendettas of memory.

• Moving ahead in your life with a solid sense of your separate self—part father, part mother, but altogether your own person.

On the assumption that you are beyond the denying or blaming stage—and what follows is not to be attempted until that stage is over—now it's possible to put the relationship on a new footing. And the way to do all that is to understand the patterns of your father's emotional history—specifically to get a fix on family triangles.

Triangling and Detriangling

"Triangling" is a term used by family therapists to describe the ways in which any two-person relationship is inevitably affected by a third. Writes Dr. Kerr,

> The [triangle] theory is an attempt to define the *facts of functioning* in human relationships—facts which can be observed to repeat over and over so consistently that they become knowable and predictable.

Family triangles are used in a variety of ways and for a variety of purposes. Within the immediate family they are employed to distribute anxiety around the "system" and to negotiate closeness and distance.

Here's how it works. When two family members are close, a third is, per force, an outsider. Thus if you and Mom are best buddies, your dad is relegated to the outside. He may make noises —such as saying to Mom, "Everything your daughter does is *perfect!*" or saying to you, "You can tell me; what did your mother *really* pay for that coat? She never tells me the truth"—that do not directly state his anxiety about feeling left out.

Instead Dad hands off his anxiety—in the first example to Mom and in the second example to you—and he gets back on the inside, while you or Mom become the outsiders. In neither case does Dad say, "Listen, I feel like a fifth wheel here. Can we have a talk?" Indeed, given the cultural rubrics of "masculinity," he'd probably rather take a bullet than to say that to *anyone,* and may in fact not be aware himself of what he's feeling.

Triangles do not simply operate in the immediate family; they echo down through many generations. For example, your father says to you of your brother's wearing an earring, "He'll be wearing a dress next. What is he, some kind of fag?"

It's tempting to write off such a father as a sexist pig. But look at it this way: Maybe he was ridiculed or severely punished by his father for being a "sissy" whenever he cried or failed to slug it out with a kid on the schoolyard, and it is *his father's* critical voice that you are really hearing.

In these ways the ghosts of the past are visited on children—and grandchildren and great-grandchildren.

Of course you won't know any of this unless you *know* your father and his history—the emotional triangles of his multigenerational past. (This same awareness can be applied to mothers and daughters, or to friendships, or to sibling attachments, or—as we shall see in the next chapter—to marital ones.)

What you see in your father today is not necessarily the whole picture. And you won't know for sure until you *detriangle*—get yourself out of the middle and encourage Dad to deal with you directly, rather than use you as a conduit or try to keep you in your old daughterly role.

Detriangling does not always go easily or take place all at once. The first hurdle may be *Mom's* resistance. She might not be thrilled with the idea of being asked to stand in the wings, away from her central maternal role, while you and Daddy seem to fall in love all over again.

Dad may have his own resistance to your efforts to change your old role and become an adult. He may—especially if he's retired—attempt to cling to or reclaim his patriarchal authority, even though you're a grown woman, perhaps with a career and/or with children or grandchildren of your own. He may not want to appear anything less than Big Daddy, now that he's been culturally disenfranchised by virtue of his age.

These areas of resistance are echoes of the family triangle—Mom, the maternal gatekeeper; Dad, the family chieftain or unblemished hero—both trying to keep daughter from growing up. *You* may like the changes in you, but they may not and may make every effort to get you to *change back.*

Try not to be discouraged by such resistance or allow it to interfere with your goals. If you can effectively detriangle and gently but firmly insist on your desire to know your parents and not be drafted into taking sides, you can uncover a wealth of information that will dramatically alter your reactions to your father (or mother) and at the same time solidify your emotional boundaries.

One woman put an end to her parents' triangulation of her—she calls it "strangulation"—this way:

> Recently I told my parents that I don't want to hear them bad-mouth each other any longer because it makes me feel disloyal to listen. My mother said, "Who else do I have to talk to?" I said, "Why don't you see a marriage counselor?" She burst into tears. My father just got very quiet. It's a pity that she sees him so negatively, and it's a pity he hasn't worked on his part in their problems. But I can't make it all better for them. I just can't be in the middle anymore. We all get along a lot better since I stopped being the intermediary.

The goals of detriangling are to think and act in a new way, rather than *react* in the old, familiar, and altogether unproductive ways—and to bring your father's history out in the open with you, one-on-one. From that you can uncover the real "why" of your father's behavior toward you.

Uncovering the Past

With those goals in mind you could begin the reconnection process in a private talk with your father, preferably in a quiet, stress-free atmosphere. You could introduce the subject with a statement something like this: "I feel that I don't know you very well, and I'd really like to get to know you better. I'd love for you to go back to the beginning and tell me all about your family."

If he agrees—and we'll discuss what to do if he doesn't—these are among the questions you can pose that are free of criticism and judgment, designed to sympathetically elicit information from him rather than to assign blame:

"What do you know about your grandparents?"

"What do you know about your parents? What was their marriage like? Who were you closer to?"

"What was it like when you were a child? How were you punished or rewarded, and for what?"

"How did your parents react when you cried or were frightened?"

"What did your parents want you to be when you grew up?"

"What did *you* want to be? How did that turn out?"

"Did your parents play favorites—did they compare you to a brother or a sister? How did you get along with your siblings—were you closer to one than another?"

"What did your parents tell you about sex? About girls?"

"Why did you get married when you did—were you ready for it?"

"Did you have in-law problems, and what were they?"

"When I was born, do you remember anything you were afraid of or happy about?"

"Was I a planned child? Was I born during a good time or a bad time—how was business? How were you and Mom getting along?"

"What was it like to become a father? What was the most difficult aspect of having a son or a daughter? What did you worry about most about us kids?"

"What did you teach me about sex? How did you want me to think or feel about my own sexuality?"

"Did you ever feel sort of out of the picture, that all you were good for was bringing home a paycheck?"

"What's the happiest moment of your whole life? What's the unhappiest moment?"

"If you could change one thing about your life, what would it be?"

It's more than likely that few people ever asked your father some or even any of these questions in quite this way. For one thing, when it comes to parenting, fathers are often considered interlopers or incapable of nurturing—at least compared with mothers—or of "touchy-feely" conversations.

Moreover most children don't know *either* parent all that well, at least when it comes to their histories. So your father may be delighted to have the opportunity to talk about things he may seldom have discussed with anyone.

In addition to the answers to these questions, it's useful to gather other information about him as well, either from him directly or by talking to Mom or other relatives. Such information includes where your father went to school, acute or chronic family illnesses, deaths, divorces and remarriages, siblings and step-siblings, his athleticism or lack of it, his military-service record and experiences, what the family finances were. You then collect as much data as possible about his parents and grandparents and their families on both sides.

As you pull together all this research, you will see patterns down through the generations. Perhaps sons were always favored over daughters. Or mothers were the matriarchs and fathers took a backseat. Perhaps stoicism was a multigenerational virtue. Alternatively maybe every family dinner was so emotional, it stopped just short of a food fight.

Sometimes these patterns all but hit you in the face. One woman said that after doing a great deal of family research she made this connection: She divorced when her son was seven; her father divorced her mother when she was eight; his father divorced his mother when he was six.

While this sounds like the stuff of horoscopes, and while all patterns are not so obvious, you will be able to see what kinds of behaviors were permitted and which were not through the generations—what was an option and what was forbidden. Most important you will see how those patterns devolved to you, and to your father's expectations of you.

Unlocking Family Secrets. One of the saddest aspects of my interviews with fathers was how often they told me secrets about themselves that they'd never told their grown children and in many cases hadn't even told their wives, believing that they had to present big, brave, perfect images of themselves. These secrets included family skeletons, such as a grandfather's jail record, or a grandmother's "shotgun" wedding, or their own physical or sexual abuse by a parent or grandparent, or early marriages and divorces, or illegitimate children.

One man I interviewed has never told his daughter that when he was thirteen, his violent father was in prison and his mother—whom he was always trying to protect—was in a mental institution. He never told her that he dropped out of school and didn't learn to read until he was an adult. He never told her that he was always afraid his wife—like his mother—would leave him, which is why he was always so angrily possessive of both his wife and his daughter. He could well be speaking for many fathers when he says,

> My daughter doesn't know anything about my past. I see no point in telling her because there's nothing glamorous about it—it's all garbage. I don't want her to know. I'm afraid she'll judge me and think I'm a loser and then feel less about herself.

Fathers don't talk about these things for a lot of reasons. It's not "manly." Or they want to be seen as heroes to their daughters. Or they just don't know how to express their feelings. Or because they've repressed their childhoods and don't want to relive them.

So it behooves daughters to try to get at those family secrets to better understand their fathers' paternal choices and behaviors. The point is not that you should be his therapist or savior or judge; rather it's to recognize the emotional circuitry of his history, which is wired directly into your own.

In seeing what formed your father, you can begin to understand how many of your feelings are a consequence of his early lessons in love or fear or hate, and how little was because of anything *you* did or didn't do.

And you may, in the process, discover things about him that will cause you to admire him: how, for example, he had to fetch his father each night from the local saloon and bring him home, or how he gave up his own college education so that another child of greater promise could go.

Settling Old Scores

Once you have completed the information-gathering process and established a more realistic, evenhanded connection, now it is possible to bring up those issues for which only he can provide answers or explanations.

One of the questions I asked virtually every daughter I interviewed was this: "If you could get your father to sit down and listen uncritically and with an open mind, what would you say to him? If you could give 'the Speech,' what would it be?"

Says Emily, twenty-eight:

> I'd like him to see me for what I am now, a grown-up. I'd like to tell him how his drinking affected me and that I'm very insecure. I'd tell him that I wish he could have been there more, that it wasn't until he walked me down the aisle at my wedding that I knew what a daddy was. I'd say that I never knew what it feels like to be a little girl with a real daddy.

Says Deeann, forty-four:

> I'd ask him why he never stood up to my mother or his mother more, why he didn't protect me from them. He didn't try to be with me or try to cultivate a relationship; it was always my responsibility. I'm sure he's had his pain, but I wonder why he didn't do more to make things better. I'd really like to know the answer to that one.

Says Rhoda, fifty-three:

> I'd say, "I wanted to feel accepted by you. You terrified me because you were such a tyrant. Why was it so hard for you? I was just an innocent child. I needed you—why couldn't you love me?" But I'd also like to thank him: He always prized my brains. Whenever I did something well, he was my champion. Not in a big way—he'd sort of peek out from behind the newspaper and say a few words—but I knew he was there for me at least that much.

All these are things you can say to your father now. You don't say, "You are a rat and deserve to die." You do say, "This is how I feel, can you help me with this? Can you explain anything for me so that I can understand what happened?"

If you can express your feelings to your father in this way, seeking truth rather than retribution, it's quite likely that you'll get some solace. He might elaborate on why he couldn't be what you wanted him to be; he might say that he just didn't know how. He might even apologize.

Then again he might not do *any* of that. *But at least you'll know that he can't; and you won't know if you don't try.* And at least you will have expressed how *you* feel, claimed *your* experience, and declared yourself as a separate adult.

When Daddy Can't—or Won't—Talk

Let us say, however, that your father is alive but you have absolutely no idea where he is because of divorce or desertion. You still need to deal with the father within you whose angry or sullen voice, or his silence, echo in your mind or emotions.

There's plenty of information you can gather about him. You can talk to living relatives from his immediate or extended family —his parents, his siblings, his uncles and aunts, cousins, godparents.

There may be old friends of his still around. There are data to be gleaned from family albums, old family letters, the family Bible, even legal documents such as birth and death certificates, divorce papers, old wills.

You might, in fact, *find* him. Some daughters who lost their fathers because of adoption or desertion track them down through Social Security or other governmental agencies. Others, whether or not they were adopted, go to adoption agencies to ask for help in working the bureaucratic system that is reluctant to yield its secrets. Even a visit to your hometown library to look at old newspapers can produce information about your father or his family on the sports or society or obituary pages.

Some fathers, such as Amanda's, mentioned earlier, are altogether willing to be rediscovered. They are relieved either of the embarrassment of inertia or of the impediments of custodial mothers who stood in the way of visitation.

There is, however, always the risk that Daddy doesn't want to have anything to do with his daughter, that he has a new life and has nothing further to add to his child's. This is an important piece of information to have: At least you *tried.* And, having tried, you can cut your losses. You have found out that which you must now accept—your father really doesn't want to be a part of your life—and lay down your bundle of fantasies.

Let us say that your father is dead. In the developmental scheme of things it's always better to have settled family scores while one's parents are alive rather than wait until all that's left are piecemeal memories. You can still do all the research just discussed. You can role-play "the Speech" with a counselor, or a close relative or empathetic friend, or a support group. Or you can set down your feelings in a letter to him.

In all these ways you can still construct an emotional dossier on your father, whether or not he is alive, and clear up many mysteries about him. Even without reconciliation or reconnection, you can complete the process of emotional separation and move on.

Special Cases: Confrontations

Many therapists and family-systems theorists argue that confrontation generally serves little purpose because it is used as an excuse to tell someone what's wrong with him or her rather than to resolve one's own emotional confusion.

In some cases, however, confrontations are healthy and useful, either because the niceties don't work and/or because of the horrendous damage a parent inflicted. Well-planned confrontations can help a daughter to integrate her own experience.

This is particularly true in the case of incest—but what follows can be applied to any devastating parental dysfunction, such as alcoholism or physical or emotional abuse.

As we have seen, incest is a family secret that is carefully guarded and vigorously denied, by father and daughter alike. In order to overcome its legacies, the daughter must find a way to deal with it.

Some survivors feel compelled to confront their fathers, and the entire family of origin, with the information, so that the daughters can gain a sense of control over their lives.

The purpose of confrontation is *not* to give one's father the opportunity to apologize and take responsibility for his behavior, or for the mother to acknowledge her role, however passive, in the incest—although it helps enormously when parents can do this, as we shall see in a moment. The larger goal is for the daughter to state the truth of her own experience and her pain, to put it out there and say, "This happened and it wasn't my fault." When she can do that, her past begins to lose its hold on her.

A word of caution is in order. Many incest victims (as well as children of some alcoholics or psychotics) *must not confront or even be with their fathers,* either for the time being or even forever, for two reasons: First, because now they must take care of themselves apart from their families of origin, and forgive and redefine themselves. Second, in some cases confrontation could result either in the victim's being physically attacked or even killed or in the abuser's harm of another family member or himself.

However, some survivors wish to confront their fathers in person to stop what incest authority Dr. Christine Courtois calls "the blackmail" of forced silence. Such daughters must carefully prepare for confrontations to make sure they can handle what in most cases is a wall of denial or outrage or scapegoating.

Preparation includes not only therapy but also telling one or two relatives who are likely to be sympathetic. In addition, the survivor needs to examine her motives closely: Protecting a sibling is a good motive; exacting remorse is not, since it may not turn out that way and she might be bitterly disappointed and even regress emotionally.

Ideally the main benefit of confrontation—when violence or retraumatization have been ruled out—is to validate one's own experience: to declare it *regardless* of a parent's reaction, so that the survivor can reclaim power over her body, her emotions, her future.

That's what Esther, thirty-eight, did, after many years of therapy. She recalls,

> I was raped by my father when I was five, and I didn't remember any of it until I was thirty—I guess it was safe to remember, and I joined an incest survivors' group. So I went to see my parents for the first time in years and told them what had happened and how I felt about it. They just sat there like stones. I said, "So that's it? You don't have anything to say?"

Although Esther hasn't seen or talked to her parents since that day seven years ago, the confrontation helped her believe that what happened actually happened and that she wasn't to blame.

It had another altogether surprising benefit. She says,

I have no doubt that my father loved me. That may sound strange, but it's true. Now I believe that I got the only affection my father was capable of expressing. It was the sickest love imaginable, but it was love. The hardest thing for me to accept has been that I don't hate my father. I don't forgive what he did; I can't be with him because all he does is deny he did anything. But I love him and I feel sorry for him. And that has freed me.

In another case the daughter confronted her father in a private conversation. He had never denied his molestation of her, and her mother knew about it—both parents and the daughter had their separate therapies to deal with it. Says the daughter,

My therapist said that if I was ever to have a good relationship with my father, I'd have to confront him. It worked. He was at my apartment for hours, and it really cleared the air. I said, "I managed to get through so many troubles in my life, especially with men, and it has a lot to do with you." He was very upset—he assured me that he was as mixed up about it as anybody could be. He was very apologetic and said he hoped we could have a better relationship. And now we do. We never had to discuss it again.

It must be restated that those same goals can be achieved without direct confrontation. One way some survivors of paternal abuse "confront" is to write letters to their fathers, knowing that in all probability they'll get no response. Other survivors confront their fathers by role-playing in therapy. Still others confront the experience by disclosing it in support groups.

Occasionally a daughter can "confront" her father in person without confronting the issue of incest (or battering or alcoholism) itself—that is, be with her father for one reason alone: to test her emotional boundaries.

Such was the case with Rochelle, forty. Of her father, she says,

My father abused me sexually for years, and I stopped seeing him for about a decade while I healed. A year ago I decided I'd try to see if I could be in his presence without panicking. I called my mother, with whom I'd kept up telephone contact, and we arranged for the three of us to meet in a restaurant.

She gave me enough assurances that he wouldn't do anything violent that I decided it would be okay. Also, I felt strong enough to handle anything he might say or do. But just in case, I went to the restaurant in my own car so that I could leave in a hurry if I had to. It was almost an anticlimax, *thank God.* He was on his best behavior. I guess he's mellowed or something. The point is, that dinner ended my terror of him forever.

Epiphanies: When Fathers Initiate Reconciliation

There are those fathers who are willing to take the first step at reconciliation with their children. These are the fathers who, in their late middle or old age, *do* accept culpability, who *do* want to help their daughters have futures of love, fulfillment, and hope, even if they were unable to do so when their daughters were growing up.

Adam, fifty-nine, a recovering alcoholic, wrote to each of his four sons and daughters explaining that he had examined his violent behavior in A.A. and now wanted to make amends. With his support group's guidance he has prepared himself for their varying responses. Some of the children want to have nothing to do with him; others are in differing stages of reattachment.

Liza, his firstborn daughter, seems to be the most amenable to renewing her relationship with her father, although that renewal is still in the incubation stage. Says Adam,

> If I had to give advice to fathers, it would be "Watch your mouth. If you tell kids they're rotten enough times, they'll be rotten and later reject you. But if you really want to make up for the past, and if you're patient, they might come back." Liza has started to come back—at least she is willing to listen. I keep in contact by calling her every week. Recently I told her, "I wanted you to be able to stand up and take care of yourself in a tough world. I'm sure it didn't seem that I loved you because I was so harsh. I just want to get this all straightened out before I croak. Now I'm ready to be a real daddy."
>
> I can't change anything that happened. I can only say what I'm feeling and hope my actions show that I'm genuine. I think she hears me.

Larry, the incest offender who voluntarily went into therapy (described at the end of Chapter 8) is also in the process of father-daughter reconciliation. He says,

> Part of the treatment for incest offenders and their families is what we call the apology session. We work separately to prepare for that session, which takes place with all of us together when everyone's ready for it. We've had that session. Now my daughter's in the angry stage; she still screams at me, "I'll never trust you again!" I'd love for her to forgive me. But it's more therapeutic for her to express her anger than to forgive me. I just pray that the day will come when she can get past the pain. I hope that that look of fear I put in her eyes will one day disappear. I'm here for her whenever she needs me or wants to talk to me. I'm here to be a father, if she'll ever let me. And if she can't, who could blame her? I did an unforgivable thing, and I have to live with it and never forget who made it happen.

In his book *Adaptation to Life,* George E. Vaillant writes,

> No whim of fate, no Freudian trauma, no loss of a loved one will be as devastating to the human spirit as some prolonged ambivalent relationship that leaves us forever unable to say goodbye.

There are millions of daughters who will never have such an epiphany with their fathers and who are dealing every day with the consequences. At the end of my interview with Larry I asked him to pretend that he was speaking to all the adult daughters whose fathers never acknowledged their role in their daughters' pain or difficulties or insecurities, whatever form the fathers' behavior took. He thought for a few minutes, closed his eyes, and said,

> Dear child, it's not your fault. Nothing I ever did that harmed you is your fault. I wish I could have shown you that I love you. I wish I could comfort you and tell you how sorry I am that I let you down so much. All I can say now is that I want you to have a happy life and that I pray you won't let whatever I did or didn't do get in your way.

18

vvvvvvvv

Redefining Our
Romantic Attachments

*My husband is the love of my life. Is he the passion of my life? No.
Our sex is wonderful, but we have other things that matter more. My
husband's the only man I ever met whom I feel totally emotionally
supported by without competing or feeling scared. I can be who I am
because he is my rock—but I am for him too. He gives me something I
never had, even with my father—a safe harbor. And nothing in marriage is more important than that.*

—HELENE, THIRTY-SEVEN

When I was a teenager, my girlfriends and I spent endless hours
trying to crack the code of masculinity, attempting to figure out
what boys were saying when they talked to us. And since boys—
except for the nerdy ones—didn't say much when they did talk, at
least not what we wanted to hear, we spent even *more* time trying
to decode their *behavior.*

"Joey gave me a stick of gum in study hall the other day," I
announced during one all-night fact-finding session at a postprom
slumber party. "What do you think *that* means?"

"It means he likes you, dummy!" shrieked my best friend,
Sandy, her eyes rolling to the ceiling in exasperation as if to suggest that any fool knows that a boy who gives a girl chewing gum
would cheerfully die for her.

"Oh, yeah?," I retorted, holding up Exhibit A of my contradic-
tory—and thoroughly wilted—evidence. "Well, he only gave me a
carnation corsage for the dance. *Your* date gave you an *orchid.*

When a boy gives you an orchid, it's practically a marriage proposal." Even I knew that much.

It is now over thirty years later, and I'm still hearing this kind of code-breaking consultation between women, only today it's about the puzzling behavior of adult men—lovers and would-be lovers, live-in partners and spouses.

"Men are just *different*," a female friend—referring to Seth, her husband of thirty-two years—sighed recently over lunch. "Get this."

> Last night we were watching a movie on TV during which a woman goes into the bedroom of a man she hardly knows and takes off her clothes. I turned to Seth and said, "What would you do in a situation like that?" He smiled lasciviously and said, "I'm not sure. Can I get back to you on that one?" I punched him and said, "Well, if a man did that to me, I'd run for my life!"
>
> We just didn't see that scene the same way, and it made me think, If a strange woman enters a man's room, he assumes she's looking for sex. But if a strange man enters a woman's bedroom, she assumes he's going to rape her. It points up a fundamental difference between men and women.

One of many fundamental differences. Now we embark on the process of sorting them out.

From reading the last two chapters you've got a sense of the triangles in your family's emotional history, the cultural training of your grandparents and parents, and the role your father played in the formation of your identity. You have some insights about why men and women think and act as they do and the genesis of the patterns in your romantic attachments.

Here is where we apply those insights in order to alter those patterns, either because the patterns aren't working or because of a desire to improve an existing relationship.

Rediscovering Love

As we have seen, the majority of men and women are aliens to one another and often can't break through the conditioning that has put them in separate camps. Yet most of them yearn for human connection, for the giving and receiving of love, and for a safe harbor with a partner.

Where once they needed parental love to survive their infancy and youth, as adults they often need love to anchor their sense of place and purpose within their own generation and to leave legacies of love for future generations. Sooner or later most people long for a grown-up version of the love they had, or wished they had, as children. They want to improve on the old model and somehow write a new emotional script. It's just that many of them can't seem to get beyond the scripts of childhood.

The goal of this chapter is to help the reader find a new way of connecting, unimpeded by the ghosts and emotional dialogues of the past; to learn to speak the mature language of the heart in a way that a partner can hear; and to open up the romantic possibilities of achieving the most intimate kind of love there is—sexualized friendship.

Double Vision

It's inevitable that men and women—composites of years of family and social training—would have so paltry an idea of what the other feels and wants.

Certainly the current mating habits—or, to be accurate, the reluctance to couple up—of many young women reflects their ambivalence about men. Women in record numbers are postponing marriage; volunteering for single motherhood; obsessing about their careers until the biological clock sounds its alarm.

Today many women can put their money where their dashed romantic hopes were. Unlike their mothers, they are not under enormous social pressure to marry or to stay in a miserable marriage. Gone are the days when women were defined solely by wifedom.

Nowhere is this more apparent than in the stratospheric divorce rate in the United States. According to anthropologist Helen Fisher, the divorce rate is high in cultures where women work outside the home and have their own incomes and low in cultures where women are economically dependent on men. In this country *75 percent of divorces are initiated by women.*

Returning to the 1990 Virginia Slims/Roper poll mentioned in the Introduction, American women are *less* satisfied with the men in their lives and find them *less* kind and gentle than did women twenty years ago. Women are twice as likely as men to feel resentment about how much their mates pitch in with housekeeping and child-rearing chores—no surprises there, given the fact that many women work double shifts as wage earner and homemaker/primary parent.

Men counter these findings with cries of "Foul! Unfair!" In response to the Virginia Slims study, *Men's Life* magazine commissioned its own study, a national survey of men ages eighteen to sixty-five to find out their attitudes about work, family, and relationships.

The men polled took particular umbrage at women's "misconception" that males are all insensitive, uncaring, leering louts. Over half of all the men—and three quarters of the married men —said that marriage is the most important thing in life. *Ninety percent* of the husbands said that their wives are their best friends. Perhaps this is because men don't seem to like *each other* all that much. When asked which gender they would choose if they had to sit next to a stranger at a picnic, twice as many men in the survey chose female over male as the other way around.

Nevertheless, like young women, men are also staying away from the altar in droves. For all that men claim to be interested in and champions of women and wedlock, in recent years the marriage rate among never-married men between the ages of thirty and forty-four has been the lowest since the Depression. As for single men in their twenties, they outnumber single women in their twenties by a margin of 6 to 5.

Why should men get married or, for that matter, even grow up? After all, they've still got *Mom* to take care of them—sorting their sons' socks, ironing their shirts, fixing their breakfasts. A recent page-one story in *The New York Times* heralded the news that of adults ages twenty-five to thirty-four still living with their parents, *32 percent* are single males, whereas only 20 percent are single females.

The conventional expert wisdom explaining this phenomenon— even taking into account a sluggish economy—is that men aren't terribly adept at taking care of themselves and that their mothers love catering to them. Most significantly such men "suffer virtually no loss of independence" while living under their parents' noses. Conversely daughters are more likely to have to abide by family rules—while doing their own laundry, no doubt—which propels them out of the parental nest *fast,* even though they make less money than the aforementioned pampered sons.

However, the "marriage bust," as it has been called, cannot be assessed only in terms of feminist choices or the Peter Pan syndrome. Rather, aversion to marriage can also be seen as a reflection of a loss of faith in romantic love, an inability to trust a member of the opposite sex.

Like men, women have in some ways become the fathers they grew up with or by whom they were rejected. Now they can afford to avoid emotional intimacy altogether.

It would appear, then, that the gender gap is wider than ever. Which is good news and bad news.

The good news is that with more women carrying their own financial weight, and with such marital traditions as dowries and getting Dad's permission now increasingly relegated to the fringes of cultural mores, love stands alone as the primary incentive for most adults to form committed partnerships.

The bad news is that men and women are more confused by each other than at any time in history, for this reason: All these cultural changes have left them without a road map for love and marriage. *That confusion falls on top of the unresolved family histories men and women bring to their partnerships.*

No wonder modern romantic love is on the ropes.

One component of romantic partnership, however, has steadfastly withstood the tests of time and social upheaval: Men and women continue to anticipate that their current or future partners will magically cure the emotional deficits of their childhoods.

The Legacies of Father Hunger. As we have seen, the tandem paternities of fathers—one for girls, one for boys—in large measure account for the different ways men and women relate to each other. The legacy of their mutual father hunger is seen in the disparate ways they express themselves and formulate expectations of one another. The most painful legacy is reflected in their love lives: Inevitably most people try to deal with their father hunger by *recapitulating their childhoods,* along gender lines, in their relationships.

Says Dr. Frank Pittman,

> Women strangle their partners by trying to get the closeness they didn't get from their fathers. But men are fatherless too. They've been raised by women who had all this emotional

power over them because their fathers were nowhere in sight. Most men have only known the male mythology of proving their manhood by escaping from Mom and by having women respond to them sexually.

So the fatherless girl and the fatherless boy are going to have quite different fantasies about what the other is supposed to do. Her fantasies have to do with wanting a wonderfully strong, nurturing man who will devote his full attention to her, because her father didn't. His fantasy is that he has to get her *sexual* attention to affirm his masculinity, but make sure she doesn't get control of him emotionally, because his father wasn't around to show him another way to be a man.

The buzz words in the psychological community for such conflicting behavior are "pursuing," usually by females, and "distancing," usually by males—ironically the exact reverse of traditional courtship. Such behavior is what men and women know. It's familiar. And unless they intercept the past, it's automatic.

Untangling Emotional Gridlocks

Given all this father hunger, these changing/unchanging habits of the heart, sometimes it seems as if there isn't a thing that women and men can do about their romantic predicaments and misunderstandings.

Before we can alter and reframe the reflections of the past in our relationships, we must acknowledge our part in perpetuating them. At a certain point we must get beyond causality and begin to do something about effect. In order to resolve our perfectly sound reasons for feeling hurt—or victimized or alienated or politically, socially, and culturally downtrodden—we must first get at the core of *how* we think about and behave with members of the opposite sex, and not just why.

One of the questions psychoanalyst Robert U. Akeret poses to the couples he counsels is this: "What's fair?" For example, a man is annoyed at his wife for getting on his case because he leaves his socks on the floor. After all, his mother always picked up after him; naturally he expects that his wife will too. But it's an unfair expectation.

It's helpful to take a brief look at how men and women are

unfair to one another, how they allow their childhood experiences —and their grudges, beefs, and biases—to get in the way of healthy love and trust. The idea of such stocktaking is to enable us to take responsibility for how we wittingly or unwittingly contribute to the unhappiness in our relationships.

Taking Responsibility: Men. In his superb book about marriage, *The Fragile Bond,* Dr. Augustus Y. Napier acknowledges the complex process of sorting out the emotional legacies of childhood, of stopping the cycle of parental loss so that it doesn't infect our attachments or get bequeathed to the next generation.

But, he writes, it is *men* who have the greater difficulty getting past those parental losses.

> Most men want to be supportive husbands and fathers. . . .
> But there is that frightened "child" aspect of such dominant men that resists being vulnerable, and that fears—in a quite irrational way—sharing power and control with their wives. The trappings of the male role are rewarding enough that many men are unwilling to risk facing their internal demons, unless they are forced to.

Men need to recognize the incalculable cost to themselves and others of their refusal to face those demons, a cost that is perpetuated by the following behaviors:

Trivializing and/or ignoring the emotional lives of their partners, children, and themselves.

Equating the expression of feelings by boys and men with being a "sissy."

Saying, and believing, that the only thing women want from them is a "meal ticket."

Claiming that the culture, or their allegedly hormone-driven aggressiveness, forces them to protect their turf with their fists.

Insisting that they "can't help it," or that testosterone is the culprit, when their only response to the tenderness or kindness of women is sexual.

Tacitly agreeing with or actively engaging in locker-room or bar-room references to female anatomy, to penis size, and to their own success rates in "scoring."

Saying of women who were sexually abused or raped, "Why didn't she do something about it?" or "She asked for it."

Treating their daughters like little dolls and their sons like budding prizefighters.

Asking the women in their lives virtually to single-handedly shoulder the burdens of housekeeping, child rearing, and calls to his parents to maintain the connection between the man and his own mother and father.

Adhering to the myth that it is only men who understand power and money and that women who compete with them are really "ballbreakers" or "dykes."

Blaming all their difficulties on women.

Taking Responsibility: Women. If women pay the price for a male-ordered society, they are not without emotional leverage in their relationships. Says Dr. Ellen Berman,

> One problem many women share is thinking of men as big babies. It's true that many men like the women in their lives to nurture them and make them feel good. This ability by women to be loving, or "babying," makes many of them feel powerful. But it allows them to avoid the fact that they don't have any real power in the outside world. Women are caught up in the myth of the sacredness of taking care of others— therefore they don't have to take care of themselves.

Thus women also contribute to sexual squaring off, abetting their own unhappiness and the remoteness of men by babying them, and in the following ways as well:

Volunteering for blame or martyrdom when anything in the office or the family goes wrong.

Recoiling from emotional (read "wimpy") men.

Believing that the only thing men want from them is sex.

Using sex as punishment or reward.

Not stating clearly what they want sexually and emotionally, hoping their partners will figure it out.

Covering up for, or conspiring with the kids against, Daddy.

Insisting that they alone know best how to nurture children.

Continuing to pamper their growing or grown sons and not teaching them such basics as housekeeping.

Being blind to the incestuous behavior of lovers or spouses.

Ignoring signs of incipient violence in the men they date and making excuses for brutality in the men they live with or marry.

Being willing to do anything or say anything to get and keep a man.

Blaming all their difficulties on men.

Now we proceed to what it is men and women are *really* talking about when they do or say any of these things to themselves and each other.

Double Trouble: What Couples Fight About

Most of us know, intellectually at least, that the majority of disagreements between men and women are merely smoke screens for underlying conflicts or stifled childhood memories. We know that the arguments into which we are helplessly drawn, like a sinister gravitational pull, are seldom only over the subject at hand. They are also about all those old issues that somehow get buried beneath new ones, like so many players mounded over one tiny, fumbled football.

We *know* this, yet we find ourselves on the verge of a heart attack over minor matters that somehow escalate to warfare.

Thus we fight about all *kinds* of things: how the toothpaste is extracted from the tube; the battle of the thermostat; a partner constantly forgetting that you like milk—skim, please, and just a drop—in your coffee; who spends how much on what; making a date with the couple that "you know I can't stand!"

That's just the small stuff. Bigger issues are repeated speeding tickets; bounced checks and insurance policies canceled for non-payment; the partner who seems to get drunk at every social engagement or every time he or she visits the old homestead; using children as pawns and forcing them to choose up sides; severe in-law problems. Biggest are breaking the law, chronic infidelity, battering, and addiction.

Then of course there are all those sexual conflicts: the man who rolls over in midsnore the instant intercourse ends; the woman who always seems to have her period; which partner wants oral sex and which hates it; whether or not the lights should be on; premature ejaculation, frigidity, impotence.

The sparks that ignite disagreements are as myriad as the problems themselves. If there is a single theme uniting them, it is this: They are the emotional residue of father hunger. The result is what Dr. Napier calls the "closeness panic" and what I, borrowing from him, call the "distance panic."

These fears are exhibited in a relationship beginning with the courtship process. Such fears don't show up right away of course— that's because the best part of romance is the first part.

If most people are at one time or another romance junkies, who can blame them? There is in courtship the undeniable appeal of having a suitor on his or her best behavior, carefully made up or closely shaven and lotion-scented, bearing gifts; going hand-in-hand to charming country restaurants, hikes in misty hills at dusk, moonlit boat rides.

What's not to like? But courtship is not the stuff of *relationships.* Courtship is the stuff of magic, the miraculous transformation of our lives from lonely, numbing sameness to "and they lived happily ever after."

Thus women in the throes of courtship look at the lover but don't really see; women listen to the lover but don't really hear. He *says* he isn't in the marriage market because he's recovering from a nasty divorce. She *hears* that he needs someone to mend his broken heart.

And should she hear even a tiny bit of what he's actually saying, she runs it through her code-breaking machine: Well, yes, he is always late. Well, yes, he forgot my birthday. But gosh, no one's perfect. Anyhow, if we ever get married, he'll change. I am so terrific he cannot help but reform. I love him more than he loves himself. How can he resist?

Easily—because the ghosts of the past are often stronger than the attractions of the present. When the fantasies start to crack, when the light of reality intrudes on the mistiness of romance, that's when men and women call on all those disparate defenses of childhood that erupt like a summer storm.

The Closeness Panic. Some conflicts are not so much about love as they are about the inability to commit—a phenomenon also known as "ambivalence about intimacy," or "cold feet."

Sheila, thirty-seven, whose parents divorced when she was eight, says that only recently has she begun to understand that her "lousy love life" is a consequence of her terror of being loved and left. Most of her adult relationships have been with men she idealizes but to whom she has never been able to give her trust. She says,

I keep getting involved with these guys who want me to worship and take care of them. But the minute they start to really
respond or want a commitment from me, suddenly I start to
pick fights with them. "Loving men" aren't normal—"leaving
men" are normal. So either I leave first or I'll do something
to make sure the man will keep his distance, like being such a
pain that he'll take off.

The Distance Panic. However, as we well know, men keep their
distance too. Men are classic intimacy avoiders because of their
need not to "need," and because they want to escape emotional
engulfment. After all, that's usually what Dad did. Men leave their
partners in lots of ways, not simply by walking out the door. They
leave through all of football and baseball seasons. They leave because they've put in a hard day.

This kind of alienating behavior is exactly what creates anxiety
in those people who are terrified of being alone and who will put
up with almost anything to avoid it.

Men who experience the distance panic express it, among other
ways, through jealous rages. These men, when they were growing
up, were generally not given—or felt ambivalent about receiving—
enough affection from their mothers, which only compounded
their father hunger.

Many members of the psychological community believe that it is
really the distance panic that causes men to withdraw emotionally
when they sense that the women they love are angry with them.
That's because most men put all their emotional eggs into one
basket: their romantic partners. And when a partner seems to be
pulling away by embarking on a new career, perhaps, or losing her
temper, many men lash out or close down rather than state their
anxieties, which are often unconscious.

Says Dr. Nina Evans,

The way we've raised most men is that feelings are forbidden,
except in the company of women. The only safe place for a
man to cry was originally with the mother, and now with the
lover. If the partner is the only person with whom the man
can be vulnerable, and if she gets angry or somehow betrays
him, he's devastated.

The distance panic, however, or at least its verbal expression, is far more common to women, who are usually the emotional pursuers in their relationships. Women tend to absorb other people's anxieties. They "make nice," they placate, they compromise so that their partners will stay. This is a replay of growing up: Women do the "feeling" work for men so that "Daddy" won't leave.

Once the wedding vows have been exchanged, closeness and distance problems become even more pronounced. Says Dr. Evans,

> It's the old story: You marry the "perfect" mate and then spend the rest of your life trying to change him. Or you marry someone because he "fills your gaps" and then you complain that you have nothing in common.

In marriage these conflicts are cemented within a legal and social framework. It's easier to leave a live-in or occasional lover than to disengage from a marriage, especially where children are involved.

Moreover, as was discussed in Chapter 10, marriage changes a relationship: Now the couple is a "family," to which all the specters of one's original family are added—rather like a double exposure—and against which they are subconsciously compared. Now the couple almost inevitably revives old family roles, often behaving toward each other as they once behaved toward their parents, or taking on the "marital" roles of their parents.

This blending of old patterns with new marital ones—this clash of closeness and distance—is exemplified by couples who were raised in different cultures and/or emotional climates.

Anne, thirty-one, who grew up in a WASP family, has been married for five years to Alberto, thirty-six, who was born in Italy. In Alberto's childhood screaming matches and sloshing tears were routine forms of communication. But in Anne's childhood, as she puts it, "You weren't ever to raise your voice unless you were about to be run over by a truck, and maybe not even then. And you *certainly* weren't supposed to express emotions."

The problem in her marriage, Anne says, is this:

> I love Alberto's warmth and effusiveness. He's the most wonderful and caring lover. But I'm terrified by his temper. He's the kind of person who blows his stack and it's over. I keep

trying to mold him into the father I never had, a man who is emotionally available but who'll never get mad. It's impossible of course—I can't have it both ways.

Then there are those people who have trouble reconciling the "closeness" of marriage with the "distance" they witnessed one unforgettable day in childhood: the day Daddy moved out. These people may know in their *heads* that their spouses love and are faithful to them, but in their *hearts* they are certain that the spouses will inevitably desert them.

Some daughters of divorce, for instance, who constantly imagine worst-case scenarios, unwittingly recapitulate the past by undermining what could be a very good marriage. Says Norma, twenty-nine,

Early in our marriage my husband, Chip, and I went to a party, and I ran into an old boyfriend. I guess I sort of came on to him, but I wasn't consciously aware of it. Chip is not the jealous type; he comes from a stable, affectionate family and is a very solid guy. So when we got home, he sat me down and said, "I don't think you have any idea what you were doing or how it made me feel. I only have a certain percentage of you. I feel like part of you is committed to me and part of you is out the door." I burst into tears, because he was right. I said, "I'm afraid if I give more of myself, you'll leave, like my father did."

Sorting It Out

The first step in resolving these intimacy and trust issues, and in redefining our romantic attachments, is to separate our emotional wants from our needs, our hopes from our expectations. As Dr. Napier has written,

We must learn to distinguish between the needs we can legitimately expect our partner to meet, and those needs which he or she cannot meet. *Our unmet needs for parenting should be addressed with a therapist.*

The trick, of course, is *identifying* the problem. One way to do that is to examine how the triangles of the past cast a shadow over our attachments. When your emotional boundaries start to fall apart in a lover's quarrel, that's the time to remember what you learned about love in your original family.

Divided Loyalties: Triangles. According to Dr. Michael Kerr, triangles often put the participants into three entirely different—and frequently exchanged—roles: One person is the anxiety "generator," as in the nagging wife; the second person is the anxiety "amplifier," as in the rebellious teenager; the third person is the anxiety "dampener," as in the emotionally distant husband.

These roles can be interchanged with or without a third person present. If, say, a talkative wife occasionally punishes her emotionally passive or distant husband by clamming up or pouting, he may suddenly find his voice, jumping into the unexpected vacuum of her uncharacteristic silence. Even people who are chronically ill or depressed can sometimes "miraculously" recover, or at least improve dramatically, when their partners become sick or die.

The reciprocal nature of emotional reactiveness gets played out in our fantasies about how we wish our partners were different. As much as we long for such change, at the same time we dread it. That's because we often use our partners to express our own unacknowledged or forbidden childhood emotions.

For example, a soft-spoken, people-pleasing woman who chooses a domineering man generally has a subconscious reason for her choice: He will act out her anger for her. Conversely when a taciturn man chooses a highly emotional woman, her psychological value to him is that she will do the "feeling" for him.

This is what is at the heart of the expression "opposites attract." People who have not separated emotionally from their parents, who have not "differentiated," find their opposite number in romance. The pursuer will find the distancer and the other way around. In the worst possible way they are meant for each other, constantly reinforcing each other's emotional scripts.

As you have gathered by now, *both* partners in these examples are inordinately dependent on each other, playing out their childhood roles. The woman who always gives in is not taking responsibility for her own angry feelings. The man who always has to have the last word and make all the decisions is not taking responsibility for his own vulnerability. With both partners unable to "individuate," the patterns of their relationship cannot change.

Detriangling. How do we break out of these patterns of the past —this reciprocity of behavior? We detriangle, just as we did with our families of origin. When we are aware of the triangles in our emotional histories, we can learn to relate to our partners in a new way—by setting limits on how much we will allow ourselves to "act out" our partners' unfinished emotional business, or they ours.

While no one can force a partner to change, there's a lot we can do to change *ourselves,* which usually leads to a partner's different way of responding and behaving.

Let's say your husband never calls to let you know when he's coming home at the end of the day. Every night you keep warming his dinner and doing a slow burn. He walks in and you pounce with your hurt feelings and slam his food on the table. What can be done in a different way?

For a start you can put his dinner in the refrigerator, slide a cassette into the VCR, and settle down for a relaxing evening's entertainment. When he does come home and asks, "When do we eat?" you reply, "Gee, I wish you had called. We finished dinner— yours is in the fridge. If you're hungry, why don't you heat it up?"

Now comes the moment of truth. If he gets furious, and if you jump up and storm into the kitchen to reheat the food, nothing in the relationship will change. But if you keep your boundaries— neither fixing his dinner nor invoking guilt or getting angry—and if you do so often enough, eventually he will have no *choice* but either to call or to fix his own dinner or to order a pizza. (Men who respond violently in such situations will be discussed in a moment.)

While this may seem to be an overly simplistic example, it's the very stuff of which marital mayhem is made.

The way to stop the distance-closeness dance is to stay within your emotional *boundaries,* not behind your emotional *defenses.* You evaluate your differences with your "fairness" check. It's simply not fair never to let a partner know one's plans. It's not fair not to state one's needs or feelings calmly but rather to act them out.

And if it's unfair, you can set limits on your own acting out, which will result in a different kind of reaction in your partner.

No relationship ever broke up because of a cold dinner. But plenty of relationships have broken up because these kinds of issues get frozen into tandem patterns: being dependent on the other person's reactions and being unwilling to take responsibility for one's own emotions and behavior.

If you are able to establish and maintain emotional boundaries, you can then get to the real issues that lie simmering beneath the superficial ones.

For a couple to close the emotional gaps that separate them, it's important for them not only to detriangle but also to examine each other's emotional histories. An extremely useful tool in this process is the sexual genogram, often used in conjunction with couples therapy.

The Sexual Genogram. This technique—developed by Ellen Berman, M.D., and Larry Hof, of the University of Pennsylvania—traces a couple's respective family trees to unearth patterns of love and trust. Explains Dr. Berman,

> A conventional genogram is a way of looking at family themes, myths, and stories over three generations. A sexual genogram is used to find out how members of your family felt about sex roles and sexuality and what they did or didn't teach you about loyalty, intimacy, and sexuality.

Here, according to Dr. Berman, is how the sexual genogram works and is applied. You begin by asking yourself questions about your family's sexual history, similar to and expanding on those outlined in the last chapter. The difference here is that *both* you and your partner conduct this exercise, first separately and then together. Such questions could include:

"What did you learn from your family about what it means to be a man or a woman? What were you taught about sexual intimacy?"

"Which parent had the most to say about sex, and who was pretty quiet or even shy about the subject?"

"How did your parents behave toward each other physically or sexually—were they openly affectionate? Did you know when they were having intercourse and how was the issue of privacy handled?"

"How did your parents behave toward you physically—were they always affectionate or withdrawn? Only in childhood? Never after puberty? Only with girls?"

"How did your parents handle your sex education? Did they discuss sex with you? What did they say?"

"Were you ever aware of a parent having an extramarital affair? What happened? How were you affected?"

"What were the sexual skeletons in your family—did a relative have an illegal abortion or a 'shotgun' wedding? Was there ever any incest? Was a relative a homosexual? How did the family handle 'secrets'?"

"If you could change how anyone in your family behaved toward you or each other in terms of expressing feelings or sexuality, what would it be?"

"What do you know about your partner's family tree? What does he know about yours?"

Often the answers to these questions can't be obtained without help from one's family of origin. In that event you can talk to parents, siblings, and other relatives—in the same ways and with the same guidelines outlined in the previous chapter—to try to get at the facts.

As has been said, your partner poses the same questions to himself and/or his parents and writes down the answers. You then exchange this information with each other. Frequently a couple whose relationship is sturdy can clear up difficulties between them simply by sharing such experiences, which will help them fine-tune their communication.

For other couples, however, swapping this sensitive information may only seem to make matters worse. Says Dr. Berman,

> When couples are really unhappy, each spouse tends to take almost any behavior as a deliberate or malicious attack. Understanding your partner's sexual and emotional history tends to make you take his or her behavior less personally. But if a couple is having serious conflicts, I don't recommend talking about this material without some sort of coach. It's enormously loaded, and your answers could be used as weapons.

In this case it's extremely important for both you and your partner to find a couples therapist who will help you gather, interpret, and integrate all this information. By working through the sexual genogram with a trained guide, a couple can discover what they learned about love in their families and what they unconsciously expect of each other sexually and emotionally. When couples can learn to discuss their feelings and experiences openly without fear of reprisal and without triangling or losing their emotional boundaries, the possibilities of profound love and improving the sexual expression of that love are enormous.

In most instances what may have started out as a sexual problem—or a financial or in-law or child-rearing one—is really an *emotional* one that, once cleared up, paves the way to solving most of the others. (Medical problems or psychosis, of course, should be sorted out and handled by a doctor.)

Says Dr. Avodah K. Offit,

> Just getting couples together for the act of working on a problem means that there is a better prognosis than anyone might expect if they were to overhear the fireworks that go on in my office. The point is that both partners are willing to get help. There is a certain commitment that's extremely important. Most of the couples I treat stay together. And the ones who don't usually have one partner who is unwilling to commit to therapy from the start.

When Your Partner Won't Talk or Get Help

Let us say that your partner digs in his heels: Therapy is for "crazy people." He's not about to discuss his personal life or air his "dirty linen" with some stranger, some headshrinker.

Anyhow, it's all in *your* head, not his, so there's no point in talking about it with you either.

Now what?

You have three choices. You can do nothing and stay within the old pattern. You can change your *reactions* to him, containing the damage of the status quo. Or you can cut your losses and end the relationship.

Deciding to Stay or Leave. Obviously you can't make such a decision if you haven't made the attempt first to work through your differences with your partner. Like fathers, when lovers or husbands are "approached right," as Dr. Berman puts it, they will often respond positively to such efforts.

Having said that, the reality may be that your partnership or marriage may have been formed early in your romantic career, when you were still half formed, still negotiating your adulthood with your family of origin, still learning to spread your wings.

Alas, one cannot make a date with maturity. Everyone has her or his own timetable for growth or change—in the case of a couple, *two* timetables, each of which may be very different. It would be *nice* if partners could wait until they're all grown up before they meet. It would also be nice if couples could ripen emotionally at the same rate.

The point is that incrementally or dramatically, people change over time, sometimes within one ongoing attachment, sometimes through several attachments. One never knows when all the questions of childhood will be answered, when all the memories will allow themselves to be released and resolved. We take emotional risks, hoping for the best. Sometimes the risks have happy results; sometimes they don't.

Before you take any action, however, you segue into what Dr. Akeret calls the warning period. You say to your partner that his behavior is intolerable to you and that he must do something about it. It is *imperative* to give this warning to men who abuse their wives and children verbally or physically, or who are addicted to drugs, alcohol, or gambling, because of the dangerously harmful consequences to the family of such behaviors.

Having given such a warning, you *cannot waffle.* If your partner shows signs of change, you give him a certain amount of time. The warning period can get murky because, once the warning has been issued, it's easy to allow your boundaries and limit setting to slip and overlook a partner's backsliding. It's easy to rationalize alarming regressions by saying, "He's in the transition stage." But certain behaviors deserve no third chances: verbal and physical abuse, incest, and addiction. You must judge whether or not a partner's behavior threatens your safety or sanity or that of your children.

Safety aside, let's say that after a reasonable period of time your partner still shows no sign of change. You can try a trial separation. Many couples, married or otherwise, do just that, sometimes for as long as a year or two, and reunite after they have taken care of their own emotional conflicts, forming strong, renewed relationships with each other.

If, however, all your efforts still fail, you may reach the conclusion that you must leave. In most cases it's better to be alone than to stay in a hopeless relationship. And if it is openly acrimonious, it will wreak incalculable harm upon your children.

A psychologist once said to me, "Don't stay married for the children; they'll never thank you." Still, where children are involved, it is *never* a good idea to leave a relationship without extensive preparation. You must be absolutely certain that the decision is the right one, that all efforts have failed.

It cannot be overstated how important it is to get some help in this decision if you are a parent. There is no more difficult role than being a single custodial mother or father: the consequences to children of a parent's unfinished emotional business and the fallout from remarrying in haste and repeating old patterns have been seen in painful detail throughout this book.

Final Thoughts

It is nearly irresistible, and utterly understandable, to long for a tender, dependable, loyal partner who will make the badness of childhood go away—to believe that romantic love will cure all the sadness and rejection and unanswered prayers of memory. As long as we hope, we also expect. And when we do not hope, we feel terrible despair.

What we are talking about, however, is *realistic* hope. Women who never experienced a loving, reliable, physically and emotionally available father often hope to resolve that loss through a lover or spouse. But it is only by being good "fathers" to themselves— that is, by not asking a partner to *be* their fantasized good daddies —that women can formulate realistic expectations in their partnerships.

As therapist Ronald Gaudia puts it,

> If you "didn't get it," meaning a loving father, in childhood, who says you need it now? Is there a hole that needs to be filled before you can move on? I don't think you ever get from a relationship what you never got from a parent. Nobody can replicate for any adult what the parent could or should have given you. Maybe an approximation. But it's not the same. You can't get the empty space filled. And once you accept that you can't, you can get something different.

"All women become like their mothers. That is their tragedy. No man does. That's his." So wrote Oscar Wilde. One can see within romantic partnerships today the unfortunate truth of his observation.

eeds to know any one thing about the man in her
)lain his behavior toward her, it is this: She must
al about his *father* rather than his mother.

n love a father imparts to his son will, in most
....d be more indelible than those of the mother. The
man who is fortunate enough to have had a father who could give
the example of masculine tenderness, as well as the model of character and strength—rather than a father who forced him to adhere
to the damaging strictures of traditional masculinity—is blessed,
as are those whom he loves.

But such men are rare. There are those men who valiantly try to
work around, if not unlearn, the lessons of their childhoods. Still,
it is a painful reality that more women than men have learned to
be both "mother" and "father" to themselves, whereas most men
only know how to be like "Dad." The tragedy for most men is that
they are too much like their fathers and not enough like their
mothers, and insufficient numbers of them are willing to do anything about it. The tragedy for women is that they must live with
the consequences in their intimate partnerships.

With patience many women are able to break through their
partners' father hunger—their "masculine" barriers against emotionality—in order to find the beguiling boys the men once were.
Not the princes, not the bullies, but the boys before they became
infected by the oughts and shoulds of traditional masculinity.

But women's emotional work, as we have seen, is simply not
enough to eradicate the cultural ramifications of father hunger. If
it were, more men would be as involved with their children as
women are. If it were, the nurturing capabilities that all men have
would not so quickly be handed over to women.

Thus it will continue to be the lot of women to do most of the
emotional work in relationships, dragging their partners by the
ears to couples therapists or workshops. It will continue to be the
lot of women to turn to other women to assuage their partners'
inability to be open to feelings and to grow.

If this is ever to change, men and women must learn to raise
their sons in a very, very different way from how they have been
raised up to now.

19

▼▼▼▼▼▼▼

The Man and Father
of the Future

Where I failed as a father is that my kids assume that there is nothing Dad cannot do. They think I know everything, and God knows I don't. They think I'm a hero, and they don't know that I'm really not. Why don't they know? Maybe because I'm afraid to tell them.

—MICHAEL, SIXTY-ONE

One sultry July night while researching this book, I drove to a suburban church near Boston to observe a men's consciousness-raising group. This was an opportunity for which I had lobbied for weeks, the result of many phone calls and explanations of my journalistic intent, reassurances that, no, I wasn't out to trash men and, yes, I am sympathetic to their emotional and cultural binds.

In the basement of the church ten men gathered for their weekly meeting, some just off commuter trains, still in corporate mufti, others fresh off the blue-collar job, clad in jeans and T-shirts. Scattered around the cheerless room were nondescript couches, chairs, and tables—leftovers from assorted attics. There were no amenities, no coffeepot percolating with fragrant brew, no cookies or cakes that are routine in women's groups. Just a bunch of guys getting right down to business.

This group ran the gamut of the middle class. There was a lawyer, a dentist, an insurance broker, a schoolteacher. One man was an electrician, another a retired bus driver. Some were widowed, others divorced. Some had individual therapy, others had tried and given up on assorted other men's groups. All were fathers.

The men greeted me with a blend of cordiality and caution. I was, for all my remonstrations, an interloper. A stranger with a tape recorder and a stack of legal release forms. *A woman.*

I carried into this night my own wariness. This will probably be a waste of time, I thought. These guys will never really be candid. They'll probably flirt or make jokes or indulge in macho posturings or verbal fencing. Or they'll digress into a rehash of last night's Red Sox game or the latest quarterly earnings of IBM. Or they'll be young eager beavers of the postfeminist offshoot of the men's movement who speak in New Age sage-and-crystals tongues.

I couldn't have been more wrong.

The first surprise was that nearly all the men were middle-aged or in their sixties, graying around the temples or softening around the midsection. The second surprise was that they avoided altogether such lingo as "codependency" and the taking of est-ian "responsibility."

The third surprise was that they ducked none of my questions— rather they spoke with the same openness that, well, that women do. They spoke not in code but in words that anyone could understand, and with a sincerity that was both undeniable and moving.

The men talked about being called upon by late twentieth-century women to demonstrate emotional skills for which the men had virtually no training. They talked about what it's like to be a man trying to learn the language of the female heart, when all they knew was the language of male dominance and competitiveness in which they themselves weren't always exactly fluent or persuasive.

They talked about the discomfort of being blamed for female oppression, about their contributions to that oppression and their varying efforts to redress it and to adjust to feminism. They talked about the difficulty of expressing professional insecurities to partners and wives already frightened about tight family budgets and a scary long-range financial picture.

Mostly they talked about the cost of "masculinity": the emotional obstacle course of being a husband and father. The sadness they felt in childhood and adulthood because their fathers were remote or rigid and unavailable. The losses the men encountered when they tried to live up to the paternal and cultural mandate to "be a man," a mandate that has wreaked varying amounts of havoc in their emotional and family lives. Their longing for the kind of intimacy that comes automatically to most women.

Here, they said, once a week in this austere room, they could finally find a real friend in other men. Here they could reveal to one another the part that gets expressed—with mixed results and limited understanding—only to lovers or wives or female friends. Here they could get the solace that only another man could give and that no "real man" would dare seek under ordinary, image-polishing circumstances in the outside world.

"I can't imagine saying to someone in the trades, 'I'm really bummed out today, let's go for a cup of coffee,' " said the electrician. "I can't *imagine* it. They'd think I'm gay. This group is the only place I can really be myself."

"Being sensitive is seen as a weakness on the job," said the lawyer. "You always have to remain strong and wear a mask. The only things you can talk about are sports or business."

"I like women, but I don't think my wife and daughter believe it—with good reason," said the dentist. "I'm so busy playing the male role, fixing things and giving directions, that I don't really listen. They complain about that. A million years ago my wife was attracted to my 'sensitivity'—somewhere along the line, she says, it dissipated. She's right."

"I did what I was trained to do," said the bus driver. "In my generation you did what was expected of you: You shut up and earned the bucks and didn't express the pain."

Driving home that night, I felt a stab of melancholy, wondering where guys like this were when I was growing up and wishing I had had a daddy like any one of them, a father who could talk to and listen to me the way these men talked and listened to each other. But then I remembered what one of the men said: "Many of our families and friends never heard us talk like this either."

Drums Along the Gender Divide

"Poor babies," the feminist reader might be thinking right about now. "So men get a few lumps. Serves them right." Indeed, when I described my evening with this men's group to a female friend and said that I sympathized with the difficulties these men face, she snapped, "Fuck 'em. They asked for it. Now let them pay."

In her book *Of Woman Born* Adrienne Rich expressed such

sentiments somewhat more elegantly: "However much [patri-archy] has failed [men], however much it divides them from them-selves, it is still *their* order, confirming them in privilege."

All true. *Still* true. *Horrifyingly true.* For these are among the legacies of American-style patriarchal privilege to women and children today:

- In the last fifteen years violent crimes against women—in-cluding date rape and assault—have increased by 50 percent, while violent crimes against men have *decreased* by 12 percent.
- Married mothers bear 90 percent of responsibility for chil-dren—that is, seeing to their well-being and care—whether or not they work outside the home.
- No-fault divorce laws on the books of at least 43 states impoverish women and benefit men. Moreover, of the 9.4 million American women with children under twenty-one in father-absent households, 59 percent have been awarded child support (average award: $60 per week) in courts of law, yet only 30 percent have received the full amount, leaving a total paternal debt of *$18 billion* in uncollected funds, affecting some 16 million chil-dren.
- Half the states have moved to cut government food allot-ments for poor women and children, or to stop all aid.
- Lack of federal funds accounts also for the paucity of parenting-education programs for pregnant women and new mothers and fathers (unlike, for example, France and Scandina-via); yet it is estimated that if $52 million were spent annually on such education, and if such education reduced serious physical abuse by only 20 percent, approximately $362 million annually would be saved in lowered costs of foster care, hospitalization and medical care, rehabilitative services, juvenile-court cases, and fu-ture productivity.
- The United States is the *only* industrialized nation (besides South Africa) that has no national guaranteed maternity leave.
- In this country only the wealthy can afford high-quality day care—millions of other children are sent to unlicensed day care centers. In contrast 98 percent of France's three-to-five-year-olds attend *free,* safe preschool programs run by well-trained person-nel.

That the United States is antichild and antifemale is a matter of disgraceful record. One of the most obscene aspects of all this is that the laws protecting women and children that do get written—or vetoed or not written or not enforced—*are the work primarily of men who are themselves fathers.*

And so we come to the purpose of this chapter: to examine how the tragic consequences of patriarchy are perpetuated through *sons,* and what is being done, and can be done, about it. For only by changing the way we raise boys in the United States can we ever hope to make even a dent in these harrowing statistics.

The hope is that today's men will produce men of the future who will rewrite the legacies of patriarchy—who will, in fact, eliminate it and replace it with a gender-neutral, but not gender-indifferent, paternity.

None of this should be construed as a clarion call for pure androgyny. There are unquestionable delights in the differences between men and women, in femininity and masculinity, which one would wish neither to ignore nor to forfeit. Nor am I so naive as to suggest that in the next generation or even the one after there will be a complete eradication of male and female roles, learned or inherent, as we know them.

But the reality is that the only totally necessary function of having different sexes, the only one without which we literally cannot live, is procreation. It still takes a male and a female to make a baby.

Thus the clarion call here is this: There is a case to be made for *androgynousness*—for the expression of one's personal best apart from artificial roles and destructive stereotypes—as the solution to the patriarchy that is damaging to everyone, male and female alike.

If there is a silver lining in all these patriarchal legacies, it is that men are finally beginning to feel and to acknowledge the punishments of masculine privilege, the dubious value of continuing to adhere to the old masculine stereotypes.

For one thing, men are becoming aware of the costs to their health of sexism and machismo, the consequences of repressing their emotional sides: The death rate for American men is 40 percent higher than for women.

For another, men are experiencing the financial costs of patriarchy. The great American dream of *their* fathers—that if they uncomplainingly put in their twenty years at a corporation, they'll be rewarded with job security and a fat pension—is now largely a myth. The financial payoff of patriarchy is not what it once was.

Third, given these costs, men are becoming aware that their safe harbor, the family, is more important than ever; yet they often don't know how to navigate the uncertain waters of emotionality that has always been the province of women. While their wives and partners are moving in and out of the domestic realm, fluent in the languages both of the work world and of kinship, in their own families many men are on foreign psychic soil.

The Men's Movement

Even as the feminist movement looks outward at a culture that is unfair to women, men are now looking inward at the price of being a man. The most dramatic example of this masculine introspection and soul-searching is the men's movement, spearheaded by its elder statesman, poet Robert Bly.

"Wild Men." In recent years an estimated 100,000 American men have been attending retreats in the woods, using the Bly paradigm of personal masculine growth. Squatting naked in tepees where they sweat in purification rites, or hunched in circles where they beat drums or grasp one another and sob, these men are grieving for the fathers they never had; seeking "blessings" from one another that they never got from their fathers; and honoring the elder males attending such retreats.

If the trappings of these retreats make these men sound as though both their intellectual oars are not exactly in the water, it must be remembered that so, too, did the behavior of certain feminists in their efforts to call attention to their cause. Some early feminists threw themselves in front of racehorses; some post-Friedan feminists burned their bras and girdles.

For all the tribalism and seeming hysteria of these male retreats, they cannot be dismissed because they are for men only or because their platform, such as it is, does not redress the legal and social wrongs of patriarchy. One cannot forget, for example, that modern feminism began with what Betty Friedan called "the problem with no name." These men are literally and figuratively feeling their way to a new kind of masculinity. Theirs is an extremely important beginning, an awakening that is critical to cultural change.

This branch of the men's movement is not immune to criticism, however. For a start there are those Blyian symbols, such as the "wild man," Bly's metaphor for "emotional strength and spontaneity," as *Newsweek* put it, and the "warrior," the masculine capacity for righteous, nonviolent indignation. Such symbols, for all of Bly's careful, poetic interpretations of them, smack of machismo—perhaps his very intention in order to stir men's attention and identification.

I have another quarrel with Bly: his excoriation, however gently expressed or well intentioned, of what he calls "soft males," those sons who lingered, he says, too long under their mothers' influence because their fathers weren't available.

Although he surely doesn't intend it, this term takes us dangerously close to homophobia; it pits those men who are slight of build and artistic of bent against a hypermasculine image. "What I'm proposing," Bly once said, "is that every modern male has, lying at the bottom of his psyche, a large, primitive man covered with hair down to his feet. Making contact with this wild man is the step the 70's man has not yet taken: this is the process that still hasn't taken place in contemporary culture."

Note the word *large* to describe the wild man. And if making contact with this wild man has not yet occurred, it's hard to imagine what all those men benchpressing weights in gyms across the country or attending Rambo films are doing.

I am also troubled by the fact that in all the literature I have read about and by Bly's disciples—including such periodicals as *Wingspan* and *MAN!*—I have yet to see the subject of *being a father to a daughter* addressed, except in passing and certainly not with nearly the same emotional weight as being a father to a son.

There is about this corner of the men's movement another disturbing reality: These forest retreats are one-shots or, maybe, annual events. Nothing about the epiphanies reached among the pine trees can last in the real world without ongoing, systematic exploration and introspection. The scramble to make a living and the existing dynamics within relationships or families when these retreat participants return home cannot be remedied by sporadic purgings.

But these retreats are a good start. Which brings us to another corner of the men's movement, part of which is a direct result of these retreats and much encouraged by Bly, part of which developed on its own: the men's consciousness-raising movement.

Male Consciousness-Raising. The men's group described at the beginning of this chapter provides the kind of integration of awareness that does produce profound and lasting change. Just as the women's consciousness-raising groups of the 1960s and 1970s helped women to parse the problem that had no name, to build everyday awareness of how women have been shortchanged and have shortchanged themselves, so, too, do men's consciousness-raising groups address similar issues.

Family therapist Augustus Y. Napier encourages such groups at the end of his book on marriage, *The Fragile Bond.* He writes,

> Only when a man feels a strong, supportive link with other men—who he will discover have similar anxieties—will he feel safe from his fears of engulfment in the feminine side of life. . . . If he is to be a truly nurturing man, he badly needs to have felt nurtured by men.

These groups are profiting from the work of organizations such as the National Organization for Men Against Sexism, which addresses the issues of sexism, fathering, men's culture, men's studies, men and aging, pornography, homophobia, child custody, men and spirituality, men and mental health, ending men's violence, and male-female relationships.

This and other organizations put together workshops and intimacy-training seminars for men—just as feminists, for instance, have put together seminars on assertiveness training for women—which helps them implement the agenda of the men's movement as a whole.

Which brings us to still another phenomenon that has begun to take hold among men in recent years: the redefinition of fatherhood.

The "New, Nurturant Father." For all the reasons we have explored, more and more men are putting family first. In one midwestern corporation, for example, 60 percent of the fathers under thirty-five are passing up transfers and promotions in order to spend more time with their families.

Increasing numbers of fathers are asking for paternity leave, better child care, and trying to find innovative ways—such as flextime and job sharing—both to parent and to earn a living. Some men are learning how to be fathers in the best sense—getting the training and education needed to do what mothers have always done, learning to tap into their long-suppressed capacities for nurturing. These men are changing the ways fathers have historically charted the "masculinity" and "femininity" of their children by encouraging both mastery and emotionality in their daughters and sons.

Like the men's movement the "fatherhood movement," it could be called, is also in its infancy. We *are* seeing changes in fathering across the socioeconomic board. Still, male resistance to such changes is extraordinary. For example, Dr. Ross D. Parke conducted an experiment in which new fathers were shown a videotape on fathering shortly after the births of their babies. The tape included information about infants' perceptual ability, play techniques, and how to take care of babies. Most of the men who saw the tape—compared with men who didn't—became more actively involved in the care and feeding of their infants.

"However," Dr. Parke writes, *"the videotape increased the fathers' involvement only if their babies were boys; fathers of girls were unaffected."* [Emphasis added.]

Thus the new fatherhood requires more than just wishes or good intentions. According to Dr. Michael Lamb, "father involvement" in fact requires four specific ingredients:

Motivation: An estimated 40 percent of fathers wish they had "more time" to devote to their children.

Skills and self-confidence: Many fathers are simply afraid; they feel they are novices in the caretaking department.

Support: A wife or partner's invitation to the father to take an equal and active parental role is crucial.

Institutional practices: Corporations must be much more open to offering child care options such as flex-time, for example.

Given all these roadblocks to paternal nurturing, it is not surprising that one researcher concluded that American fathers are, compared with fathers in other cultures in Europe, Africa, and elsewhere, "deviant" in their lack of involvement with their children.

Seen in this light, involved fathering in this country may be an act of singular and courageous commitment in *spite* of cultural constraints.

As the forty-year-old father of a son and a daughter told me,

> My wife and I are attempting to raise our children in nonsexist ways. But it's very difficult in this society to counteract stereotypes, especially in trying to bring up a son. So our son will be the guinea pig and will suffer for it.
>
> Sometimes it gets funny. In our house both he and his sister share such chores as emptying the dishwasher. One day he went to school and asked his male buddies, "Are you *forced* to do the dishes?" Most of them, he said, aren't. But other times the consequences of our child rearing are really painful to watch. Another time our son was talking to his male friends about homosexuality, and one of the boys said he couldn't be friends with a homosexual. My son said, "If I were gay, which I'm not, I'd still be me." He's going to suffer a lot for his parents' opinions.

To be sure, there are myriad problems to be addressed in this new paternity. I do not think it beyond the realm of possibility to suggest that such problems in the long run can be surmounted if men and women can learn to relate to one another in a new and different way. When the father hunger of both sexes can be addressed and reduced, the faces of marriage and family will change and with them many of the social ills that have been described.

The Call for a Family Revolution

It is in all our interests—both men and women—to see to it that these changes in men coalesce into a groundswell that grows far beyond the pioneering grassroots level.

"Why can't a woman be more like a man?" wondered Henry Higgins in George Bernard Shaw's *Pygmalion*. The better question is why can't a man be more like a woman, and the answers to that one have been covered in copious detail throughout this book.

Which brings us to the most important question of all: How do we mount a family revolution? How do we persuade men once and for all and in huge numbers to become more involved in the emotional and physical lives of their children? How do we convey the urgency of appeasing the father hunger of their children and of examining the damaging consequences of their own father hunger?

What will it take for men to revive their inherent nurturing capacities and continue equally to nurture and embolden both their female and male children throughout their lives? What will it take for men and fathers to make that which has always been a private matter—the family—a public concern, taking its place at the top of our priorities?

How do you get a man to become the father he probably never had?

For a start, fathers of grown sons and daughters must honestly assess their own parenting and examine how their kids have turned out, factoring in the ways the fathers themselves may or may not have failed their children on their journeys of self-discovery and growth.

Men must remember their own fathers. They must recall their own childhood wounds. They must remain constantly, vigilantly, passionately aware of the costs to themselves of a patriarchal culture.

Ultimately, however, the decision to be an involved father comes down to a sense of morality: It is simply the right thing to do. And if the men who acknowledge the "rightness" of involved fathering *do something about it,* "right" can create the best kind of might.

Men must be in the vanguard of these changes, and not just women. Men must make the leap of faith that while the trappings of masculinity are in many ways rewarding, they cannot make up for the loss to themselves, and to their children, of their absence as fathers.

Men have the power to effect changes that women, in spite of their vigorous advocacy, have not been able to bring about by themselves. Once men become advocates for their own children and for all children, the laws that have been written over the centuries by men who ignore the needs of children one by one will fall away, replaced by new laws. The yardsticks of masculinity and the cultural requirements of machismo will fall away, replaced by the yardstick of *humanity.* The poverty of single or divorced mothers struggling to be both mothers and fathers to their children will wither away. The rates of rape and incest and battering will plummet.

Children will be the better for it. The family will be the better for it. Even the safety of our towns and cities will be the better for it.

And fathers themselves will be better for it. For fathers need their children to become whole, caring, fully developed human beings, just as children need their fathers.

In my book *When You and Your Mother Can't Be Friends,* I encouraged mothers to set aside their pride and their own psychological or cultural losses and say to their daughters, "Here is where I failed you. I am not the same person today I was when you were born and were growing up. I am ready to accept my part in your emotional confusion. Can we talk about it?"

I urge fathers to say the same things to their sons and daughters. With very few exceptions, there isn't a single grown man or woman who would not give a great deal to hear his or her father make such a statement. When a father has the courage and sensitivity to admit his failures, admit that he tried to do his best and that sometimes it wasn't good enough, admit that he was not a hero but only a man, *it is one of the greatest gifts he can give to his children.*

Such an admission frees sons and daughters to see his humanity rather than his male pride. It frees them to see his "feminine" qualities that were buried under millennia of male-ordered cultural mandates. It frees them to treasure the mother and father within themselves and to love one another without the hindrances of hidden emotional agendas.

More than anything, it frees sons to become the new, loving, engaged fathers of the future: men who will judge themselves by their capacities for love and growth rather than by their incomes, penis size, and all the arbitrary and damaging measurements of male worth.

Women can't rewrite the sexist present alone. Men have written the patriarchal past, and we are all living with the consequences. But together men and women can change the future, for their sons, their daughters, and each other.

It is my greatest hope that such change will finally come about, and the reason I wrote this book.

Notes

Unattributed quotations are from interviews conducted by the author.

Introduction

p. xix "In 1990 a Virginia Slims/Roper opinion poll. . . ." "The 1990 Virginia Slims Opinion Poll: A 20-Year Perspective of Women's Issues," p. 98, A Study Conducted by the Roper Organization Inc., The Roper Center, University of Connecticut, Storrs, Connecticut 06268.

Chapter 1: What Are Fathers For?

p. 4 ". . . 'great gray-green, greasy Limpopo River. . . .' " "The Elephant's Child," *The Just-So Stories* by Rudyard Kipling (London: Macmillan, 1902).

p. 5 ". . . 'both safe harbor and ship. . . .' " Interview with Claudia Tate, *Black Women Writers at Work,* edited by Claudia Tate (New York: Continuum, 1983), p. 122, cited in *Writing a Woman's Life,* by Carolyn G. Heilbrun (New York: Ballantine Books, 1988), p. 61.

p. 6 ". . . even develop the paternal version. . . ." "Development of the Father-Infant Relationship," by Michael W. Yogman, in *Theory and Research in Behavioral Pediatrics,* Vol. 1, edited by Hiram E. Fitzgerald, Ph.D., Barry M. Lester, Ph.D., and Michael W. Yogman, M.D. (New York: Plenum Press, 1982), p. 230.

p. 7 "Perhaps in compensation for their biological. . . ." "In Search of Fathers: A Narrative of an Empirical Journal," by Ross D.

Parke, in *Methods of Family Research: Biographies of Research Projects,* edited by Irving E. Siesgel and Gene Brody (Hillsdale, N.J.: Lawrence Erlbaum Associates, 1990), p. 156.

p. 7 "Babies know the differences between. . . ." "Development of the Father-Infant Relationship" by Yogman, p. 239.

p. 7 ". . . particularly girls, who become attached. . . ." "The Role of the Father in the Separation-Individuation Process," by Ernest L. Abelin, in *Separation-Individuation,* edited by J. B. McDevitt and C. F. Settlage (New York: International Universities Press, 1971), cited in "Fathering and the Separation-Individuation Process," by Luevonue M. Lincoln, *Maternal-Child Nursing Journal* 13 (no. 2, Summer 1984): 107.

p. 7 "Although all babies are emotionally connected. . . ." *On Human Symbiosis and the Vicissitudes of Individuation,* by Margaret S. Mahler (New York: International Universities Press, 1968), pp. 14–15, cited in Lincoln, p. 103.

p. 7 ". . . they notice and need their fathers. . . ." "Fathers and Child Development: An Integrative Overview," by Michael E. Lamb, in *The Role of the Father in Child Development,* second edition, edited by Michael E. Lamb (New York: John Wiley & Sons, 1981), p. 13, citing "Father Participation in Infancy," by F. A. Pederson and K. S. Robson, *American Journal of Orthopsychiatry* 39 (1969): 466–472.

p. 7 "According to Ross D. Parke, Ph.D., ..." *Fathers,* by Ross D. Parke (Cambridge, Mass.: Harvard University Press, 1981), p. 32.

p. 7 "So important is this fatherly. . . ." "Development of the Father-Infant Relationship," by Yogman, p. 253.

p. 7 ". . . separation-individuation. . . ." *The Psychological Birth of the Human Infant,* by Margaret Mahler, Fred Pine, and Anni Bergman (New York: Basic Books, 1975).

p. 8 "John Condry and Sandra Condry. . . ." "Sex Differences: A Study of the Eye of the Beholder," by John Condry and Sandra Condry, *Child Development* 47 (1976): 812–819, in *Annual Progress in Child Psychiatry and Child Development,* edited by Stella Chess, M.D., and Alexander Thomas, M.D. (New York: Brunner/Mazel, 1977), pp. 289–300.

p. 9 "It is no surprise, then, that most fathers. . . ." *Fathers,* by Parke, p. 43.

p. 9 "In fact families with sons. . . ." "Sons, Daughters and Divorce: Does the Sex of Children Affect the Risk of Marital Disruption?" by P. S. Morgan, D. N. Lye, and G. A. Condron (in press), *American Journal of Psychology,* cited in "Marital Transitions: A Child's Perspective," by E. Mavis Hetherington, Margaret Stanley-Hagen, and Edward R. Anderson, *American Psychologist* 44 (No. 2, February 1989): 306.

p. 9 "And when there is a divorce. . . ." "Divorce: A Child's Perspective," by E. Mavis Hetherington, *American Psychologist* 34 (No. 10, 1979): 851–58. See also "Post-Divorce Relationships as Mediating Factors in the Consequences of Divorce for Children," by R. D. Hess and K. A. Camara, *Journal of Social Issues* 35 (1979): 79–96.

p. 9 "Because fathers *are* a whole lot harder on. . . ." "Disciplinary Encounters Between Young Boys and Their Mothers and Fathers: Is There a Contingency System?," by H. Lytton, *Developmental Psychology* 15 (1979): 256–68.

p. 9 " 'When I was born. . . .' " *Home Before Dark: A Biographical Memoir of John Cheever by His Daughter,* by Susan Cheever (Boston: Houghton Mifflin Company, 1984), p. 126.

p. 10 "They hold their infant daughters. . . ." *Fathers,* by Parke, p. 44.

p. 10 ". . . 'firmer, larger-featured, better coordinated. . . .' " Ibid., p. 45, citing "The Eye of the Beholder: Parents' Views on Sex of Newborns," by J. Rubin, F. J. Provenzano, and Z. Luria, *American Journal of Orthopsychiatry* 43 (1974): 720–31.

p. 10 ". . . but fathers' involvement is more volitional. . . ." "The Father-Daughter Relationship: Past, Present, and Future," by Michael E. Lamb, Margaret Tresch Owen, and Lindsay Chase-Lansdale, in *Becoming Female: Perspectives on Development,* edited by Claire B. Kopp (New York: Plenum Press, 1979), p. 97.

p. 10 "Studies show that infants wriggle. . . ." Ibid.

p. 10 ". . . it is fathers who most often decree. . . ." Parke, *Fathers,* p. 61, citing "Mothers, Fathers, and Peers as Socialization Agents of Sex-Typed Play Behaviors in Young Children," by J. H. Langlois and A. C. Downs, *Child Development* 51 (1980): 1,217–47.

p. 11 "By the time little girls are around two. . . ." "Fathers and 'Femininity' in Daughters: A Review of the Research," by Miriam M. Johnson, *Sociology and Social Research* 67 (No. 1, October 1982): 9.

p. 11 ". . . punish rambunctiousness in the former. . . ." "Teaching Old Dogmatists New Tricks: Contributions from Child Development Literature to Freud's Oedipal Theory," by Carol E. Griffith, *Contributions to Human Development,* Vol. 18 (Basel: Karger, 1987), p. 19, citing "Sex Differences in Parent-Child Interaction Styles During a Free Play Session," by M. Tauber, *Child Development* 50 (1979): 981–88.

p. 11 "And while they want their sons to master. . . ," by Parke, *Fathers,* p. 75, citing "Another Look at Sex Differentiation in the Socialization Behaviors of Mothers and Fathers," by Jeanne Block, *Psychology of Women: Future Directions of Research* (New York: Psychological Dimensions, 1979).

p. 11 "Fathers are more likely to flirt. . . ." "Interest in Persons as an Aspect of Sex Difference in the Early Years," by Evelyn W. Goodenough, *Genetic Psychology Monographs* 55 (1957): 287–323, cited in "Fathers and 'Femininity' in Daughters: A Review of the Research," by Miriam M. Johnson, *Sociology and Social Research* 67 (No. 1, Oct. 1982): 5.

p. 11   "In family gatherings fathers tend to interrupt. . . ." "Father-Child Interaction: Implications for Gender-Role Socialization," by Phyllis Bronstein, in *Fatherhood Today: Men's Changing Role in the Family,* edited by Phyllis Bronstein and Carolyn Pape Cowan (New York: John Wiley & Sons, 1988), p. 111, citing "Sex Differences in Parent-Child Conversations: Who Interrupts Whom," by E. B. Grief, presented at the biennial meeting of the Society for Research in Child Development, San Francisco, April 1979.

p. 11   ". . . whereas with sons conversation is likely to include threatening language. . . ." "Guns and Dolls," by Laura Shapiro, *Newsweek,* May 28, 1990, p. 62.

p. 11   ". . . and or instruction." "Father-Child Interaction," by Bronstein, p. 111, citing "Mothers', Fathers', and Preschool Children's Interactive Behaviors in a Play Setting," by M. C. Bright and D. F. Stockdale, *Journal of Genetic Psychology* 144 (1984): 219–32.

p. 12   ". . . a concern far more prominent in fathers than in mothers." "Sexual Preference, Femininism and Women's Perceptions of Their Parents," by Miriam M. Johnson, Jean Stockard, Mary Rothbart, and Lisa Friedman, *Sex Roles* 6 (No. 1, 1981): 1,018, cited in "Fathers and 'Femininity' in Daughters," by Johnson, p. 9; see also *Patterns of Child Rearing,* by R. R. Sears, E. E. Maccoby, and H. Levin (Evanston, Ill.: Row, Peterson, 1956).

p. 14   ". . . the second individuation-separation phase." See "The Second Individuation Process of Adolescence," by Peter Blos, *The Psychoanalytic Study of the Child,* Vol. 22 (1967); also *Son and Father: Before and Beyond the Oedipus Complex,* by Peter Blos (New York: The Free Press, 1985).

p. 14   "Fathers avert their bodies more. . . ." "Families, Lies and Videotapes," by E. Mavis Hetherington, Ph.D., Presidential Address, Meetings of the Society for Research on Adolescence, Atlanta, Georgia, March 23, 1990, p. 20.

p. 18   "Drawing in part on what he acknowledged. . . ." For a discussion of Freud and current thinking about his work, see *Feminism and Psychoanalytic Theory,* by Nancy J. Chodorow (New Haven: Yale University Press, 1989), pp. 165–77.

p. 18   "Put simply, Freud believed that women. . . ." For an excellent overview and critique of Freud's theories, see "Teaching Old Dogmatists New Tricks: Contributions from Child Development Literature to Freud's Oedipal Theory," by Carol E. Griffith, *Contributions to Human Development,* Vol. 18 (1987), pp. 1–35.

p. 20   ". . . 'fathers often become external attachment figures. . . .' " *The Reproduction of Mothering: Psychoanalysis and the Sociology of Gender,* by Nancy J. Chodorow (Berkeley and Los Angeles: University of California Press, 1978), pp. 96–97.

p. 21 ". . . 're-engulfing' mother. . . ." *Son and Father*, by Blos, p. 20.

p. 22 "He would see a mere 27.5 percent of American families. . . ." "Changes in American Family Life," Current Population Reports Special Studies, Series P-23, No. 163, U.S. Department of Commerce, Bureau of the Census, August 1989, p. 18.

p. 22 "He would see nearly a quarter of all. . . ." Ibid., p. 13.

p. 22 "He would see seven million children of gay. . . ." "Daddy Is Out of the Closet," *Newsweek*, January 7, 1991, p. 60.

p. 22 ". . . and real estate laws defining. . . ." "Lesbian Child-Custody Cases Test Frontiers of Family Law," by David Margolick, *The New York Times*, July 4, 1990, pp. 1, 10.

p. 22 ". . . some thirty thousand artificially inseminated. . . ." "Not the Right Father," by Barbara Kantrowitz, *Newsweek*, March 19, 1990, p. 51.

p. 22 "By six weeks or so. . . ." "The History of Female Sexuality in the United States," by Myrna I. Liew, in *Women's Sexual Development: Explorations of Inner Space*, edited by Martha Kirkpatrick, M.D. (New York: Plenum Press, 1980), p. 32.

p. 23 "When the newborn is around seven months. . . ." "Physiological Aspects of Female Sexual Development: Conception Through Puberty," by Cori Baill and John Money, in *Women's Sexual Development*, edited by Kirkpatrick, p. 50.

p. 23 "Infant girls tend to be less physically. . . ." *Success and the Fear of Success in Women*, by David W. Krueger, M.D. (New York: The Free Press, 1984), p. 4, citing "Relations Between Behavior Manifestations in the Human Neonate," by R. Bell, *Child Development* 31 (1960): 463–77.

p. 23 ". . . greater skin sensitivity. . . ." Ibid., p. 4, citing "Electrotactual Threshold in the Human Neonate," by L. Lipsitt and N. Levy, *Child Development* 30 (1959): 547–54.

p. 23 ". . . keener sense of smell." "Guns and Dolls," *Newsweek*, May 28, 1990, p. 58.

p. 23 "Boys have greater muscle mass. . . ." Ibid., p. 59.

p. 23 "In the erogenous zone, male orgasm. . . ." "Maternity and Paternity in the Developmental Context: Contribution to Integration and Differentiation as a Procreative Person," by Judith S. Kestenberg, M.D., *Psychiatric Clinics of North America* 3 (No. 1, April 1980): 63–64.

p. 23 ". . . orgasm is intensified by the congestion. . . ." "A Biosocial Perspective on Parenting," by Alice S. Rossi, *Daedalus*, Spring 1977, p. 17, citing "The Evolution and Nature of Female Sexuality in Relation to Psychoanalytic Theory," by M. M. Sherfey, *Journal of the American Psychoanalytic Association* 14 (No. 1, 1966): 28–128.

p. 23 ". . . 'the ease with which males. . . .' " Ibid., p. 12.

p. 23 ". . . Little boys exhibit greater visual acuity. . . ." *Success and the Fear of Success in Women,* by Krueger, p. 5, citing *On the Psychology of Women* by J. Sherman (Springfield, Ill.: Thomas, 1971).

p. 23 ". . . little girls are better with language." Ibid., citing Sherman.

p. 23 ". . . research also shows that mothers. . . ." Ibid., p. 6, citing "Sex, Age, and State as Determinants of Mother-Infant Interaction," by H. Moss, *Merrill-Palmer Quarterly* 13 (1967): 19–36.

p. 24 "Recent studies of the effect of genes. . . ." "Personality Puzzle: What Researchers Studying Twins Can Tell Us About Ourselves," by James Thornton, *Self,* March 1990, pp. 227, 229, citing studies of identical twins by Thomas J. Bouchard et al., University of Minnesota.

p. 24 " 'There is no substantial experimental. . . .' " *Success and the Fear of Success in Women,* by Krueger, p. 5, citing *Love and Love Sickness: The Science of Sex, Gender Difference, and Pair-Bonding* by J. Money (Baltimore: Johns Hopkins University Press, 1980).

p. 25 ". . . 'The men are a more highly selected. . . .' " "Guns and Dolls," *Newsweek,* p. 57.

p. 25 " 'The only useful answer to the question. . . .' " "Do Human Brains Have Gender?" by Madeline Chinnici, *Self,* July 1990, p. 151.

p. 25 " 'One is not born, but rather becomes. . . .' " *The Second Sex,* by Simone de Beauvoir (New York: Alfred A. Knopf, 1983), p. 267.

p. 25 "Researchers believe that the combination. . . ." " 'The Second Other': The Role of the Father in Early Personality Formation and the Dyadic-Phallic Phase of Development," by Stanley I. Greenspan, in *Father and Child: Developmental and Clinical Perspectives,* edited by Stanley H. Cath, Alan R. Gurwitt, John Munder Ross (New York: Basil Blackwell, 1988), pp. 128–29; see also "Some Suggested Revisions Concerning Early Female Development," by Eleanor Galenson and Herman Roiphe, citing *Man and Woman, Boy and Girl,* by J. Money and A. Ehrhardt (Baltimore: Johns Hopkins University Press, 1972), in *Women's Sexual Development,* by Kirkpatrick, pp. 85–86.

p. 26 " 'The basic imprint of gender. . . .' " *Success and the Fear of Success in Women,* by Krueger, p. 23.

p. 26 " 'The sex that is attributed. . . .' " Ibid., p. 24, citing *Man and Woman, Boy and Girl,* by J. Money and A. Ehrhardt.

p. 27 ". . . 'not that we have to make men and women. . . .' " "Real Man Redux," by Michael S. Kimmel, *Psychology Today,* July 1987, p. 52.

p. 27 ". . . 'Femininity . . . is not what *is.* . . .' " "Femininity," by Robert J. Stoller, in *Women's Sexual Development,* edited by Kirkpatrick, p. 128.

p. 27 "As Dr. Miriam M. Johnson put it. . . ." "Fathers and 'Femininity' in Daughters: A Review of the Research," by Miriam M. Johnson, *Sociology and Social Research* 67 (No. 1, October 1982): 2.

p. 27 "But the greatest impact on a woman's. . . ." *The Female Orgasm: Psychology, Physiology, Fantasy,* by Seymour Fisher (New York: Basic Books, 1973), p. 5.

Chapter 2: Silent Partner

p. 31 "Dr. Stella Chess, for example. . . ." Referring to the New York Longitudinal Study by Drs. Stella Chess and Alexander Thomas, *Daughters: From Infancy to Independency,* by Stella Chess, M.D., and Jane Whitbread (New York: Doubleday & Co., 1978), pp. vii, 110.

p. 31 " 'We were unprepared for. . . .' " Ibid., p. 221.

p. 31 "To take another example, Dr. Seymour Fisher. . . ." *The Female Orgasm,* by Fisher, p. 7.

p. 31 "The seminal study of the father-daughter relationship. . . ." "Effects of Father Absence on Personality Development in Adolescent Daughters," by E. Mavis Hetherington, *Developmental Psychology* 7 (No. 3, 1973): 313–26.

p. 33 "Paternal neglect. . . ." "Fathers and Child Development: An Integrative Overview," by Michael E. Lamb, in *The Role of the Father in Child Development,* edited by Lamb, p. 30.

p. 34 "But the less involved the father. . . ." *The Female Orgasm,* by Fisher, p. 230.

p. 34 "In a 1987 study. . . ." "Depressive Mood in Female College Students: Father-Daughter Interactional Patterns," by Judith S. Brook, Martin Whiteman, David W. Brook, and Ann Scovell Gordon, *Journal of Genetic Psychology* 149 (1988): 495–96.

p. 34 "The psychological absence of fathers can be. . . ." "Fathers and Child Development: An Integrative Overview," by Michael E. Lamb, in *The Role of the Father in Child Development,* edited by Lamb, p. 30.

p. 36 ". . . an estimated 90 percent. . . ." "Marital Transitions: A Child's Perspective," by E. Mavis Hetherington, Margaret Stanley-Hagan, and Edward R. Anderson, *American Psychologist* 44 (No. 3, February 1989): 305.

p. 36 ". . . up to half have no regularly scheduled. . . ." "Missing Fathers," by Edward Teyber and Charles D. Hoffman, *Psychology Today,* April 1987, p. 36.

p. 36 ". . . 42 percent haven't seen their fathers. . . ." "Father's Vanishing Act Called Common Drama," by Tamar Lewin, *The New York Times,* June 4, 1990, p. A18.

p. 36 "Only 7 percent of children. . . ." Ibid.; see also "Marital Transitions," by Hetherington et al., pp. 307–309.

p. 37 "One study found that up to. . . ." "Husbands' and Wives' Paid Work, Family Work, and Adjustment," Wellesley, Mass.: Wellesley College Center for Research on Women (Working Papers), by J. H. Pleck, 1982; and *The 1977 Quality of Employment Survey,* by R. P. Quinn and G. L. Staines, Ann Arbor, Michigan, Survey Research Center, 1979, cited in "Introduction: The Emergent American Father" by Michael E. Lamb, *The Father's Role: Cross-Cultural Perspectives,* edited by Michael E. Lamb (Hillsdale, N.J.: Lawrence Erlbaum Associates, 1987), p. 20.

p. 37 "Paternal reticence results in. . . ." "The Role of the Father in Cognitive, Academic, and Intellectual Development," by Norma Radin, in *The Role of the Father in Child Development,* edited by Lamb, p. 418.

p. 38 ". . . writer Letty Cottin Pogrebin calls Teflon. . . ." "The Teflon Father," by Letty Cottin Pogrebin, *Ms.,* September/October 1990, p. 95.

p. 38 " 'The longer the absence . . . the greater this need.' " "Some Further Observations and Comments on the Earliest Role of the Father," by Ernst L. Abelin, *International Journal of Psycho-Analysis* 56 (1975): 297.

p. 38 "And, in extreme cases, they express it. . . ." "Fathers of Transsexual Children," by Robert J. Stoller, M.D., in "Primary Femininity," *Journal of the American Psychoanalytic Association* 27 (1979): 863 (Presented at the Sixty-sixth Annual Meeting of the American Psychoanalytic Association, Quebec, Canada, April 29, 1977).

p. 40 ". . . the false-self personality. . . ." *The Maturational Processes and the Facilitating Environment,* by D. W. Winnicott (New York: International Universities Press, 1965).

p. 40 " '[Children develop] the art of not. . . .' " *The Drama of the Gifted Child,* by Alice Miller (New York: Basic Books, 1981), p. 10.

p. 42 "According to Philippe Ariès. . . ." *Centuries of Childhood: A Social History of Family Life,* by Philippe Ariès (New York: Vintage Books, 1962).

p. 42 "So, too, in Greece and Rome. . . ." "Historical Perspectives on the Father's Role," by Jonathan Bloom-Feshbach, in *The Role of the Father in Child Development,* edited by Lamb, p. 86, citing *The History of Childhood,* by L. DeMause (New York: Harper, 1975).

p. 42 "Prepubertal children were thought. . . ." *Centuries of Childhood,* by Ariès, p. 106.

p. 42 "Child labor wasn't eliminated. . . ." See *Toil and Trouble: A History of American Labor,* by Thomas R. Brooks (New York: Delacorte Press, 1964), pp. 106–110.

p. 42 ". . . 'the little thing which had disappeared. . . . ,' " *Centuries of Childhood,* by Ariès, p. 38.

p. 43 "Indeed it wasn't until. . . ." *Mothers on Trial: The Battle for*

Children and Custody, by Phyllis Chesler, Ph.D. (New York: McGraw-Hill Book Company, 1986), p. xii.

p. 43 "As for the actual financial *support,. . . .*" Ibid.

p. 43 "Sociologist Joseph Pleck. . . ." "Introduction: The Emergent American Father," by Michael E. Lamb, in *The Father's Role: Cross-Cultural Perspectives,* edited by Lamb, p. 4–6, citing "Changing Fatherhood," by J. H. Pleck, unpublished manuscript, Wellesley College, 1984.

p. 43 "The Industrial Revolution changed. . . ." *Mothers and Such: Views of American Women and Why They Changed,* by Maxine L. Margolis (Berkeley: University of California Press, 1984), p. 12.

p. 43 "As Barbara Ehrenreich has pointed out. . . ." *For Her Own Good: 150 Years of the Experts' Advice to Women,* by Barbara Ehrenreich (New York: Anchor Press/Doubleday, 1978), p. 10.

p. 43 ". . . 'As long as fathers rule but do not nurture . . .' " *Father-Daughter Incest,* by J. Herman (Cambridge, Mass.: Harvard University Press, 1981), p. 206, cited in *Healing the Incest Wound: Adult Survivors in Therapy,* by Christine A. Courtois, Ph.D. (New York: W. W. Norton & Company, 1988), p. 167.

p. 44 "Dr. Michael E. Lamb divides paternal behavior. . . ." "Introduction: The Emergent American Father," by Michael E. Lamb, in *The Father's Role,* edited by Lamb, pp. 8–11.

p. 44 ". . . *almost all mothers, working or not.* . . ." Ibid., p. 8.

p. 44 " 'Like prisoners who "do time". . . .' " "Fatherhood and Social Change," by Ralph La Rossa, *Men's Studies Review 6* (No. 2, Spring 1989): p. 6.

p. 44 "Contrary to popular opinion. . . ." "The Varying Linkages of Work and Family," by J. T. Mortimer and J. London, in *Work and Family: Changing Roles of Men and Women,* edited by P. Voydanoff (Palo Alto, Calif.: Mayfield, 1984), cited in "Intimate Fathers: Patterns of Paternal Holding Among Aka Pygmies," by Barry S. Hewitt, in *The Father's Role,* edited by Lamb, p. 323.

p. 44 "But recent studies indicate that while. . . ." "Fatherhood and Social Change," by La Rossa, p. 5.

p. 47 ". . . since there are 13 million stepfathers. . . ." "Stepfathers: The Shoes Rarely Fit," by Jon Nordheimer, *The New York Times,* October 18, 1990, p. C1.

p. 47 "According to studies conducted by Dr. Hetherington. . . ." "Families, Lies and Videotapes," by E. Mavis Hetherington, Ph.D., presidential address, Meetings of the Society for Research on Adolescence, Atlanta, Georgia, March 23, 1990.

p. 49 ". . . male intimacy with children is a *developmental.* . . ." See *The Seasons of a Man's Life* by Daniel J. Levinson, with Charlotte N. Darrow, Edward B. Klein, Maria H. Levinson, Braxton McKee (New York: Alfred A. Knopf, 1978).

Chapter 3: The "Other" Woman (Mom)

p. 52 "At the turn of the century. . . ." "Mothers Who Don't Know How," by George F. Will, *Newsweek,* April 23, 1990, p. 80.

p. 53 "Researchers have observed a version. . . ." "Sex, Age, and State as Determinants of Mother-Infant Interaction," by H. A. Moss, in *Readings on the Psychology of Women,* cited in "Father-Child Interaction: Implications for Gender-Role Socialization" by Phyllis Bronstein (New York: Harper & Row, 1972), cited in *Fatherhood Today: Men's Changing Role in the Family,* edited by Phyllis Bronstein and Carolyn Pape Cohen (New York: John Wiley & Sons, 1988), p. 120.

p. 54 "Indeed of all pairings in the family. . . ." See *When You and Your Mother Can't Be Friends: Resolving the Most Complicated Relationship of Your Life,* by Victoria Secunda (New York: Delacorte Press, 1990).

p. 55 "Indeed some researchers believe fathers. . . ." "Engrossment: The Newborn's Impact Upon the Father," by Martin Greenberg and Norman Morris, in *Father and Child: Developmental and Clinical Perspectives,* edited by Stanley H. Cath, Alan R. Gurwitt, and John Munder Ross (New York: Basil Blackwell, 1988), p. 97.

p. 56 "And her attitude toward Dad. . . ." "Discovering Daddy: The Mother's Role," by Richard N. Atkins, in *Father and Child,* edited by Cath et al., p. 144.

p. 56 "In the normal course of events. . . ." For a discussion of "reciprocal role learning," see "The Father-Daughter Relationship: Past, Present and Future," by Michael E. Lamb, Margaret Tresch Owen, and Lindsay Chase-Lansdale, in *Becoming Female: Perspectives on Development,* edited by Claire B. Kopp, in collaboration with Martha Kirkpatrick (New York: Plenum Press, 1979), pp. 92–93.

p. 57 "In an important study . . . *immeasurable* significance." *The Managerial Woman,* by Margaret Hennig, Ph.D., and Anne Jardim, Ph.D. (New York: Anchor Press/Doubleday, 1977), pp. 82, 77.

p. 57 ". . . 'did not see themselves as having. . . .' " Ibid., p. 101.

p. 58 "In effect fathers are 'crowded out'. . . ." "Father Influences Viewed in a Family Context," by Frank A. Pederson, in *The Role of the Father in Child Development,* second edition, edited by Michael E. Lamb (New York: A Wiley-Interscience Publication, John Wiley & Sons, 1981), p. 303.

p. 59 "In fact one of the most important indicators. . . ." "Primary Caregiving Fathers of Long Duration," by Norma Radin, Ph.D., in *Fatherhood Today,* edited by Bronstein and Cowan, p. 128.

p. 60 ". . . 'One of the curses that weigh heavily. . . .' " *The Second Sex,* by Simone de Beauvoir (New York: Alfred A. Knopf, 1983), p. 281.

p. 60 "As one researcher noted, mothers are. . . ." "Sex-Role Perception: Portrayal and Perception in the Fantasy Play of Young Children," by Wendy S. Matthews, *Sex Roles* 7 (1981); 979–87, cited in "Fathers and 'Femininity' in Daughters: A Review of the Research," by Miriam M. Johnson, *Sociology and Social Research* 67 (No. 1, October 1982): 12.

p. 63 "And in their deprivation. . . ." " 'The Second Other': The Role of the Father in Early Personality Formation and the Dyadic-Phallic Phase of Development," by Stanley I. Greenspan, in *Father and Child,* edited by Cath et al., p. 134.

p. 64 " 'We rarely see abuse by one spouse. . . .' " "Abusive Fathers," by Brandt F. Steele, in *Father and Child,* edited by Cath et al., p. 489.

p. 65 ". . . 'tight . . . *alliance against the father.'* " *Linked Lives: Adult Daughters and Their Mothers,* by Lucy Rose Fischer, Ph.D. (New York: Harper & Row, 1986), p. 30.

p. 67 "In her fifteen-year study of sixty divorced. . . ." *Second Chances: Men, Women, and Children a Decade After Divorce,* by Judith S. Wallerstein and Sandra Blakeslee (New York: Ticknor & Fields, 1990), pp. 97–98.

p. 67 ". . . rather than risk winning where her mother. . . ." *Daughters of Divorce: The Effects of Parental Divorce on Women's Lives,* by Diedre S. Laiken (New York: William Morrow and Company, 1981), pp. 110–111.

p. 67 " '*I have found that the quality. . . .' " Second Chances,* by Wallerstein et al., p. 187.

p. 68 "Ten years after the divorce, one third. . . ." Ibid.

p. 68 "According to Dr. E. Mavis Hetherington. . . ." "Marital Transitions," by Hetherington et al., pp. 303–312.

p. 68 ". . . 43 percent of divorced custodial mothers. . . ." Ibid., p. 307, citing "Demographic Trends and the Living Arrangements of Children," by D. J. Hernandez, in *Impact of Divorce, Single-Parenting, and Stepparenting on Children,* edited by E. M. Hetherington and J. D. Arasteh (Hillsdale, N.J.: Lawrence Erlbaum Associates, 1988), pp. 3–22.

p. 69 "In Wakerman's study. . . ." *Father Loss: Daughters Discuss the Man That Got Away,* by Elyce Wakerman (New York: Doubleday & Company, 1984), p. 29.

p. 71 ". . . most studies on sexual abuse agree. . . ." "Father-Daughter Incest," by Irving Kaufman, in *Fathers and Child,* edited by Cath et al., p. 500.

p. 72 "Since 80 percent of divorced fathers. . . ." "Marital Transitions," by Hetherington et al., p. 303.

p. 72 "Judith Wallerstein found in her study. . . ." *Second Chances,* by Wallerstein et al., p. 255.

p. 73 "Stepmother becomes the repository. . . ." *Daughters of Divorce,* by Laiken, pp. 156–65.

Chapter 4: The Good-Enough Father

p. 82 "One researcher suggests that there is. . . ." "The Father in Midlife: Crisis and the Growth of Paternal Identity," by Calvin A. Colarusso and Robert A. Nemiroff, in *Father and Child: Developmental and Clinical Perspectives,* edited by Stanley H. Cath, M.D., Alan R. Gurwitt, M.D., and John Munder Ross, Ph.D. (New York: Basil Blackwell, 1982), p. 316, citing *Parenthood,* by E. James Anthony and Theresa Benedek (Boston: Little, Brown, 1970), p. 167.

p. 82 ". . . 'most attuned,' 'less well-attuned,' and 'least well-attuned'. . . ." "Patterns of Expectant Fatherhood: A Study of the Fathers of a Group of Premature Infants," by James M. Herzog, in *Father and Child,* edited by Cath et al., p. 303.

p. 83 "Sex for the least well-attuned men. . . ." Ibid., p. 306.

p. 83 ". . . a large percentage of them. . . ." Ibid., p. 313.

p. 83 ". . . that figure rose to nearly *100 percent.*" Ibid., p. 309.

p. 84 " 'If you are always searching for. . . .' " Ibid., p. 313.

p. 84 "Another study confirmed. . . ." "The Expectant Father," by Jerrold Lee Shapiro, Ph.D., *Psychology Today,* January 1987, pp. 38–42. Dr. Shapiro studied 227 expectant fathers ages eighteen to sixty of varying backgrounds.

p. 85 "Simply because she is not male. . . ." "Role of the Father," by Christine Adams-Tucker, M.D., and Paul L. Adams, M.D., in *Women's Sexual Development: Explorations of Inner Space,* edited by Martha Kirkpatrick, M.D. (New York: Plenum Press, 1980), p. 228.

p. 85 "Sometimes it is the result of his hatred. . . ." "A Note on the Father's Contribution to the Daughter's Ways of Loving and Working," by Lora Heims Tessman, in *Father and Child,* edited by Cath et al., p. 229.

p. 85 "But some fathers pray for daughters. . . ." "Aspects of Prospective Fatherhood," by Alan R. Gurwitt, in *Father and Child,* edited by Cath et al., p. 298, citing "Fatherhood and Providing," by T. Benedek, in *Parenthood: Its Psychology and Psychopathology,* edited by E. J. Anthony and T. Benedek (Boston: Little, Brown, 1970), p. 172.

p. 87 "Drs. Stella Chess and Alexander Thomas. . . ." *The Dynamics of Psychological Development,* by Alexander Thomas, M.D., and Stella Chess, M.D. (New York: Brunner/Mazel, 1980), p. 69.

p. 87 "Some women are temperamentally better suited. . . ." See "Primary Caregiving Fathers of Long Duration," by Norma Radin, Ph.D., in *Fatherhood Today: Men's Changing Role in the Family,* edited by

Phyllis Bronstein and Carolyn Pape Cowan (New York: John Wiley & Sons, 1988), p. 133.

p. 87   "Approximately 2 percent. . . ." "For Today's Fathers, Their Holiday Seems a Bit Set in Its Ways," by Woody Hochswender, *The New York Times,* June 17, 1990, p. 22.

p. 88   "A study of Australian fathers. . . ." *Fathers,* by Ross D. Parke (Cambridge, Mass.: Harvard University Press, 1981), pp. 106–107, citing "Fathers As Caregivers: Possible Antecedents and Consequences," by G. Russell (paper presented to a study group on "Fathers and Social Policy," University of Haifa, Israel, 1980).

p. 88   "A study of the children. . . ." Ibid., p. 106, citing "Child-rearing Fathers in Intact Families: An Exploration of Some Antecedents and Consequences," by Norma Radin (paper presented to a study group, "The Role of the Father in Child Development, Social Policy, and the Law," University of Haifa, Israel, 1980).

p. 88   ". . . 'more nurturing than children'. . . ." "Divorced Fathers with Custody," by Shirley M. H. Hanson, Ph.D., in *Fatherhood Today,* edited by Bronstein and Cowan, p. 182.

p. 88   "In his book *Seasons of a Man's Life.* . . ." *Seasons of a Man's Life,* by Daniel J. Levinson with Charlotte N. Darrow, Edward B. Klein, Maria H. Levinson, and Braxton McKee (New York: Alfred A. Knopf, 1978).

p. 89   ". . . 'the double life-cycle perspective'. . . ." *Fathers and Daughters: A Father's Powerful Influence on a Woman's Life,* by William S. Appleton (New York: Berkley Books, 1984), p. 6.

p. 92   "As Dr. Appleton points out. . . ." Ibid., p. 39.

p. 95   "Child maltreatment is on the rise. . . ." "How to Protect Abused Children," by Barbara Kantrowitz, *Newsweek,* November 23, 1987, p. 68; see also "Highlights of Official Child Neglect and Abuse Reporting," 1986, published by the American Humane Association.

p. 95   "Psychological abuse is at the heart. . . ." See *The Psychologically Battered Child: Strategies for Identification, Assessment, and Intervention,* by James Garbarino, Edna Guttmann, and Janis Wilson Seeley (San Francisco: Jossey-Bass, 1986).

p. 95   ". . . from 20 to 39 percent. . . ." The 20-percent figure is from *Fathers and Daughters,* by Appleton, p. 150; 39 percent is from *The Female Orgasm,* by Fisher, p. 201.

p. 96   "Good parenting has been defined. . . ." "The Development of Paternal Attitudes," by Judith S. Kestenberg, Hershey Marcus, K. Mark Sossin, and Richard Stevenson, Jr., in *Father and Child,* edited by Cath et al., p. 206.

p. 96   "In fact a study of divorced custodial fathers. . . ." *Fathers,* by Ross D. Parke, Ph.D., p. 93, citing K. E. Gersick, "Fathers by Choice: Divorced Men Who Receive Custody of Their Children," in *Divorce and*

Separation, edited by G. Levinger and O. C. Moles (New York: Basic Books, 1979).

p. 96 ". . . 'the more feminine a gay man appears. . . .' " "Homophobia: Scientists Find Clues to Its Roots," by Daniel Goleman, *The New York Times,* July 10, 1990, p. C11, quoting psychiatrist Richard Isay.

p. 96 "Androgynous fathers are involved with their babies. . . ." *Fathers,* by Parke, p. 30, citing "The Measurement of Psychological Androgyny," by S. L. Bem, *Journal of Consulting and Clinical Psychology* 42 (1974): 155–62.

p. 98 "According to Judith S. Kestenberg. . . ." "Maternity and Paternity in the Developmental Context," by Judith S. Kestenberg, M.D., *Psychiatric Clinics of North America* 3, No. 1 (April 1980): 75.

p. 99 ". . . fathers, even more than mothers, knock. . . ." *Fathers,* by Parke, p. 62.

p. 100 "In renegotiating the relationship. . . ." "Daughters and Lovers: Reflections on the Life Cycle of Daughter-Father Relationships," by Rudolf Ekstein, in *Women's Sexual Development: Explorations of Inner Space,* edited by Martha Kirkpatrick, M.D. (New York: Plenum Press, 1980), pp. 214–16.

Chapter 5: The Doting Father

p. 106 " 'I have seen many more women. . . .' " *Fathers and Daughters,* by William S. Appleton, pp. 43–44.

p. 107 "In his book *The Fragile Bond.* . . ." *The Fragile Bond: In Search of an Equal, Intimate and Enduring Marriage,* by Augustus Y. Napier, Ph.D. (New York: Harper & Row, Publishers, 1988), p. 178.

p. 108 "As one researcher put it, 'Occasionally, the selfsame father. . . .' " "The Role of the Father," by Christine Adams-Tucker, M.D., and Paul L. Adams, M.D., in *Women's Sexual Development: Explorations of Inner Space,* edited by Martha Kirkpatrick, M.D. (New York: Plenum Press, 1980), p. 232.

p. 109 "Such fathers, Dr. Henry Biller writes. . . ." "The Father and Sex Role Development," by Henry B. Biller, citing *The Psychology of Women,* Vol. 1, by H. Deutsch (New York: Grune & Stratton, 1944), in *The Role of the Father in Child Development,* edited by Michael E. Lamb, second edition, revised and updated (New York: McGraw-Hill Book Company, 1987), p. 338.

p. 110 ". . . fall into a category of emotional maltreatment as defined by Dr. James Garbarino. . . ." *The Psychologically Battered Child: Strategies for Identification, Assessment, and Intervention,* by James Garbarino, Edna Guttmann, and Janis Wilson Seeley (San Francisco: Jossey-Bass, 1986), p. 8.

p. 114 "In the family, according to Dr. Michael Kerr. . . ." *Family Evaluation: An Approach Based on Bowen Theory,* by Michael Kerr, M.D., and Murray Bowen, M.D. (New York: W. W. Norton & Company, 1988), pp. 64–67.

p. 116 "Research shows that American men and women. . . ." "Close Encounters," by Stephen Thayer, *Psychology Today,* March 1988, p. 32.

p. 117 " 'Mother may often remind. . . .' " "Divorce and the Child: 'The Father Question Hour,' " by Stanley H. Cath, in *Father and Child: Developmental and Clinical Perspectives,* edited by Stanley H. Cath, Alan R. Gurwitt, and John Munder Ross (New York: Basil Blackwell, 1988), p. 474.

p. 119 " '. . . parents who infantilize. . . .' " Napier, *The Fragile Bond,* p. 179.

p. 120 "Psychologist Carl Hindy. . . ." "Patterns in Love Charted in Studies," by Daniel Goleman, *The New York Times,* September 10, 1985, p. C1.

p. 120 " 'Because she so often sees. . . .' " *The Culture of Narcissism: American Life in an Age of Diminishing Expectations,* by Christopher Lasch (New York: Warner Books, 1979), p. 294.

p. 122 ". . . he is addicted to his daughter's love. . . ." *Family Evaluation,* by Kerr et al., pp. 77–78.

p. 122 "Recent research into the mechanics of empathy. . . ." "Studies on Development of Empathy Challenge Some Old Assumptions," by Daniel Goleman, *The New York Times,* July 12, 1990, p. B8.

p. 122 "But new studies suggest. . . ." Ibid.

p. 122 " '. . . the warmth alone is not enough. . . .' " Ibid.

Chapter 6: The Distant Father

p. 129 ". . . 'a barrier of silence.' " *The Psychologically Battered Child: Strategies for Identification, Assessment and Intervention,* by James Garbarino, Edna Guttmann, and Janis Wilson Seeley (San Francisco: Jossey-Bass, 1986), p. 26.

p. 129 "They are, Dr. Garbarino tells us. . . ." Ibid., pp. 27, 53–55.

p. 132 ". . . overfunctioners. . . ." *Family Evaluation: An Approach Based on Bowen Theory,* by Michael E. Kerr and Murray Bowen (New York: W. W. Norton, 1988), p. 56.

p. 132 ". . . 'underfunctioners'. . . ." Ibid., pp. 55–56.

p. 134 " 'Whether the men passively disappear. . . .' " "The Politics of Mood," by Ronald Taffel, *The Family Therapy Networker,* September/October 1990, p. 51.

p. 135 " 'I don't think it off-the-wall. . . .' " "The Masculine Mystique," by Frank Pittman, *The Family Therapy Networker,* May/June 1990, p. 48.

p. 137 " '[Americans] owe nothing. . . .' " *Democracy in America,* by Alexis de Tocqueville 1835, edited and abridged for the modern reader by Richard D. Heffner (New York: A Mentor Book, New American Library, 1956), p. 194.

p. 138 ". . . 'reengulfing mother'. . . ." *Son and Father: Before and Beyond the Oedipus Complex,* by Peter Blos (New York: The Free Press, 1985), p. 19.

p. 140 "Many authorities on eating disorders. . . ." For a discussion of anorexia nervosa, see *Adolescence: The Farewell to Childhood,* by Louise J. Kaplan, Ph.D. (New York: Simon & Schuster/Touchstone, 1985), pp. 249–83.

p. 140 "Emotionally distant fathers. . . ." see "Fathers and Child Development: An Integrative Overview," by Michael E. Lamb, *The Role of the Father in Child Development,* edited by Michael E. Lamb, second edition, revised and updated (New York: A Wiley-Interscience Publication, 1981), pp. 27–30.

p. 141 " 'The greater a woman's difficulty. . . .' " *The Female Orgasm: Psychology, Physiology, Fantasy,* by Seymour Fisher (New York: Basic Books, 1973), p. 7.

p. 141 ". . . inadequate fathering is more of a factor. . . ." "The Father and Sex Role Development," by Henry B. Biller, in *The Role of the Father in Child Development,* edited by Lamb, pp. 347–438.

Chapter 7: The Demanding Father

p. 148 "The consensus among experts. . . ." "Coping and Family Transitions: Winners, Losers and Survivors," by E. Mavis Hetherington, *Child Development,* 60 (1989): 8.

p. 148 "First, the daughter's cognitive abilities. . . ." "The Role of the Father in Cognitive, Academic, and Intellectual Development" by Norma Radin, in *The Role of the Father in Child Development,* edited by Michael E. Lamb (New York: John Wiley & Sons, 1981), p. 418.

p. 148 "According to Dr. Seymour Fisher. . . ." *The Female Orgasm: Psychology, Physciology, Fantasy,* by Seymour Fisher (New York: Basic Books, 1973), pp. 201, 258.

p. 150 ". . . 'be in favor of "women's liberation". . . .' " "A Note on the Father's Contribution to the Daughter's Ways of Loving and

Working," by Lora Heims Tessman, Ph.D., in *Father and Child,* edited by Cath et al., p. 229.

p. 152 ". . . 'threatening the child with extreme. . . .' " *The Psychologically Battered Child: Strategies for Identification, Assessment, and Intervention,* by James Garbarino, Edna Guttmann, Janis Wilson Seeley (San Francisco: Jossey-Bass, 1986), p. 25.

p. 154 ". . . physical abuse is most common. . . ." "Abusive Fathers," by Brandt F. Steele, in *Father and Child,* edited by Cath et al., p. 483.

p. 154 "Parental violence is split about equally. . . ." "Highlights of Official Child Neglect and Abuse Reporting 1986," American Humane Association, 1988, p. 29.

p. 154 "Curiously the domineering father at home. . . ." Steele, "The Abusive Father," in *Father and Child,* edited by Cath et al., p. 484.

p. 156 "An estimated 50 percent of child abuse. . . ." *The Recovery Resource Book,* by Barbara Yoder (New York: A Fireside Book/Simon & Schuster, Inc., 1990), p. 274.

p. 156 ". . . between 30 and 40 percent. . . ." "Current Trends in Child Abuse Reporting and Fatalities: The Results of the 1989 Annual Fifty-State Survey," The National Center on Child Abuse Prevention Research, March 1990, p. 11.

p. 156 "And so, as addictions specialist. . . ." *The Recovery Resource Book,* by Yoder, p. 34.

p. 156 "In 1989, of the 2.4 million children. . . ." "Current Trends in Child Abuse Reporting and Fatalities," pp. 2, 8.

p. 156 "Violence toward children is on the rise. . . ." Ibid., p. 15.

p. 156 "Moreover, according to David C. Leven. . . ." Letter to the editor from David C. Leven, *The New York Times,* September 13, 1990, p. A26. Mr. Leven is executive director of the Prisoners' Legal Services of New York.

p. 159 "Dr. Joseph Pleck. . . ." "Real Man Redux," by Michael S. Kimmel, *Psychology Today,* July 1987, p. 51.

p. 160 "The domineering father is terrified. . . ." *The Fragile Bond: In Search of an Equal, Intimate and Enduring Marriage,* by Augustus Y. Napier, Ph.D. (New York: Harper & Row, 1988), p. 192.

p. 160 "Dr. Marjorie Leonard, in writing about such fathers. . . ." "Fathers and Daughters: The Significance of 'Fathering' in the Psychosexual Development of the Girl," *International Journal of Psycho-Analysis* 47 (1966): 330.

p. 160 "According to Brandt F. Steele. . . ." "Abusive Fathers," by Steele, in *Father and Child,* edited by Cath et al., pp. 485–86.

p. 161 ". . . malignant narcissism. . . ." "Experts Differ on Dissecting Leaders' Psyches from Afar," by Daniel Goleman, *The New York Times,* January 29, 1991, p. C9.

p. 161   ". . . 'manipulate with no sense of how others. . . .' " Ibid.

p. 161   ". . . 'Children who have grown up being assailed. . . .' " *For Your Own Good: Hidden Cruelty in Child-Rearing and the Roots of Violence,* by Alice Miller (New York: Farrar, Straus & Giroux, 1984), p. 91.

p. 163   " 'Emotionally based conflict. . . .' " *Family Evaluation: An Approach Based on Bowen Theory,* by Michael E. Kerr, M.D., and Murray Bowen, M.D. (New York: W. W. Norton & Company, 1988), p. 83.

p. 165   "Research shows that the more dependent. . . ." *The Female Orgasm,* by Fisher, p. 103.

p. 165   "A recent study by the U.S. Justice Department. . . ." "In Crime, Too, Some Gender-Related Inequities," by Tamar Lewin, *The New York Times,* January 20, 1991, p. E9.

p. 165   "And when it comes to rape, the United States. . . ." "Women Under Assault," by Eloise Salholz, *Newsweek,* July 16, 1990, citing statistics from the Senate Judiciary Committee, p. 23.

Chapter 8: The Seductive Father

p. 169   "A nationally known child abuse. . . ." "Damages Are Awarded to 2 Sisters for Abuse," *The New York Times,* May 18, 1990, p. D16.

p. 169   "A famous movie actress. . . ." "Learning to Live Again," by Sandra Dee, *People,* March 18, 1991, pp. 87–94.

p. 169   "A former Miss America. . . ." "A Miss America Says She Was Incest Victim," AP, *The New York Times,* May 12, 1991, p. L19.

p. 169   ". . . The white, middle- or upper-middle class. . . ." "Highlights of Official Child Neglect and Abuse Reporting 1986," American Association for Protecting Children, a division of the American Humane Association, 1988, pp. 22, 26, 32. Regarding higher incest rates among high-income as opposed to low-income families, see *Healing the Incest Wound* by Christine A. Courtois, Ph.D. (New York: W. W. Norton & Company, 1988), p. 19, citing *The Secret Trauma: Incest in the Lives of Girls and Women,* by D. E. H. Russell (New York: Basic Books, 1986).

p. 170   "Not surprisingly incest is the least reported. . . ." *By Silence Betrayed: Sexual Abuse of Children in America,* by John Crewdson (Boston: Little, Brown, 1988), p. 81.

p. 170   ". . . in 1989 there were approximately 384,000. . . ." "Current Trends in Child Abuse Reporting and Fatalities: The Results of the 1989 Annual Fifty-State Survey," prepared by the National Center on Child Abuse Prevention Research, a program of the National Committee for Prevention of Child Abuse, March 1990, pp. 2, 8, based on 16 percent of 2.4 million reported maltreatment cases annually.

p. 170 "... a twenty-fold increase. ..." "Highlights of Official Child Neglect and Abuse Reporting," American Association for Protecting Children, a Division of the American Humane Association, p. 23.

p. 170 "Eighty-two percent of the perpetrators. ..." Ibid., pp. 26, 32.

p. 170 "Unofficial reports, however. ..." Ibid., pp. 20, 26. See also Crewdson, *By Silence Betrayed,* pp. 31, 70.

p. 170 "Some authorities believe that for every. ..." *Incest as Child Abuse: Research and Application,* by Brenda J. Vander Mey and Ronald L. Neff (New York: Praeger, 1986), p. 46.

p. 171 "... as many as *fifteen million.* ..." "Incest and the Law," by Carol Lynn Mithers, *The New York Times Magazine,* October 21, 1990, p. 44.

p. 171 "... it usually begins. ..." Courtois, *Healing the Incest Wound,* pp. 5–6.

p. 172 "... 'Physical attraction and affection. ...' " *Thou Shalt Not Be Aware: Society's Betrayal of the Child,* by Alice Miller (New York: New American Library, 1986), p. 161.

p. 173 " '[Incest] refers to. ...' " Courtois, *Healing the Incest Wound,* pp. 12–13, quoting from "Incest as a Causative Factor in Anti-Social Behavior: An Exploratory Study," by J. Benward and J. Densen-Gerber, *Contemporary Drug Problems* 4 (No. 3, 1975): 326.

p. 174 "... 'Incestous abuse can include. ...' " Courtois, *Healing the Incest Wound,* p. 13.

p. 177 "Most incest is not forced. ..." Courtois, *Healing the Incest Wound,* p. 17, citing *The Secret Trauma,* by Russell.

p. 178 " '*Actual* violence occurs. ..." Ibid.

p. 179 "... 'it is not the mother. ...' " *Incest as Child Abuse,* by Vander Mey and Neff, p. 86.

p. 179 "... abused children almost never lie. ..." *By Silence Betrayed,* by Crewdson, pp. 169–70.

p. 180 "... extensively coached children. ..." "Why Children Lie in Court," by Jerome Cramer, *Time,* March 4, 1991, p. 76.

p. 180 "A Harvard Medical School and Massachusetts General. ..." "The Father's House and the Daughter in It: The Structures of Western Culture's Daughter-Father Relationship," by Lynda S. Boose, *Daughters and Fathers,* edited by Lynda E. Boose and Betty S. Flowers (Baltimore: Johns Hopkins University Press, 1989), p. 71.

p. 181 "Some studies suggest. ..." Courtois, *Healing the Incest Wound,* p. 55, citing *The Secret Trauma,* by Russell.

p. 181 "... 'she is picked by both parents. ...' " "Father-Daughter Incest," by Irving Kaufman, in *Father and Child,* edited by Cath et al., p. 500.

p. 183 ". . . they share one common characteristic. . . ." *By Silence Betrayed,* by Crewdson, pp. 60–69.

p. 183 "Most of these men are not psychotic. . . ." *Healing the Incest Wound,* by Courtois, p. 51.

p. 183 ". . . incestuous father harbors . . . hatred and fear of women. . . ." *Incest as Child Abuse,* by Vander Mey and Neff, p. 135.

p. 183 ". . . incest becomes a way of passive-aggressively. . . ." Ibid.

p. 183 ". . . the incestuous father suffers from. . . ." "Abusive Fathers," by Brandt F. Steel, in *Father and Child,* edited by Cath et al., pp. 485–86.

p. 183 "But if there is one common thread. . . ." Kaufman, in *Father and Child,* edited by Cath et al., pp. 494–99.

p. 187 "She may develop stomach problems. . . ." For somatic and other symptoms of incest, see Courtois, *Healing the Incest Wound,* pp. 102–107.

p. 190 ". . . 'will unconsciously do the same to the child. . . .' " Miller, *Thou Shalt Not Be Aware,* p. 161.

Chapter 9: The Absent Father

p. 196 "Up to half of all children born in the 1970s. . . ." "Marital Transitions: A Child's Perspective," by E. Mavis Hetherington, Margaret Stanley-Hagan, and Edward R. Anderson, *American Psychologist* 44 (No. 2, 1989): 303, citing P. C. Glick and S. Lin, "Recent Changes in Divorce and Remarriage," *Journal of Marriage and the Family* 48 (1986): 737–47.

p. 197 "Lacking the intellectual and emotional. . . ." "Children of Divorce: A Ten-Year Study," by J. Wallerstein, S. B. Corbin, and J. M. Lewis (1988). In *Impact of Divorce, Single-Parenting and Stepparenting On Children,* edited by E. M. Hetherington and J. Arasteh (Hillsdale, N. J.: Lawrence Erlbaum Associates), pp. 198–214.

p. 197 "On the other hand divorce can cause older children. . . ." "Marital Transitions," by Hetherington et al., p. 305.

p. 198 "Boys living with single mothers. . . ." Ibid., pp. 305–306, citing "Effects of Divorce on Parents and Children," by E. M. Hetherington, M. Cox, and R. Cox, in *Nontraditional Families,* edited by Michael E. Lamb (Hillsdale, N.J.: Lawrence Erlbaum Associates, 1982), pp. 233–88.

p. 198 ". . . and tend to be more aggressive. . . ." Ibid., p. 306, citing "Interparental Conflict and Cooperation: Factors Moderating Children's Post-Divorce Adjustment," by K. A. Camera and G. Resnick, in *Impact of Divorce, Single-Parenting and Stepparenting on Children,* edited by Hetherington et al. (Hillsdale, N.J.: Lawrence Erlbaum Associates, 1988), pp. 169–95.

p. 198 "Interestingly, the same aggressiveness. . . ." Ibid., citing "Child Care After Divorce and Remarriage," by F. F. Furstenberg, in *Impact of Divorce,* edited by Hetherington et al., pp. 245–61.

p. 198 "According to Dr. E. Mavis Hetherington. . . ." "Effects of Father Absence on Personality Development in Adolescent Daughters," by E. Mavis Hetherington, *Developmental Psychology* 7 (No. 3, 1973): 313–26.

p. 198 "Noncustodial fathers spend time. . . ." See F. F. Furstenberg, "Child Care After Divorce and Remarriage" (1988), in *Impact of Divorce,* edited by Hetherington et al., pp. 135–54; see also "Post Divorce Relationships as Mediating Factors in the Consequences of Divorce for Children," by Robert Hess and Kathleen Camara, *Journal of Social Issues* 35 (1979): 79–96.

p. 198 ". . . and are twice as likely to help sons. . . ." *Second Chances: Men, Women, and Children a Decade After Divorce,* by Judith S. Wallerstein, Ph.D., and Sandra Blakeslee, p. 158.

p. 199 ". . . families who belonged to churches. . . ." Ibid., p. 7.

p. 200 "According to Dr. Hetherington. . . ." "Effects of Father Absence," by Hetherington, pp. 321, 325.

p. 201 ". . . Fewer than one third of the fathers. . . ." "The Father-Child Relationship: Changes After Divorce," by Judith S. Wallerstein and Joan B. Kelly, in *Father and Child: Developmental and Clinical Perspectives,* edited by Stanley H. Cath, Alan R. Gurwitt, and John Munder Ross (New York: Basil Blackwell, 1988), p. 461.

p. 202 "According to recently published findings. . . ." "Father's Vanishing Act Called Common Drama," by Tamar Lewin, *The New York Times,* June 4, 1990, p. A18, referring to a study by Frank Furstenberg and Kathleen Mullan Harris.

p. 202 ". . . Dr. Wallerstein found that remarkably few divorcees. . . ." *Second Chances,* by Wallerstein et al., p. 236.

p. 202 ". . . as attorney Paula Roberts. . . ." "Fathers' Vanishing Act Called Common Drama," by Lewin.

p. 205 "In her longitudinal study. . . ." "The Father-Child Relationship: Changes After Divorce," by Wallerstein et al., in *Father and Child,* edited by Cath et al., pp. 455–62.

p. 205 ". . . many men became depressed. . . ." Ibid., p. 458.

p. 205 "Younger fathers seemed. . . ." *Second Chances,* by Wallerstein et al., p. 222.

p. 206 ". . . seventy percent of these fathers. . . ." Ibid.

p. 206 ". . . Ten years after the divorce. . . ." Ibid, pp. 40–41.

p. 207 ". . . 'off-time'. . . ." See "Sociological Perspectives on the Life Cycle," by Bernice L. Neugarten and Nancy Datan, *Life Span Developmental Psychology: Personality and Socialization,* edited by Paul B. Baltes and K. Warner Schaie (New York: Academic Press, 1973).

p. 208   "Studies show that widows. . . ." "Effects of Father Absence," by Hetherington, p. 322.

p. 208   "Consequently their daughters have fewer. . . ." Ibid., See Table 6, p. 320.

p. 208   "Indeed, according to Dr. Hetherington. . . ." Ibid., p. 324.

p. 209   "Elyce Wakerman, who conducted a study. . . ." *Father Loss: Daughters Discuss the Man That Got Away* (New York: Doubleday & Company, 1984), p. 29.

p. 209   ". . . 'repressed mourning'. . . ." Ibid.

p. 211   "According to Dr. Hetherington and others. . . ." "Girls Without Fathers," by E. Mavis Hetherington, *Psychology Today,* February 1973, p. 52.

p. 212   "Researchers have noted, for example. . . ." "The Father as a Member of the Child's Social Network" by Michael Lewis, Candice Feiring, and Marsha Weinraub, in *The Role of the Father in Child Development,* edited by Michael E. Lamb, second edition, revised and updated (New York: John Wiley & Sons, 1981), p. 283, citing *Attachment and Loss,* by J. Bowlby, Vol. 3, *Loss: Sadness and Depression* (New York: Basic Books, 1980).

p. 213   "In Elyce Wakerman's study. . . ." Wakerman, *Father Loss,* p. 176.

p. 214   "On the other hand, in Dr. Wallerstein's. . . ." *Second Chances,* by Wallerstein et al., pp. 65–66.

Chapter 10: Habits of the Heart

p. 222   " 'Love is blynd'. . . ." "The Merchant's Tale," from *The Canterbury Tales,* by Geoffrey Chaucer, c. 1387.

p. 222   ". . . '. . . and lovers cannot see. . . .' " *The Merchant of Venice,* by William Shakespeare, Act II, scene vi.

p. 223   "Dr. Phillip Shaver. . . ." "Patterns in Love Charted in Studies," by Daniel Goleman, *The New York Times,* September 10, 1985, p. C1.

p. 223   ". . . 'fail to develop stable expectations. . . .' " Ibid.

p. 226   "Indeed, in terms of how people behave. . . ." *Family Constellation: Its Effects on Personality and Social Behavior,* by Walter Toman, third edition (New York: Springer Publishing Company, 1976), p. 70.

p. 226   "Since firstborns try to live up. . . ." Ibid., p. 68.

p. 226   "Middle children tend to be. . . ." Ibid., pp. 68–69.

p. 227   "Because they are more loosely attached. . . ." *The Birth Order Book,* by Dr. Kevin Leman (New York: Dell Publishing Company, 1985), p. 120. See also *First Child, Second Child,* by Bradford Wilson and George Edington (New York: McGraw-Hill Book Company, 1981).

p. 227 "A study of revolutionary scientific. . . ." "The Order of Innovation," by Kenneth L. Woodward, *Newsweek,* May 21, 1990, p. 76, citing study by Frank J. Sulloway at MIT.

p. 227 ". . . the child's *gender* must be factored. . . ." Toman, *Family Constellation,* p. 121.

p. 227 ". . . *Sibling connections, or lack of them.* . . ." Ibid., p. 79.

p. 227 ". . . '. . . siblings are often the first partners. . . .' " "Blueprints from the Past: A Character Work Perspective on Siblings and Personality Formation," by Sandra Watanabe-Hammond, in *Siblings in Therapy: Life Span and Clinical Issues,* edited by Michael D. Kahn and Gail Lewis (New York: W. W. Norton & Company, 1988), p. 356.

p. 227 ". . . 'rank conflicts'.. . . . 'sex conflicts'. . . . Peer conflicts. . . ." *Family Constellation,* by Toman, pp. 84–89.

p. 228 "Among the couples least likely. . . ." Ibid., pp. 88, 203.

p. 230 ". . . 'level of differentiation' . . ." *Family Evaluation: An Approach Based on Bowen Theory,* by Michael E. Kerr, M.D., and Murray Bowen, M.D. (New York: W. W. Norton & Company, 1988), p. 94.

p. 230 "For instance a parent who dislikes. . . ." *The Sibling Bond,* by Stephen P. Bank and Michael D. Kahn (New York: Basic Books, 1982), p. 204.

p. 230 ". . . 'part of the fabric which was woven. . . .' " "The Stolen Birthright: The Adult Sibling in Individual Therapy," by Stephen P. Bank, in *Siblings in Therapy,* edited by Kahn et al., p. 342.

p. 231 "As long as the kids. . . ." *The Sibling Bond,* by Bank et al., p. 57.

p. 231 "Indeed it is a daughter's perceived mandate. . . ." *Family Evaluation,* by Kerr et al., pp. 137–138.

p. 232 "According to recent research. . . ." "Personality: Major Traits Found Stable Through Life," by Daniel Goleman, *The New York Times,* June 9, 1987, p. C1.

p. 232 " 'What does change is one's role. . . .' " Ibid., p. C5.

p. 233 "According to authorities on invulnerability. . . ." "Risk, Vulnerability, and Resilience: An Overview," by E. James Anthony, in *The Invulnerable Child,* edited by E. James Anthony, M.D., and Bertram J. Cohler, Ph.D. (New York: The Guilford Press, 1987), pp. 3–48.

p. 233 "This hardiness was observed. . . ." Ibid., p. 40, citing *Cradles of Eminence,* by V. Goertzel and M. D. Goertzel (Boston: Little, Brown, 1962).

p. 233 ". . . 'good copers'. . . ." Ibid., p. 16.

p. 236 "Sociologist A. Aron. . . ." *The Fragile Bond: In Search of an Equal, Intimate and Enduring Marriage,* by Augustus Y. Napier, Ph.D. (New York: Harper & Row, Publishers, 1988), p. 226, citing "Relationships with Opposite-Sex Parents and Mate Choice," by A. Aron, *Human Relations* 27 (1974): 17–24.

p. 236 "But family therapist Augustus Y. Napier. . . ." Napier, *The Fragile Bond,* p. 226.

p. 237 "By the age of thirty-five or so. . . ." *Lifeprints: New Patterns of Love and Work for Today's Women,* by Grace Baruch and Rosalind Barnett and Caryl Rivers (New York: New American Library, 1984), p. 195.

p. 238 " 'The way a parent handles. . . .' " *The Sexual Self,* by Avodah K. Offit, M.D. (Philadelphia: J. B. Lippincott Company, 1977), p. 37.

p. 239 "Nearly half of people in their early thirties. . . ." "Living in Sin," *American Demographics,* April 1990, p. 12.

Chapter 11: The Favored Daughter

p. 243 ". . . 'A man who has been the indisputable favorite. . . .' " *The Life and Works of Sigmund Freud: The Formative Years and Great Discoveries 1856–1900,* by Ernest Jones, M.D., Vol. 1 (New York: Basic Books, 1953), p. 5.

p. 243 "It all has to do with . . . locus of control. . . ." "Issues in Defining and Measuring Subjective Well-Being and Ill-Being," paper by Ed Diener, Psychology Department, University of Illinois, 1989, p. 44.

p. 246 ". . . an important ingredient. . . ." "The Father in Sex Role Development," by Henry B. Biller, in *The Role of the Father in Child Development,* edited by Lamb, p. 342. See also *Fathers* by Ross D. Panes (Cambridge, Mass.: Harvard University Press, 1981), p. 51, citing "Parent-Infant Interaction: Progress, Paradigms and Problems," in *Observing Behavior, I, Theory and Applications in Mental Retardation,* edited by P. Sackett (Baltimore: University Park Press, 1978).

p. 246 "Studies show that beautiful children. . . ." *Changing the Body: Psychological Effects of Plastic Surgery,* by John M. Goin and Marcia Kraft Goin (Baltimore: Williams and Wilkins, 1981), pp. 71–80.

p. 246 " 'As the girl ripens . . .' " *American Beauty,* by Lois W. Banner (Chicago: The University of Chicago Press, 1983), p. 101, citing *The Woman Beautiful,* by Ella Adelia Fletcher (New York: Brentano's, 1901), p. 10.

p. 246 "Not surprisingly researchers have found. . . ." "The Father-Daughter Relationship: Past, Present, and Future," by Michael E. Lamb, Margaret Tresch Owen, and Lindsay Chase-Lansdale, in *Becoming Female: Perspective on Development,* edited by Claire B. Kopp, in collaboration with Martha Kirkpatrick (New York: Plenum Press, 1979), p. 103.

p. 247 "Ed Diener and his colleagues. . . ." "Happiness Is the Frequency, Not the Intensity, of Positive Versus Negative Affect," by Ed

Diener, Ed Sandvik, and William Pavot, in *Subjective Well-Being: An Interdisciplinary Perspective,* edited by Fritz Strack, Michael Argyle, and Norbert Schwartz (New York: Pergamon Press, 1991), pp. 119–39.

p. 247   "Indeed the ability to ride out. . . ." "Issues in Defining and Measuring Subjective Well-Being and Ill-Being," by Ed Diener, p. 37.

p. 252   ". . . 'opportunistic-competent'. . . ." "Coping with Family Transitions: Winners, Losers, and Survivors," by E. Mavis Hetherington, *Child Development* 60 (1989): 11–12.

p. 254   "Dr. Seymour Fisher in his studies. . . ." *The Female Orgasm: Psychology, Physiology, Fantasy,* by Seymour Fisher (New York: Basic Books, 1973), p. 327.

p. 254   ". . . 'something of an embarrassment. . . .' " *The Sexual Self,* by Offit, p. 70.

p. 254   "As incest authority Christine A. Courtois. . . ." *Healing the Incest Wound: Adult Survivors in Therapy,* by Christine A. Courtois, Ph.D. (New York: W. W. Norton & Company, 1988), p. 102.

p. 256   " 'I lived at the center . . .' " "David," by Mary Gordon, in *Fathers: Reflections by Daughters,* edited by Ursula Owen (New York: Pantheon Books, 1983), pp. 112–13.

p. 257   " 'The most fundamental way to think. . . .' " *Family Evaluation,* by Kerr et al., p. 117.

p. 258   "Consequently many heroines are psychological . . . virgins. . . ." See "The Role of the Father," by Christine Adams-Tucker, M.D., and Paul L. Adams, M.D., in *Women's Sexual Development: Explorations of Inner Space,* edited by Martha Kirkpatrick, M.D. (New York: Plenum Press, 1980), p. 233.

Chapter 12: The Good Daughter

p. 265   "According to authorities on birth order. . . ." *First Child, Second Child,* by Bradford Wilson and George Edington (New York: McGraw-Hill Book Company, 1981), pp. 122–23.

p. 265   ". . . these children settle for less. . . ." Ibid., p. 133.

p. 265   ". . . and are likelier to abide. . . ." *The Birth Order Book: Why You Are the Way You Are,* by Dr. Kevin Leman (New York: Dell Publishing Co. Inc., 1985), p. 127.

p. 265   "The well-meaning parent. . . ." *Children: The Challenge,* by Rudolf Dreikurs, M.D., with Vicki Stoltz, R.N. (New York: Hawthorn/Dutton, 1964), p. 38.

p. 267   "Her parents' 'weakness'. . . ." See *Family Evaluation: An Approach Based on Bowen Theory,* by Michael E. Kerr, M.D., and Murray Bowen, M.D. (New York: W. W. Norton & Company, 1988), p. 210.

p. 267 ". . . they are called 'enablers'. . . ." *Another Chance: Hope and Health for the Alcoholic Family,* second edition, by Sharon Wegscheider-Cruse (Palo Alto, Calif.: Science and Behavior Books, 1989), pp. 89–103.

p. 267 "Maltreated children tend to believe. . . ." *The Psychologically Battered Child: Strategies for Identification, Assessment, and Intervention,* by James Garbarino, Edna Guttmann, and Janis Wilson Seeley (San Francisco: Jossey-Bass, 1986), p. 62.

p. 267 ". . . 'caring competent' children of divorce. . . ." "Coping with Family Transitions: Winners, Losers, and Survivors," by E. Mavis Hetherington, *Child Development* 60 (1989): 12.

p. 268 " 'Rather, these new roles. . . .' " *Second Chances: Men, Women, and Children a Decade After Divorce,* by Judith S. Wallerstein and Sandra Blakeslee (New York: Ticknor & Fields, 1990), p. 203.

p. 269 "Daughters who are considered to be extremely feminine. . . ." *The Female Orgasm: Psychology, Physiology, Fantasy,* by Seymour Fisher (New York: Basic Books, 1973), p. 369.

p. 269 ". . . while boys affirm their masculinity. . . ." Fisher, *The Female Orgasm,* p. 98, citing "A Cognitive-Developmental Analysis of Children's Sex-Role Concepts and Attitudes," by L. Kohlberg, in *The Development of Sex Differences,* edited by Eleanor Maccoby (Stanford, Calif.: Stanford University Press, 1966), pp. 82–173.

p. 270 ". . . 'Father-deprived girls are more likely. . . .' " *Father Power,* by Henry B. Biller and Dennis Meredith (New York: David McKay Company, 1974), p. 176.

p. 270 " 'If a person grows up under strong pressure. . . .' " *Family Evaluation,* by Kerr, p. 69 note.

p. 270 ". . . 'As [emotional boundaries]. . . .' " Ibid., p. 77.

p. 271 ". . . just as there is an urge for closeness. . . ." Ibid., p. 78.

p. 276 "One of Dr. Seymour Fisher's findings. . . ." *The Female Orgasm,* by Fisher, p. 211.

p. 277 ". . . the whole issue of sex is 'messy'. . . ." Ibid., p. 338. For a discussion of female sexuality and morality, see "The History of Female Sexality in the United States," by Myrna I. Liew, in *Women's Sexual Development: Explorations of Inner Space,* edited by Martha Kirkpatrick, M.D. (New York: Plenum Press, 1980), p. 35.

p. 278 "Unlike consistently orgasmic women, they have vivid. . . ." *The Female Orgasm,* by Fisher, pp. 230–31, 237.

p. 278 "For such daughters separation anxiety. . . ." Ibid., p. 280.

p. 279 "Their erotic appetite. . . ." "Effects of Father Absence on Personality Development in Adolescent Daughters," by E. Mavis Hetherington, *Developmental Psychology* 7 (No. 3, 1973): 323.

Chapter 13: The Competitive Daughter

p. 290   "According to Harvard psychologist Jerome Kagan. . . ." "The Bold and the Bashful," by Geoffrey Cowley, in "How Kids Grow," *Newsweek Special Issue,* Summer 1991, p. 25.

p. 290   "One is the 'Dionysian' sort. . . ." *Please Understand Me: Character & Temperament Types,* by David Keirsey and Marilyn Bates (Del Mar, Calif: Gnosology Books, Ltd., 1984), pp. 30–39.

p. 291   ". . . the 'Promethean' temperament." Ibid., pp. 47–57.

p. 291   "The desire to be the opposite sex. . . ." "Daughter John," by Bonnie Blodgett, *In Health,* July/August 1990, pp. 26–28.

p. 291   "According to Dr. Ken Zucker. . . ." Ibid.

p. 293   " 'Conflict . . . may reveal depth in parent-child. . . .' " "The Father-Daughter Relationship: Past, Present and Future," by Michael E. Lamb, Margaret Tresch Owen, and Lindsay Chase-Lansdale, in *Becoming Female: Perspectives on Development,* edited by Claire B. Kopp, in collaboration with Martha Kirkpatrick (New York: Plenum Press, 1979), p. 106.

p. 293   ". . . 'brilliant . . . personally secure, vital. . . .' " "The Father in Sex Role Development," by Henry B. Biller, in *The Role of the Father in Child Development,* second edition, edited by Michael E. Lamb (New York: John Wiley & Sons, 1981), p. 345, citing "Fathers and Autonomy in Women," by M. M. Lozoff, in *Women and Success,* edited by R. B. Kundsin (New York: William Morrow and Company, 1974).

p. 300   "Fatherless girls tend to get higher grades. . . ." *Father Loss: Daughters Discuss the Man That Got Away,* by Elyce Wakerman (New York: Doubleday & Company, 1984), p. 262, citing "Race, Daughters, and Father-Loss: Does Absence Make the Girl Grow Stronger?" by Janet G. Hunt and Larry L. Hunt, *Social Problems* 25 (No. 1, October 1977): 97.

p. 300   "Behind this workaholism . . ." *Success and the Fear of Success in Women,* by Krueger (New York: The Free Press, 1984), pp. 145–47.

p. 301   " 'Women who can comfortably. . . .' " "The Father in Sex Role Development," by Henry B. Biller, in *The Role of the Father in Child Development,* second edition, revised and updated, edited by Michael E. Lamb (New York: John Wiley & Sons, 1981), p. 345.

p. 303   ". . . the safer course is to . . . channel all their emotions. . . ." *Healing the Incest Wound: Adult Survivors in Therapy,* by Christine A. Courtois, Ph.D. (New York: W. W. Norton & Company, 1988), p. 114.

p. 303   ". . . and to become social isolates." Ibid., p. 218.

p. 303   ". . . what Elyce Wakerman calls the 'restitution' theory." *Father Loss,* by Wakerman, p. 264.

p. 304 ". . . 'aloof, perfectionistic and self-disciplined'. . . ." "The Father and Sex Role Development," by Henry B. Biller, in *The Role of the Father in Child Development,* edited by Michael E. Lamb, p. 346, citing "Fathers and Autonomy in Women," by M. M. Lozoff, in *Women and Success,* edited by R. B. Kundsin (New York: William Morrow and Company, 1974).

p. 305 "In a landmark study of achieving women. . . ." *The Managerial Woman,* by Margaret Hennig and Anne Jardim (New York: Anchor Press/Doubleday, 1977).

p. 305 "By their mid- to late thirties. . . ." Ibid., p. 138.

p. 305 "These women were able to take a chance on love. . . ." Ibid., pp. 143–46.

p. 306 ". . . 'impotizing,' as Dr. Avodah K. Offit. . . ." *The Sexual Self,* by Avodah K. Offit, M.D. (New York: J. B. Lippincott Company, 1977), p. 103.

Chapter 14: The Fearful Daughter

p. 314 ". . . 'strike as many notes, deep, full. . . .' " *The Notebooks of Henry James,* edited by F. O. Mathhiessen and Kenneth B. Murdock (New York: Oxford University Press, 1947), p. 106.

p. 314 ". . . describe introverts as 'territorial and 'intuitive'. . . ." *Please Understand Me: Character & Temperament Types,* by David Keirsey and Marilyn Bates (Del Mar, Calif.: Gnosology Books, Ltd., 1984), pp. 15, 18, citing *Psychological Types,* by Carl G. Jung (New York: Harcourt Brace, 1923).

p. 314 "Timid youngsters—roughly 15 percent. . . ." "Personal Health," by Jane Brody, *The New York Times,* November 16, 1989, p. B19.

p. 314 ". . . they are 'slow-to-warm-up'. . . ." *The Dynamics of Psychological Development,* by Alexander Thomas, M.D., and Stella Chess, M.D. (New York: Brunner/Mazel, 1980), p. 71–72.

p. 315 "Dr. Philip G. Zimbardo. . . ." "Personal Health," by Brody, *The New York Times,* November 16, 1989, p. B19.

p. 315 "In the normal course of developmental events. . . ." *The Sexual Self,* by Offit, pp. 31–39.

p. 316 ". . . in a Yale/Harvard study. . . ." "Personal Health," by Brody, *The New York Times,* November 16, 1989, p. B19.

p. 316 "Lastborn children. . . ." *First Child, Second Child: Your Birth Order Profile,* by Bradford Wilson, Ph.D., and George Edington, M.A. (New York: Zebra Books, Kensington Publishing Corp., 1987), pp. 142–43.

p. 316   "This is particularly true of 'change of life'. . . ." Ibid., p. 152.

p. 316   "In fact in examining the core components. . . ." *The Female Orgasm: Psychology, Physiology, Fantasy,* by Seymour Fisher (New York: Basic Books, 1973), pp. 110–11, citing *Identification and Child Rearing,* by R. R. Sears, L. Rau, and R. Alpert (Stanford, Calif.: Stanford University Press, 1965).

p. 317   "In Dr. Judith S. Wallerstein's study. . . ." *Second Chances: Men, Women, and Children a Decade After Divorce,* by Judith S. Wallerstein and Sandra Blakeslee (New York: Ticknor & Fields, 1990), p. 117.

p. 318   "An estimated 7 million American women. . . ." "Women's Depression Rate Is Higher," by Daniel Goleman, *The New York Times,* December 6, 1990, p. B18.

p. 319   "As Donna Moreau, clinical director. . . ." "Why Girls Are Prone to Depression," by Daniel Goleman, *The New York Times,* May 10, 1990, p. B15.

p. 319   "A 1988 study of college women. . . ." "Depressive Mood in Female College Students: Father-Daughter Interactional Patterns," by Judith S. Brook, Martin Whiteman, David W. Brook, and Ann Scovell Gordon, *Journal of Genetic Psychology* 149 (1988): 485–504.

p. 319   "In 1990 a report by the Task Force on Women. . . ." "Women's Depression Rate Is Higher," by Goleman, p. B18.

p. 319   "As many as 40 percent. . . ." *Healing the Incest Wound: Adult Survivors in Therapy,* by Christine A. Courtois, Ph.D. (New York: W. W. Norton & Company, 1988), p. 89, citing "Impact of Child Sexual Abuse: A Review of the Literature," by A. Brown and D. Finkelhor, *Psychological Bulletin* 99 (1986): 66–77.

p. 319   " 'If there is absolutely no possibility. . . .' " *For Your Own Good: Hidden Cruelty in Child-Rearing and the Roots of Violence,* by Alice Miller (New York: Farrar, Straus & Giroux, 1984), p. 7.

p. 321   ". . . what Dr. Offit calls the 'schizoid'. . . ." *The Sexual Self,* by Offit, pp. 92–97.

p. 322   "These daughters often remain bound. . . ." "Father-Daughter Incest," by Irving Kaufman, in *Father and Child: Developmental and Clinical Perspectives,* edited by Stanley H. Cath, M.D., Alan R. Gurwitt, M.D., John Munder Ross, Ph.D. (New York: Basil Blackwell, 1982), p. 505.

p. 323   ". . . a study of phobic women whose anxieties. . . ." *Success and the Fear of Success in Women,* by David W. Krueger, M.D. (New York: The Free Press, 1984), p. 112, citing "Phobias After Marriage: Women's Declaration of Dependence," by A. Symonds, *American Journal of Psychoanalysis* 31 (1971): 144–51.

p. 326   ". . . sexual abuse can underscore the inherent lesbianism. . . ." *Healing the Incest Wound,* by Courtois, pp. 278–81.

p. 327 "Sexual dysfunction takes a variety of forms." For a discussion of sexual dysfunction, see *The Sexual Self,* by Offit, pp. 141–76.

p. 330 ". . . 'neuroses are a result of repression. . . .' " *For Your Own Good,* by Miller, p. 7.

p. 330 ". . . it can be conceptualized as a reciprocal process. . . ." *Family Evaluation: An Approach Based on Bowen Theory,* by Michael E. Kerr, M.D., and Murray Bowen, M.D. (New York: W. W. Norton & Company, 1988), pp. 237, 241.

p. 330 ". . . 'Chronic psychosis and depression can be. . . .' " Ibid., p. 87.

Chapter 15: The Maverick Daughter

p. 337 " 'Beneath the surface . . . there is a strong. . . .' " *The Fragile Bond: In Search of an Equal, Intimate and Enduring Marriage,* by Augustus Y. Napier, Ph.D. (New York: Harper & Row, Publishers, 1988), pp. 198, 200.

p. 341 " '[The Apollonian wants] to be what he is meant. . . .' " *Please Understand Me: Character and Temperament Types,* by David Keirsey and Marilyn Bates (Del Mar, Calif.: Gnosology Books Ltd., 1984), p. 59.

p. 342 ". . . to 'provoke establishment of rules. . . .' " *Success and the Fear of Success in Women,* by David W. Krueger, M.D. (New York: The Free Press, 1984), p. 77.

p. 344 ". . . a reflection of their own anxiety-determined. . . .' " *Family Evaluation: An Approach Based on Bowen Theory,* by Michael E. Kerr, M.D., and Murray Bowen, M.D. (New York: W. W. Norton & Company, 1988), p. 8.

p. 344 " 'It is easier to 'help'. . . ." Ibid., p. 214.

p. 345 " '. . . different and exceptional, even as the one. . . .' " *The Psychologically Battered Child: Strategies for Identification, Assessment, and Intervention,* by James Garbarino, Edna Guttmann, and Janis Wilson Seeley (San Francisco: Jossey-Bass, 1986), p. 85.

p. 346 " 'It is a tragic irony. . . .' " *Second Chances: Men, Women, and Children a Decade After Divorce,* by Judith S. Wallerstein, Ph.D., and Sandra Blakeslee (New York: Ticknor & Fields, 1990), p. 116.

p. 346 "Most of the mavericks in my sample. . . ." For a discussion of the causality of paternal behavior and female promiscuity, see "Promiscuity as a Function of the Father-Daughter Relationship," by Allan Gerson, *Psychological Reports* 34 (1974): 1,013–14.

p. 347 "Studies of prostitutes. . . ." *Healing the Incest Wound: Adult Survivors in Therapy,* by Christine A. Courtois, Ph.D. (New York: W. W. Norton & Company, 1988), p. 114.

p. 347   ". . . 'disorder of hope'. . . ." Ibid., p. 113, quoting *Psychological Trauma,* by B. van der Kolk (Washington, D.C.: American Psychiatric Association Press, 1987).

p. 348   "'. . . may . . . produce someone who cannot enjoy. . . .'" *The Sexual Self,* by Offit, p. 37.

p. 351   ". . . there is a kind of hollowness that haunts. . . ." "Children at High Risk for Psychosis Growing Up Successfully," by E. James Anthony, in *The Invulnerable Child,* edited by E. James Anthony, M.D., and Bertram J. Cohler, Ph.D. (New York: The Guilford Press, 1987), pp. 180–81.

Chapter 16: Rediscovering Our Fathers

p. 373   "Many, if not most, incest victims dare not remember. . . ." For an excellent description of the collecting of memories of sexual abuse, see *The Courage to Heal: A Guide for Women Survivors of Child Sexual Abuse,* by Ellen Bass and Laura Davis (New York: Perennial Library, Harper & Row, 1988), pp. 70–85.

p. 374   "One woman, an attorney, was in court. . . ." "Incest and the Law," by Carol Lynn Mithers, *The New York Times Magazine,* October 21, 1991, p. 53, describing incest-law reform advocate Shari Karney of Los Angeles.

p. 374   " 'These men just get away with it!' " Ibid.

p. 376   " 'It wasn't until I joined CoDA. . . .' " "The 12-Stepping of America," *New Woman,* by Victoria Secunda, June 1990, p. 49.

Chapter 17: Reframing the Father-Daughter Relationship

p. 385   " 'The [triangle] theory. . . .' " *Family Evaluation: An Approach Based on Bowen Theory,* by Michael E. Kerr, M.D., and Murray Bowen, M.D. (New York: W. W. Norton & Company, 1988), p. 134.

p. 394   "Many incest victims . . . *must not confront or even be with* . . ." For a discussion of deciding on and preparing for confrontation, see *Healing the Incest Wound,* by Courtois, pp. 325–39.

p. 397   " 'No whim of fate, no Freudian drama. . . .' " *Adaptation to Life,* by George E. Vaillant (Boston: Little, Brown, 1977), p. 2.

Chapter 18: Redefining Our Romantic Attachments

p. 400 "According to anthropologist Helen Fisher. . . ." "Too Many Divorces? The Real Miracle May Be So Few," by Dr. Helen Fisher, *Bottom Line Personal,* October 12, 1989, p. 11.

p. 400 ". . . *75 percent of divorces.* . . ." *The Fragile Bond: In Search of an Equal, Intimate and Enduring Marriage,* by Augustus Y. Napier, Ph.D. (New York: Harper & Row, 1988), p. 338.

p. 400 "Returning to the 1990 Virginia Slims. . . ." "The 1990 Virginia Slims Opinion Poll: A 20-Year Perspective of Women's Issues," a study conducted by the Roper Organization, Inc., pp. 8, 30. For further information, write to Virginia Slims, P.O. Box 311028, Chicago, Illinois 60641.

p. 401 ". . . *Men's Life* magazine commissioned its own study. . . ." "A Generation of Men Grows Up," by Carl Arrington, *Men's Life,* Fall 1990, pp. 64–70. (Note: This magazine is defunct.)

p. 401 ". . . the marriage rate among never-married men. . . ." "Why Wed? The Ambivalent American Bachelor," by Trip Gabriel, *The New York Times Magazine,* November 15, 1987, p. 24.

p. 401 "As for single men in their twenties. . . ." "For Every Five Young Women, Six Young Men," by Keith Bradsher, *The New York Times,* January 17, 1990, p. C1.

p. 401 "A recent page-one story. . . ." "More Young Single Men Hang On to Apron Strings," by Jane Gross, *The New York Times,* June 16, 1991, p. A1.

p. 401 ". . . 'suffer virtually no loss. . . .' " Ibid.

p. 404 " 'Most men want to be. . . .' " Napier, *The Fragile Bond,* p. 141.

p. 407 ". . . 'the closeness panic'. . . ." Ibid., p. 254.

p. 408 "These men, when they were growing up. . . ." Ibid., pp. 307–308.

p. 410 " 'We must learn to distinguish. . . .' " Ibid., p. 346.

p. 411 ". . . anxiety 'generator' . . . 'amplifier' . . . 'dampener'. . . ." *Family Evaluation: An Approach Based on Bowen Theory,* by Michael E. Kerr, M.D., and Murray Bowen, M.D. (New York: W. W. Norton & Company, 1988), p. 142.

p. 411 "Even people who are chronically ill or depressed. . . ." Ibid., pp. 56–57.

p. 413 ". . . the sexual genogram. . . ." "The Sexual Genogram," by Larry Hof and Ellen Berman, *Journal of Marital and Family Therapy* 12 (No. 1, January 1986): 39–47.

p. 417 " 'All women become like their mothers.' " "The Importance of Being Earnest," Act I, quoted from *The Picture of Dorian Gray and Other Writings by Oscar Wilde,* edited by Richard Ellman (New York: Bantam Books, 1988), p. 417.

Chapter 19: The Man and Father of the Future

p. 422   " '. . . however much [patriarchy]. . . .' " *Of Woman Born: Motherhood as Experience and Institution,* by Adrienne Rich (New York: W. W. Norton & Company, 1986), p. 83.

p. 422   "In the last fifteen years, violent crimes. . . ." 1990 NOW Legal Defense and Education Fund fundraising letter from Helen Neuborne, Executive Director, 99 Hudson Street, New York, New York 10013.

p. 422   "Married mothers bear 90 percent. . . ." "Introduction: The Emergent American Father," by Michael E. Lamb, in *The Father's Role: Cross Cultural Perspectives,* edited by Lamb (Hillsdale, N.J.: Lawrence Erlbaum Associates, 1987), pp. 3–25.

p. 422   "No-fault divorce laws. . . ." "Onward Women!" by Claudia Willis, *Time,* December 4, 1989, p. 83.

p. 422   ". . . of the 9.4 million American women. . . ." "New Tools for States Bolster Collection of Child Support," by Tamar Lewin, *The New York Times,* June 15, 1991, p. A1, A9.

p. 422   "Half the states have moved to cut. . . ." "Many States Cut Food Allotments for Poor Families," by Robert Pear, *The New York Times,* May 29, 1990, p. A1.

p. 422   "Lack of federal funds. . . ." "Intervening with New Parents: An Effective Way to Prevent Child Abuse," by Deborah Daro, D.S.W., working paper for the National Center on Child Abuse Research, a program of the National Committee for Prevention of Child Abuse, February 1988, p. 29, citing *Confronting Child Abuse: Research for Effective Program Design,* by D. Daro (New York: The Free Press, 1988).

p. 422   "The United States is the *only.* . . ." "Mommy vs. Mommy," by Nina Darnton, *Newsweek,* June 4, 1990, p. 67.

p. 422   "In contrast, 98 percent. . . ." "About Education," by Fred M. Hechinger, *The New York Times,* August 1, 1990, p. B8.

p. 423   "The death rate of American men. . . ." "Drums, Sweat and Tears," by Jerry Adler, *Newsweek,* June 24, 1991, p. 51.

p. 424   "In recent years an estimated 100,000. . . ." "Robert Bly, Wild Thing," by Charles Gaines, *Esquire,* October 1991, p. 127.

p. 425   ". . . 'emotional strength and spontaneity'. . . ." "Heeding the Call of the Drums," by Jerry Adler, *Newsweek,* June 24, 1991, p. 52.

p. 425   ". . . 'soft males'. . . ." "Call of the Wildmen," by Trip Gabriel, *The New York Times Magazine,* October 14, 1990, p. 39.

p. 425   " 'What I'm proposing. . . .' " Ibid.

p. 426   " 'Only when a man feels a strong. . . .' " *The Fragile Bond: In Search of an Equal, Intimate and Enduring Marriage,* by Augustus Y. Napier Ph.D. (New York: Harper & Row, 1988), pp. 286, 287.

p. 426   ". . . The National Organization for Men Against Sexism. . . ." For information, write N.O.M.A.S., 794 Penn Avenue, Pittsburgh, Pennsylvania 15221.

p. 426   "In one midwestern corporation. . . ." "Dad: New & Improved," by Lisa Schroepfer, *American Health,* June 1991, p. 68.

p. 427   " 'However . . . the videotape. . . .' " *Fathers,* by Ross D. Parke, Ph.D. (Cambridge, Mass.: Harvard University Press, 1981), p. 112.

p. 427   "According to Dr. Michael Lamb, 'father involvement' in fact requires. . . ." "Introduction: The Emergent American Father," by Michael E. Lamb, in *The Father's Role: Cross-Cultural Perspectives,* edited by Michael E. Lamb (Hillsdale, N.J.: Lawrence Erlbaum Associates, 1987), pp. 17–22.

p. 427   ". . . one researcher concluded that American fathers. . . ." "Intimate Fathers: Patterns of Paternal Holding Among Aka Pygmies," by Barry S. Hewlett, in *The Father's Role,* edited by Lamb, p. 327.

Bibliography

Anthony, E. James, M.D.; and Bertram J. Cohler, Ph.D., editors. *The Invulnerable Child*. New York: The Guilford Press, 1987.

Appleton, Dr. William S. *Fathers and Daughters: A Father's Powerful Influence on a Woman's Life*. New York: Berkley Books, 1984.

Ariès, Philippe. *Centuries of Childhood: A Social History of Family Life*. New York: Vintage Books, 1962.

Bank, Stephen P.; and Michael Kahn. *The Sibling Bond*. New York: Basic Books, 1982.

Banner, Lois W. *American Beauty*. Chicago: The University of Chicago Press, 1983.

Baruch, Grace; and Rosalind Barnett (with Caryl Rivers). *Lifeprints: New Patterns of Love and Work for Today's Woman*. New York: New American Library, 1984.

Bass, Ellen; and Laura Davis. *The Courage to Heal: A Guide for Women Survivors of Child Sexual Abuse*. New York: Perennial Library, Harper & Row, Publishers, 1988.

Biller, Henry, Ph.D.; and Dennis Meredith. *Father Power*. New York: David McKay Company, 1974.

Blos, Peter. *Son and Father: Before and Beyond the Oedipus Complex*. New York: The Free Press, A Division of Macmillan, 1985.

Boose, Linda E.; and Betty S. Flowers, editors. *Daughters and Fathers*. Baltimore: The Johns Hopkins University Press, 1989.

Bronstein, Phyllis; and Carolyn Pape Cowan, editors. *Fatherhood Today: Men's Changing Role in the Family*. New York: John Wiley & Sons, 1988.

Brownmiller, Susan. *Against Our Will: Men, Women and Rape*. New York: Simon & Schuster, 1975.

Cath, Stanley H.; Alan R. Gurwitt; and John Munder Ross, editors. *Father and Child: Developmental and Clinical Perspectives.* New York: Basil Blackwell, 1988.

Chess, Stella, M.D. *Daughters: From Infancy to Independence.* New York: Doubleday & Company, 1978.

Chodorow, Nancy J. *Feminism and Psychoanalytic Theory.* New Haven: Yale University Press, 1989.

———. *The Reproduction of Mothering: Psychoanalysis and the Sociology of Gender.* Berkeley and Los Angeles: The University of California Press, 1978.

Courtois, Christine A., Ph.D. *Healing the Incest Wound: Adult Survivors in Therapy.* New York: W. W. Norton & Company, 1988.

Crewdson, John. *By Silence Betrayed: Sexual Abuse of Children in America.* Boston: Little, Brown and Company, 1988.

Daniels, Norman. *Am I My Parents' Keeper? An Essay on Justice Between the Young and the Old.* New York: Oxford University Press, 1988.

de Beauvoir, Simone. *The Second Sex.* New York: Alfred A. Knopf, 1983.

Dreikurs, Rudolf, M.D.; with Vicki Soltz, R.N. *Children: The Challenge.* New York: Hawthorn / Dutton, 1964.

Ehrenreich, Barbara. *For Her Own Good: 150 Years of the Experts' Advice to Women.* New York: Anchor Press/Doubleday, 1978.

Eicher, Terry; and Jesse D. Geller, editors. *Fathers and Daughters: Portraits in Fiction.* New York: NAL Books, 1990.

Fischer, Lucy Rose, Ph.D. *Linked Lives: Adult Daughters and Their Mothers.* New York: Harper & Row, 1986.

Fisher, Seymour. *The Female Orgasm: Psychology, Physiology, Fantasy.* New York: Basic Books, 1973.

Fitzgerald, Hiram E., Ph.D.; Barry M. Lester, Ph.D.; and Michael Yogman, Ph.D., editors. *Theory and Research in Behavioral Pediatrics,* Vol. 1. New York: Plenum Press, 1982.

Fraser, Sylvia. *My Father's House: A Memoir of Incest and of Healing.* New York: Ticknor & Fields, 1988.

Garbarino, James; Edna Guttmann; and Janis Wilson Seeley. *The Psychologically Battered Child: Strategies for Identification, Assessment, and Intervention.* San Francisco: Jossey-Bass, 1986.

Gaylin, Willard, M.D. *Rediscovering Love.* New York: Penguin Books, 1987.

Gilligan, Carol. *In a Different Voice: Psychological Theory and Women's Development.* Cambridge, Mass.: Harvard University Press, 1982.

Gilligan, Carol; Nona P. Lyons; and Trudy J. Hanmer. *Making Connections: The Relational Worlds of Adolescent Girls at Emma Willard School.* Troy, N.Y.: Emma Willard, 1989.

Goin, John M.; and Marica Kraft Goin. *Changing the Body: Psychological Effects of Plastic Surgery.* Baltimore: Williams and Wilkins, 1981.

Hammer, Signe. *Passionate Attachments: Fathers and Daughters in America Today.* New York: Rawson Associates, 1982.

Heilbrun, Carolyn. *Writing a Woman's Life.* New York: Ballantine Books, 1989.

Hennig, Margaret, Ph.D.; and Anne Jardim, Ph.D. *The Managerial Woman.* New York: Anchor Press/Doubleday, 1977.

Jones, Ernest, M.D. *The Life and Works of Sigmund Freud: The Formative Years and the Great Discoveries 1856–1900,* Vol. 1. New York: Basic Books, 1953.

Kahn, Michael D., Ph.D.; Karen Gail Lewis, Ed.D., editors. *Siblings in Therapy: Life Span and Clinical Issues.* New York: W. W. Norton & Company, 1988.

Kaplan, Louise J., Ph.D. *Adolescence: The Farewell to Childhood.* New York: Simon & Schuster/Touchstone, 1985.

———. *Female Perversions: The Temptations of Emma Bovary.* New York: Doubleday & Company, 1991.

———. *Oneness and Separateness: From Infant to Individual.* New York: Simon & Schuster/Touchstone, 1978.

Keirsey, David; and Marilyn Bates. *Please Understand Me: Character and Temperament Types.* Del Mar, Calif.: Gnosology Books, Ltd., 1984.

Kerr, Michael E., M.D.; and Murray Bowen, M.D. *Family Evaluation: An Approach Based on Bowen Theory.* New York: W. W. Norton & Company, 1988.

Kirkpatrick, Martha, M.D., editor. *Women's Sexual Development: Explorations of Inner Space.* New York: Plenum Press, 1980.

Kopp, Claire B., editor, in collaboration with Martha Kirkpatrick. *Becoming Female: Perspectives on Development.* New York: Plenum Press, 1979.

Krueger, David W. *Success and the Fear of Success in Women.* New York: Macmillan/Free Press, 1984.

Laiken, Diedre S. *Daughters of Divorce: The Effects of Parental Divorce on Women's Lives.* New York: William Morrow and Company, 1981.

Lamb, Michael E., editor. *The Father's Role: Cross-Cultural Perspectives.* Hillsdale, N.J.: Lawrence Erlbaum Associates, 1987.

———. *The Role of the Father in Child Development,* second edition, revised and updated. New York: John Wiley & Sons, A Wiley-Interscience Publication, 1981.

Lasch, Christopher. *The Culture of Narcissism: American Life in an Age of Diminishing Expectations.* New York: W. W. Norton & Company, 1979.

Leonard, Marjorie. *The Wounded Woman: Healing the Father-Daughter Relationship.* Boulder, Colo.: Shambala, 1983.

Levinson, Daniel J.; with Charlotte N. Darrow; Edward B. Klein; Maria

H. Levinson; Braxton McKee. *The Seasons of a Man's Life.* New York: Alfred A. Knopf, 1978.

Mahler, Margaret; Fred Pine; and Anni Bergman. *The Psychological Birth of the Human Infant.* New York: Basic Books, 1976.

Miller, Alice. *The Drama of the Gifted Child: The Search for the True Self.* New York: Basic Books, 1981.

———. *For Your Own Good: Hidden Cruelty in Childrearing and the Roots of Violence.* New York: Farrar, Straus & Giroux, Inc., 1984.

———. *Thou Shalt Not Be Aware: Society's Betrayal of the Child.* New York: New American Library, 1986.

Napier, Augustus Y., Ph.D. *The Fragile Bond: In Search of an Equal, Intimate and Enduring Marriage.* New York: Harper & Row, Publishers, 1988.

Offit, Avodah K., M.D. *The Sexual Self.* New York: J. B. Lippincott Company, 1977.

Owen, Ursula, editor. *Fathers: Reflections by Daughters.* New York: Pantheon Books, 1983.

Parke, Ross D. *Fathers.* Cambridge, Mass.: Harvard University Press, 1981.

Pogrebin, Letty Cottin. *Growing Up Free: Raising Your Child in the 80's.* New York: McGraw-Hill Book Company, 1980.

———. *Family Politics: Love and Power on an Intimate Frontier.* New York: McGraw-Hill Book Company, 1983.

———. *Deborah, Golda and Me: Being Female and Jewish in America.* New York: Crown, 1991.

Rich, Adrienne. *Of Woman Born: Motherhood as Experience and Institution.* New York: W. W. Norton & Company, 1986, 1976, Tenth Anniversary Edition.

Secunda, Victoria. *By Youth Possessed: The Denial of Age in America.* Indianapolis: The Bobbs-Merrill Company, Inc. (Macmillan), 1984.

———. *When You and Your Mother Can't Be Friends: Resolving the Most Complicated Relationship of Your Life.* New York: Delacorte Press, 1990.

Singer, June, Ph.D. *Androgyny: Toward a New Theory of Sexuality.* New York: Anchor Press/Doubleday, 1976.

Thomas, Alexander, M.D.; and Stella Chess, M.D. *The Dynamics of Psychological Development.* New York: Brunner/Mazel, 1980.

Toman, Walter. *Family Constellation: Its Effects on Personality and Social Behavior,* third edition. New York: Springer Publishing Company, Inc., 1976.

Trepper, Terry S.; and Mary Jo Barrett, editors. *Treating Incest: A Multimodal Systems Perspective.* New York: The Haworth Press, 1986.

Vaillent, George E. *Adaptation to Life.* Boston: Little, Brown and Company, 1977.

Vander Mey, Brenda J.; and Ronald L. Neff. *Incest as Child Abuse: Research and Application.* New York: Praeger, 1986.

Wakerman, Elyce. *Father Loss: Daughters Discuss the Man That Got Away.* New York: Doubleday & Company, 1984.

Wallerstein, Judith S., Ph.D.; and Sandra Blakeslee. *Second Chances: Men, Women, and Children a Decade After Divorce.* New York: Ticknor & Fields, 1990.

Wegscheider-Cruse, Sharon. *Another Chance: Hope and Health for the Alcoholic Family,* second edition. Palo Alto, Calif.: Science and Behavior Books, 1989.

Wilson, Bradford, Ph.D.; and George Edington, M.A. *First Child, Second Child: Your Birth Order Profile.* New York: Zebra Books, Kensington Publishing Corp., 1981.

Winnicott, D. W. *The Maturational Processes and the Facilitating Environment.* New York: International Universities Press, 1965.

Index